# AT THE OPERA

# At the Opera

## TALES OF THE GREAT OPERAS

by Ann Fiery

Illustrations by Peter Malone

CHRONICLE BOOKS

SAN FRANCISCO

*Many thanks to Sally Barrows, without whose editorial acumen this book might never have existed.*

*—A.F.*

Text copyright © 2003 by Ann Fiery.
Illustrations copyright © 2003 by Peter Malone.

Library of Congress Cataloging-in-Publication Data available.

ISBN 0-8118-2774-7

Manufactured in China.

Designed by Pamela Geismar
Typset in Perpetua with Dalliance Flourishes

Distributed in Canada by Raincoast Books
9050 Shaughnessy Street
Vancouver, British Columbia V6P 6E5

10 9 8 7 6 5 4 3 2 1

Chronicle Books LLC
85 Second Street
San Francisco, California 94105

www.chroniclebooks.com

For Clio, my favorite muse.

*— Ann Fiery*

*Frontispiece*, Orfeo ed Euridice

*The story of opera begins with the story of Orpheus and his ill-fated journey into the underworld to reclaim his beloved wife, Euridice, from death. It was the subject of Peri's* Euridice *(1600), usually considered the first extant opera. Claude Monteverdi developed the form musically and dramatically with his retelling of the myth in* La Favolo d'Orfeo *(1607). But it was not until 150 years later that Christoph Willibald Gluck, though not technically opera's inventor, first married the naturalistic drama with the emotionally expressive music we now look for in the art. His* Orfeo ed Euridice *took Europe by storm in 1762, provoking outrage in the music academies and a host of imitators in the theaters. The French philosopher Jean Jacques Rousseau commented after seeing Gluck's opera, "If one can experience two hours of such great pleasure, I can understand that life may be worth living."*

*Page 8*, Dido and Aeneas

*John Blow's seldom performed* Venus and Adonis *(c. 1682) was the first of the few operas written in English. But Henry Purcell's* Dido and Aeneas, *which premiered at Mr. Josias Priest's Boarding School for Girls in London in 1689, remains acclaimed today for its extraordinary psychological portrait of the Queen of Carthage doomed by her love for the Greek hero Aeneas.*

# CONTENTS

# FOREWORD

The lavish spectacle, the thrilling drama, the honeyed voices rising to golden heights—opera's enchantment lies in its glorious excess. For those of us who savor enormous emotions and lyrical fervor, the operatic era that began with Mozart and ended with Richard Strauss offers a sumptuous feast for the ears, eyes, and soul. It was during this period that opera emerged from aristocratic seclusion and became the most wildly popular musical entertainment in Europe. What we now call opera was born in Italy in the seventeenth century with Claudio Monteverdi's *Orfeo,* and for the first hundred years of its existence, it was performed almost exclusively by court musicians for royal audiences, primarily in Italy and France. In the early years of the eighteenth century, however, this new and exciting mixture of music and drama was recognized by several wily theater managers as a potential gold mine and, accordingly, opera was brought before the eyes of the theatergoing masses. It was an immediate sensation. A public hungry for entertainment relished the magical tunes, the lurid tales, the gorgeous gowns, the beautiful voices. No less captivating were the rivalries between singers, the promotional ploys of competing theater managers, and the flamboyant lives of composers. Audiences were passionately partisan: They loved and hated with almost the same ardor as the characters in an opera. Feverish fans booed Rossini because he was impudent enough to recycle a story that had already been used by another composer; they threatened to lynch the tenor who cracked on a high B; they lined the streets with flowers when the soprano Jenny Lind made an appearance.

One result of this devotion was a flowering of the form. Operas were in incessant demand. The impresarios who ran the theaters were desperate for supply. Accordingly, in the 125 years between 1785 and 1910, thousands of operas were commissioned from thousands of composers. Most of them are now lost and forgotten, and somewhere among the host of the missing are probably works of genius. But among the hundreds that are still with us are the indisputable jewels of the operatic crown—rich, satisfying, shimmering as brightly now as they did a century ago—the eternal favorites. And then, within that list of delights are the beloved few, the operas that are performed again and again, the operas that changed the history of opera, the operas that embodied the spirit of their age. Here are the stories of those magnificent works.

# THE MARRIAGE OF FIGARO

*— Le nozze di Figaro —*

The *Marriage of Figaro* is the most frequently performed opera in the world, and for good reason. The astonishing loveliness of Mozart's music is paired with a brilliant arrangement of arias, ensembles, and recitative, and the result is the sparkling apotheosis of operatic charm.

It's hard to believe that this beguiling farce was considered scandalously subversive in 1786, the year it was composed. Today, the three intertwined love plots seem sweetly unexceptional, similar to any number of complex farces that appeared in the late eighteenth century, with much bursting in and out of rooms, discovering of lovers in closets, trading of garments, and dismayed confusion—cleared up, of course, in the final moments of the drama. But the play by Pierre de Beaumarchais upon which Mozart's opera was based, also called *Marriage of Figaro,* was deemed a revolutionary and immoral work and was banned in France soon after it was written, in 1784. Though the clerical censors decried the sexual shenanigans of the characters, the truly objectionable aspect of the play was the well-justified humiliation of the noble Count Almaviva by his servants. The spectacle of the lower classes outwitting the upper, not to mention the servants' moral superiority to their master, was enough to send anyone wearing a crown into a tailspin, and it was only after Mozart's librettist, Lorenzo da Ponte, promised Emperor Joseph II that he would excise "anything that might offend good taste or public decency" that Mozart was allowed to proceed with his plan to create the opera for Vienna. Accordingly, much of Beaumarchais's social satire disappeared from Mozart's version, and Figaro himself was transformed from a vengeful cynic into a playful conniver. So captivating was the resulting confection that the radicalism of its politics slipped down the gorge of its royal audience, and *The Marriage of Figaro* became an instant favorite throughout Europe.

# ACT ONE

Before the story begins to unfold, we would do well to become acquainted with the important members of the House of Almaviva. The most important, of course, is Figaro, who has been rewarded for his instrumental role in arranging the marriage of the Count and Countess Almaviva (which involved plucking her out from under the protuberant eyes of her guardian, Dr. Bartolo) by being elevated to the position of the Count's valet. Now, Figaro is in love with Susanna, who, coincidentally, is the Countess's chambermaid, and a very pretty and intelligent young lady. Happily, she is in love with Figaro, but unhappily, she is also being pursued by the Count. This old roué, forgetting the vows of true love he took some years before—in *The Barber of Seville,* to be exact—has become bored with his wife, though she is beautiful and virtuous and in love with him. But he doesn't like to appear the cad. In fact, he likes to appear progressive, admirable, noble, even, and to this end he has abolished the barbaric old custom of the *droit du seigneur* on his lands. This, remember, is the tradition that the lord may enjoy any female servant before her marriage can be consummated, and Count Almaviva is much congratulated by all and sundry for his liberalism in revoking such an indecent rite. Nonetheless, Count Almaviva feels perfectly certain that it would be ridiculous to let Susanna marry Figaro before he has had her himself, and, with this in mind, he is intent on seducing her, posthaste. The Count's household also contains a page, Cherubino, a young man from an impoverished noble family who has been sent to Almaviva's to learn refined manners and meet elevated and influential people. Unfortunately, Cherubino is not interested in manners or elevation; he's interested in girls—all girls. Today, Cherubino is cherishing a mad passion for the Countess, but yesterday, he loved Barbarina, the gardener's daughter.

The immediate problem as the opera begins is that Susanna has just interrupted Figaro's happy preparations for their marriage to point out that their bedroom is far too close to the Count's for comfort. Figaro is outraged to learn of the Count's campaign and begins immediately to plan his defeat: "*Se vuol ballare . . .* You may feel like dancing, little Count, but it's I who calls the tune."

Figaro's gleeful caper is cut short by the entrance of his old enemy, Dr. Bartolo, accompanied by his housekeeper, Marcellina, rouged and laced like a teenager, which she most emphatically is not. It seems that Figaro borrowed some money from the old lady, and worse, has promised to marry her if he cannot repay it. Marcellina is much more interested in the marriage than the money; and Dr. Bartolo is much more interested in revenge than the money; and together they plot to ruin Figaro's engagement to Susanna, who comes into the room just in time to exchange a series of obsequious insults with Marcellina. Susanna easily defeats her opponent and the housekeeper retires from the field.

A bit later, as Susanna arranges her mistress's clothes, Cherubino enters the room and seizes the opportunity to capture a ribbon belonging to the Countess, she being his current inamorata. Not that he's exclusive. Cherubino is also in love with Susanna herself, not to mention Barbarina.

Poor Susanna. As if Cherubino weren't annoying enough, the Count now appears. Cherubino, who has

had enough run-ins with Almaviva lately, hides himself behind a large armchair, leaving Susanna to evade the Count's attentions while trying to distract him from the page's hiding place. Oblivious to Susanna's lack of interest in him and fancying himself quite the suitor, the Count pleads for an assignation in the garden—whoops! Basilio the music master can be heard yodeling in the anteroom. In a panic, the Count looks about for a place to hide and decides on the armchair. Just in the nick of time, Susanna interposes herself between the page and the Count and hides Cherubino under a dress artfully thrown over the back of the chair. Now, with both men hidden, Basilio comes blundering in, full of gossip about Cherubino's attentions to the Countess. He so inflames the Count with jealousy that he promptly pops out of hiding, and Susanna is terrified that he will in a moment discover the page and run him through with his sword. The enraged Count declares that Cherubino must be packed off, for only yesterday he found the young fool in Barbarina's room, under the table. Here the Count demonstrates how he lifted up the tablecloth, and lo and behold, as he narrates, he finds Cherubino crouched beneath the armchair. Of course the Count assumes that Susanna has been trysting with the page, and his rage is redoubled. The realization that Cherubino has overheard his attempts to seduce the girl further infuriates him, and he decides on the spot to send the boy into the army.

At the height of this imbroglio, the wily Figaro reappears with a group of peasant girls who sing the praises of the Count for abolishing the hated *droit du seigneur.* Of course, the Count must receive them graciously, and Figaro tops off the scene by asking the Count to unite him and Susanna in matrimony. Almaviva, not to be outdone, assures Figaro that nothing would give him greater pleasure but begs to be allowed enough time to offer a really lavish ceremony, and Figaro's little plot is foiled. After dismissing the little girls, the Count offers Cherubino his heartiest good wishes for a magnificent career in the army, and Figaro enthusiastically seconds him: "*Non più andrai, farfallone amoroso . . .* No more, you amorous butterfly, will you go fluttering around, disturbing the peace of all the girls." Warming to his subject, he describes the charms of military life, "Lots of honor, little money, and, instead of the fandango, marching through the mud. Over mountains, through valleys, in snow and days of listless heat . . ."

Inspired, everyone departs from the room in a march.

# ACT TWO

In the second act, the plot thickens. This is to be expected of a plot, but in this case, it thickens almost to the point of incomprehensibility. It begins with the Countess in her room mourning her lonely state: "*Porgi amor . . .* O love, bring some relief to my sorrow." Her sad seclusion is soon interrupted by Susanna and Figaro, and together they hatch a scheme to return the Count to his wife's arms. Figaro has written an anonymous letter suggesting that the Countess is to have an assignation with a lover that very night; this, asserts Figaro, will so agitate the Count that he will have no time to prevent Susanna's wedding and, in the presence of the Countess, will not dare to oppose it. Further, Figaro proposes to have Cherubino (who has somehow not quite left for the army yet) meet the Count in the garden, dressed as a woman. The Countess will discover the pair, and thus embarrassed, the Count will do her bidding forever. This, they all agree, is a lovely plan.

Cherubino is sent for, to make ready his disguise. All ablush, he offers to sing the Countess a little song he has just written. *"Voi che sapete . . . You who know what love is,"* he begins, looking at her languishingly, "see if it is what I have in my heart." His soulful ballad is wasted on Susanna, who is itching to get him into his costume. She begins to dress him, though she is woefully hampered by Cherubino himself, who's busily flirting with the Countess. The two of them are thus engaged, Susanna having run to get another ribbon, when the unthinkable happens—the Count knocks on the Countess's door, demanding to know why it's locked. The quick-thinking (and terrified) Cherubino makes a dive for the Countess's dressing room while the poor woman stalls her husband with inexpert excuses. When she finally opens her door, the Count storms in, filled with suspicions and carrying the anonymous letter. Of course, the callow Cherubino chooses this moment to stumble over a table inside the dressing room, rousing the Count to new heights of jealousy. In vain, the Countess protests that she's heard nothing, and the Count decides to break down the door to discover the lover who's undoubtedly hidden within. Returning, Susanna assesses the situation and while the Count is out gathering up his door-breaking tools, she quickly convinces Cherubino to let her take his place in the dressing room. Relieved, he leaps from the balcony and runs away as fast as his little legs will carry him. The Count and Countess return; she, driven to desperation by the impending discovery, admits that Cherubino is hiding within. What's more, she adds, he's not exactly dressed. The Count explodes in a rage, but the Countess responds with dignity, "Your anger does me wrong. Your suspicion is an insult."

Well he should listen, but of course he does not. Wrenching the key from her, he is about to—when Susanna calmly opens the door. The Count and Countess are dumbfounded, but they soon recover themselves, the Count enough to be ashamed of his imprecations, and the Countess enough to take advantage of his repentance. He is just begging her forgiveness, when Figaro bounds into the room to announce that the musicians are all ready to begin the wedding march. "Let us hasten to the wedding!" he crows, taking Susanna by the arm.

"Not so fast," says the Count, waving the anonymous letter in the air. Figaro, of course, disavows all knowledge of the letter, of Cherubino, of the garden, of everything, and he is so dexterous in his denials that he has almost managed to convince the Count when Antonio the gardener comes stomping in with a shattered flowerpot. This, he reports with outrage, is what comes of throwing men from the balconies! The Count, ever alert, deduces that the gardener has seen a man leaping from the Countess's window, and he begins accusing his wife all over again. Figaro points out that Antonio is drunk. This cuts no ice with the Count, and Figaro hastily changes tactics, admitting that it was he, Figaro, who jumped from the balcony. This fabrication, in turn, requires Figaro to concoct a whole series of lies, each more precarious than the last, until the Count, still suspicious but unable to prove a thing, has to admit defeat.

Now who should appear but Marcellina and Dr. Bartolo, come to complain to the Count about Figaro's breach of contract. This is exactly the kind of impediment to Susanna's marriage that the Count has been seeking, and he solemnly announces that he must take it all under consideration. Here, with all parties in consternation, the act ends.

# ACT THREE

Not the least daunted by the events of the morning, the Countess and Susanna pursue their original scheme to entrap the Count. Susanna is sent to the Count to arrange a tryst, though her heart is so clearly not in it that she can scarcely pay attention to his entreaties. When he catches a glimpse of her whispering to Figaro, the Count deduces that he is being tricked. In his anger, he reveals his true self: *"Vedro mentr'io sospiro . . . Must I see a servant of mine made happy, while I am left to sigh?"*

The possibility of revenge appears in the person of Don Curzio, a lawyer who comes in to plead Marcellina's case before the Count. Of course, the Count rules in favor of the housekeeper, rendering Figaro

*The solo arias in* The Marriage of Figaro, *lovely though they are, have generally been considered less masterful than the ensemble pieces, particularly the ensemble finales of each act, which are often regarded as the pinnacle of Mozart's operatic art. Traditionally, the finales of opera buffa, Italian comic opera, were obliged to conform to a strict pattern, which was described by Mozart's librettist, Lorenzo da Ponte, in the following way:*

*"This finale, which has to be closely connected with the rest of the opera, is a sort of little comedy in itself and requires a fresh plot and a special interest of its own. This is the great occasion for showing off the genius of the composer, the ability of the singers, and the most effective 'situation' of the drama. . . . In this finale it is a dogma of theatrical theology that all the singers should appear on the stage, even if there were three hundred of them, by ones, by twos, by threes, by sixes, by tens, by sixties, to sing solos, duets, trios, sextets, sessantets; and if the plot of the play does not allow of it, the poet must find some way of making the plot allow of it, in defiance of his judgement, of his reason, or of all the Aristotles on earth; and if he then finds his play going badly, so much the worse for him!"*

*Instead of this kind of rote avalanche of sound, Mozart's buildup to the Act Two finale, in which the Count is provoked and frustrated by all the other characters, shows his genius as a musical and dramatic architect. Each section presents a contrast of tempo and time signature from the one that preceded it, offering either an escalation of emotion or a moment of repose, as the action of the story warrants. Together, the harmonics and dramatics of each segment surge forward and relax, all the while progressing inexorably toward the climatic ending of the act.*

aghast, Marcellina jubilant, Dr. Bartolo self-satisfied, and the Count triumphant—that is, until Figaro lays down his final card. He cannot be married, he declares, without the consent of his noble parents. His nobility is news to all parties, and they demand proof. He describes the lovely embroidered clothes, the jewels, and the gold that were found in his swaddling clothes, not to mention the birthmark on his arm.

"A spatula upon your right arm?" inquires Marcellina breathlessly.

Thus the truth is revealed: Marcellina is not only old enough to be Figaro's mother—she *is* Figaro's mother. And Dr. Bartolo is his father. As Marcellina clasps her newfound son to her capacious bosom, Susanna enters and, mistaking the situation, boxes Figaro's ears, but soon all is explained and familial embraces are exchanged all around. So moved is Bartolo by this reunion that he proposes to Marcellina on the spot, and the two couples begin to plan a double wedding.

While this jolly scene is taking place in one part of the palace, the Countess is reflecting on her lonely state in another. Her melancholy is interrupted by Susanna, who tells her the latest revelations. Together they write a letter, arranging Susanna's rendezvous with the Count for that evening in the garden. The Countess seals the note with a pin, adding "send back the seal" to the envelope; a flurry of voices outside warns them that a crowd approaches, and Susanna hastily hides the note in her bosom.

It's Barbarina with a group of village girls, come to present a bouquet to the Countess. One charming young maid catches the Countess's eye; the girl reminds her of someone, but who? The Countess bestows a kiss upon her cheek—and at that very moment the Count and Antonio burst upon the scene, remove the girl's bonnet, and clap a boy's cap on her instead. Voilà! It's Cherubino!

The Countess is astonished, but the Count is beside himself with fury. Just as he is about to give the lad the full brunt of his rage, Barbarina clears her throat. "Remember, your lordship," she begins, "when you said to me, 'Barbarina, if you'll love me, I'll give you whatever you want?' So, please give me, sir, Cherubino for a husband, and I'll love you as much as I love my kitten."

The Count is caught. He can't break a promise, though he swears, "What man, god, or demon is it that turns everything I do against me!" Despite his wrath, Susanna manages to convey the letter to the Count, and though he pricks his finger on the pin, the message fills him with contentment. Figaro has seen the letter, the pin, and the Count's smug smile, and he deduces that some amorous adventure is underway.

The act ends with the Count directing all to make ready for a grand wedding banquet and ball, declaring, "You shall see how I treat those dear to me."

# ACT FOUR

The stream of events becomes a cataract in this final act, which opens in the famous garden of the palace. Barbarina comes rushing along, looking for a pin she was charged by the Count to return to Susanna; she has lost it, she tells Figaro, and she doesn't know what to do. Reasonably enough, Figaro concludes that Susanna is the author of the billet-doux he saw the Count receive, and of course he is thrown into despair. He turns to his newfound mother in his hour of need, but her sympathies seem to lie with Susanna, and soon he is creeping through the garden with Basilio and Dr. Bartolo, hoping to catch Susanna and the Count *in flagrante.*

Charging the two old men with the surveillance of the bushes, Figaro steals off to nurse his jealousy and rave against the perfidy of womankind.

The Countess and Susanna now appear, each dressed in the garb of the other. Rejoicing in her approaching nuptials with Figaro, the genuine Susanna sings, *"Deh vieni, non tardar, o gioia bella . . .* Come, do not delay, oh bliss." Unfortunately, the concealed Figaro, blinded by the bushes, concludes that she rapturously awaits the Count, and he becomes even more infuriated. Enter Cherubino, who, failing to find Barbarina, decides to make do with Susanna—the Countess in disguise—and begins to kiss her hands and whisper sweet nothings in her ear. In vain the Countess tries to swat him away, fearing he will be the ruination of her plot. The Count comes rustling through the shrubbery and indignantly spies the page aiming for his own target. At the very moment that Cherubino launches his kiss, the Count lunges for him, and receives the kiss himself. Figaro, beside himself with this double-barreled assay on his purported wife-to-be, emerges from the bushes just in time to receive the slap that the Count had intended for the page. Susanna, who has been watching the comedy from her hiding spot in the arbor, bursts into laughter, as the page, thinking better of the whole episode, hies himself off. With Figaro lurking in the shadows, the Count renews his attempts on Susanna, but, of course, it's not really Susanna, it's the Countess. Murmuring about her slender fingers and delicate skin, he draws her into a grotto, causing the enraged Figaro to exclaim with disgust. At this, the real Susanna warns him to speak more softly and Figaro, recognizing her voice, realizes what's happened. Never one to let an opportunity for teasing go by, he pretends to be taken in by the disguise, and begins to woo Susanna as though she were the Countess, much to her dismay and his amusement. Soon enough, though, they call a truce and are happily reconciled.

Throughout the garden recesses, true love is triumphing. The Count catches Cherubino in a bush and, mistaking Susanna for the Countess, attempts to expose their treachery. Imagine his chagrin when he learns that he has been duped and that the lady he's been seducing is none other than his wife. Finally realizing that he has a treasure in the Countess, the Count begs pardon all around, and everyone concludes their day of follies with rejoicing and renewed affection. ~∽

# DON GIOVANNI

Opera boasts no villain more unrepentant than the great and terrible Don Giovanni. In the course of the magnificent work that bears his name, the Don assaults every woman he encounters, kills one man, beats another half to death, and humiliates his serving man regularly—yet nowhere expresses any semblance of remorse, anxiety, or sympathy for his victims. Even as he is dragged away to hell, Don Giovanni refuses to save himself by renouncing his crimes; refuses, even, to be afraid. In his relentless consumption of women, his disregard for the dignity of others, and his steadfast inability to experience human emotion, the Don is a monster. But he's a glorious monster, heroic in his willingness to accept the consequences of his monstrosity. While every other character in the opera calls out for help at one point or another, Don Giovanni does not. He neither wants nor expects kindness, companionship, or pity, even in his final extremity.

His profound amorality makes the Don seem like a modern creation rather than the hero of an eighteenth-century opera composed by Wolfgang Amadeus Mozart. And yet, by Mozart's time, the legend of Don Juan was already old, so old that its origins are obscure. By 1787, when Mozart got to it, the tale had appeared in numerous forms, including a play by Molière and, more usefully for Mozart and Lorenzo da Ponte, his librettist, an opera by Giuseppe Gazzaniga. Notwithstanding the Don's pervasiveness, the story was dismissed as ridiculous and vulgar by nearly every critic and intellectual of the era. The only explanation for its frequent adaptation was its indisputable popularity with everyone else. This drawing power is probably what attracted Mozart to the tale, for he was composing the opera for Prague, then considered a provincial backwater where the audience was likely to prefer the spectacular to the elevated. Though it was received with acclaim in that city, *Don Giovanni* was disdained in Mozart's own Vienna. Emperor Joseph II declared that though the music of *Don Giovanni* was beautiful, it was meat too tough for the teeth of the Viennese. "Give them time to chew on it," replied Mozart. And, of course, he was right: A mere quarter-century after its composition, reverent musicians and audiences were hailing *Don Giovanni* as the pinnacle of Mozart's genius.

# ACT ONE

The story begins with Leporello, the definitely craven and possibly crafty manservant of Don Giovanni, a young nobleman whose passion is the possession of every woman he lays eyes on. That is what he is about even now. As Leporello paces nervously back and forth in the garden of the Commendatore's palace, the Don is within, laying siege to Donna Anna, the Commendatore's prim and pious daughter. The sounds of a scuffle alert Leporello to the impending need for a quick getaway, and, sure enough, there is Don Giovanni, masked, his escape obstructed by Donna Anna, who is clinging to his arm and screaming for help. The Don, annoyed by her unpleasant shrieks, is trying to extricate himself from her grip when the aged Commendatore emerges from the palace with his sword drawn, intent on rescuing his daughter. As she flees, the Commendatore, maddened with rage, advances on the Don. Unalarmed, unmoved, the Don strikes the old man a fatal blow, killing him carelessly and watching with mild curiosity as he struggles for his final breath. Leporello, aghast, tries to remonstrate with the Don, though he should know better by now, but he is ignored. They depart, and immediately the distraught Donna Anna returns, accompanied by her fiancé, Don Ottavio, a careful, cautious, and virtuous man. They discover the grisly sight of the Commendatore's corpse and, overwhelmed with grief, Donna Anna demands that Don Ottavio swear to avenge her father. With a fine combination of vigor and self-congratulation, he does so.

Meanwhile, Don Giovanni is expounding to Leporello on his favorite topic: his next seduction. Just as he is relaying his plan, he stops. "Quiet!" he hisses, "I sniff a woman!" And presto, a lady swathed in veils emerges from the shadows of the street. Though the two men don't recognize her, it's Donna Elvira, one of Don Giovanni's previous victims, abandoned by the cad three days after he swore eternal love. With a single-mindedness bordering on obsession, she is combing the city for the Don, either to reclaim him or to tear out his heart. As she explains her dire scheme, the Don licks his salacious lips—a betrayed gentlewoman is just what he likes—and sweeps forward to console her. Upon discovering Donna Elvira within the veils, the Don is momentarily shaken from his nonchalance. She, however, is primed with invective. "Don Giovanni!" she begins, "You here! You monster, you criminal, you pack of lies."

As the recriminations pour forth from her lips, the Don's initial boredom turns to irritation: "This woman is a nuisance," he says and slips away, leaving Leporello to offer what solace he can—which is not much.

The servant urges the outraged lady to calm herself, for she is neither the first nor the last the Don has treated so ruthlessly. To prove his point, Leporello produces a fat little book: *"Madamina, il catalogo è questo . . . My dear lady, this is a list of the beauties my master has loved . . . In Italy, six hundred and forty, in Germany, two hundred and thirty-one,"* and on he goes through the roster, assuring Donna Elvira that the Don never discriminates against the fat or the thin, the old or the young, the noblewoman or the peasant, but enjoys them all equally. With this comforting thought, Leporello soon departs, followed by the fuming Donna Elvira.

In the lush countryside near Don Giovanni's palace, a small band of peasants is singing and dancing in celebration of the impending union of one of their number, the lovely young Zerlina, and her betrothed, Masetto. Their innocent pleasure is interrupted by the return of Leporello and Don Giovanni. The latter immediately targets Zerlina for his list and begins his campaign by inviting the group to his house for a party. Masetto and his friends will go ahead with Leporello, directs the Don, while he will follow with Zerlina. This arrangement immediately arouses Masetto's suspicions. However, when Don Giovanni coldly suggests that he will find resistance regrettable, the young man resentfully acquiesces.

Once the others have left, the Don commences his seduction. With flattery, assurances of his sincerity, and a proposal of marriage, he succeeds in dazzling the poor girl. *"Là ci darem la mano . . .* There you will give me your hand," he murmurs, pointing at his sumptuous villa, "there you will tell me yes."

After voicing a few half-hearted scruples about Masetto, Zerlina capitulates, but just as the Don is about to consume his prey, Donna Elvira makes an unexpected appearance. Revealing to Zerlina the Don's true character, she quickly whisks the girl away. Who should appear at this juncture but Donna Anna and Don Ottavio? They have come to their old friend Don Giovanni in their hour of need, seeking his assistance in apprehending the vile murderer of the Commendatore. Realizing that the pair has no idea that they are addressing the vile murderer himself, Don Giovanni solemnly commiserates and promises to help them. But now the ubiquitous Donna Elvira returns, hurling further accusations at the Don before the astonished Donna Anna and Don Ottavio. "She's mad. Pay no attention," whispers the Don smoothly.

*Lorenzo da Ponte was a priest, but he clearly regarded his vow of celibacy as a mere technicality. He was thrown out of Venice for scandalous behavior, and in the Venice of the 1780s, that took some doing. After a number of adventures, da Ponte ended up in Vienna, where he turned a talent for writing into a career as a librettist, though he had no previous musical or theatrical experience. In 1783, da Ponte and Mozart became acquainted, and the poet-priest promised the composer a libretto. Mozart had his doubts, though: "Who knows whether he will be able to keep his word—or be willing either? As you know, these Italian gentlemen are very polite to one's face—we know all about them! If he is in league with Salieri, I shall get nothing out of him as long as I live."*

*Inspired by the prospect of payment, da Ponte kept his promise, writing* Le nozze di Figaro, Don Giovanni, *and* Così fan tutte *for Mozart. In his memoirs, da Ponte describes the composition of the libretto for* Don Giovanni; *his method would make the Don himself proud:*

*"I sat down at my writing table and stayed there for twelve hours on end, with a little bottle of Tokay on my right hand, an inkstand in the middle, and a box of Seville tobacco on the left. A beautiful maiden of sixteen was living in my house with her mother, who looked after the household. (I should have wished to love her only as a daughter—but—) She came into my room whenever I rang the bell, which in truth was fairly often, and particularly when my inspiration seemed to cool."*

Donna Anna and Don Ottavio find her tragic demeanor strangely moving, and as she tells her pitiful story of betrayal, they are filled with doubt. Finally, tearing her hair, Donna Elvira retires and the Don beats a hasty retreat as well. This precipitous departure confirms Donna Anna's worst fears; all at once she is certain that the Don and her assailant are one and the same. Falteringly, she tells Don Ottavio the details of the night before—how she, alone in her room, was seized by a man wrapped in a cloak. How he tried to silence her before she wrenched herself free and ran after him as he fled. Her anguish renewed, Donna Anna asks Don Ottavio to swear once more that he will revenge her assault and her father's murder; then, overwhelmed, she leaves to compose herself. Vowing to discover the truth, Ottavio follows.

The exasperated Leporello enters, swearing for the millionth time that he's going to quit the Don's service. And here's the Don now, blithely indifferent to all the trouble he's caused. Leporello explains that he brought home the peasants, fed them, plied them with wine, smoothed Masetto's ruffled feathers, and kept them all in a festive spirit. Then, at the height of the party, who should drop in but Donna Elvira, with Zerlina under her wing and scandal to spread about Don Giovanni.

"And what did you do?" asks the Don.

"When I guessed that she had finished, I led her out and locked the door in her face."

"Well done, excellently done," says Don Giovanni heartily. "The thing could not be going better," he declares. He dilates upon the pleasures before him: a whole house full of young and intoxicated women. *"Finch'han dal vino calda la testa . . .* Now that the wine has set their heads whirling, go and prepare a wonderful party . . . To my list tomorrow morning, you will have to add at least ten names!" he laughs in anticipation.

Outside Don Giovanni's villa, Zerlina and Masetto are quarreling. Jealous, he reproaches her for succumbing to the Don's advances, but she assures him that nothing whatever occurred. Cheerfully, she suggests that he go ahead and wallop her, *"Batti, batti, o bel Masetto,"* as long as he'll agree to make up afterward. Just as she has succeeded in mollifying him, Don Giovanni is heard approaching. Masetto decides that he will hide to spy upon Zerlina with the Don and see for himself if she's faithful.

The Don enters and quickly homes in on Zerlina, first coaxing and then pulling her toward a secluded garden nook, where—surprise—he comes face-to-face with a grim Masetto. Diplomatically relinquishing the girl's arm, Don Giovanni suggests that they should join the rest of the party inside the villa. As that harmonious threesome departs, another arrives. Donna Anna, Don Ottavio, and Donna Elvira come into the garden wearing masks. Spurring one another on, they vow to reveal the Don's perfidy, but they are interrupted by a shouted invitation from Leporello at the window to join the festivities.

Inside, the Don commands the musicians to strike up a tune. He whirls Zerlina in a wild dance while Masetto grows more furious every minute. The simmering tensions of the dancers are matched by the musical melee as three different dance tunes are played by dueling orchestras. Expertly, Don Giovanni maneuvers Zerlina out of the room as Masetto looks on helplessly. Barely a moment passes before her screams are heard. Exhilarated at the thought of catching the Don red-handed, Don Ottavio, along with Donna Anna and Donna Elvira, rush to rescue her, but they are thrown into confusion by the reentrance of Don Giovanni, sword in hand, dragging Leporello after. The cagey Don charges his poor servant with the infamous crime and raises his sword. "Die!" he bellows.

"What are you doing?" asks Leporello confusedly.

Outraged at this new trick, Ottavio, Anna, and Elvira unmask themselves and denounce Don Giovanni. "Traitor! We know everything!" they cry. "Tremble, tremble, scoundrel! Now the whole world shall know of your horrible, black crime, of your arrogant cruelty!" Don Ottavio draws his pistol.

Even the Don falters in the face of their combined forces, but he soon recovers: "I do not lack courage, I am not lost or worried. Even if the world itself should end, nothing could make me afraid!" Bolstered by his own bravado, Don Giovanni makes a dash through the crowd and escapes.

# ACT TWO

Don Giovanni and Leporello are arguing again, this time outside Donna Elvira's lodging. Leporello declares that almost being killed by the Don was positively the last straw. The Don replies that he has no sense of humor, which outrages Leporello even further, but the two resolve their differences with the exchange of a little cash.

Don Giovanni has a new scheme and, of course, he needs Leporello's help.

"As long as we leave the women alone," says Leporello.

"Leave the women alone?" responds the Don incredulously. "You're mad. You know that they are more necessary to me than the bread I eat! Than the air I breathe!"

"Do you have the gall, then, to betray them all?" asks Leporello.

"Love is much the same in any form. He who remains faithful to one is being cruel to the others. I, who have an overabundance of sentiment, love them all," replies the Don airily, and proceeds to unveil his newest plot: the seduction of Donna Elvira's maid. This will best be accomplished, he says, if Leporello and he exchange clothes, since the nobility is not very popular among the servant class. The long-suffering Leporello agrees and they quickly don one another's cloaks.

Donna Elvira appears on her balcony, deep in thought. Why, she sighs, does her heart still beat for Don Giovanni? The diabolical Don seizes the opportunity to complete her humiliation by thrusting the disguised Leporello forward and speaking for him. With practiced cunning, he persuades the credulous Donna Elvira to come down to him. Even Leporello is astounded at the Don's heartlessness, but he agrees to lure Elvira away and when poor, lovesick Donna Elvira appears, Leporello enters into the deception with gusto, tossing endearments around like candy. In the shadows, Don Giovanni is finding this most amusing, but time is awasting and, to get his maid-seduction project underway, he leaps out at the pair in the guise of a robber. They scatter as the Don laughs. Picking up Leporello's mandolin, he begins his serenade, *"Deh vieni alla finestra, o mio tesoro . . .* Come to the window, my treasure," he croons.

Unexpectedly, Masetto and a crowd of peasants appear in the square. Brandishing weapons, they are in search of Don Giovanni and vow to kill him. The disguised Don eagerly offers his support, sending the stalkers off in the direction taken by Leporello and Donna Elvira, whom he describes in the minutest detail to ensure their capture. Masetto stays behind with the costumed Don to plan the murder and, on the pretext of inspecting his weapons, Don Giovanni steals Masetto's sword and beats him brutally. Leaving the peasant groaning in the street, the Don departs unscathed.

A few moments later, Zerlina comes searching for Masetto. Despite the gravity of his wounds, she effects a miraculous cure.

Night has fallen and, in the dark courtyard before Donna Anna's palace, Leporello—in the costume of the Don—and Donna Elvira seek shelter. Nervously, Leporello is seeking some way out before his disguise is

discovered, but as he sidles up to a gate, his way is blocked by the entrance of Don Ottavio and Donna Anna. Switching courses, Leporello heads for a second exit, but this time he is stymied by the appearance of Zerlina and Masetto. All at the same moment, the four notice him and jubilantly cry, "Death to the ingrate who has betrayed me!"

"He is my husband," shrieks Donna Elvira. "Have mercy!"

But Don Ottavio is determined to obtain revenge. Unsheathing his sword, he runs toward the miscreant—who falls to his knees and reveals himself as Leporello, to general consternation.

Though Donna Anna is too discomfited to remain, the others vie for the chance to punish the servant for his part in their troubles. Leporello, sensing that abject groveling is his best bet, begs everyone's pardon profusely, all the while edging toward the door. Choosing a propitious moment, he flees, and Don Ottavio follows.

Left alone, Donna Elvira contemplates her mortification and realizes that, despite her sufferings, she would still forgive the ungrateful Don Giovanni if he returned to her.

The quiet of a lonely cemetery is shattered by Don Giovanni scrambling over a wall. Having extricated himself from yet another predicament, the Don is laughing triumphantly when he is joined by Leporello, who as usual is much aggrieved. The unrepentant Don jokes with him as they resume their proper garb, but in the midst of his hilarity, a ghostly voice intones, "You will have your last laugh before dawn." The moonlight, breaking through the clouds, sheds a silvery light on a great stone statue of the Commendatore.

Leporello's voice quavers as he reads the inscription beneath the statue: "Here I await revenge upon the godless one who sent me to my death."

Don Giovanni finds this amusing. "The old buffoon! Tell him that tonight I expect him for dinner," he blasphemously commands his servant.

Only the Don's dire threats convince the trembling Leporello to extend the invitation, but when he does, the grim statue nods its head. At this, Leporello nearly melts with fear, but Don Giovanni is unmoved. "So you'll come to dinner?" he repeats to the statue.

"Yes!" it replies in funereal tones, startling even the Don.

At her palazzo, Don Ottavio is begging Donna Anna to marry him at once. When she refuses, he accuses her of cruelty, but she reassures him that she will marry him as soon as a suitable mourning period has elapsed.

The fateful hour has arrived. In Don Giovanni's palace, the table has been magnificently set for dinner. The Don enters and commands the musicians to begin. As they play a few old chestnuts like *"Non più andrai"* from *The Marriage of Figaro,* Leporello watches Don Giovanni feast on exquisite morsels and surreptitiously takes a few bites himself.

Suddenly, Donna Elvira enters in a state of nervous agitation. She has come to make a last attempt to reform Don Giovanni, but the callous Don rebuffs her. Finally, her hopes dashed, Donna Elvira rushes to the doorway. There, she freezes and utters a horrifying scream before running away through another door. Curious, the Don sends Leporello to see what has happened. As the servant starts over the threshold, he, too, lets out a bloodcurdling shriek.

"What a scream! Leporello, what is it?"

His teeth chattering, Leporello describes a man of stone who marches through the hall, but the Don dismisses this as mere fantasy. A resonant knock on the door interrupts them and, as Leporello hides under the table, the giant statue enters.

"Don Giovanni, you invited me to dinner and I have come."

The unflappable Don orders another place set at the table, but the statue refuses such mortal food. "Tell me," it says, "will you come and dine with me?"

"No one will say of me that I have ever been afraid," Don Giovanni murmurs, and he assents.

"Give me your hand upon it!"

As the Don clasps the stone hand, a deadly chill overtakes him.

"Repent!" commands the statue, grasping him tightly. "Change your ways, for this is your last hour!"

"No, no, I will not repent!" the Don shouts. "Let me be!"

The two struggle, but Don Giovanni is resolute in his refusal. "Ah! Your time is up!" says the statue at last, and as it disappears, flames rise around the Don and the ground beneath his feet begins to tremble.

The horrifying voices of the damned ring through the chamber and now, finally, Don Giovanni experiences pain. "Who lacerates my soul?" he cries. "Who torments my body? What torture! What agony! What a hell! What a terror!"

Engulfed in flames, Don Giovanni is dragged, screaming, to hell. As he dwindles and fades, his shrieks grow more distant, until finally the room is silent.

Leporello peeks out from under the table. Suddenly, the door is flung open and the Don's victims enter: Donna Elvira, Donna Anna, Zerlina, Don Ottavio, and Masetto storm in, accompanied by a Minister of Justice. They have come to arrest Don Giovanni, but Leporello tells them of the Don's demise. This news is met with general rejoicing: Donna Anna promises to marry Don Ottavio in a year; Donna Elvira decides to join a convent; and Zerlina and Masetto decide to go home and have dinner. As for Leporello, he is finally free to get a new master. Cheerfully, the group declares, "This is the end which befalls evildoers! And in this life scoundrels always receive their just deserts!"

Thus unmourned, Don Giovanni comes to his end. ⤳

# COSÌ FAN TUTTE

The last of the great Mozart–da Ponte triumvirate of operas is *Così fan tutte,* which may be translated, loosely, as "All women are like that." The story, while distressing to our postfeminist sensibilities, had the status of an urban legend in earlier eras: A man who wagers that his wife is a paragon of virtue suffers the humiliation of losing his bet. Shakespeare addressed the theme in *Cymbeline* and Boccaccio took it up in the *Decameron,* to name two of its most illustrious incarnations. The tale is defiantly antisentimental, which may have contributed to the tepid reception of the opera when it premiered in 1790. One critic has called *Così fan tutte* "the apotheosis of insincerity"; in a Europe teetering on the edge of Romanticism, the opera's cynical treatment of love and loyalty was enough to brand it immoral. Franz Xaver Niemetschek, an early and extremely reverent biographer of Mozart, felt obliged to distance his hero from his creation: "Everyone was astonished that this man could have demeaned himself to waste his heavenly melodies on such a worthless libretto. It did not, however, lie within his power to refuse the commission, and the libretto was specially provided." Though there is no evidence that Mozart was actually commissioned to create *Così,* his drastically reduced income for 1789 is ample reason to believe that he desperately needed the opera to please its audience. It is an irony tinged with tragedy that the bright and brittle aristocratic world portrayed in the opera had all but disappeared by the time it was performed.

## ACT ONE

In a café, two strapping young Neapolitan officers, Ferrando and Guglielmo, are deep in disputation with the worldly-wise Don Alfonso. Ferrando is blond, a bit pensive, and madly in love with Dorabella, whereas Guglielmo is dark, more cheerful, and madly in love with Fiordiligi, Dorabella's sister. They are extolling the beauty and constancy of these maidens—with particular emphasis on the constancy. Don Alfonso is shaking his head. There is no such thing as a faithful woman, he announces. Ferrando and Guglielmo immediately offer to run him through with their swords, but Don Alfonso is unmoved: If they're women, they're fickle. Again, the officers protest, and so it goes until Don Alfonso, tiring of their sentimentality, says, "Wait a moment. What if I give you tangible proof today that they are like other women?" Don Alfonso bets the two young men one hundred gold pieces that their women will betray them, and as he concocts his plan, Guglielmo and Ferrando concoct their own—for spending their hundred gold pieces in splendid celebrations of love.

In a garden near the sea, Dorabella and Fiordiligi are gazing rapturously at the portraits of their lovers that they wear in lockets. While Fiordiligi admires Guglielmo's mouth, Dorabella exclaims over Ferrando's eyes. Oh, how happy they are! they exclaim. Their love is most certainly eternal and immovable.

In walks Don Alfonso with some dreadful, horrible, dire news: Ferrando and Guglielmo have been called away to battle. Once the calamity has been announced, the two officers appear mournfully in the garden. "Now you must fulfill the lesser duty," the girls announce, "of plunging your swords into both our hearts." In vain, the men try to comfort their lovers. At the sound of the boat, Fiordiligi announces that she's fainting, Dorabella that she's dying. Against the background of a cheerful marching song, the two couples make passionate farewells while Don Alfonso looks on, trying not to laugh. As the boat sails away and the swooning ladies totter off, Don Alfonso reflects on the foolishness of their sentiment and then he, too, takes his leave.

Despina, the chambermaid, has just entered the drawing room with the sisters' chocolate on a tray, and now she's giving vent to her frustration with the life of service. Why should she have to stand by and watch them drink the chocolate she's had to stir for so long? "O amiable ladies, who gave the substance to you and the aroma to me?" And, putting theory into practice, she takes a big swallow of cocoa.

Just at that moment, Dorabella and Fiordiligi enter the room. Despina chokes, but as it turns out, they're in such despair that they can pay the chocolate no mind. They ask for poison. They ask for the sword. When Despina learns from the collapsed sisters that their trouble is only the temporary absence of their lovers, she is astounded. They should view this event as an opportunity, she advises. They've lost two men, but that leaves all the others. Dorabella and Fiordiligi recoil, but Despina goes on: To hope for constancy in any man is the height of foolishness. Thus, women should follow suit: "Let us love for our convenience and for vanity," she declares jubilantly, as the sisters, aghast, flee.

Now, the two masterminds meet. Don Alfonso finds Despina and, with the help of a few coins, converts her to his cause. Despina agrees that she'll do her best to promote the interests of two of Don Alfonso's friends, who just happen to be outside, dying to meet the lovely Dorabella and Fiordiligi. With a flourish, Don Alfonso ushers them in: It's Guglielmo and Ferrando, in deep disguise as two Albanian noblemen, replete with enormous moustaches. Though she frankly finds their appearance "the very antidote of love," Despina promises to help them win favor and the three men surreptitiously congratulate each other on the success of their costumes.

Hallooing for Despina, Fiordiligi and Dorabella burst into the room. Instead of one servant, they find three supplicants: Despina and two vigorously moustached young men, who plead, "Forgive us, ladies. See, languishing at your lovely feet, two wretches, swains who worship your merit."

The outrage of the two sisters can scarcely be imagined. Filled with fury, they call on the gods to attest to their virtue. Even when Don Alfonso claims the two Albanians as long-lost friends, the girls are not mollified. Whipped to heights of flattery, the two officers rhapsodize about the ladies' charms, but Fiordiligi avows that their infamous words will not profane her heart, and the two prepare to leave in a huff. In vain does Guglielmo describe his manifold charms, including, of course, his moustaches, "the triumph of men, the plumes of love." Fiordiligi and Dorabella march out with their heads held high and the two soldiers burst into laughter, certain that the hundred gold pieces will be theirs.

Back in the garden, Dorabella and Fiordiligi are busy mourning their lost lovers when suddenly the Albanians lurch in, clutching vials of poison and followed by the expostulating Don Alfonso. Together, the two noblemen gulp down the poison, declaring that the sisters' cruel rejection drove them to it. Dorabella and Fiordiligi find the sight of the supine Albanians quite upsetting and, in this as in all troubles, they call for Despina.

With a quick look at Don Alfonso, Despina declares that a doctor must be retrieved immediately, and the two depart. After a good deal of fluttering and fussing, the girls decide that, given the extremity of the situation, it is permissible to pat the Albanians' heads and feel for their pulses. Moved, they admit that the death of the Albanians would make them weep, news that Ferrando and Guglielmo find a bit discomfiting. But here comes the doctor with Don Alfonso, a very peculiar-looking doctor—namely, Despina in disguise. The young ladies are far too occupied to notice the resemblance and earnestly answer the doctor's questions. Despina then produces a large magnet and proceeds to wave it over the stricken bodies of the Albanians, curing them instantly. Saved from death, the two men embrace the girls and kiss their hands, which, Don Alfonso assures them, is merely an aftereffect of the poison. The sisters find their resistance to Albanian charms weakening— until the noblemen ask them for kisses, which provokes an indignant protest.

# ACT TWO

Dorabella, Fiordiligi, and the inimitable Despina are chatting about feminine wiles. *"Una donna a quindici anni . . .* a woman, by the age of fifteen," begins Despina, "must know what's what, where the devil hides his tail, what is good and what is bad. She must know the cunning ways that make lovers fall in love, feign laughter, feign tears, invent fine excuses." On and on she goes, offering the girls a catalog of necessary skills: flirting, lying, hiding, appeasing, commanding.

Dorabella, a quick study, decides to adopt the proffered philosophy. "Enjoying ourselves a little and not dying of melancholy isn't betraying our word, sister," she announces. "I'll take the little dark one."

"And for me," declares Fiordiligi, "the blond one. I want to laugh and joke a bit." Thus, unknowingly, each has chosen her sister's lover.

Back in the garden by the sea, Ferrando and Guglielmo, still incognito, stand on a gaily decorated boat, singing love songs to the sisters on the shore. Disembarking, they approach Dorabella and Fiordiligi with melting looks and wooing words. The girls are at first struck dumb by this sentimental assault, but soon each girl is strolling with her new swain.

Dorabella succumbs to Guglielmo in no time, replacing Ferrando's portrait with the other's gift of a heart-shaped pendant while Guglielmo looks on, pitying his friend his faithless lover. Fiordiligi retains the remnants of her virtue, though she can feel her resistance crumbling. To avoid temptation, she flees her Albanian, returning to the villa. Abandoning their overwrought ladies for a moment, Ferrando and Guglielmo rendezvous in the garden to compare notes. "Friend, we've won!" crows Ferrando. Fiordiligi, he assures Guglielmo, is chastity personified. "And my Dorabella?" he inquires. "How did she behave?"

Not one to spare feelings, Guglielmo shows his friend the discarded portrait that Dorabella replaced with the pendant. The enraged Ferrando determines to kill the faithless girl and is only just restrained by the argument that she isn't worth the trouble. Guglielmo, from the lofty position of one who has not (yet) been thrown over, offers his considered opinion of women as solace for his despondent friend. Ferrando admits that, treacherous or not, Dorabella is still the one he loves. This profession is heard by Don Alfonso, who congratulates him on his constancy. Though Don Alfonso reminds him that the game is not yet over, Guglielmo remains confident in the adherent nature of his charms.

However, even now Fiordiligi is admitting to Dorabella and Despina that she, too, is in love—and not with Guglielmo. Though her sister and her servant urge Fiordiligi to capitulate, she gallantly attempts to maintain her resistance by suggesting that she and Dorabella don uniforms and join their fiancés at the front. Guglielmo, watching her from a concealed spot, again congratulates himself on the quality of the love he inspires. But when Ferrando, in his Albanian getup, declares, "Your heart, or my death," poor Fiordiligi's virtue suffers a mortal blow.

Falling into his arms, she cries, "Cruel man, you've won . . . do with me what you will." While Don Alfonso restrains Guglielmo from rushing in and killing her, the newly paired Ferrando and Fiordiligi rapturously confess their love and hurry from the room. Who can blame Ferrando when he returns for a quick bit of gloating?

Together, the two young men vow to exact revenge, but Don Alfonso advises them to marry the sisters instead. Nature, he tells them, couldn't go to the trouble of creating two women of a different clay, just for them. "Tutti accusan le donne ed io le scuso . . . Everyone accuses women and I excuse them, if a thousand times each day they change their love. The lover who, at the end, finds himself disappointed, shouldn't lay the blame on another, but on himself, since young and old, beautiful and ugly—repeat after me—all women are like that!"

"All women are like that!" chime in Ferrando and Guglielmo.

Despina enters with the news that the ladies are prepared to marry their Albanian lovers. Newly armed with tolerance, the soldiers agree.

The final scene opens with Despina and Don Alfonso gleefully arranging the wedding festivities. "A finer comedy has never and will never be seen," they laugh. The blushing brides and bemused grooms exchange compliments and toasts, with Guglielmo muttering darkly about shameless hussies off to the side.

Don Alfonso announces the arrival of the notary who will perform the marriage. It's Despina in disguise, of course, and she embarks on the formalities with notarial dignity, sputtering about contracts, dowries, and counterdowries. The impatient lovers interrupt, urging her to marry them at once. But what's this? The sounds of a military march can be heard outside! Don Alfonso proclaims that the missing officers are landing at the shore that very moment!

Needless to say, this news throws the sisters into turmoil, and everyone tries to flee. In the commotion, the pseudo-Albanians slip away, only to reenter a few minutes later as Guglielmo and Ferrando, pointedly rejoicing in their return "safe and sound to the loving embraces of our most faithful lovers." But why, they inquire with elaborate solicitude, are the girls so pale, so silent?

Don Alfonso hastens to assure them that the sisters are merely stunned with delight, while Fiordiligi and Dorabella murmur, "If I don't die, it will be a miracle."

Swaggering about, Guglielmo discovers the notary and demands an explanation for his presence. Thinking quickly, Despina reveals herself and swears she's been at a costume party. Don Alfonso, refusing to be foiled by this development, drops the marriage contract to the floor, where Ferrando can pick it up and feign horror at the evidence.

"Good heavens! You've signed here: You can't deny it! Betrayal! Betrayal! Ah, let the revelation be made, and in streams, rivers, oceans, blood will then flow!" the two officers yelp. Humbly, Dorabella and Fiordiligi admit their mistake and, with their usual drama, announce themselves worthy only of death.

Don Alfonso, enjoying himself mightily, suggests that Guglielmo and Ferrando look in the next room, where the putative Albanians hid themselves at the arrival of the officers. The two girls quake with terror—until Guglielmo and Ferrando return, without the plumes of love but in the garb of the Albanian noblemen, and reveal the plot. Despina and the two sisters are suitably humiliated, but Don Alfonso is triumphant.

Fervently, the sisters promise that they'll adore their lovers forever, and fervently the men answer, "I believe you, my lovely joy, but don't want to test it." Despina, meanwhile, is suffering the humiliation of having been taken in by Don Alfonso. But all together they declare, "Fortunate is the man who can take the good with the bad and in all events and trials allows himself to be led by reason. What makes others weep is for him a source of laughter and in the midst of the world's buffeting, he will find a lovely calm."

# THE MAGIC FLUTE

*— Die Zauberflöte —*

Composed in 1791, the last year of Mozart's life, *The Magic Flute* is a world away from the rococo sophistication of *Così fan tutte,* both musically and morally. For the first time, Mozart was composing an opera for the people of Vienna rather than for their emperor. The commission to write a new opera came from Emanuel Schikaneder, an impresario who also was a famous Shakespearean actor, an inveterate carouser, and, like Mozart, a Freemason. He had a brilliant idea for a libretto—a sort of fairy tale, with plenty of special effects (including storms and trick animals) and lots of comic relief, all done up in the Oriental style that had made such a hit at two competing playhouses that year. Mozart agreed, and the result was *The Magic Flute,* an opera that has been called both the "strangest of Mozart's operas" and "the first and perhaps the only great masterpiece of music ever created deliberately for 'the masses.'" Beethoven was a devoted admirer, as was Wagner. George Bernard Shaw declared that its grand aria, *"O Isis und Osiris,"* was "the only music which might be put into the mouth of God without blasphemy."

Schikaneder's libretto is a hodgepodge of crowd-pleasing comedy, awe-inspiring pyrotechnics, and heartrending romance. But it is also a spiritual fable; the dreamy peregrinations of the plot are rife with Masonic symbols and thinly veiled references to Masonic beliefs. The acquisition of wisdom is the true subject of the opera; the moral center of the story comes into focus during Sarastro's second-act aria, when he avows that "evil cannot survive when all people love one another. Anyone who does not accept this knowledge does not deserve to be a human being." This coda, the foundation of Masonic belief, was undoubtedly an article of faith for both Mozart and Schikaneder, and the humanism and progressiveness that pervade the opera make it more earnest as well as more mysterious than any of Mozart's previous works.

# ACT ONE

Prince Tamino, the royal scion of a mighty Eastern kingdom, finds himself journeying through dark and dreadful mountains. Brought up in splendor and indulgence, the Prince wanders alone and unarmed through the rocks, intent only on pleasing himself. Imagine his horror when a great viper uncoils itself from its stony den and slithers toward him. The frightened prince runs like the wind, but the snake pursues him, roiling and heaving ever closer. In vain, Tamino cries out for help, and, as the snake draws back to strike, he faints away with terror. As he lies unconscious, three dark ladies appear and join forces to smite the serpent dead with their spears. These ladies, servants to the Queen of the Night, admire their handiwork before turning their attention to the handsome young prince lying before them. After a bit of squabbling about who should guard him, they decide that it is only fair that they all go to inform the Queen, and so, with a few backward glances at their prize, they depart for her palace.

No sooner have they left than Prince Tamino awakes, wondering how he has escaped with his life. Before he has time to do much more, however, a piping tune comes wafting out of the nearby forest and a strange-looking figure marches onto the scene. *"Der Vogelfänger bin ich ja . . .* Yes, I'm the bird-catcher," he chortles, beaky nose in the air, "always jolly, known to all." This is Papageno, who is quite pleased with himself. Cheered by this odd birdman, Tamino introduces himself as a royal visitor from another land, and though Papageno is taken aback by the news that there *is* another land, he welcomes the Prince and explains that he serves the Queen of the Night. Tamino assumes that Papageno is the one who delivered him from the snake and Papageno, after quickly checking to make sure that the beast is dead, regales his new friend with the gory details of his single-handed strangulation of the serpent.

*"Papageno!"* shout the three ladies, abruptly returning, outraged at this barefaced lie.

No amount of backpedaling can save the bird-catcher; the ladies promptly lock his lips with a golden padlock, then turn their attentions to Prince Tamino. They are bearing, they announce, a portrait of the Queen's daughter, Pamina, and if the Prince finds her appealing, fortune, honor, and fame might well be his.

There is a long silence while Tamino gazes at the portrait as though bewitched. Finally, he speaks: *"Dies Bildnis . . .* This portrait is quite entrancing, like nothing I've ever seen before. I feel this heavenly image filling my heart with a new emotion. Could it be love?"

The ladies interrupt his reverie to congratulate him. The Queen, they say, has heard every word and, in her beneficence, has resolved to grant him her daughter's hand after he has saved the girl.

"Saved?" asks Tamino.

A mighty, wicked demon named Sarastro has spirited her away, they explain, throwing Tamino into a ferment of anxiety and chivalrous rage that is abruptly halted by a roar of thunder. The Queen of the Night swoops down, her dark hair swirling around her ghostly white face, her great gray eyes shining like stars. In a grand voice she welcomes Tamino and describes the terrible moment of Pamina's abduction. *"Zum Leiden bin ich auserkoren . . .* Suffering is my destiny," she pronounces, tragically. However, suffering does not preclude commanding. "You shall be my daughter's savior! Yes!" she cries. "And if you are victorious, she shall be yours forevermore!" With this vow, the Queen departs in another whirlwind.

The three ladies give him instructions for effecting the rescue, while poor Papageno chimes in with muffled "hmmm-hmmms" through his locked lips. Finally, the ladies relent and, after a little homily on the evils of lying, remove the golden padlock. To prepare Tamino for his journey to Sarastro's palace, they bestow upon the Prince a magic flute that has the extremely helpful property of filling all who hear its music with love and joy. And for Papageno, who is to accompany the Prince—

"No, thank you very much," protests the bird-catcher. "You yourselves have told me that Sarastro is as fierce as a tiger." Hastily, Papageno tries to make his escape. The implacable ladies pay him no mind. Thrusting a set of silver bells into his hand, they assure him that he will find in them ample protection.

Over their shoulders, the departing ladies tell them that three boys, young, pretty, good, and wise, will guide them on their journey.

At the lavish palace of Sarastro, Pamina has just made an unsuccessful attempt to escape her jailer, the Moorish ghoul Monostatos. As Monostatos gleefully rebinds her fetters and hisses threats, Papageno peers through the window. Having somehow misplaced the Prince, he is pleased to find some company. Bounding through the door, he comes face-to-face with Monostatos and they both recoil in horror. "This surely is the devil," they cry in unison, and the craven jailer scurries away in terror.

A careful inspection of the miniature portrait convinces Papageno that he has indeed found the Queen's daughter, and he tells her about Prince Tamino—how he saw the picture, fell in love, and vowed to rescue her. The lovely Pamina finds this all a little surprising, but she can see that Papageno has a tender heart and she decides to trust him. "What use is my tender heart," complains the bird-catcher, "when Papageno has no Papagena?"

Pamina assures him that he will find love in the end. *"Bei männern welche Liebe fühlen . . .* The man who can love has kindness of heart." Together they agree that love is the center of life.

Meanwhile, the three boys have led Tamino to the Temple of Sarastro, where they leave him standing before three giant portals. Tamino approaches the first door with bravado.

"Stand back!" thunders a voice.

Tamino jumps back and tries the second door. Again, the voice orders him away. Finally, with more trepidation, he knocks on the third door and is greeted by an old priest, who asks him what he seeks.

"Love and virtue," responds Tamino.

The priest rebukes him: "You cannot be guided by love and virtue, because you are inflamed by death and revenge."

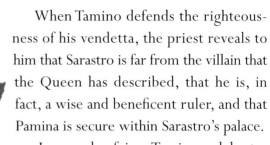

When Tamino defends the righteousness of his vendetta, the priest reveals to him that Sarastro is far from the villain that the Queen has described, that he is, in fact, a wise and beneficent ruler, and that Pamina is secure within Sarastro's palace.

In a rush of joy, Tamino celebrates Pamina's safety by taking out his magic flute and playing a tune. From behind the rocks, from around the pillars of the temple, and, seemingly, from the very air, majestic and beautiful beasts appear, lulled by the magical music. Lions, peacocks, and foxes cluster around the Prince as he plays and return to their hiding places when he puts the flute down, distracted by the distant sound of Papageno's bells. Filled with anticipation, the Prince rushes off to find the bird-catcher.

If only he had waited, for who should enter the temple glade but Papageno and Pamina, rushing to find Tamino. The ghoulish warden, having recovered from his fright, comes charging after them, shrieking for his slaves to bring the ropes, bring the fetters, capture the miscreants, tie them up! In the nick of time, Papageno pulls out his chimes and plays a pretty song. Much against their will, Monostatos and his henchmen are overcome by the tune and are whirled away in an uncontrollable dance.

Hardly have Pamina and Papageno finished rejoicing in this reprieve than a mighty chorus announces the arrival of the dread Sarastro. Papageno fervently wishes that he were a mouse, a snail, anything that could hide away, but Pamina bravely approaches Sarastro's chariot and humbly begs forgiveness for her flight. The fault, she adds, was not hers alone, for "the evil Moor demanded love."

With a kindly smile, Sarastro grants her pardon, though he declines to free her.

"But my mother—" begins Pamina.

"Your happiness would be destroyed if I left you in her hands," says Sarastro, just as Monostatos reappears, dragging Tamino behind him in chains. While Monostatos blusters about, trying to impress Sarastro and hinting for a reward, Tamino and Pamina finally see each other for the first time.

"It is she," murmurs the Prince.

"It is he," murmurs Pamina.

Impelled by the magical force of love, they embrace, provoking an explosion from Monostatos. "What insolence! Part them at once! He meant to steal Pamina from you," the warden explains to Sarastro. "But I was able to track him down."

Sarastro agrees that such watchfulness deserves a reward and gives Monostatos a good one: seventy-seven strokes of the bastinado!

Turning his attention to the young lovers, Sarastro tells them of the initiation rite to come, which will prove their worthiness of each other.

# ACT TWO

In the center of a forest of silver palm trees stands a giant pyramid, surrounded by eighteen thrones; this is the Temple of Light. Marching toward the temple in a solemn processional are eighteen priests of the sun, each carrying a palm branch. Once they are seated on their thrones, Sarastro begins his address. "Tamino, the son of a king," he says, "intends to tear aside the dark veil and to behold the sanctuary of supreme light. Today our duty must be to watch over this man and to extend to him the hand of friendship." Tamino has been chosen to wed Pamina, Sarastro informs the assembly, but he must prove his virtue, discretion, and charity before

*There is much fussing among musicologists about the sudden U-turn that* The Magic Flute *takes at the end of Act One. It's true that the Queen of the Night's abrupt transformation from grieving mother to vengeful villain is startling, and Sarastro's corresponding mutation from kidnapper to beneficent ruler certainly occurs without much explanation. Scholars have developed several theories; some believe the opera to be a political allegory, with the Queen of the Night representing the capricious Empress Maria Theresa. Others believe that Mozart had already composed much of the first act when another opera based on the same fairy tale appeared at a Vienna theater, causing Schikaneder to make hasty revisions to the latter part of his libretto. Though there were undoubtedly interpolations and alterations in the action of the story —why, for example, is Pamina suicidal at the beginning of the second-act finale when she has been assured of a reconciliation with Tamino in an earlier trio?—the transformations that the characters undergo may simply be part of the Masonic creed that informs the work. Freemasons of the era placed a great deal of emphasis on the hidden nature of great truths. Wisdom was not accessible to the uninitiated, and the unveiling of hermetic knowledge was the primary theme of induction into the order. As Tamino progresses further in his journey toward wisdom, the true nature of the Queen of the Night becomes clearer, echoing the journey of the Mason from the darkness of ignorance to the blinding light of truth. Unfortunately, the degree to which these and other transformations are inspired by Masonic mysteries will never be known, since neither Mozart nor Schikaneder left any evidence of their thoughts on the subject.*

the couple can be permitted to enter the Temple of Light together. "*O Isis und Osiris*," intones Sarastro, "grant to this new couple wisdom's spirit. Let them see the fruit of their trials. But if they should die, reward their brave endeavor; take them to your dwelling on high."

The rite begins: Tamino finds himself in the midst of a great thunderstorm. Papageno, sitting beside him, is so terrified he can scarcely move—and he's sure he's caught the flu. Two priests appear and warn Tamino that his second trial is one of silence—he must not speak to any woman, including Pamina. Tamino is stalwart, but Papageno has his doubts. After much argument, Papageno reluctantly acquiesces to the forthcoming trials, but no sooner have the priests departed than the three ladies of the Queen appear, full of dire predictions about Tamino's fate. Promptly forgetting his vow of silence, Papageno begins to question them. However, a chorus of initiates soon damn the ladies to the underworld, where they properly belong.

While Tamino is unfolding mysteries in one part of Sarastro's palace, Pamina has been overcome by languor in the garden. She sleeps there, all unaware that Monostatos is creeping closer. Undeterred by the beating he had been promised, the ghoulish warden goggles lasciviously at Pamina's sleeping figure. But his lustful ruminations are suddenly interrupted by a great swooping maelstrom—it is the Queen of the Night, and she is in a rage. Monostatos hides behind a tree just close enough to hear the exchange between the Queen and her daughter.

*The Magic Flute premiered on September 30, 1791, and was accounted a great success almost immediately. Sadly, Mozart had little time to enjoy this triumph, for he died on December 5, afflicted by the idea that he had been the victim of poison. Though few scholars now give any credence to the old rumor that he was killed by the rival composer Salieri, Mozart's sense of persecution was certainly real enough. It had all begun the previous summer, when a mysterious visitor delivered a letter "without a signature" offering Mozart a substantial sum for a requiem mass, the sole stipulation being that Mozart was not to inquire into the identity of the patron. Accepting the commission, Mozart began work on the requiem, though he was already in the middle of two operatic works,* The Clemency of Titus *and* The Magic Flute. *When he was called suddenly to Prague later that summer, the messenger reappeared, "like a ghost," according to Constanze Mozart, to ask about his progress on the requiem. This visitation discomfited Mozart greatly and later in the year he became haunted by the notion that he was writing the piece for his own funeral. He continued to work on the requiem, but could not bring himself to finish it. As he lay dying, he was much preoccupied with the unfinished work, even attempting to organize rehearsals in his sickroom; but his final words were about* The Magic Flute. *He imagined that he was at the theater, where his sister-in-law, Josepha Hofer, was singing the part of the Queen of the Night: "Quiet, quiet! Hofer is just taking her top F;—now my sister-in-law is singing her second aria . . . how strongly she strikes and holds the B-flat: 'Hear, hear, hear the mother's curse!'" Soon thereafter, Mozart died.*

Pamina's natural joy on seeing her mother is soon extinguished by the Queen's words: Tamino, once initiated, will be lost to Pamina forever. The girl protests: Might she not love the Prince just the same?

This stirs the Queen to a fury. "You would love a man who might cause my downfall at any moment?!" she cries and pulls a knife from within the soft folds of her robes. "Do you see this dagger? It has been sharpened for Sarastro. You shall kill him and bring to me the powerful circle of the sun! *Der Hölle Rache kocht in meinem Herzen . . .* Hell's revenge burns within my heart! If through you Sarastro does not die, you are no longer my daughter!" and, tossing the dagger at Pamina's feet, the Queen swirls away in a wrathful twist of wind.

Stunned, Pamina looks after her. "But," she says weakly, "I cannot."

The sly Monostatos chooses this moment to emerge from his hiding spot and put his newest plan into action. He will reveal her murderous plot to Sarastro, he informs poor Pamina, unless she consents to love him. Pamina resolutely refuses; then, as Monostatos is filling the air with threats and curses, Sarastro himself enters. Though the warden does his best to incriminate Pamina, Sarastro knows better. He banishes Monostatos from the kingdom and as the ugly fellow slips away, Sarastro promises that he will exact no revenge upon the Queen. *"In deisen heil'gen Hallen . . .* In these sacred halls, we forgive all our enemies. He who does not rejoice in such teaching does not deserve to be a man."

Meanwhile, the two priests are still giving Tamino and Papageno advice. Tamino is setting new standards for silence, but Papageno is hungry, thirsty, and easily distracted. How can he remain silent when an ancient crone appears bearing water and announces that her name is Papagena, that she is really eighteen years old, and that she has a sweetheart named—Papageno! As soon as she has revealed her name to him, she flutters off like a bird, and the three boys who have guided Tamino descend from the sky in an elegant hot-air balloon, ornamented with great curling bows and scrolls. They have been sent by Sarastro to deliver the magic flute to Tamino and the silver bells to Papageno—and to offer them a delicious array of food and drink. This last is a great relief to Papageno, but Tamino expresses his gratitude only by playing his magic flute.

The enchanted melody brings Pamina running ecstatically to her prince. But he, adhering to his vow of silence, does not respond to her; she walks alone and in despair, sure that he has abandoned her. Sarastro appears, offering as comfort the prediction that she and the Prince will be reunited after Tamino's final trial.

Papageno, too, becomes separated from Tamino. Approaching the Temple, he bangs on the doors and receives the same thunderous warning that Tamino has. This reduces him to shivers and, observing his craven behavior, the two priests return to inform him that though he will never be first among the initiates, they will grant him a single wish. Papageno opts for a glass of good wine, but once that is swallowed, he makes another request: He would also like a nice girlfriend or wife! Benevolently, the priests acquiesce, and the old crone reappears. Papageno holds out as long as he can, but when the old woman tells him that he must marry her or be condemned to a diet of bread and water forever, he finally consents. Instantaneously, the crone is transformed into the young and pretty Papagena. Soon enough, though, the old priest comes and takes her away.

Despite Sarastro's assurances, Pamina is convinced that Tamino has abandoned her. Inconsolable, she wanders in the palace gardens. The three boys descend in their balloon and, divining her suicidal intentions, take her dagger away and promise to carry her to her beloved.

And they do. Accompanied by a pair of men in black armor, Tamino stands before two great mountains, one containing roaring flames and the other a gushing waterfall; within these, he will undergo the test of the elements. At the last minute, Pamina rushes to Tamino's side and begs to accompany him. The two men in armor give their permission, and Tamino picks up his magic flute. As he plays it, the couple proceeds through the test of the elements unharmed. Triumphant, they emerge from this final trial to be greeted as full initiates into the Temple of Light.

Papageno, meanwhile, is miserably looking for his Papagena. Like Pamina, he decides to end it all, and like Pamina, he is prevented from killing himself by the three boys, whose balloon just happens to drift by. They suggest he try the silver bells, which Papageno has forgotten all about. Of course! Papageno rings the bells as fast as he can and—poof!—Papagena appears.

Both of them are stunned.

"Pa, pa, pa, Papagena!" stutters Papageno.

"Pa, pa, pa, Papageno!" stutters Papagena back.

Once they stop stuttering, they swear eternal love, decide to have a million little Papagenos and Papagenas, and run off to start their life together.

Monostatos, who has joined forces with the Queen of the Night, makes one last attempt to overthrow Sarastro. Joined by the three wicked ladies, they try to invade the temple, but Sarastro's power proves too great for them and in an explosion of thunder and lightning the pack of villains is swallowed into the earth. The initiates celebrate their triumph, and everyone lives happily ever after. ⁓꙲

# FIDELIO

**A**s Ludwig van Beethoven lay dying in 1827, he bequeathed the manuscript of his only opera, *Fidelio,* to a friend, saying, "Of all my children, this is the one that cost me the worst birth-pangs and brought me the most sorrow; and for that reason it is the one most dear to me." Consider this, in a family that includes the Fifth and Ninth Symphonies, the *Moonlight* Sonata, and the late quartets—to be the favored child among such siblings is a rare honor.

But it was indeed a difficult labor: *Fidelio* was composed by Beethoven not once, but four times. It began its life in 1805 as *Leonore,* with three acts and an overture that is now known, confusingly, as "Leonore no. 2." The premiere in Vienna was a resounding failure, not only because the city had been invaded by Napoleon Bonaparte the previous week, but because the opera itself was dismissed as a "miserable mixture of low manner and romantic situations." Aghast at this response, Beethoven withdrew the opera after only three performances. The following March, he offered a revised, shortened version featuring the bravura "Leonore no. 3" overture, which nowadays is occasionally sandwiched between the first and second scenes of Act Two. However, this second version met with no better a fate; the composer removed the score in a huff after deciding that the management was cheating him out of his royalties. The opera then languished for some eight years before a trio of singers attached to the Kärntnertor Theater asked Beethoven for permission to revive it. He agreed on the condition that he could make major alterations, and on May 23, 1814, a completely revised version with a new overture appeared. Entitled *Fidelio,* the opera was reduced to two acts, with much of the story simplified by a new librettist, Georg Friedrich Treitschke. Though it was well received, the opera was not fixed in its final form until the middle of the summer. Aside from his obvious dissatisfaction with the overture, Beethoven's primary problem was resolving the conflict between the opera's heroic themes and its cozy domestic scenes, which emphasized speech mixed with songs. Despite his efforts, Beethoven's revisions were not enough for some latter-day interpreters of *Fidelio,* who preferred their heroism unmitigated and cut vast portions of the homey dialogue in favor of the higher emotional pitch of the dungeon scenes.

# ACT ONE

Two years before our story opens, Leonore had watched helplessly as her husband, Florestan, was dragged away in chains by masked guards. In the long months since, she has had no word, no sign that he is alive, but she has never ceased to search for him. Now, following little more than her intuition, she believes that she has found the prison where he is incarcerated, and in desperation she has disguised herself as a young man, Fidelio, and obtained a position as the assistant to the head jailer, Rocco. Though Rocco and his family haven't the slightest suspicion that their new employee is really a woman, the situation is not without peril, for Marzelline, Rocco's daughter, has taken a decided interest in the young man. As the story opens, Marzelline is doing her best to avoid the attentions of her father's other assistant, Jaquino, with whom she had been in the midst of a protracted courtship before Fidelio's appearance on the scene. Jaquino is annoyed to find that he has been ousted from Marzelline's affections and when she settles down to ironing in the prison courtyard, it seems a propitious moment for a romantic tête-à-tête—but he is perpetually interrupted by deliveries at the porter's gate. Desperately, Jaquino proposes, but she answers with an absentminded, "Oh, really? I suppose we're engaged then."

A loud knocking comes from the gate and the exasperated Jaquino goes to open it. While he's gone, Marzelline takes courage, and when he returns, she breaks the news: She will never marry him.

"But you promised me so often," Jaquino protests.

Marzelline denies it, but even her denials are halfhearted, because her mind is on Fidelio—when will he return from the city?

Her father, Rocco, is thinking the same thing. He comes into the courtyard just as Leonore (in her Fidelio guise) returns, bearing the sturdy new set of chains that he had sent her out to purchase. After Rocco congratulates her on her shopping skills, Leonore finds herself in a predicament: On one side is Marzelline, looking at her dreamily; on the other is her employer, dropping broad hints about what a fine son-in-law she would be; and in front of her is Jaquino, glowering. In a fit of benevolence, Rocco grants Fidelio the un-asked-for favor of his daughter's hand, and he offers the happy couple his philosophy of life: *"Hat man nicht auch Gold beineben . . .* Unless you have money as well as love, you will never be truly content. Gold is a lovely, lovely thing, oh, a precious thing is gold."

Choosing this opportunity to introduce her secret agenda, Leonore avows that her deepest desire is to be of greater help to Rocco. For example, she suggests cleverly, he looks exhausted after he returns from his daily trip to the deepest dungeon—perhaps she could help him with that arduous task.

Rocco demurs. He has the strictest orders to attend to that prisoner himself, though it is certainly tiring. But, he says, the prisoner will not last much longer. Rocco has been given orders to reduce his ration gradually, and now the captive receives no more than two ounces of bread and a little water each day; no light, no straw, nothing else! Affecting a professional coolness, Leonore tries to restrain her desperate anxiety about the identity of the prisoner.

Suddenly the massive front gate swings open and Pizarro, the Governor of the prison, stalks into the courtyard, flanked by a troop of soldiers and officers. Leonore and Marzelline hastily withdraw into the warden's house as Pizarro demands the latest dispatches from Rocco. Leafing through them, he finds an anonymous letter, which he (foolishly) reads aloud: "I am writing to inform you that the Prime Minister has learned of several victims of arbitrary oppression who languish in the prisons under your supervision. He leaves tomorrow to make a surprise investigation." Grinding his teeth, Pizarro muses on the situation. "God! If he should discover Florestan, whom he believes long since dead! Still, there is a solution!" The Governor's mouth twists into a diabolical grin. "Vengeance shall be mine! To twist the knife in his heart! What bliss. Now I have the chance to slay the would-be slayer, and in his dying moments to shout in his ear: Triumph!"

Pizarro orders his captain to put a watch on the road from Seville. As soon as the Prime Minister's carriage is seen, the trumpeter is to signal. The troops march away and Pizarro is left alone with Rocco. The Governor knows his man: He tosses a purseful of coins at Rocco before broaching the delicate subject of murder.

"Murder?" stammers Rocco. After hemming and hawing for a bit, he finally gathers his courage and announces, "No sir, the taking of life is no part of my duties."

With an aggrieved sigh, Pizarro agrees that he will do the murdering himself. But Rocco must go down at once "to that man down there—"

"The one who's scarce alive?" asks Rocco.

*The soprano Wilhelmine Schröder-Devrient was considered the definitive Leonore in the mid-nineteenth century, and no wonder—she learned the part from Beethoven himself. However, her description of one of his rehearsals reveals the difficulties of working with the illustrious composer: "Waving his baton to and fro with violent movements, a puzzled expression on his face, and celestial inspiration in his eyes, he stood among the playing musicians and did not hear a note. When, in his opinion, a note was to be played piano, he would creep almost under the music stand; when he wanted forte, he would leap upwards with the most curious gestures and utter the strangest sounds. . . . It was inevitable that the deaf composer caused the most complete confusion among the singers and orchestra and everyone got quite out of time . . . But Beethoven observed nothing of all that, and so we somehow managed to finish the rehearsal, with which he seemed to be quite satisfied, for he laid aside the baton with a cheerful smile. It was unthinkable, however, that he should be entrusted with the performance, and Kappellmeister Umlauf had the heartbreaking task of telling him that the opera could not be put on with him conducting."*

For those who keep track of details: The "Leonore no. 1" overture was composed for a proposed revival of the opera in Prague in 1806 but was mistakenly believed to precede the "Leonore no. 2" overture when the manuscript was found in 1832.

"Yes, that one," says Pizarro—"and dig a grave in his cell."

Rocco assuages his conscience by reflecting that death will probably be a deliverance for the suffering prisoner.

Though she cannot hear what they are saying, Leonore has been spying on this conference, and now, as they depart, she bursts into the courtyard in a state of desperation. *"Abscheulicher!* Monstrous fiend!" she cries, looking after Pizarro's retreating figure. "Where are you scurrying? What are you plotting?" But soon she regains hope and vows to take any measure necessary to save her husband.

Pizarro having left the prison grounds, Leonore has persuaded Rocco to allow the prisoners the rare privilege of a bit of fresh air. As they emerge, pale and hollow-eyed, from their cells, the captives rejoice, *"O welche Lust . . .* Oh what joy to be in free air, to draw our breath with ease." As an officer appears on the ramparts, the prisoners warn one another to restrain their joy and slowly walk into the garden.

Rocco walks into the courtyard, rubbing his hands with satisfaction. Pizarro, he says, has given his permission for Fidelio to both marry Marzelline and assist him further in the dungeons. "This very day, I shall take you down to the cells."

Leonore is exhilarated, though she tries to moderate her enthusiasm. Rocco promises that she shall accompany him to the deepest cell, "down to the captive I have been giving less and less to eat."

"To free him?" cries Leonore impetuously.

"Oh, no," Rocco assures her, "to bury him." He explains Pizarro's plot to her, and their part in it. Thinking that Fidelio's trembling is a sign that he is daunted by the labor, Rocco explains that the grave will be easily made.

Suddenly, Marzelline and Jaquino burst in—Pizarro has learned that the prisoners are enjoying a respite, and he is in a rage. Sure enough, the Governor storms in, but the jailer delicately brings up the imminent satisfaction Pizarro will get by killing Florestan, which mollifies the villain somewhat, though he demands that the captives be returned to their cells instantly. As the prisoners file back into the building, Leonore anguishes over their unjust fate.

# ACT TWO

In the clammy darkness of the deepest dungeon, a solitary prisoner sits on a stone ledge. The only light is a thin, gray gloom emanating from tiny grates cut into the wall, revealing a staircase. With a dull clank of his chains, Florestan shifts on his bench. *"Gott! welch' Dunkel hier . . .* God! What darkness here. What ghastly silence!" As he contemplates his death, which he knows will come soon, he has a vision of an angel: "Has not my tomb become lighter? I see an angel that seems to be my Leonore, leading me to freedom." Covering his face with his hands, Florestan slips into unconsciousness just as Leonore and Rocco enter his cell.

Her first thought is that the prisoner is dead, but Rocco tells her that he's merely asleep. Despite her surreptitious looks, she cannot see the captive's face. Meanwhile, Rocco is all business, climbing into the cistern with his pickax and shovel. Pretending to busy herself with a large stone, Leonore vows that she shall set the captive free, no matter who he may be.

As Rocco stops to take a long swig from his flask, Florestan raises his head. "Had a little rest, then?" inquires Rocco.

"Rest? How could I rest?" responds Florestan, turning his head toward the jailer.

"God! It is him!" exclaims Leonore under her breath.

Meanwhile Florestan begs his jailer, clearly for the hundredth time, to reveal the identity of the prison's governor.

Relenting, Rocco tells him, "Well, then, the governor is Don Pizarro."

"Pizarro! The traitor I dared to expose! O send a messenger to Seville to find Leonore Florestan, and tell her that I am a prisoner here," he begs.

But Rocco's benevolence goes only so far. "That is impossible. It would completely ruin me and do you no good."

Florestan sags against the stone wall. "If I am condemned to end my life here, let it not be in the slow agony of thirst and starvation. In pity give me just a drop of water."

Rocco gestures for Fidelio, and Leonore leaps to provide the prisoner with the jailer's flask. Shamed into compassion by his assistant, Rocco allows Fidelio to give Florestan a piece of bread as well.

"Oh, thank you, thank you," cries the starving man to Leonore. "May you be rewarded in a better world."

Stung by his exclusion from this gratitude, Rocco announces, "I've often been moved by your sufferings

here, but I was strictly forbidden to help you." The grave is finished now and, sympathy notwithstanding, Rocco sends up a signal for Pizarro to descend.

In no time, the villain appears in Florestan's cell with his cloak drawn up to conceal his face.

"Shall I remove his chains?" inquires Rocco.

"No, but unchain him from the rock," answers the coward, drawing his dagger. *"Er sterbe!* He shall die!" But first, Pizarro pulls aside the cloak to reveal himself. "Pizarro, whom you should have feared, is here to take his revenge," he gloats.

Just as he lunges forward, Leonore throws herself between the two men. "First kill his wife!" she cries, astonishing them all.

Florestan recovers first. "My heart stands still with joy," he exclaims, but Pizarro is recovering his rage.

"What incredible audacity," he sputters. "Am I to be frightened by a woman? You shared his life—now share his death!" He lifts his dagger.

But Leonore is not so easily vanquished. Drawing a small pistol from her doublet, she points it at Pizarro. "Another sound and you're dead!" she warns, as the call of a trumpet is heard, signaling the arrival of the Prime Minister. "You are safe now, thank God!" she exults, throwing her arms around Florestan. Cursing fate, Pizarro ascends the stairs and Rocco follows, shaken by the scene he has witnessed.

Left behind in the dank cell, Leonore and Florestan rhapsodize about the unutterable bliss of reunion: *"O namenlose Freude!"* Together, they thank God for the joy he has given them.

Into the courtyard in front of the castle enters the Prime Minister, Don Fernando. He is accompanied by Pizarro and his troops. The townspeople cluster about, and Marzelline and Jaquino lead in the prisoners.

The Prime Minister announces that he has come at the King's behest, to offer mercy to any unjustly held prisoners. As the populace rejoices, Rocco pushes his way through the crowd. "Help these unfortunates, my lord," he calls to the Prime Minister, and stepping aside, he reveals Florestan and Leonore.

"He whom I thought dead, the noble spirit who fought for truth?" exclaims Don Fernando.

"Yes, it is he," replies Rocco, "and Leonore!" Quickly telling the story of Leonore's disguise as Fidelio, Rocco exposes Pizarro's plot.

Desperate to escape justice, Pizarro attempts to implicate Rocco in his crimes, but the townspeople know better and at a sign from the Prime Minister, the villain is taken away in chains.

As they depart, Don Fernando turns to Leonore. It is her privilege, he declares, to remove the chains from the prisoner. Leonore takes the proffered key and liberates her husband. He immediately embraces his wife. At the sight of this triumph of love over evil, the assembled crowd—Prime Minister, townspeople, and prisoners alike—offers an exhilarating paean to Leonore's courage and nobility, and to that of all loving wives. ⦿

# THE BARBER OF SEVILLE

## — Il Barbiere di Siviglia —

On December 15, 1815, Gioacchino Rossini signed a contract with Rome's Teatro Argentina to compose an opera to be staged the following February. The timetable sounds daunting, but the twenty-four-year-old composer was more than equal to the task: It took him a mere fourteen days to complete *The Barber of Seville.* However, Rossini helped himself to a few short-cuts. The first of these was the story itself, which was based on a popular 1775 play by Pierre de Beaumarchais. Not only were the tale and its characters well known (which is probably the reason Rossini chose them), but they had already appeared in Giovanni Paisiello's beloved opera entitled, of all things, *Il barbiere di Siviglia.* To avoid confusion, Rossini called his work *Almaviva, ossia L'inutile precauzione (Almaviva,* or *The Useless Precaution),* but this proved to be a useless precaution and Paisiello partisans were mortally offended at what they perceived as a wholesale theft of their master's property. Another timesaving measure Rossini employed was the recycling of some of his own work: The brilliant overture to *Barber* was transported in full from his 1815 *Elisabetta, Regina d'Inghilterra.*

The premiere of *The Barber of Seville,* on February 20, 1816, was one of the great opera fiascos of all time. In addition to comical mishaps such as a cat wandering onto the stage and Don Basilio getting tangled up in his own robes, the audience was full of Paisiello fans who hissed and booed the young composer. Rossini fled the theater fearing for his life, but the opera's second performance was a success and by the third performance, *The Barber of Seville* was being hailed as a masterpiece, an appraisal that has been widely held ever since.

Rossini went on to write thirty-four more operas in the next fifteen years, including such crowd pleasers as *Cenerentola* (Cinderella) and the haunting *William Tell.* Then, at the age of thirty-nine and the height of his popularity, he retired from operatic composition. The reasons have always been mysterious. He was ill, true, and his financial arrangements with several opera houses had made him rich enough to quit in comfort, but the great master of the form lived for another thirty-nine years, growing ever fatter and more celebrated, without writing another operatic note.

# ACT ONE

The Count Almaviva, renowned for his great fortune and even greater nobility, emerges from the shadows into one of the narrow streets of old Seville to greet the little band of musicians he has hired to play under a certain balcony. Utmost discretion must be exercised, he tells them. "No one must hear us," he whispers. "Softly, softly."

The musicians begin to play accompaniment to the Count's serenade: *"Ecco, ridente in cielo . . . All the world is waking . . . Oh! When will you arise? Do you doubt that I adore you? . . . Oh! To tell you how I love you . . ."*

Alas, his song ends without any sign of having been heard. "Hopes dashed again!" groans the Count, sinking into despair. Gloomily, he tosses a purseful of money to his nervous valet, who distributes it to the players with maximum officiousness. Overwhelmed by the sight of so much cash, they cluster around Almaviva, kissing his hands and thanking him effusively—and loudly.

"Quiet!" whispers the Count furiously. "Stop your chattering, you fools! You'll wake the whole neighborhood!"

The musicians obligingly pocket their money and depart. But Almaviva cannot bring himself to leave. Alone, he paces back and forth, never taking his eyes from the fateful window and muttering all the while about love, love, love.

Suddenly, the quiet of the dawn is punctured with a song. "La la la, la," trills an ebullient voice. A short, wiry figure comes dashing through the piazza, singing at the top of his lungs. *"La, la, la, lera! Largo al factotum della città!* I'm Figaro! Busy, useful, important Figaro, the Barber of Seville. I shave all the important people. I'm the busiest and cleverest fellow in town! The luckiest, the best, and the smartest! Bravo, Figaro! Bravo, bravissimo, bravo for Figaro! I know everyone! They tell me all their secrets. I give them advice. I know everything and life is fabulous! What could be better? Time for work!"

Dazzled by this whirlwind, the Count steps forward impulsively and Figaro, recognizing him as the great and noble Almaviva, gives a flustered greeting and prepares to make himself scarce.

"Wait," says Almaviva thoughtfully. "You may be the very person I need. Are you discreet?"

"Terrifically discreet! But what are you doing in Seville, sir?"

Casting caution to the wind, Almaviva tells Figaro all—that in this very house lives the most enchanting girl in the world, the daughter of a doctor, that he lost his heart to her the moment he saw her, that he is madly in love, that he is pining away for a glimpse of her, that he waits for her day and night.

"Well, well, well," says Figaro jovially. "You're in love? With the maiden that lives behind that window there? You're in luck! The cheese has fallen on the macaroni!"

"What do you mean?" cries the Count.

"I," says Figaro grandly, "am their barber, their hairdresser, their surgeon. I cure them all, including their dogs and little kittens."

"Wonderful!" says the Count.

"And listen! Your beloved Rosina, she's not the doctor's daughter, she's his ward, so all we have to do is— quiet!"

The door to Rosina's balcony is opening. Quick as a flash, the Count and Figaro dive for cover. A young girl with large brown eyes and a deceptively demure expression looks down over the balustrade. In her hand is a small piece of paper.

"Perhaps he is not coming today," she murmurs to herself. "How can I give him this letter, then?"

"Good morning, my dear." The excessively rotund Dr. Bartolo emerges behind Rosina. "How's the weather? And what is that little paper you've got there?" he inquires suspiciously.

Rosina lets the sheet flutter out of her hand. "Oh dear, I must have dropped it. Will you go get it for me?"

Grumpily, the Doctor stomps off to retrieve the paper. As soon as his back is turned, the lovely Rosina leans over the balcony and beckons to the Count. "Hurry!" she whispers, pointing to the letter. The Count neatly plucks it from the street just as Bartolo begins his futile search.

"I don't see it," grumbles the Doctor. "Perhaps she is trying to dupe me." He shakes his fist in Rosina's direction. "Get inside at once, young lady! And remind me to wall that balcony up!"

"What a life," sighs Rosina, as she reluctantly retreats.

"Poor darling," sighs the Count.

"Hurry! Hurry! What's it say?" demands Figaro, plucking the letter from the mooning Count. "'Your persistent attentions have aroused my curiosity,'" he reads. And then the good news—the Doctor was about to go out, and Rosina asked that her admirer reveal his name, his station, and his intentions during this brief absence.

As if on cue, Bartolo thumps out the door. "I warn you, young lady," he bellows, "you're to receive no callers except Don Basilio while I'm gone." To himself, he muttered, "I'd better marry her soon. This morning, I'll make the arrangements." Locking the door, he disappears.

"Marry her! Never!" declares Almaviva. "And who is this Basilio?"

"A snake!" replies Figaro. "He makes his living arranging weddings, but he also teaches music to Rosina. By the way, aren't you going to answer Rosina's letter?"

"Yes, but I shall not tell her my name or rank. I must discover her true feelings—does she love me for myself or merely for the prospect of becoming the Countess Almaviva. You must help me."

The Barber of Seville *is probably the most illustrious example of opera buffa, Italian comic opera. Aside from being just plain funny, an opera buffa exhibits several distinctive musical features. The first is lightning-quick singing, such as Figaro's famous entrance aria, "Largo al factotum." The second is the use of crescendi, in which a simple musical phrase is repeated, softly at first, then more and more loudly, with intensifying instrumentation at each repetition. Though Rossini did not invent the crescendo, he used it to such magnificent effect—as in the overture to* Barber—*that it became known as the "Rossini crescendo."*

"Well, go out and speak with her, at least. Or serenade her. That'll get her. Go on! Sing!" Figaro commands.

Ingeniously, the Count bursts into song: *"Se il mio nome saper voi bramate . . .* If you want to know who is singing—I am Lindoro, who adores you! Who wants to marry you. I have nothing to offer you except my heart's devotion."

Rosina appears, seduced by the lovely music. She smiles down on the enraptured Almaviva, but just as she begins to reply, her window slams shut. Someone has come in, ruining the lovers' meeting.

The Count is in despair. "How can I bear it?" he cries, shaking Figaro by the shoulders. "You must help me! You must think of a plan! What's the matter with you? You're speechless—ohhhhh," Almaviva realizes the problem. "Don't worry; you'll be paid handsomely for your services."

Figaro brightens. "Plus money for expenses?"

"Of course."

"Ah. Strange how the thought of money sets my genius into motion," Figaro muses. And then, "I've got it. You will go to Bartolo's house dressed as a soldier. You will be one of the regiment that is arriving today—"

"Oh, yes. As a matter of fact, the Colonel is pal of mine."

"All the better! You'll tell them that you've been quartered there, in his house, and—wait, another idea is coming to me!—you'll pretend you're a little drunk!"

"Why do I have to be drunk?" demands Almaviva.

"No one ever suspects that a drunkard is anyone other than a drunkard, that's why."

"Brilliant!"

Trying to look modest, and failing, Figaro sends the Count off to get a uniform. Thus, the one effusing about love and the other about money, they set out in opposite directions.

Meanwhile, inside Dr. Bartolo's house, Rosina is wandering about with yet another letter. *"Una voce poco fa . . ."* she sings to herself. "Yes, Lindoro is the one. No one can stop me. My plans are laid. I am very docile, very obedient, very sweet. *But,* if you push me around, I'll let you have it. I always have the last laugh. Now, what am I going to do with this letter? I need someone to carry it—but who? Ah, yes! The barber! He'll help us." Rosina hastens from her room, only to find Figaro waiting for her outside the door. He has been busy giving a sneezing powder to the maid and a sleeping powder to the groom, on the theory that it would be helpful if the servants were somewhat distracted. But now, just as he and Rosina begin to lay their plans, Dr. Bartolo returns home in a foul temper. Figaro, sensing impending excitement, hides himself behind a curtain.

Don Basilio arrives to find Bartolo writhing with suspicions of Rosina's duplicity. "Oh, I'll get her one way or another—with love or by force! I'll marry Rosina tomorrow. Tomorrow! You hear me?" fumes the Doctor.

"You put it so well," Don Basilio says unctuously. "But allow me to reveal to you my latest secret findings." Ceremoniously, he removes his cloak, ignoring the doctor's impatience. "I've seen him," he announces. "It's the Count Almaviva!"

"Almaviva?" repeats the doctor incredulously. "It's Almaviva who courts Rosina?"

"Yes," says Don Basilio, "that's the one."

"Goddammit!" explodes Bartolo, "we've got to stop this nonsense immediately."

"Yes," says Basilio, rubbing his hands, "and I suggest that we invent a story, yes, a story, that reflects badly on him. For you know, my dear doctor, that people love to believe the worst of others. We'll simply circulate a story that ruins his reputation."

"But," falters the Doctor, "how, exactly, do we start a scandal?"

Don Basilio is more than pleased to explain the mechanism to his old friend. *"La calunnia e un venticello . . .* Rumor is like a feather floating on the breeze. First it's a whisper, then a murmur, then, as ears open to hear it, it expands, never stopping, never slowing, ever increasing, ever growing. And finally, it unleashes its terrible power like an explosion, destroying a reputation with a mighty blast!"

A slow smile spreads over Bartolo's face. "Why, this is just the thing! But my dear friend, we must work quickly. In fact, I think we should write up the marriage contract this very morning. Then I can marry Rosina tomorrow and put an end to all this flirting and fussing." And off go the two scoundrels to complete their dirty plans.

Instantly, Figaro pops out from behind his curtain, spluttering with indignation. "Confusion to the Doctor! The devil take him! We'll take care of him and his plans!" He reflects for a moment. "The first thing to do is tell Rosina."

As luck would have it, Rosina enters the room at that moment. "Tell me what you've heard," she begs. And Figaro proceeds to inform her of the Doctor's dastardly plan.

"Oh yes? So that's his plan. Well, they'll have to deal with me first. But Signor Figaro," Rosina pauses, suddenly looking coy, "a little while ago, you were under my window with a, a man . . . "

Eagerly, Figaro obliges her with all the particulars on Lindoro: He is handsome. Brainy. Soulful. Impoverished. And madly in love. At this last tidbit, Rosina is covered in maidenly blushes. But that doesn't

stop her from quickly ascertaining that the object of Lindoro's affections is none other than her own delightful self. "It's me!" she cries exultantly. "I'm his beloved! Of course," she adds to herself in a whisper, "it's really not so surprising, since I knew it all along."

"He's dying for a word from you," Figaro assures her. "If you would but write a tiny note, he will rush to your side."

After a show of embarrassment, Rosina produces a letter from her pocket.

"Already written? Whenever a man thinks he's being clever, a woman teaches him a lesson!"

"When shall I see Lindoro?" asks Rosina eagerly.

"He's on his way right now," Figaro assures her as he departs. "He will be here any moment, don't you worry."

And, sure enough, there is soon a knock at the front door. Dr. Bartolo bustles into the hallway, just in time to see the door open and a disheveled cavalryman appear. Of course, it's none other than Count Almaviva, disguised as Lindoro, in turn disguised as a somewhat tipsy officer of the cavalry.

"Hey!" he yells. "How come no one's here to greet me?" He catches sight of the Doctor. "Oh. Dr. Balordo. Or Bertoldo? Or Barbaro? Oh, what's the difference? Are you really a doctor?"

Bartolo draws himself up as tall as possible. "Of course."

"Good!" shouts the soldier. "That's what I am, too! I am a doctor of the horses! We're colleagues! And you shall have the pleasure of providing me with a bed. See, I've an order right here." He waves a paper at the Doctor, who snatches it in a fury.

"I don't have to house you, you scoundrel. I've an exemption!" he cries.

Rosina peeks out of the drawing room, taking care to elude Bartolo's eyes. "Who's this soldier?" she says to herself, strangely apprehensive.

The Count approaches and says softly, "It is I, Lindoro."

Having been booed off the stage at the premiere, Rossini was loath to believe the reports of Barber's success that came to him during the second performance. Too anxious to go to the theater, Rossini had stayed behind in his apartments and fallen asleep. Hours later, he was awakened by a clamor in the street. Seeing torches, the composer feared that the crowd was bent on vengeance and rushed downstairs to hide himself in the stable. It was Manuel Garcia, his Almaviva, who found him and explained that the mob wanted only to laud him. Rossini is said to have replied, "To hell with them, their cheers, and everything else. I'm not coming out." Garcia returned to the crowd to deliver this message and was beaned with an orange for his trouble. The crowd threatened to set fire to the house, but still the composer would not budge, and finally they dispersed, leaving Rossini to creep back up to his room, which he found quite chilly, since two windows had been smashed by his enthusiastic audience.

Equally softly, Rosina responds, "Oh, my Lindoro, oh, my heavens!"

The Doctor bustles about, looking for his exemption, while Rosina and Lindoro exchange tender looks and secret words. "Aha!" Bartolo cries at last, flapping the paper in the air—which allows Rosina to escape detection yet again.

"To hell with it," cries the Count. "I intend to stay here!" He whips out his sword and begins to wave it about. Bartolo scrambles out of the way and in the ensuing confusion, Almaviva and Rosina manage to exchange letters. Finally catching sight of her, Bartolo fills the air with accusations.

In rushes Don Basilio, smelling trouble.

In rushes Figaro, trying to calm them all.

Suddenly, there's a knock at the door. It's the guard, come to restore the peace! Everyone begins to tell their story to the officer at once:

"This intruder—" shouts the Doctor, pointing at the Count.

"He will not comply with my orders—" shouts the Count.

"He's been drinking," explains Rosina.

"He's a villain," says Basilio.

"Hmm," says the Officer to the Count. "I'm afraid I must arrest you. Time to go—to jail!"

"Get back!" says Almaviva in a commanding voice. Startled, the soldiers comply, and the Count hands a document to the Officer. Glancing at it quickly, the Officer dismisses his men with a single gesture.

The household stands frozen in amazement.

# ACT TWO

That afternoon, Dr. Bartolo is still fussing about the mysterious soldier. He is sure that the soldier is connected somehow to Almaviva, but he can't quite put his finger on it. A knock on the fateful front door interrupts his cogitations.

This time, the Count has assumed the costume of Don Alonso, a poor music teacher. In a pinched and squeaky voice, he informs the Doctor he has come in place of Don Basilio, who has been stricken, suddenly, with a fever.

"Ill?" cries Bartolo. "I'll go to him!"

Realizing his mistake, Almaviva catches him by the coattails in the nick of time. "Just a moment," he says in a low voice. "I know a secret."

"I can't hear you!" hollers the Doctor.

"Well—" says the Count in a whisper, stalling.

"Louder, damn it! Speak louder!" shouts the Doctor.

In desperation, Almaviva pulls Rosina's letter from his pocket. "I found this," he says, waving it before

Bartolo, "in Almaviva's chambers! And since I knew that I was to give Rosina her music lesson, I thought it would behoove me to reveal it . . . my plan was to show it . . . " He subsides in feigned embarrassment.

"Go on!" orders the enraptured Doctor.

"My idea was to show it to the girl and tell her that I got it from Almaviva's mistress, you see, and that he gave it to her as a joke."

"Shh-shh," says Bartolo, glancing around. "It's a wonderful plan, a lovely scandal. Oh, you have a mind as subtle as Don Basilio's. Yes, indeed, I'll reward you handsomely, my good fellow. I'll call Rosina, yes indeed. I am your servant. Ha! I'll call her now."

Left alone, the Count tries to justify himself. "What could I do? I'll tell Rosina I had no choice. Oh, there she is! How my heart leaps at the sight of her."

Unlike the Doctor, Rosina recognizes her Lindoro immediately and soon the two lovers are ensconced on the piano bench side by side while the Doctor, ever suspicious, lurks nearby.

*"Contro un cor che accende amore . . . "* sings Rosina in angelic tones, and soon enough, Bartolo has been lulled to sleep. Seizing the opportunity, Rosina confesses her love to Lindoro and begs him to save her from the tyranny of Bartolo. Lindoro responds with ardent promises of a happy future. Just as the lovers are swearing eternal love to one another, the fat Doctor begins to rouse himself, and Rosina returns to her song.

"Oh, what a talent!" effuses the Count, pretending to be a music master.

"Yes, yes, you have talent," Bartolo pronounces in his pompous manner, "but that thing you've been singing is very stupid. When I was a lad—" His lecture is interrupted by the appearance of Figaro. "What are you doing here?" demands the Doctor.

"Today is the day for your shave," announces Figaro with an innocent look.

"Come back tomorrow!"

"Couldn't possibly. I'm very busy tomorrow."

"Fine. No shave today."

"That's it! I've had it! This house will drive me crazy! This morning you're in an uproar, and this afternoon you say, 'Shave me tomorrow.' Harumph." Slamming his basin about, Figaro prepares to stomp off in a huff.

"Oh, these artists! Honestly," the Doctor protests. "All right! Here are the keys. Go get a towel. No, wait. I don't know if you're to be trusted. I'll go myself."

As the door closes behind the Doctor, Figaro leans close to Rosina. "Is the key to your balcony door on that ring?"

"Yes," she whispers.

"No, no," says the Doctor, coming back into room. "It's not safe to leave a young girl with such a rascal. You go get the towels."

"Me? A rascal?" Delightedly, he takes the keys from the Doctor. "We've done it!" he whispers to Rosina.

No sooner has Figaro departed than a terrible crash is heard.

"Agh! The clumsy idiot!" screams the Doctor, tearing out of the room.

They are gone only long enough for the Count to propose to Rosina and for her to accept him rapturously before the peace is shattered by the cacaphonous return of Figaro and the Doctor.

"Everything smashed!" the Doctor is groaning.

"You're lucky it's not worse," insists Figaro. "I could have broken my neck." Surreptitiously, he waggles the key at the lovers. After much to-do, the Doctor is settled in his chair for his shave. Figaro begins to lather him up, when the door opens and Don Basilio enters.

Figaro begins to lather the Doctor frenziedly. The resourceful Count, thinking quickly, expostulates, "My dear Basilio, what about your raging fever? What could induce you to leave your sickbed?"

Getting the drift, Figaro grabs Basilio's wrist. "But this is dreadful! Look at him shaking and quaking! It must be—yes, it is—*scarlet fever!*"

"Eeeek!" shriek Basilio and Bartolo together.

"You must take some of this medicine," says the Count, stealthily slipping a purseful of money into Basilio's ready palm.

"And go to bed," add Figaro, Rosina, and Bartolo together. "At once!"

"Hmm," Basilio says, thoughtfully squeezing the Count's purse. "Far be it from me to ignore your excellent suggestions."

"Good-bye, good-bye, good-bye," chorus the others eagerly. "Good-bye for now, Don Basilio!"

Don Basilio waves gratefully at the Count and departs. The Doctor is now drowning in lather and chatter, courtesy of the ever-busy Figaro, and the Count is making whispered arrangements with Rosina for their elopement that very night at the stroke of twelve.

Unfortunately, Bartolo has very keen hearing. *"What?"* howls the Doctor. "You deceived me! You devils, you scoundrels! Ah, ah, aaaaahh! I think I'm about to *burst!*"

Enraged, he chases Figaro and the Count out of one door and locks Rosina behind another. He sets the maid to guard the girl and dashes off to find Don Basilio himself.

Together, the two old villains hatch a plot, which the Doctor puts into action at once. He shows Rosina the fateful letter she wrote Lindoro as proof that her lover has betrayed her. At first, Rosina is crushed, but after the Doctor leaves her, she begins to reflect. She wavers, she wonders, but her heart tells her that Lindoro is true. She prays that the future will prove her right. "Reveal to me his innocence," she pleads to the heavens.

It is midnight, and a thunderstorm rages over Seville. Figaro and Almaviva, wrapped in cloaks, once again approach the house of Dr. Bartolo in secrecy. Ascending the famous balcony via ladder, the Count unlocks Rosina's door and softly calls his beloved.

Rosina appears, but she is in a temper. "How could you?" she cries, pushing away the man she knows as Lindoro. "I thought you loved me, you deceiver! I know what you're up to! You are abducting me to sell me to that villain Count Almaviva!"

"So that's it!" cries the Count joyfully. "My darling, *I* am the Count Almaviva," and he throws back his cloak to reveal himself to her in the glittering attire of a Spanish nobleman.

The astonished Rosina can scarcely believe her eyes. "Is this real?" she murmurs to herself.

Drunk with love, Almaviva and Rosina go on whispering sweet nothings to each other as the minutes pass by, and Figaro begins to grow apprehensive. "Stop your spooning," he hisses. "Stop your mooning! Uh-oh! I see a lantern. Oh! Another lantern! Oh dear!" To their tripartite dismay, the crucial ladder has been removed by an enemy hand. Hastily, the three hide in the shadows of the balcony.

Don Basilio appears, dragging a notary behind him.

"Ah," breathes Figaro with relief. "It's Basilio. He's come with a notary. How splendid. Just leave this to me!" He calls from the shadows, "Oh Signor Notary! Here you are, just in time to marry my niece to the Count Almaviva. Have you brought the marriage contract with you? Oh, that's fine!"

"Wait a minute," calls out Don Basilio. "Where's Bartolo?"

Thinking quickly, the Count pulls an enormous jeweled ring from his finger. "Hey, Don Basilio, here's a ring for you—but if you don't take it, I'll have to shoot you," he adds, pulling a pistol out of his cloak.

Without hesitating, Basilio reaches for the ring with one hand and signs the marriage license with the other. Figaro likewise signs the document.

"We are married!" announces the Count. "I'm so happy!"

Overjoyed at the success of his scheme, Figaro is in the process of kissing everyone in sight when Bartolo enters with yet another contingent of soldiers. Pointing his pudgy finger at Almaviva, he demands his immediate arrest.

"Get back!" commands the Count.

"How dare you speak to me in that tone? Who are you?" the Officer inquires, scandalized.

"The Count of Almaviva is who I am!"

"Oh damn!" yells Bartolo.

"And this is my wife, the Countess," continues Almaviva.

"But—" says Bartolo.

"Be silent!" commands Almaviva. "Know that if you resist me now, my anger will be immense and unending. Rosina is free now; you no longer have power over her. And you, my darling," he says, turning to his wife, "you are a prisoner no more. Rejoice in your liberty."

"This is all your fault!" cries the Doctor to Basilio.

"What could I do? The Count was persuasive," shrugs Don Basilio.

"Don't argue," breaks in Almaviva, "be happy. Even you, Doctor, should be happy, for I will bequeath to you all of Rosina's dowry. Now, my friends, what say you to my marriage?"

Together the assembled crowd roars, "May nothing ever come between you! May your marriage last forever!" And with that, the whole group begins to sing and dance around the freshly minted couple, especially Figaro, who is certain that the happy ending is all due to him—the helpful, busy, useful, important Barber of Seville. ～⧉

# WILLIAM TELL

~⚬⚬⚬~

To the casual listener, it seems almost impossible that *The Barber of Seville* and *William Tell* are the work of the same composer. While the former seems to look back to Mozartean classicism, *William Tell* is the prototypical Grand Opera, the jumbo-sized ancestor of all other nineteenth-century operatic spectacles. Created for the Paris Opéra in 1829, it was Rossini's last, for reasons that continue to be endlessly speculated upon. Some believe that the reception of *William Tell* so disappointed the composer that he retired from the field. Certainly, the critics raved, but after its first few seasons, the work was rarely performed in full. The reasons are not difficult to understand; as one critic wrote, "Lasting nearly five hours in the theater . . . it requires vast scenic apparatus, a genius for a conductor, and the finest tenor on earth." Even during its initial run, *William Tell* lost the first scene of the third act and most of the fourth act, and, just a few years later, the only bit remaining in the Paris Opéra repertory was Act Two, which contains the juicy *"Sombre forêt"* and the stunning trio, *"Quand l'Helvétie."* This showpiece act was trotted out for various galas and ballets, and the rest of the opera was more or less discarded. There is a legend that the director of the Opéra, meeting Rossini on the street one afternoon, and anxious to make good with the illustrious composer, announced effusively that Act Two of *William Tell* would be staged that night. "What!" exclaimed Rossini, *"All* of it?"

## ACT ONE

In 1307, the cantons of Switzerland lie crushed under their Austrian overlords. In villages ringed by magnificent mountains and softened by gentle fields, where peasants till the soil and shepherds guard their flocks, the joy of venerable traditions is tinged with the bitterness of subjugation.

In just such a village, nestled between a grand mountain and a glistening lake, the townspeople have gathered for the Shepherd's Festival. William Tell watches them, lost in thought. Though the scene before him is peaceful, Tell cannot take pleasure in it; his joy has been poisoned by the loss of his fatherland. "Has life not lost all its meaning?" he broods. But his wife, Hedwig, and son, Jemmy, are caught up in the festive mood and when the old shepherd Melchthal comes down the mountain path, leaning on the arm of his son, Arnold, they rush with the other villagers to greet him.

"The festival of shepherds is an ancient rite," Hedwig explains to Jemmy. "It is when young lovers are transformed into happily married couples."

Arnold, hearing her speak of love, turns suddenly grim, but his gloom is lost in the eagerness of the peasants who surround Melchthal, urging him to preside over the wedding ceremony. The old shepherd agrees and says gently to Arnold, "Would that I were to hear your marriage vow this day."

"My vow? No, never!" Arnold says to himself, watching his father depart. Alone, he reveals that he has lost his heart to Mathilde, an Austrian princess, whom he rescued from the path of an avalanche. He curses his futile love, doomed by her rank and her connection to the Austrian regime, and even more does he curse himself for having served in the army of the oppressors. From far away comes the haunting sound of horns; it is the tyrant Gessler, who rules the canton with an iron fist. He is returning from the hunt, and knowing that Mathilde rides with him, Arnold decides, guiltily, to seek her out.

Turning to leave, Arnold comes face-to-face with William Tell, who urges him to unburden his heart. Carefully evading the issue of love, Arnold blames himself for his traitorous service in the Austrian forces. Tell forgives him easily, and Arnold earnestly swears loyalty to the revolutionary movement, though he questions the likelihood of victory. "What glory do you hope will come from danger?" he asks.

"I do not know that glory will come to me, but I must challenge my fate," declares Tell.

Inspired by Tell's passion for freedom, whatever the cost, Arnold promises, "When the time comes, William, I will fight by your side." But no sooner has he made up his mind than he is torn apart by the conflict between his love for his father and country and his love for Mathilde. So distraught does he appear that Tell doubts him again.

The sounds of the festival drift through the air. "Listen to the sacred wedding songs," urges Tell, "and do not remind the shepherds of their wrongs; today, their pleasure should be unmixed with pain. But soon, one day not long from this . . . hatred and death to the traitor!"

"Hatred and death to the traitor!" echoes Arnold, hardening his heart against the claims of love.

Their warlike resolve is tamed by the sight of three bridegrooms coming down the mountain path. In a shaded bower, Melchthal blesses their marriages, and each word is like a dagger in Arnold's heart. When the hunting bugles sound again, he steals away to catch a glimpse of Mathilde.

Enraged by the proximity of Gessler and his men, Tell ignores his own counsel and begins an impassioned address to the villagers: "Listen to the godless tyrant! Listen! He proclaims that now and forever is the fountain dry that gave us heroes' blood. And we, unhappily, are slaves and cowards! A people with no strength begets no heroes!"

Hedwig rushes to calm him, and Tell notices Arnold's absence. Leaving his wife to keep the festivities merry, Tell goes in search of him.

Suddenly, the laughter and congratulations are cut short; the shepherd Leuthold approaches, shaking and breathless. In his hands is a blood-stained ax. "Save me!" he gasps. Stuttering with fear, Leuthold tells how his only daughter caught the eye of one of Gessler's henchmen, who, with the support of the tyrant, tried to kidnap her. "I had to save my child," explains Leuthold. "I struck him with my weapon. That is his blood."

"Oh, heaven," cries Melchthal. "You had the courage of a father, but who will help you now?"

"I could find safety across the water," says Leuthold urgently, turning to one of the fishermen. "I beg you! Take me there!"

Stuttering about currents and rocks, the terrified fisherman refuses.

The soldiers can be heard moving closer to the village. Their cry becomes clearer now: "Leuthold, you are doomed!"

Hearing the commotion, William Tell comes rushing down the mountain path. Seeing that no one dares to ferry Leuthold across the lake, he instantly offers to do so himself. Quickly, they board a boat and row for the far shore.

One grim voice rises above that of the other soldiers. Rudolph, Gessler's loathsome lieutenant, roars, "Death and destruction are at hand!" as he approaches the village.

Despite rough waters, Tell lands safely on the opposite shore, just as Rudolph and his soldiers appear among the assembled peasants.

"He is safe!" exult Hedwig and Jemmy.

"Heaven heard my prayer!" says Melchthal.

"This rejoicing is an insult!" bellows Rudolph, confronting Melchthal, Hedwig, and Jemmy. "Tell me at once, you filth: Who put the murderer beyond my grasp?"

*William Tell was almost universally admired by contemporary composers, but admiration made for some strange bedfellows: According to Vincenzo Bellini, William Tell reduced all other operas of its day, including his own, to pygmies. Gaetano Donizetti said that though Rossini had written the first and last acts, "God wrote the second act." And Richard Wagner, the man who made a career out of scorning operatic excess in favor of an avant-garde that consisted solely of his own "music of the future," believed that Tell's third-act "Sois immobile" reached "the highest peaks of lyric expression."*

*Rossini's response to this last compliment was characteristic: "So I was writing the music of the future without realizing it?"*

The villagers are paralyzed with fear.

"Have courage, friends," urges Melchthal.

"Be warned!" Rudolph says. "Reveal the culprit's name at once!"

"Villain!" cries Melchthal, losing his temper. "This soil does not breed informers!"

Rudolph turns on him, enraged. "Surround that man," he shouts to his soldiers. "Take him to Gessler! Now destroy the village. Set fire to everything! Leave no trace of human dwelling. Let havoc and ruination be their lot!"

Jemmy, incited to bravery, echoes Rudolph's order. "Yes, set fire to everything. But God will avenge us, and one day may you fall victim to my father's dreaded bow."

Finally, despite the villagers' efforts to shield him, Melchthal is bound and dragged away.

# ACT TWO

Night is falling in a valley set between towering mountains and the hunting party of Austrian nobles is returning home, congratulating themselves on the thrilling chase. Gradually, their whooping and carousing fades, and quiet returns.

Glancing about to make sure she's undiscovered, Mathilde enters the glade. She had been hoping that she would see Arnold. "You alone fill my thoughts," she sighs, "and make me feel afraid." The dark woods offer her

some comfort: "*Sombre forêt . . .* Brooding forest, wild moors, I prefer you to the splendors of a palace. In the mountains alone can my heart find peace." She begs the stars, just now appearing, to direct Arnold to her.

As if in answer to her prayers, Arnold walks toward her between the trees. But he is pensive, certain that he can never win the love of an Austrian princess.

"Wait," cries Mathilde. "Let me confess the secret of my heart. For you alone it suffers and beats. For you alone."

Astonished and enraptured, Arnold takes her hand. "If you love me, if you

*Arnold is a famously demanding tenor role. As one nineteenth-century French critic wrote,* William Tell *"has exterminated three generations of tenors in twenty years." Indeed, the first Arnold, Adolphe Nourrit, was forced to abandon the spectacular fourth-act aria, "Asile hérédi-taire," after the second performance, because the high C gave him so much trouble. When the opera premiered in Italy in 1831, Gilbert-Louis Duprez took the role of Arnold and produced the innovation of the high C sung as a chest tone rather than a falsetto head tone, which created a sensation. When Duprez brought a complete ver-sion of* Tell *back to Paris in 1837, a rivalry developed between the pro-Nourrit and the pro-Duprez factions. So undone was Nourrit by the new style of singing champ-ioned by Duprez that he fled to Italy, where he committed suicide in 1839.*

return my passion, then I can hope that some day my heart will be at rest. But," he reflects, growing despon-dent again, "there are so many obstacles between us."

"Don't lose hope," Mathilde replies. "Return to the field of battle and win new laurels there. Victory alone will give you the right to claim my hand."

Swept up in love, Arnold abandons his newfound revolutionary fervor and vows to rejoin the Austrian forces. Together, the lovers joyously plan their future, until they hear someone approaching. Quickly, they promise to meet at dawn in a small chapel nearby, and Mathilde slips away.

William Tell, accompanied by his friend Walter Furst, break through the gloom. "We interrupted a pleas-ant tête-à-tête, I see," says Tell grimly.

"What if I were in love? And what if I were loved in return?" says Arnold.

"She is an enemy of our people," says Tell. "Do you have any idea, Arnold, what it means to love your country?"

"What country? We no longer have one! I must leave this place of fear and hate. In happier places honor awaits me," says Arnold.

"*Quand l'Helvétie est un champ de supplices* . . . While your compatriots shed their blood, you would take up your sword and fight for Gessler? Give your life for the traitor's cause?" asks Tell.

"Gessler has killed an old man," interrupts Walter impatiently. "The murdered man awaits revenge and he asks it—needs it—from you."

A look of horror dawns on Arnold's face. "My father!" he cries.

"Yes, your father, dead by the tyrant's hand," says Walter.

"My father . . . my—my heart fails me," Arnold gasps. "The villain dared to cut him down and my blade was not unsheathed. My father! You died cursing me, while I was betraying my country. Oh, God!"

"He raves," says Tell, moved by Arnold's grief, "but now the scales have fallen from his eyes."

"I shall never see him again," sobs Arnold, stricken. "What shall I do?"

"Your duty," replies Tell instantly.

"The villain will die! I swear by my father's soul!"

"Calm your fury now, and you can at the same time avenge your father and your country," Tell directs him.

"What are we waiting for?" says Arnold impatiently.

"Night, which will favor our plan, has already lowered its protective veil," explains Tell. "Soon our confederates will come. With them, we will carve out a happier destiny. Liberty or death!"

Aflame with lust for vengeance and justice, Arnold, too, cries, "Liberty or death!"

And distantly through the woods comes the sound of tramping feet. The men of three cantons are arriving to join forces with William Tell. "William," they cry, "you have made three peoples into one. Your words have set every heart on fire!"

"We swear," begins Tell, and the men of the three cantons join in, "we swear by all our wrongs, by our fathers and our burdens borne too long, we swear to the God of kings and shepherds to utterly destroy the vile oppressors! To arms!" they cry.

"To arms!" repeats Arnold.

"To arms!" they roar in unison.

# ACT THREE

As dawn breaks, Arnold and Mathilde meet, as promised, in a secluded mountain chapel. In despair he reveals to her the news of his father's murder, which horrifies her. Upon learning that Gessler was the architect of Melchthal's death, she urges Arnold to flee.

"Escape? Save myself?" he repeats. "I think only of my father."

In the distance, the chanting of Gessler's soldiers can be heard. "He goes to Altdorf today," explains Mathilde, "to hold a festival."

"Their singing is an insult to my grief," says Arnold. "His doom awaits him."

Recognizing that Arnold's mission will probably end in death, the lovers part, mourning their lost hopes.

The main square of Altdorf, ringed with fruit trees, has been decorated for the festival. To one side is a dais, where Gessler reclines on a massive throne, and on the other is a pole, with Gessler's hat perched atop. As a gratuitous insult, the tyrant has required that every citizen make an obeisance to this "trophy."

Drunk with power, the Austrian soldiers are singing paeans to Gessler: "Glory to Gessler, whom the whole world fears!"

The Swiss women, who have been commanded to perform their traditional dances, murmur among themselves, hoping for better days. Resistant yet fearful, the Swiss men join them in their complaints, while Gessler preens.

They begin their performance resentfully, but soon they are caught up in the pleasure of dancing, and they welcome the spring with ballet and song. When the dance is over, everyone is expected to bow down to Gessler's trophy. All except William Tell and Jemmy acquiesce. Affronted, the soldiers drag the two before Gessler, but Tell is unrepentant.

"I respect your authority and I honor your laws, but I will bow my head to none but God," says Tell defiantly.

"By his audacity, I recognize this man," says the lieutenant Rudolph. "This is William Tell, the traitor who aided Leuthold's escape!"

"Arrest him!" commands Gessler, and the soldiers seize Tell's bow and arrows and hold him captive. "Your bragging makes my blood boil! I'll break you like a tree struck by lightning!"

While Gessler smiles in sadistic anticipation, Tell speaks to Jemmy in an undertone: "Go, my beloved son. Run to your mother and get her to set alight the beacon on our mountain's highest peak. This will signal the three cantons to begin the battle." Obediently, Jemmy starts to run off.

"Stop!" roars Gessler. "Is this your son?" he asks.

"My only child," answers Tell, turning pale.

"And do you wish to save him?"

"Save him? What has he done wrong?"

Gessler laughs. "All of your friends admire your skill as an archer," he says slowly, walking to a nearby tree to pick an apple. "This apple will be placed on your son's head, and you shall remove it with an arrow. While I watch."

"My son's head?" Tell asks, trembling. "I'm lost! How can you command this? Impossible. This cruelty is too great!"

"Obey me!"

"I cannot."

"Kill the son," says Gessler gleefully to his minions.

"No!" shouts Tell. "Gessler, you have won. I will abase myself for the life of my son. I kneel to you!"

Gessler is unmoved: Tell must shoot the apple off Jemmy's head. Jemmy whispers to his father, "Give me your hand and place it on my heart. Feel! It beats with love, not fear!"

Fortified by these words, Tell picks up his bow. From his quiver, he chooses an arrow; secretly, he hides another inside his cloak. "Let me embrace him once more," he begs Gessler, who signals his assent. "*Sois immobile* . . . Keep still," Tell whispers to his son, "with your eyes fixed on heaven, otherwise you may move when you see the arrow flying. The slightest movement could mean death. And Jemmy, think of your mother."

Jemmy runs back to his place and the apple is placed on his head. Tell lifts his bow, takes aim, and fires. The arrow hits the apple dead center, and Jemmy is untouched. The townspeople are exultant, and Jemmy runs to his father while Gessler curses.

"I feel faint," murmurs the distraught Tell. "My joy overwhelms me." He falls to his knees, and the second arrow drops to the ground.

"What's that arrow for?" asks Gessler.

"For you, had I killed my son," answers Tell bluntly.

Enraged, Gessler commands his soldiers to manacle Tell, but as they bind both father and son in chains, Mathilde rushes into the square, demanding that Gessler release Jemmy, at least. Even Rudolph concurs, and Gessler reluctantly frees Jemmy, though this does nothing to placate the growing fury of the townspeople.

Foolishly, Gessler ignores their muttering. "I shall personally take him to Kussnacht, across the lake."

"Cross the lake? With a storm coming?" asks Rudolph skeptically.

"Certainly we shall not falter with such a skilled oarsman as our captive," says Gessler.

"Have mercy! Mercy!" cry the townspeople.

Gessler laughs. "This is my mercy. I will feed your William Tell to the reptiles. Their horrible mouths will make him a splendid tomb."

This decree is met with curses by the townspeople and delight by the soldiery. Jemmy and Mathilde, equally aghast, join together, and Mathilde vows that she will do all that is humanly possible to save the father as well as the son.

# ACT FOUR

In the chill of evening, Arnold approaches his father's abandoned home. With the Swiss conspirators gathering in the woods, his long-sought revenge is imminent, yet the stillness of the old chalet fills him with a mysterious dread. Shivering, he hesitates on the threshold. *"Asile héréditaire . . .* My childhood home, where my eyes first saw the light of day, I come here now for the last time."

He is startled out of his reverie by an approaching battle cry. A group of Swiss patriots have marched to Melchthal's chalet and greet Arnold with fiery zeal. "William is a prisoner," they cry. "We must rescue him, and we need arms!"

"My father and William have long had a cache of spears and swords down by the shore. Come! Let us not lose a moment! We shall have revenge upon the villain. To arms!" shouts Arnold, filled with fervor.

"Hurry! Revenge!" shout the patriots. "William shall not die!" Together, they make haste for Altdorf.

On the cliffs above Lake Lucerne, a cluster of women surrounds Hedwig as the sky grows dark with clouds. Believing that both her husband and her son are dead, Hedwig longs to join them. Her despair ends with Jemmy's cry, "Mother!" Running toward her is the son she expected never to see again, accompanied by his rescuer, Mathilde.

Once reunited with Jemmy, Hedwig turns to the Austrian princess to seek another favor. "O angel of peace, use your power to save my husband!" When they tell her that William is rowing across the lake, she cries, "But a storm is coming! Death awaits him!"

Suddenly, Jemmy remembers his father's directive—he must light a beacon that will signal the beginning of the uprising. He runs to set Tell's house afire, saving only the weapons from within. As he does so, the brooding storm erupts. Hedwig and the other women kneel to pray: "Save William in his hour of peril. Save him for the love of our country!"

As the storm reaches its crescendo, Leuthold rushes to the scene. "Follow me!" he cries. "The storm is driving William to the shore nearby." As the house blazes behind them, the women, Jemmy, and Leuthold hasten down to the lake, to better see the boat scudding toward the beach. Tell, wrestling against the wind, maneuvers it close to shore and then leaps upon a rock. Handily, he pushes the boat away, sending Gessler and his cronies back out into the turbulent waters. They are immediately lost to sight.

Tell runs toward the huddled group and gathers his family in his arms. "What are those flames I see?"

"It's our house, Father. I saved only your weapons," answers Jemmy, handing Tell his crossbow and arrows.

"Come when you will, Gessler," says Tell.

As if he had heard the summons, the tyrant appears on a nearby cliff. "Let the wretch find mercy in death's embrace!" he shouts.

"It's him!" screams Hedwig.

"Stand back," orders Tell, raising his bow. "Switzerland must be free! Die, Gessler!" He looses the arrow and Gessler, mortally wounded, falls backward to a watery death.

Walter Furst appears, leading a band of patriots. Rejoicing, they praise Tell as Switzerland's liberator.

"No," Tell objects. "We cannot be certain of freedom until the walls of Altdorf have been razed."

"We now command those walls," announces Arnold, entering.

"Victory! Victory!" roars the crowd, as the storm clouds disperse and the sky turns blue.

"The sun is shining," observes Hedwig.

*"Tout change et grandit en ces lieux . . .* All is transformed—the sky opens and the air is clear," says Tell.

"Nature lays bare her splendor for our eyes," says Arnold wonderingly.

"In answer to our prayers, liberty has been returned to us!" says William Tell, and together, all the Swiss people give thanks. ~⚮

# THE ELIXIR OF LOVE

### L'elisir d'amore

In contrast to Vincenzo Bellini, his chief rival in composing the classic operas of the bel canto repertoire, Gaetano Donizetti was no exquisite *artiste*. In true Romantic poet style, Bellini composed only one opera a year, lingering over each of his scores until every note was perfect. Donizetti, on the other hand, produced more than seventy operas and numerous other musical compositions in his fifty-one years. Upon hearing that Rossini had completed *The Barber of Seville* in fourteen days, Donizetti commented, "That does not surprise me; he has always been lazy." Of course, some of Donizetti's works showed the ill effects of having been churned out too quickly, but an amazing number are still with us and still delightful. Many of Donizetti's best-known operas are in the Romantic vein, replete with mist-shrouded castles, bewitched lakes, star-crossed lovers, betrayed queens, and, most of all, hair-tearing, roof-raising mad scenes. Sopranos loved Donizetti, for he was generous with the big tunes and the big scenes that were a requirement for the true bel canto extravaganza, and he was also relaxed enough to supply a fresh aria if a diva felt she needed further opportunity for vocal display. However, Donizetti's greatest contribution may well have been his comic operas. Tempering the post-Rossinian era of gloomy tragedies and Grand Opera with such lively and tuneful works as *The Elixir of Love* and *Don Pasquale,* Donizetti was the last great composer of opera buffa, traditional Italian comic opera. But his was an ebullience with heart; one benefit of Donizetti's Romantic milieu was that it deepened the emotional resonance of his characters and their music. A prime example is Nemorino, the hapless hero of *The Elixir.* He is a buffoon, certainly, but he's also touchingly sympathetic, and when he blooms into self-confidence in his final aria, the lovely *"Una furtiva lagrima,"* the audience cheers him on instead of hoping for one more comic pratfall.

# ACT ONE

On one of those idyllic farms that appear only in the theater, a group of cheerful young peasants rests from harvesting duties under one tree while Adina, the rich and somewhat spoiled landowner, reads in the shade of another. Not far from her, the young farmer Nemorino sits on a bench and stares at Adina with the mournful, unblinking gaze of a cow. Every once in a while, he shifts his position to catch a slightly different angle of her adorable face. But, he admits, she feels nothing for him, because he is a fool, only a fool.

Laughing, Adina tosses her book down. "How lovely! How peculiar!" she exclaims. Her friend Giannetta and the others beg her to tell them the story, and Nemorino sidles closer to listen in. Adina reads them the tale of Tristan's hopeless love for Isolde, how in despair he went to a magician, who gave him a miraculous elixir. No sooner had he taken a sip of the potion than Isolde's heart began to melt with love, and in an instant she became his for eternity. "I wish I had that recipe," the beautiful Adina concludes with a pout.

Over the cacophony of laughter, a military drumroll sounds and Sergeant Belcore marches in, leading his troops with maximum swagger and flourish. Somewhat incongruously, he hands Adina a diminutive bouquet of flowers. Twirling his luxuriant moustache, he embarks on a comparison of himself and his little bouquet with the Trojan Paris, who handed the apple to the most beautiful girl. "But," he says, goggling his eyes suggestively at Adina, "I am more glorious and happier than he, for as a reward for my gift, I'll receive your heart."

"He's modest, this one," comments Adina, and the peasants laugh.

Twirling his moustache ever more vigorously, Belcore urges Adina to confess that she can't resist him. "Why delay?" he inquires. "My adored, let's admit defeat—what day would you like to get married?"

Nemorino, at the edge of the crowd, gasps in horror.

"I'm in no hurry," says Adina, rolling her eyes. "I want to think it over a bit."

This is small comfort for poor Nemorino.

Chortling at the thought of Adina being as easily won as Belcore presumes, Giannetta and the harvesters return to the fields. Belcore, quite certain of imminent victory, marches away with his soldiers. This leaves Adina alone with Nemorino, a state that clearly bores her to distraction, for she immediately jumps ups and begins to search vigilantly for some missing, perhaps mythical, item. But Nemorino is persistent. "A word, Adina," he says tremulously.

"Humph! The same old nuisance! The same old sighs!" exclaims Adina impatiently. "You would do better to go to town and see your uncle, who is, I hear, dangerously ill."

"His suffering is nothing compared to mine," says Nemorino plaintively. "I cannot bear to leave."

"What if he dies and leaves his money to someone else?"

"What do I care whether I die of hunger or of l-l-l-l-ove?" stutters Nemorino.

Adina throws up her hands. He may as well give up, she tells him, for she will never, not ever, love him.

"But *why?*"

"Ask the sweet breeze why it flies without settling, and it will tell you that it is its nature to be fickle and inconstant," says Adina poetically. "You must renounce all thought of me; you must leave me."

"Adina! I cannot."

Adina counsels him to cure his madness by taking a new lover every day, for each new love drives out the old. "This," she explains, "is how I enjoy life; this is how I remain free."

Doggedly, Nemorino replies that he will never change, for one can never drive out the first love from one's heart. Back and forth they argue—Adina for diversity, Nemorino for true love—without changing their opinions in the least.

The village is bustling with the ordinary comings and goings of shoppers, grocers, farmers, and busybodies, all mingling and jingling—until a trumpet blast sends an eddy of surprise through the crowd.

Slowly, creakily, a great golden carriage rolls into the middle of the square and a corpulent figure in a rather dirty golden robe appears from within.

"A baron? A marquis?" the townspeople whisper to one another. "Perhaps a duke!"

But no! It is Doctor Dulcamara, and he is, he explains, extremely, terribly, wonderfully important. *"Udite, udite . . .* Listen, listen, you rustics, pay attention, hold your breath. I am the great medico called Dulcamara whose illustrious power and innumerable marvels are known throughout the universe and . . . and . . . and lots of other places." He can, he informs them, cure all their ills. And they, lucky ones, can have, for nearly nothing, Dulcamara's miraculous specific, known to remedy apoplectics, asthmatics, asphitics, hysterics, diabetics, the agony of earaches, scrofula, and rickets—and all this, not for thirty scudi, not for twenty, no, but for only, merely one scudo!

The townspeople are agog. "Only one scudo," they whisper, and cluster around the carriage to buy the prodigious potion.

Nemorino hangs back, summoning up his courage. After the crowd disperses, he shyly approaches the great Dulcamara. "Would you by any chance have the love potion of Queen Isolde?"

"Huh? What?" grunts Dulcamara.

"The elixir that awakens love," explains Nemorino.

"Ah yes, *that* one. Of course. Used quite a lot nowadays."

And quickly working out an exchange by which Nemorino is relieved of every cent he has, Dulcamara produces a bottle of the precious elixir. Nemorino is overwhelmed by his good fortune in finding the doctor, and Dulcamara is overwhelmed by his good fortune in finding such a simpleton. Just as the doctor is preparing to depart, Nemorino remembers to ask for instructions.

Very gravely, Dulcamara suggests that he shake it, uncork it, and drink it right down. Its astounding effects will be apparent immediately—or, actually, in a day, he says, backpedaling to give himself time for a getaway.

"And the flavor?" inquires the fearful Nemorino.

"Excellent!" pronounces Dulcamara confidently—for it is, after all, quite a nice Bordeaux, he whispers. Swearing the younger man to secrecy, Dulcamara leaves Nemorino to polish off the treasured elixir in a few mighty gulps.

In no time Nemorino is feeling quite cheerful—even better than cheerful—downright ecstatic. "Lalalalalalalala," he sings happily to himself.

Suddenly, Adina enters. She can't believe her eyes when she finds Nemorino, the heartbroken Nemorino, warbling away like a bird.

"Lalalalala—" Nemorino breaks off when he catches sight of Adina. Then he thinks, "Why not play it a bit cooler, since by tomorrow she'll be consumed with love anyway?" He recommences his song, "Lalalalalala!"

Adina looks at him in wonder. How he's changed, she thinks. But perhaps he's just pretending. "You're profiting from my lesson," she says acidly.

"Indeed," he replies blithely, "I'm putting it into operation."

After a few moments of watching him ignore her, Adina begins to feel a bit piqued. After a few more moments, she longs to see his old hangdog devotion. Several more "lalalalas" and she is determined to get revenge. At this delicate juncture, Sergeant Belcore appears, marching as vigorously as usual while complimenting himself on his military and romantic prowess. "In war and in love, I go for hand-to-hand combat," he announces to one and all. Seeing Adina, he decides it's time for an all-out campaign and, to his surprise, he finds Adina oddly compliant.

"Tell me, my pretty angel, when shall we be married?" Belcore leers.

"Very soon," says Adina.

"But when?" presses Belcore.

"In six days," she says, looking hard at Nemorino, who, disconcertingly, bursts into laughter. "How can he be so jolly when he hears that I'm getting married?" Adina whispers, grinding her teeth.

Nemorino is still chuckling—for he is certain of his victory before the six days have passed—when Giannetta runs in with a message for Belcore. He and his troops have been called away, and they must leave tomorrow morning.

As the soldiers curse their luck, Belcore turns to Adina imploringly. Couldn't she perhaps wed him sooner, say, this very afternoon?

Nemorino gulps. "This very afternoon?"

Adina glances at Nemorino and is gratified to find him looking tragic. "Yes. Well, then. Today," she acquiesces.

"Today?" says Nemorino in a strangled voice.

"And why not?" she replies coldly.

In vain he begs her to wait, just one day. It's for her own good, he promises her, for tomorrow she would regret it as much as he. Belcore, enraged at this interference, offers to knock his block off.

With a superior smile, Adina explains to Belcore that Nemorino has a crazy idea that he loves her. "Do excuse him," she says, and then, to herself, "I'll make him suffer."

Nemorino continues to plead and Belcore to threaten, while Giannetta and the village girls look on, amused. "Look at that big simpleton. He expects to get the better of the sergeant, the fool."

In a pretense of avid enthusiasm, Adina joins arms with Belcore and invites him to make haste to the notary.

"Help! Doctor! Help!" squeaks Nemorino, while Adina generously invites the village to the wedding party. As the betrothed couple departs, the villagers and peasants mock poor Nemorino.

# ACT TWO

At Adina's farm, the party has already begun, though the marriage has yet to take place. The villagers are dancing, singing, and drinking to the health of the happy couple. Even Dulcamara is there, grabbing all the food he can lay his hands on. Belcore, stupendously self-satisfied, is regaling the crowd with his philosophy of life. "Love and wine will always be my two gods. Every trouble is made up for by women and wine!"

"If only Nemorino were here," says Adina to herself, adding quickly, "I would so like to see his discomfort."

As his contribution to the entertainment, Dulcamara offers to sing a little duet with the bride. Officiously, he rustles through his pockets until he finds the score he seeks. "Ah, yes, 'The Pretty Gondolier Girl and Senator Threetooth,'" he announces. "Pay attention." He clears his throat and begins, "*Io son ricco e tu sei bella* . . . I am rich and you are pretty, I have money and you have charm. My sweetheart, what more could you want?" Taking the part of the Gondolier Girl, Adina protests that the honor is too great for her and she must marry a man of her own station. And so they sing along, until the notary arrives and they must all depart to sign the marriage contract—though Adina feels a stab of regret that Nemorino is not there to witness her marriage.

As Dulcamara lingers at the banquet table, who should come moping into the garden but Nemorino, certain that the doctor is his only hope. "I am desperate, I am beside myself. Doctor, I absolutely must be loved before tomorrow, right now, on the spot."

This is certainly possible, Dulcamara assures him. All he need do is repeat the dose. However, Nemorino has no money. The doctor advises his patient that he will be waiting in the village pub in a quarter hour, which should be ample time to find the needed cash.

And it is. Belcore reappears in the garden, baffled by Adina's sudden insistence that the wedding be postponed until the evening. There he finds Nemorino, who confesses his dire need for some money. Belcore has a simple solution: "Well, stupid!" he begins, "if you have no money, enlist as a soldier and you will have twenty scudi." He extols the charms of the military life: glory, honor, girls!

After a period of befuddled cogitation, Nemorino decides to take the chance. Belcore is still rambling on about glory, honor, and girls (mostly about girls), when Nemorino agrees to sign the enlistment papers. Pocketing the twenty scudi, Nemorino squirms impatiently through Belcore's congratulatory speech. Finally, the sergeant comes to a stop, and Nemorino rushes away at a gallop.

In a village courtyard, Giannetta and a cluster of village girls are deep in the midst of a gossip session.

"Is it possible?" ask several girls together.

"More than possible," announces Giannetta firmly.

The peddler has told Giannetta in strictest confidence that Nemorino's uncle has died and left the young man a considerable—no, immense—fortune! "But quiet!" warns Giannetta. "It mustn't get about," for Nemorino himself knows nothing of it.

Solemnly swearing that they won't breathe a word, the girls disperse, each reflecting on Nemorino's newfound status as a good catch.

Suddenly, the catch himself appears in the courtyard. The villagers watch him curiously. He has consumed another bottle of the miraculous elixir and already he can feel the effects.

"Your most humble servant," says Giannetta, simpering.

Nemorino gapes. "Giannetta!" One by one the village girls sidle by him, curtseying. "Whatever is the matter with these young girls," Nemorino cries, flummoxed by their coy looks. "Oh! I have it! This is the work of the magic potion!"

Adina and Dulcamara arrive from different directions. They stop in amazement at the sight before them: girls flirting with—Nemorino! Catching sight of the doctor, Nemorino thanks him feverishly for the potion. "This is wonderful! Through the power of the potion, I've already stirred the hearts of all the girls!"

"Oh, yes! He's a fellow who deserves our respect and esteem!" the girls exclaim, as Adina looks on, astounded. Giannetta solicitously asks if Nemorino would like to dance, and happily he accepts. Soon a quarrel breaks out among the girls as to who will dance next with the marvelous, the charming Nemorino.

In vain, Adina calls Nemorino to her side. She's worried, she says, because she's heard that he signed up as a soldier. Nemorino pays her no mind, so certain is he of the potion's mighty effect. "Oh! how sudden was

Enrico Caruso, possibly the greatest and certainly the most famous tenor the world has ever known, made a specialty of Nemorino. Audiences loved him in the role, for it dovetailed nicely with the satisfying mythology of Caruso as rustic genius, natural wonder. But in December 1920, there came a ghastly performance of Elixir that revealed the tenacity and professionalism underneath the "voice of gold." Dorothy Caruso, the tenor's wife, wrote an account of that evening: "Enrico came running out over the little bridge, laughing and looking as foolish and stupid as possible. . . . The audience applauded wildly. Standing close to the footlights, he began at once to sing. When he had finished he turned his back and reached for his handkerchief. I heard him give a little cough, but he came in on his cue, finished the phrase and turned away again. When he faced the audience, the front of his smock was scarlet. A whisper blew through the house but stopped as he began to sing. This time it was an aria and he couldn't turn his back. From the wings Zirato's hand held out a towel. Enrico took it, wiped his lips, and went on singing. Towel after towel was passed to him and still he sang on. All about him on the stage lay crimson towels. At last he finished the aria and ran off. The act was ended and the curtain came down. Cold and blind with terror, I sat without moving. For long moments the theatre was as silent as an empty house. Then, as if a signal had been given, a thunder of sound and movement shook the audience. I heart shouts and screams, voices crying 'Stop him!' 'Don't let him go on!'"

That performance was, of course, cancelled, but Caruso's doctors allowed him to sing again two days later. Two weeks later, he made what was to be his final appearance on stage, in Halévy's La juive. He died eight months afterward, of complications from pleurisy.

this change," fumes Adina, as she watches Nemorino dancing off. "O Love, you take your revenge for my indifference; the one who rejects me is the one I am forced to love."

Dulcamara offers his sympathy—and the love potion of Queen Isolde.

"Isolde?" Adina says sharply. "Is this the potion you gave Nemorino?"

"He asked me for it in order to win the heart of who knows which cruel beauty."

"He was terribly in love?"

"He languished and sighed, and, to obtain a drop of the magic drug, he sold his freedom by enlisting as a soldier!"

"*Quanto amore!* . . . Such love! And I was pitiless. I tortured this noble heart," sighs Adina.

Slyly the doctor pulls out a bottle of the magic potion and offers it to the girl, who rejects it with a smile, explaining that she has something better than any elixir. "A tender look, a smile, a caress, can conquer the most stubborn man. My formula is in my pretty face, and not even Nemorino will be able to escape me!"

Laughing, the doctor agrees, and the pair departs. Soon enough, Nemorino wanders back to the courtyard, tired of flirtation and foolishness. He wants only Adina. "*Una furtiva lagrima* . . . A furtive tear sprang to her eye, and she seemed to envy those carefree girls. Why should I look any further? She loves me, yes, she loves me! I can ask for nothing more. I could die of love."

He turns and there she is, standing before him. He resolves to pretend indifference until she declares her love. But Adina has another plan; she has bought back his enlistment from Belcore because, she says, everyone would miss him if he left.

"Now she'll come out with it," Nemorino whispers.

"Farewell," says Adina politely, putting out her hand.

"What! Have you nothing more to tell me?" asks Nemorino.

"Nothing else," she replies.

"Well then, take it back," he says, handing her the paper. "If I'm not loved, I'd rather die a soldier's death."

At this, the truth comes out. Adina assures him that she loves him tenderly, that she longs to make him just as happy as she once made him miserable, and of course Nemorino's joy knows no bounds. Their rejoicing is interrupted by Belcore and his troops, with Dulcamara and the villagers following along. The sight of the lovers brings the sergeant to an abrupt halt. "What's this I see?" he yelps. Adina admits that it's Nemorino she loves, and Belcore recovers with astonishing speed, for, after all, "the world is full of women; and Belcore will catch thousands upon thousands."

Dulcamara, never one to pass up an opportunity, offers the sergeant a sample of the amazing potion, and though Belcore curses him for a charlatan, everyone else gathers round to buy a bottle. With the blessings of Nemorino and Adina, the old quack drives off, the air ringing with cheers for him and his elixir of love. ⁓

# NORMA

~⟨∂⟩'⟨∂⟩~

Literally, *bel canto* means "beautiful song," and thus seems as though it should apply to any opera worth its salt. In practice, however, the term refers to a specific type of singing—expressive, exhibitionistic, highly ornamented, and requiring the full fusillade of trills, arpeggios, and displays of virtuoso agility—that reached its zenith in the operas of Vincenzo Bellini and Gaetano Donizetti. Bel canto opera had been around for quite a while; the *opere serie* of the mid-eighteenth century were essentially bel canto compositions, even if they lacked Romantic charm, and individual singers could always find a way to display their pyrotechnics, no matter what the opera. Where Bellini and Donizetti excelled, though, was in finding stories of madness, delirium, passion, and fury that provided suitable opportunities for heroic singing. Furthermore, both composers simplified their orchestration to emphasize the melodic line and the voice itself, which not only pushed the singer to the forefront, but made for pleasingly hummable tunes. As a result, the works of Bellini and Donizetti are regarded as the quintessential bel canto operas.

It's important to remember that a composer's efforts are bootless without the services of a singer who can deliver the vocal and theatrical goods. Bellini was lucky in his sopranos; the early nineteenth century was rife with fabulous, temperamental sopranos, such as Giuditta Pasta, who originated Norma at Milan's La Scala in 1831, and the ever-dramatic Maria Malibran, who was not so much singer as spectacle. But after about 1850, Bellini's works were rarely performed—at least until the 1950s, when a much-lauded revival of the style was precipitated by the emergence of a constellation of heavenly sopranos, with Maria Callas at its center. Thanks in large part to these voices, Bellini and *Norma* have enjoyed a return to the repertoire and will probably never leave it again.

# ACT ONE

The year is 50 B.C., and though the wild forests of Gaul have been recently subdued by the Roman forces, the Gallic people seethe with rebellious fervor. In a sacred grove, the Druid priest Oroveso speaks to the assembled warriors. The moment for the uprising has not yet come, he warns them. Only when Oroveso's daughter, the great priestess Norma, gives the signal will the time be ripe to throw off the yoke of subjection. Eager to fight, the Druids march to a nearby hill to beseech the new moon to inspire Norma's anger.

Only a few moments later, the grove's silence is disturbed again, by the Roman consul, Pollione. His companion, the centurion Flavio, mentions Norma, and Pollione pales. "You have spoken a name that chills my heart."

"What are you saying?" responds Flavio incredulously. "She is your beloved, the mother of your children!"

Pollione confesses that his love for Norma is dead, replaced by his passion for another woman, Adalgisa, though she, like Norma, is a supposedly virgin priestess at the temple of the Druid gods.

"Do you not fear the wrath of Norma?" Flavio asks.

Groaning, Pollione nods. "It will be terrible. I dreamed I was at the altar of Venus in Rome with Adalgisa, when a sudden shadow descended between us and she was enfolded by the great Druidic cloak. Lightning flashed and the day was veiled in darkness; then my beloved was no longer by my side. From afar, a monstrous voice echoed through the temple, saying, 'This is Norma's vengeance upon her faithless lover!'" He trembles at the memory.

Flavio hears the sound of voices approaching. Urgently, he drags the reluctant Pollione to safety, just as a crowd of Druids, warriors, and bards enter in a thunderous march. An excited whisper runs among them—Norma is coming to perform her rites!

A phalanx of priestesses parts, and there is Norma upon the altar, her magnificent hair crowned with the mystical vervain, her great dark eyes searching the heavens. Slowly, she turns her burning gaze upon the people below her. "*Sediziose voce* . . . Are there those who raise seditious voices, voices of war, before the altar of God?" she thunders, castigating those who dare to question her prophecy. Though Oroveso pleads and the tumultuous crowd protests, she maintains that the hour of vengeance has not arrived. "One day Rome shall die; but not at your hands. She will die through her own vices, as if consumed by them. Await that hour, and meanwhile, peace!" Absorbed again in her vision, she joins her priestesses in a prayer to the moon. "*Casta Diva* . . . Chaste goddess," she intones, "who bathes these hallowed trees in silver, temper the burning hearts of thy people." She cuts the mistletoe with a golden sickle, bringing the ceremony to an end.

Reluctantly her people acquiesce, but they still mutter lustfully of the revenge they would exact upon Pollione. Norma counterfeits agreement, but hiding her face from her followers, she whispers that her heart would not know how to rise up against her lover. She begs the gods to restore the luster to Pollione's love, wishing desperately that everything between them would be as it was.

Slowly, led by Norma, the crowd marches away, leaving a single priestess at the altar: Adalgisa. Try as she might, she cannot resist the temptation to see Pollione; but when he enters the sacred grove, she begs him to leave and vows she will return to the temple forever.

He can never leave her, he asserts. "You do not know what it would cost me to renounce your love."

"And you do not know the pain that loving you has cost me," she replies. "For me, guilty violator of my oath, both heaven and God are veiled from my sight."

Pollione offers her a purer heaven and holier gods—in Rome. Thus he breaks the news of his departure. As he begs her to accompany him, she begs him to leave her. But finally, as Pollione describes how their love will flourish in Rome, Adalgisa is conquered. "My God I shall renounce," she swears, "but to you I shall always be faithful."

In front of the cottage where she has hidden the offspring of her illegal union, Norma watches her sons playing. But she is distracted and agitated, and when her servant, Clotilde, comes, Norma directs her to hide the children away.

"What strange fear troubles you?" asks the servant.

"I do not know. Many passions torment my soul. I love and yet I hate my children. I suffer when I see them, I suffer when I do not," answers Norma. She knows that Pollione is leaving for Rome and suspects he will abandon her. Her dark thoughts are interrupted by an approaching visitor: Adalgisa!

She has come, consumed by her guilty love and entirely unaware that Norma was her predecessor in Pollione's heart, to confess her terrible sin to the priestess. At Norma's urging, Adalgisa's secret comes out: She's in love—and she has promised her lover to abandon the temple and her fatherland.

Norma questions her closely, sympathetically, about the beginning of her romance, and Adalgisa innocently recounts the story. How she was praying at the altar when her glance fell on him and "I seemed to find

> The passionate intensity of Bellini's operas—to say nothing of their eminent tunefulness—soon gave him the reputation of being an exquisitely sensitive poet, the embodiment of the Romantic ideal. His contemporary, the poet Heinrich Heine, who was no piker in the sensitive poet department, scoffed at Bellini's refined public image: "His features had something vague in them, a want of character, something milklike, and in his milklike face flitted a sometimes painful-pleasing expression of sorrow.
>
> It was this shallow sorrow that the young maestro seemed most willing to represent in his whole appearance. His hair was dressed so fancifully sad; his clothes fitted so languishingly around his delicate body; he carried his cane so idyllike, that he reminded me of the young shepherds we find in our pastorals, with their crooks decorated with ribbons. His whole walk was so innocent, so airy, so sentimental. The man looked like a sigh in pumps and silk stockings."

a new heaven in his face." Her words evoke sweet memories in Norma and she commands the girl to continue. Adalgisa begs for Norma's forgiveness, and the priestess pityingly releases her from her vows and wishes her great happiness. "But—the youth you love—which one of us is he?" asks Norma.

"He is not a Gaul. His country is Rome," replies Adalgisa, and with a gasp, Norma learns what she dreads to know. As she recoils from this blow, Pollione himself enters the clearing, terrified to see his new love with his old.

Wheeling about, Norma turns on him. *"Tremi tu?* . . . You tremble? For whom? Do not tremble for her, faithless man, for she is not to blame," she roars. "Tremble for yourself, traitor—for your children—for me!" As she curses him, Adalgisa begins to understand what has happened. Repulsed by Pollione's faithlessness, she vows to renounce him, despite his pleas. Meanwhile, Norma rails on: "Leave me, yes, worthless man! Forget your children, your promises, your honor. Over the seas, borne on the winds, my burning hatred will pursue you!"

Bitterly, Pollione curses the fate that brought him Norma's love, while Adalgisa swears that she will never be the cause of Norma's sorrow. Three spine-tingling clangs of the gong interrupt them; Norma must attend the sacred assembly. "Ah, the sound of death," Norma hisses over her shoulder at Pollione. "Go! Death is ready for you."

# ACT TWO

Norma is pacing back and forth before the bed upon which her children sleep, a dagger in her hand. "They will not see the hand that strikes them," she mutters. "No remorse, oh, my heart." Better to die by her hand than suffer as slaves of a stepmother in Rome, she reasons. "Strike! Ah, no! They are my children—mine!"

Dropping the dagger, she sends Clotilde to fetch Adalgisa. The young priestess comes running, and Norma begs for one final favor. Adalgisa fervently swears that she will do anything, and Norma consigns the children to Adalgisa's care, directing her to take them to Pollione. "May he be less cruel a husband to you. I forgive him, and now I shall die." Adalgisa's protestations are met with impatient dismissal: "Take them with you," Norma interrupts, "and protect them."

Her fierce desperation touches Adalgisa's heart, and the young priestess promises that she will go to the Roman camp to urge the Consul to return to Norma, but Norma responds proudly that she will never stoop to begging. Seeking a way to soften her resolve, Adalgisa points to the sleeping children nearby, asking her to take pity on them, even if she feels no pity for herself.

"Why do you try to weaken me?" cries Norma. "Such illusions and hopes are not for one about to die."

However, Adalgisa slowly wins the proud woman over to her plan and, embracing, they vow to remain loyal companions forevermore.

Once again the Druids and Gallic warriors are gathered around the altar. Emboldened by the news of Pollione's departure, they clamor for war and vengeance. Oroveso tries to assuage their anger by reminding them that their pretended docility will make their attack more powerful when it comes, and the disgruntled warriors slowly file away.

All is silent when Norma appears, expecting to meet a repentant Pollione at the altar. But it is Clotilde who arrives, bearing bad tidings: Pollione has refused to return to her.

"She has betrayed me!" Norma cries, but Clotilde assures her that an anguished Adalgisa is coming to the temple to offer up her vows. "And he?" asks Norma.

"He has sworn to carry her off, even from the altar of God," replies Clotilde fearfully.

Norma's face grows pale with rage. Like a lion, she roars, "The traitor presumes too much! But my vengeance will strike first and blood—Roman blood—shall flow like water." She turns and beats savagely upon the great golden shield. As Druids, Gauls, bards, and priestesses rush in, Norma strides to the altar and cries, "War! Massacre! Death!"

Electrified, the mob breaks into an anthem of violence, *"Guerra! guerra! . . .* War! War! Blood! Slaughter, extermination, and vengeance begin already and will soon be complete!"

But the carnage cannot commence without a ritual sacrifice. Who is the victim to be? asks Oroveso. Calmly, his daughter assures him that the altar will never lack for victims. "But what is that tumult?" she asks, seeing a disturbance in the temple.

It is Pollione, captured in the cloister of the virgins.

"Now I am avenged," breathes Norma, as the bound Consul is dragged forward and accused of blaspheming the sacred temple.

"It is I who must strike," intones Norma, pushing her way through the crowd to take the dagger from Oroveso. She raises the knife over Pollione—but something stays her hand.

"Strike! Strike!" chants the crowd.

Stalling for time, she replies that she must question the blasphemer alone to uncover his accomplice within the cloister. The mob reluctantly departs and Norma, exulting in her power over him, demands that Pollione give up Adalgisa in return for his life. "Swear it!" she commands.

But Pollione refuses.

"Do you not know that my fury is greater than yours? Do you not know that with this dagger, your children—"

"My God, what are you saying?" cries Pollione.

She admits that she could not strike them, but warns that "in an instant, I could forget I am a mother."

Pollione begs her to kill him instead, but Norma scoffs. "You alone? All the Romans, by the hundreds, shall be mown down, destroyed. And Adalgisa—"

"No!" cries the Consul.

"—having violated her vows, will die in flames," continues the implacable Norma, as Pollione pleads with her. "Already, I feed upon your anguish for her death. At last, I can make you as unhappy as I am."

In vain, he begs her to show mercy to Adalgisa, but Norma calls for the priests and warriors to return. "To appease your wrath, I announce a new victim. A perjured priestess has broken her holy vows, has betrayed her nation, and our fathers' gods."

A ripple of shock runs through the crowd; they demand to know the name of the traitor, but Norma tells them to light the sacrificial pyre first.

"Who is she?" they cry wrathfully.

"It is I," replies Norma.

For a moment there is an astonished silence.

"My heart fails me," whispers Pollione. He turns to the mob, pleading, "Do not believe her."

"Norma does not lie," says the priestess regally. She fixes Pollione with her proud gaze. *"Qual cor tradisti* . . . the heart you betrayed, the heart you lost; in this hour, see what a heart it was."

Transfixed by the nobility he sees in her, Pollione feels the dead love within his heart stir to life. "Too late, I have realized that you are a woman sublime, and I have lost you," he says. "Let us die together; yes, let us die. My last word will be that I love you. But before you die, forgive me."

Oroveso, bewildered and distraught, begs his daughter to recant. "Norma! Are you guilty? Speak!"

"Yes, beyond mortal power to imagine," she replies firmly, earning execration from the crowd. Only the thought of her children seems to give her pause in her inexorable journey toward death. Turning to her father, Norma confesses, "I am a mother," and implores him to have pity on his own blood. Though he is at first loathe to accept the progeny of this guilty union, she extracts his promise and then, calmly, she turns toward the flaming pyre.

"Your pyre, Norma, is mine," says Pollione, clasping her hand. "There beyond, sanctified, begins our eternal love."

And, while her people rain curses on her head and her father weeps, Norma and Pollione are led to their deaths. ~~∽

# DIE MEISTERSINGER VON NÜRNBERG

—— *The Mastersingers of Nuremberg* ——

Now, a century and a quarter after his death, Richard Wagner is so weighted down by the freight of his mythology that it is nearly impossible to listen to his music simply. Wagnerians have made loving Wagner a formidable task, with their stern reverence for every note and their exegesis of each opera as though it were a sacred text. Wagner, too, makes it difficult to love Wagner: His appalling egocentrism, his callous treatment of his friends, his anti-Semitism, and his insistence on the superiority of German culture cloud our approach to his magnificent works. For his operas are magnificent, and if we could hear them in the context of their creation, their idealism might be utterly appealing. Wagner's "Music of the Future" was a complete revolution against the operatic conventions of the day—down with soaring arias, duets, trios, and quartets that do nothing except display the virtuosity of the singers; down with ridiculous plots written by second-rate poets; and down, especially, with opera as a series of discrete "numbers" strung together on a flimsy thread of recitative.

What Wagner provided instead was the *Gesamtkunstwerk,* the total work of art. They were not operas, they were "music-dramas," transcendent concatenations of music, poetry, scenery, and singing based on German folk legends. Instead of tunes and numbers, Wagner created *leitmotivs,* leading motifs, music that represented characters and ideas throughout the work, ultimately intertwining into one organic whole. Wagner's repudiation of all that went before required courage and surpassing confidence, but his creation of an entirely new form of opera necessitated a multivalent genius. Librettist, composer, and producer all rolled into one, Wagner shook the musical world by its heels in the 1860s. The breadth of his vision is still impressive, of course, but we have grown blasé about titanic productions, and what has kept Wagner firmly on his throne is the ecstatic tapestry of his music. In the early twentieth century, one delirious American music student, upon hearing *The Ring of the Nibelungs* for the first time, summed up the intoxicating effect of Wagner's music: "A new world burst forth! Life would never be the same again, the commonplace was banished from our several lives forever! . . . The music—the music was truth itself . . . a revelation of the primitive impulses and sources of all things."

*Die Meistersinger,* composed in the interstices of the great Ring project and first performed in 1868, embodies all of Wagner's criteria for the Music of the Future and adds comedy to boot. Despite the occasional polemic, it is Wagner's most endearing opera; one commentator called it "the longest single smile in the German language."

# ACT ONE

In Nuremberg's church of Saint Katherine, a handsome young knight, Walther von Stolzing, is paying little heed to the soaring hymns of the congregation. His attention is fixed on Eva, the charming daughter of the prosperous goldsmith Pogner. She is also finding it difficult to keep her mind on spiritual matters and the two have been exchanging long glances across the pews. Now, as the service comes to an end, Eva craftily manages to shed the company of her nurse, Magdalena, for a few moments, in order to receive Walther's whispered avowals of love. When Magdalena returns, the presence of her own lover, the apprentice David, inspires her to delay their departure a little, and from her Walther learns that though Eva is not betrothed, her hand has been promised to the victor of the next contest of the Mastersingers, which is to be held tomorrow. Eva innocently assumes that Walther must be a Mastersinger himself, and is shocked to learn that he is not. Defiantly, she declares that she will have the knight or no one, a piece of forwardness that appalls Magdalena. However, she takes up the young lovers' cause by instructing David to help Walther learn the rules of the Mastersingers, that he might enter their guild today and win the contest tomorrow. As luck would have it, David, who is apprenticed to the Mastersinger Hans Sachs, and a few of his companions are even now setting up the church for the meeting of the Mastersingers' Guild in which the candidates for new membership will be tested. Eva and Magdalena depart, and the determined knight listens attentively to David's explanation of the Mastersingers' complex regulations, growing more and more confused as the apprentice describes "strophes," the permissible forms of melody, and the job of the Marker, who marks down each breach of law committed by the singer during his trial. Anyone who receives more than seven marks, David declares solemnly, is finished!

Now the Masters are assembling in the church. First enters Pogner, Eva's father, followed by Beckmesser, an elderly, whey-faced clerk who is determined to win Eva's hand and is much concerned with Pogner's stipulation that the girl must acquiesce to the union. What, he fusses, is the point of winning the contest, when the prize may refuse to be won? Pogner dismisses his complaints just as Walther approaches, begging for the opportunity to be admitted into the guild. The knight is well known to Pogner and he gladly grants Walther a trial. The roll is called as the cobbler Hans Sachs slips into his chair. The Masters agree that competing for Pogner's daughter will reveal the true depths of their devotion to art. Beckmesser continues to agitate against the girl having a say in her fate, but Pogner assures him that if Eva refuses the contest's winner, she may not marry another man. Sachs argues for making the people of Nuremberg the judges of the contest, but he is shouted down by the old guard, for, they say, what do the people know of music? Eventually, he accedes to the majority and settles back to hear the candidates for admission to the Mastersingers' Guild.

Pogner recommends Walther, and the Masters begin to examine him on his musical training. Walther admits that his musical education has come chiefly from an old book—and from the "meadows and forests." The Masters are taken aback, but they allow Walther to continue. Beckmesser, as Marker, retreats into his special chamber with a board and chalk, and Master Kothner reads out the redoubtable roster of rules. The young knight settles himself on the stool—for the singer must sit, according to regulation—and, when Beckmesser curtly orders him to begin, Walther sings, *"Fanget an! . . . Begin! Thus spring cried to the forest."* His swelling song is continually interrupted by Beckmesser's groans and the sound of chalk cracking against the board. Discomfited, Walther incorporates nature's brutality into his song, but, rising, he chronicles its defeat by the forces of new life—

"Have you finished yet?" Beckmesser interrupts, holding up his chalk-covered board. "There's no more room on the slate." The Masters laughingly agree that the young man's composition was full of faults.

"Not so fast, Masters!" interjects Hans Sachs. The song and melody are new, he concedes, but not confused; they proceed according to their own rules. Why not let the knight proceed?

The voice of reason and moderation is met with derision. The Masters declare that the matter is finished: The young man has been undone. Sachs, meanwhile, encourages Walther to finish his song, and with increasing desperation, the knight begins anew. But no one—except Sachs—listens, and when the cacophony of voices grows too great, Walther strides out of the church in disgust. In a tide of chatter and hand-wringing, the Masters and apprentices leave soon after and finally, looking discouraged, Hans Sachs also departs.

# ACT TWO

Dusk is falling on an old square in Nuremberg. On one corner stands Sachs's simple, sturdy house and opposite stands Pogner's grand residence. David and the other apprentices are hanging up garlands of flowers in preparation for the next day's Festival of St. John. Magdalena slyly approaches David to inquire about the knight's progress with the Mastersingers. David tells her that Walther was outsung and undone. Outraged, Magdalena rushes into Pogner's house, leaving David ripe for ridicule by his companions, who solemnly offer him their heartfelt congratulations on his marriage. David is just about to lose his temper when Sachs steps in and pulls David back into his workshop. The boys disperse and the street is quiet for a few moments, until

Eva and her father come strolling slowly around the corner, returning from a walk. Sighing over the next day's contest, Eva asks, "Dear Father, must it be a Master?"

"Listen carefully," replies Pogner, smiling. "It must be the Master of *your choice*."

At that moment, Eva's attention is caught by Magdalena, who is signaling frantically from the door. Inside, Eva learns that Walther has been unsuccessful in his attempt to join the Mastersingers. In despair, the young girl goes across the street to visit her old friend Hans Sachs.

Naturally, the conversation turns to the coming contest, and in her anxiety that Beckmesser might be the only candidate, Eva hints to Sachs that he should contend for her hand as well. Smiling, he demurs: He's too old for her, and none of Eva's coaxing will change his mind. Casually, she asks him about Walther's singing trial, and Sachs carefully answers with a seeming dismissal of Walther's talents. Eva's fiery defense of the young knight tell Sachs all he needs to know, and he resigns himself to assisting her in the realization of her heart's desire while he denies his own. In the midst of this exchange, Magdalena comes calling for Eva, and the young girl leaves Sachs's workshop, though Sachs opens his door slightly to keep an eye on her doings. Her father has been calling for her, says Magdalena, and Beckmesser is preparing to serenade her window any minute. In the hopes of rousing David to jealousy, Magdalena accedes to Eva's pleas to impersonate her at the window. Midway across the square, Eva catches sight of Walther hastening toward her. She runs to him and casts herself into his arms. As Magdalena slips away to take her place at the window, Walther recounts the afternoon's experience, filled with indignation about the Mastersingers' web of rules and their insolence. He grows angrier and angrier, but Eva gradually calms him and, leading him to the shadows of the lime tree, promises to elope with him. She slips home to prepare.

As the night watchman ambles by, chanting his ancient song, Sachs, who has overheard the lovers' exchange, vows to do his best to foil this ill-considered elopement and bring the romance to a more legitimate conclusion. Eva returns, costumed in Magdalena's clothes and ready to fly. Sachs craftily opens his upper door, allowing a full stream of light to flood the square, effectively trapping the young couple in their hiding place. Just as they decide to risk a dash to freedom, the sour-faced Beckmesser comes creaking into the square with lute in hand, set to commence his serenade. As though by coincidence, Sachs pulls his workbench out into the street, and at this, Eva draws Walther deep into the foliage of the lime tree. Affecting not to notice Beckmesser's busy preparations, Sachs begins to hammer loudly, shouting a thunderous work song.

"Damned yelling!" complains Beckmesser furiously.

Sachs takes no notice, but continues to sing lustily. Smiling, he hollers to Beckmesser that he is working on Beckmesser's own shoes, specially ordered for the festival.

"Devil take the shoes! Can I have a little peace and quiet here?" shouts Beckmesser.

Sachs ignores him, and Eva, catching on, suggests to Walther that Sachs has a scheme in mind. Magdalena, disguised as Eva, now opens the window, throwing Beckmesser into a positive frenzy. He pleads with Sachs to stop his hammering and howling; Sachs, politely obtuse, declines. But, Sachs adds, he would be glad to

learn the art of marking. In fact, he offers, he will be the Marker for Beckmesser's serenade, tapping out the errors with his hammer. Sourly judging that Sachs marking is better than Sachs singing, Beckmesser agrees, and after numerous instructions to the cobbler, he begins to warble in a toneless quaver.

Bang!

"Are you joking? What was wrong?"

Sachs ingenuously suggests a better rhyme. Growling, Beckmesser carries on with his torturous song, accompanied by Sachs's pounding. From behind a discreet curtain, Magdalena, dressed as Eva, shows every sign of disenchantment, so Beckmesser sings louder and louder. Now the din is waking the neighbors, who lean out their windows, calling, "Who's yelling? Who's screeching so loud?"

David has been wakened by the noise, and as he leans out his window, he catches sight of Magdalena, seemingly in a romantic meeting with a lute-playing swain. Enraged, David leaps out into the street swinging his cudgel, knocks the instrument out of Beckmesser's hands, and jumps upon his enemy in a frenzy of vengeance.

Magdalena screams as Beckmesser struggles to extricate himself from the boy's grasp and the neighbors shriek and exclaim. Soon, burghers and their apprentices are pouring into the street to join the fray, shouting and walloping each other with indiscriminate enthusiasm. Old hatreds are reborn, professional prejudices aired: The butchers blame the coopers, the barbers denounce the smiths, the weavers accuse the tanners, and a magnificent melee is soon fully underway. The Mastersingers march sternly into the square demanding order, but they go unheard and the riot escalates.

Eva and Walther decide that they have no choice but to flee. Brandishing his sword, Walther forces his way through the crowd. Sachs, spying his opportunity, bounds from his shop and grasps the young man by the arm. Just as the women, watching from their windows, decide to take matters into their own hands and pour water on the rioters, Sachs half-carries the terrorized Eva to her door. Then he catches up with David, whom he kicks back into the workshop before him as he drags Walther behind. Just in time, Sachs bars his workshop door. As water comes flying out of upstairs windows on all sides, the watchman's horn is heard and at this, the rioters suddenly scatter. Doors and windows bang shut and in a matter of minutes, quiet descends. When the befuddled night watchman enters the square, it is once again the peaceful haven of an hour before.

# ACT THREE

The next morning, relieved that his master has forgiven him for his part in the previous night's melee, David is singing for Sachs the carol he will perform at the St. John's Day festival. When he is finished, Sachs sends him off to array himself for the day. Now alone, the cobbler returns to his thoughts: *"Wahn! Wahn! . . . Madness! Madness! Everywhere madness! Why do people torment and flay each other in useless, foolish anger?"*

Walther enters, newly arisen and still under the influence of his dreams. Sachs encourages him to record the fleeting images in verse. Walther protests—no poem of his would ever be acceptable as a master-song. Sachs disputes this, telling Walther that the Masters' original purpose was to retain the freshness of youth and love. Sachs offers to write the verse into a song according to the Masters' precepts as Walther recites it. Slowly, Walther begins to sing the words to his Prize Song, telling of the scents of morning, unthought-of joy, a garden that holds the Tree of Life, and a beautiful woman who joins him there. Under Sachs's guidance, this vision takes the shape of a master-song. Deeply moved, Sachs convinces Walther to prepare to enter the contest. Together, they go upstairs to ready themselves for the festival.

The workshop is quiet for a few moments, until Beckmesser limps through the door. He is dressed in ostentatious velvets and silks, but he is bruised and battered from the previous night's events. As he looks about the room, his eye falls on Sachs's transcription of Walther's song. Assuming that the love song is Sachs's creation, he concludes that Sachs himself is contending for Eva's hand and quickly pockets the paper.

Sachs enters the room and greets Beckmesser with surprise. Surely his shoes aren't still hurting, Sachs inquires solicitously.

"The devil take you!" explodes Beckmesser. "Never have I worn such thin shoes. I can feel the smallest stone through the soles!"

Hiding a smile, Sachs explains that it was the fault of his marking, as the soles got pounded with each mark. Beckmesser can contain himself no longer. He reproaches Sachs for ruining his chances of winning Eva, for upsetting his serenade, for making him a laughingstock. Sachs denies the charges and reveals that he has no intention of entering the contest. In disbelief, Beckmesser cross-examines him and produces Walther's verse as evidence of Sachs's deceit. Much to his astonishment, Sachs, knowing that Beckmesser will be

*For all his rigorous theories, even Wagner was not always a Wagnerian, and* Die Meistersinger *proves it. It is, of all things, a comedy (at least intermittently). Furthermore, the opera is set in historical Nuremberg, rather than in the mythical past, and features an actual historical character, the poet and songwriter Hans Sachs. It is also remarkably tuneful. However, if the four-and-a-half-hour running time didn't give away the work's authorship, the rampant German nationalism would. The allegorical nature of the story is also telling: The hero is a young knight whose nontraditional yet beautiful songs are disparaged by a hidebound guild of Mastersingers relying on outmoded regulations rather than emotional truth. The chief villain of the piece, Beckmesser, who strongly resembles a music critic Wagner despised, is overcome by the noble Hans Sachs, and the opera concludes with Sachs's vision of a musical future in which holiness and Germanness will be discovered to be one and the same. As the curtain falls, the young knight receives his rightful adulation from a joyous public, true love is victorious, and small-minded critics are thoroughly reformed.*

incapable of singing it correctly, immediately makes him a present of the poem. The clerk's suspicions turn to delight, for a song by Sachs will ensure his success. Cackling gleefully, he is on the verge of hobbling away when a new fear crosses his sallow face: "Swear one thing: You'll never say that this song was written by you."

Sachs assures him truthfully that he will never claim the song as his, and rejoicing in his good fortune, Beckmesser leaves.

The next visitor to the workshop is Eva, dressed in a shimmering white gown. Ostensibly, she has come about her shoes, but as Sachs fusses about her feet, Walther enters the room dressed in magnificent knightly garb and the real reason for her visit becomes clear. The young lovers stare at one another, transfixed. Without moving, Walther begins to sing, "Did the stars stop still in their lovely dance? In her tresses—above all women glorious to behold—so light and clear, a garland of stars lay gleaming."

"Listen, child! That's a master-song," comments Sachs.

Walther continues with his song, as Eva listens breathlessly. As the last notes linger in the air, she begins to weep on Sachs's shoulder. Silently, Sachs draws Walther to her and tears himself away, leaving the couple in an embrace. Then he busies himself around the workshop, soliloquizing assiduously about shoes.

Wiping her eyes, Eva interrupts him, explaining that she now has no choice, for her love for Walther is compulsion. But if she had been forced to choose among the Mastersingers, she assures Sachs, she would have chosen him.

Smiling sadly, Sachs says that he has heard the tale of Tristan and Isolde and would not want the part of King Marke. With a shake, he rouses himself and calls for David and Magdalena. They hurry in and David is greeted with the ritual blow on the shoulder, which brings his days of apprenticeship to an end and frees him to marry Magdalena. Together, Sachs, Walther, Eva, David, and Magdalena ruminate about the transformations the day will bring.

In an open meadow near the river, the people of Nuremberg have gathered for the festival. Prosperous burghers, lively journeymen, and riotous children mingle on the grounds, which are decorated with flags and flowers. A platform stands in the middle with brightly colored tents surrounding it. As each of the town guilds arrives, the members sing its anthem. A boat docks at the riverbank landing and gaily dressed peasant girls disembark. They are greeted by the apprentices and soon couples pair off for a lively dance.

In due time the Mastersingers arrive. Pogner leads Eva to the stage, where she sits in the place of honor. Sachs rises and steps forward, and as he does, the crowd breaks into a roar of acclamation and praise. Touched by their esteem, Sachs describes the singing contest and the great prize to be awarded the victor.

Beckmesser is called first. He complains in a whisper to Sachs about the difficulty of the verse. A ripple of disapproval runs through the audience, subsiding as Beckmesser begins. But what a beginning! Beckmesser has set the words to the quavering tune of his serenade song and warbles away painfully about morning time and gardens. But soon the hastily memorized verses begin to slip away; words are hopelessly mixed and meaning is mangled.

The Mastersingers look at each other in consternation. Is he mad? The townspeople are less circumspect. "To the gallows!" they cry sarcastically, bursting into laughter. The town clerk descends from his platform in a rage, shouting that it's not his fault, it's not his song at all. "It's by Sachs. Your Sachs has given it to me!" Furious, Beckmesser rushes into the crowd and is seen no more.

The audience is perplexed: Can this horrible song be the work of Sachs?

Sachs replies that he would never dare to boast that such a beautiful song was his own composition. For it *is* beautiful, he assures them, when sung properly. And so he calls upon Walther to perform. The Mastersingers, though noting an infraction of the rules, allow Sachs to proceed, and Walther ascends the platform and begins his Prize Song.

The listeners can scarcely believe that this is the same work. Even the Mastersingers are struck by the beauty of it and sigh softly to themselves. "It's bold and strange," they admit, "but well rhymed and singable."

Encouraged by this reception, Walther sings as never before, and the people of Nuremberg hang on every note. As it draws to a close, they urge the Mastersingers to grant the prize to the knight, which, of course, they do.

But Walther is not to be so easily won. In his pride, he refuses, and the Mastersingers are dismayed. Sachs comes forward with wise words for Walther: "Do not scorn the Masters' art. Make it your task instead to rejuvenate their traditions and join them in repelling foreign influences. Honor your German Masters and holy German art!"

And, to the cheers of the audience, Walther acquiesces. Eva places the wreath of the victor around his head. Then all turn to Sachs for one final expression of honor and gratitude. ⁓ῷ

# DER RING DES NIBELUNGEN

## — The Ring of the Nibelungs —

**W**agner's *Ring* is the greatest musical composition ever written, at the very least in terms of size. An uninterrupted performance of the *Ring* would last more than fifteen hours, but no one, not even Wagner himself, has ever seriously entertained the concept of an uninterrupted *Ring*. Instead, the four operas—*Das Rheingold, Die Walküre, Siegfried,* and *Götterdämmerung*—are usually given in a series, sometimes on four different nights within one season and sometimes spread over four seasons. Tying together a number of ancient Teutonic legends, the *Ring* cycle embodies all the criteria for the "holy German art" that Wagner advocated: It is powerful, it is beautiful, it celebrates the greatness of Germany, it is unbesmirched by Italian and French influence, and yet it is progressive. The greatness of the *Ring* rests not on its music alone, but on the totality of Wagner's idea: This is *Gesamtkunstwerk* with a vengeance. Not only every note but also every word, every piece of scenery, every costume, every stage direction, every lighting effect—indeed, everything—was conceived and directed by the composer.

Such a masterwork could not, of course, be tossed off in a matter of a few years. A twenty-eight-year undertaking, the *Ring* represents its author's transformation from a little-known maverick to the most revered composer in Europe. Wagner began the *Ring* in 1848, with a libretto entitled *Siegfried's Tod* (The Death of Siegfried), which told the story that now appears in the final opera of the cycle, *Götterdämmerung*. Before long, Wagner wanted to further chronicle Siegfried's heroic past, and accordingly composed an opera which is now embedded within *Siegfried*. Following the same compulsion to preface, he then wrote the libretto for *Die Walküre* and, finally, the prelude to the whole saga, *Das Rheingold*. In 1853, after the "poems," as Wagner called them, were completed, he embarked upon the scores, but in 1857 he lay down the *Ring* and dashed off two little trifles entitled *Tristan und Isolde* and *Die Meistersinger von Nürnberg*. Thus, the first performance of a *Ring* opera did not take place until 1869, when King Ludwig II of Bavaria demanded proof that the streams of cash he had been sending the composer for many years had, as promised, been funding a masterpiece. So Wagner staged *Das Rheingold* and *Die Walküre* at Munich's Hofoper.

He had to do it, but he didn't have to like it. There was no opera house in existence that met Wagner's standards for his music-dramas. Most couldn't come close to producing such technical effects as the "steam curtains" that Wagner envisioned cloaking his scene changes, not to mention the swimming Rhinemaidens, Brünnhilde's circle of fire, and the destruction of Valhalla. Then there was the lamentable social atmosphere of most opera houses; Wagner despised the dilettantes who came to see and be seen and, even worse, chattered during the music. The theaters themselves were vulgar, in his view, decked and draped with ornament and garish color, pandering to bourgeois taste. Wagner's solution, like all of his thinking, was visionary, colossal, and nearly impossible: He would build an opera house to his own specifications where his music would be played exactly as he directed. Hence, Bayreuth. A small, rural town in Bavaria, Bayreuth became the center of the musical world in 1876, when, after years of preparation, the Bayreuth Festspielhaus opened with a performance of the entire *Ring* cycle, fully directed and ordained, in every detail, by Wagner himself. No artistic event has ever provoked the passion of the *Ring*'s inaugural production. Wagner himself was plunged into despair: "I know now that I and my work have no place in these times of ours," he told his wife. Others greeted the premiere as the cultural event of the century. Pyotr Tchaikovsky called it "one of the most significant events in the history of art." And, of course, King Ludwig, who sat in a specially constructed box, was ecstatic. He wrote to Wagner, "You are a god-man, the true artist by God's grace who brought the sacred fire from heaven to earth to cleanse, sanctify, and redeem it!"

The Bayreuth Festival became an annual event, staging not just the *Ring* but, eventually, all of Wagner's operas in the course of a month-long season each year. As a temple to Wagnerism, the Festspielhaus boasts some unusual features. It is the largest freestanding wooden structure ever erected, and its dimensions yield a long reverberation time that is ideal for the kind of "heavy sound" that abounds in Wagner's music. The orchestra is nearly hidden underneath the stage. The music wells up out of a hooded opening, and the musicians are ranged below in a descending pit. This setup puts considerable stress on the conductor. As the only person who can see what is happening on the stage and hear all the instruments, he or she is responsible for unifying music and performance, which is why a season at Bayreuth is seen as the ultimate test of a conductor's skill and endurance. As conductor Georg Solti said of his tenure at Bayreuth, "If anybody had told me when I was at music school that I would one day be in a pit where I couldn't hear anything or see all the players, I would have become a doctor."

# DAS RHEINGOLD

~ ◦◦ ~

The wondrous prelude—it is hardly an overture— to *Das Rheingold* is nothing more, or less, than an aural wave pattern that swells and rises in an undulating 6/8 rhythm to encompass and, figuratively, give birth to all of the sounds that will follow.

## SCENE ONE

In the clear, green waters of the Rhine, three Rhinemaidens cavort merrily. Woglinde and Wellgunde give themselves up to the joy of the moment, while the wiser Flosshilde reminds the others that they are shirking their responsibilities. But even Flosshilde cannot resist the temptation to mock the repulsive dwarf Alberich, who clambers along the riverbank, vainly trying to lure the nymphs to his side. Alberich grows more infuriated each time he is thwarted, but all four are suddenly silenced by a dazzling golden light, which penetrates the water in rays of liquid fire. The innocent Rhinemaidens inform Alberich that the magical light comes from the beams of the rising sun mingling with their glorious golden hoard, the Rhinegold. They confide that their father has ordered them to guard the gold, but that they are doing a very bad job of it. It's true, they say, that a ring fashioned from the gold would confer infinite power on its owner, but they are certain that no one would forge such a ring, for the only way to do so is to forswear love forever.

The lighthearted Rhinemaidens have reckoned without Alberich, though, for their taunts have soured him on love and, scampering wildly toward the source of the light, he renounces the emotion. As he closes his greedy hands over the treasure, Woglinde, Wellgunde, and Flosshilde begin to wail and cry for help. But the dwarf easily makes his getaway with the precious gold.

# SCENE TWO

The glistening green water has been replaced by a swirling white mist, which parts to reveal a mountain meadow, carpeted in soft grass and bedecked with flowers. In the distance, a glittering castle can be seen; this is Valhalla, the fortress of the gods.

Fast asleep on the grass are Wotan, the ruler of the gods, and Fricka, his wife. Power and immortality notwithstanding, the lives of the gods are not free of domestic carping, which commences when Wotan awakes to find Fricka enraged that he has promised the giants Fafner and Fasolt the possession of Fricka's sister, Freia, the goddess of love, in return for the construction of Valhalla. Wotan attempts a counterattack—didn't Fricka beg him to build a palace? Bitterly, she replies that she only wanted a castle to keep him from philandering. Dodging this blow, Wotan assures her that he has never intended to give Freia up to the giants. Then, returns his wife, you'd better protect her, for here she comes. Freia enters the scene at a run, fleeing from Fafner and Fasolt.

The thumps of monstrous footsteps are now heard as the two heavy-headed giants come to claim their prize. With an air of nonchalance, Wotan asks them their fee for the construction of Valhalla, but the giants quickly remind him that the fee was already pledged: Freia. "Has this contract set you out of your minds?" says Wotan disingenuously. "I cannot sell Freia."

Fasolt, who is infatuated with the goddess, accuses Wotan of deceit. "What you are, you are only by contracts," he warns, but Wotan persists in dismissing his promise. Fafner, the more practical of the brothers, suggests that they simply carry her off.

Desperately, Wotan stalls the giants and succeeds long enough for Loge, the fire god, to arrive. Loge, it seems, has promised to find Wotan a way out of his pact. And he has tried, first inspecting Valhalla for flaws that would nullify the agreement, then searching across the world for a goddess substitute. But no one was willing to give up his love. In fact, continues the wily Loge, in all the world, there is only one who has forsworn love: Alberich, one of the Nibelung dwarfs, who stole the Rhinegold from the Rhinemaidens in order to make a ring that will allow him to rule the world. And by the way, he adds to Wotan, the Rhinemaidens want you to help them get it back.

Wotan reminds Loge that he has enough problems, but meanwhile, Fasolt has been pondering Loge's words. He has always hated the Nibelungs, he announces, and Fafner adds that they have much to fear from Nibelung power. Determined to crush Alberich's bid for supremacy, Wotan decides that he must obtain the ring himself. Loge advises him to steal it, for after all, Alberich is not its rightful owner. Casting aside the Rhinemaidens' claims, Wotan resolves to filch all of the Rhinegold as well as the ring. This way, the giants shall have a payment in gold instead of goddess, and he shall have the omnipotent ring. Fafner and Fasolt agree,

conditionally. They will keep Freia until sundown and if Wotan does not return with the gold by then, she will be theirs forever. As Freia cries out, the giants march off with the goddess over their shoulders, and Wotan plunges into the bowels of the earth to visit the Nibelungs.

# SCENE THREE

All is not well in the steaming caverns of the Nibelungs. With the aid of his ring-induced power, Alberich has forced his fellow dwarfs to toil incessantly for his profit. Day and night, they mine the earth for precious metals and forge them in the burning heat. Alberich also torments his brother, Mime, whom he has ordered to manufacture a magical golden helmet he calls the Tarnhelm, which cloaks its wearer in invisibility, or indeed, in any guise he desires. Grabbing the helmet from Mime, Alberich makes use of his new imperceptibility to pinch and poke his brother, all the while congratulating himself on his ascendancy.

When Wotan and Loge arrive, they find Mime collapsed on the rocks. But Loge and Mime are old acquaintances, and the beleaguered dwarf eagerly enumerates his tribulations, winding up with a description of the powers of the Tarnhelm. Now comes Alberich himself, in visible and vicious form, driving a band of cowering Nibelungs before him. Wotan immediately sets about flattering Alberich with extravagant praise for his newfound wealth. Exhilarated to find that even the immortals envy him, Alberich brags about his omnipotence and even asserts that he will soon rule over the gods themselves.

Observing that Wotan is on the verge of a fury that will blow his cover, Loge cleverly begins to build a trap. Professing disbelief in Alberich's claims for the Tarnhelm, Loge begs him to demonstrate its uses. Eager to show off, Alberich turns himself into a monumental dragon. Wotan and Loge applaud his dexterity but challenge him to transform himself into something small—a toad, for instance. That would certainly be too hard for him, they say.

His pride piqued, Alberich indignantly changes into a toad—and Wotan calmly captures him underneath his foot. Loge reaches down and retrieves the Tarnhelm from the tiny beast, which causes Alberich to reassume his dwarfish form, still underneath Wotan's heel. Cursing, he is carried in chains up to the immortals' mountaintop.

# SCENE FOUR

Gleefully, Wotan and Loge mock Alberich's dreams of grandeur while their prisoner spits invective and threats. Tiring of his insolence, Wotan informs Alberich that he may buy his freedom with his entire hoard of gold. Comforting himself with the thought of his all-powerful ring, Alberich summons the Nibelungs to bring his treasure to the mountaintop. Roundly damning them all, he delivers the gold to Wotan and asks Loge to return him the Tarnhelm.

Loge coolly announces that the Tarnhelm is part of the ransom, and though Alberich shakes with fury, he reflects that with the ring's help, he can always make another magic helmet. But now Wotan approaches and demands the ring.

Alberich rails and raves, "Take heed, haughty god! If I sinned, I sinned only against myself: But you, immortal one, sin against all that was, is, and shall be if you recklessly seize my ring!"

Wotan, furious at this impertinence, wrenches the ring from the dwarf's finger. "Now I possess what will make me the mightiest of mighty lords!" he exults.

Loge tells the newly freed Alberich to make himself scarce, but before he goes, the despairing dwarf snarls to the gods, "Am I free now? Truly free? Then I give you my freedom's first greeting! Since by curse it came to me, accursed be this ring! . . . Whoever possesses it will be consumed by care, and whoever has it not be gnawed with envy . . . Its owner shall guard it profitlessly, for through it he shall meet his executioner. Forfeited to death, faint with fear shall he be fettered; the length of his life he shall long to die, the ring's master to the ring a slave, until again I hold in my hand what was stolen! . . . My curse you cannot escape." Concluding his dire speech, Alberich limps toward the Nibelung cave.

Wotan, unmoved by this recital, turns his attention to Fasolt and Fafner, who have returned with Freia. Freia's two brothers and Fricka also have arrived to learn the outcome of Wotan's journey. He has retrieved the gold, he announces, but Fasolt is filled with regret. The only way he can bear to part with the goddess is if her form is completely obscured by the golden hoard. With distaste, the fire god and Freia's brothers set about their work, until she is concealed behind a wall of treasure.

But Fafner objects. He can still see strands of the goddess's golden hair above the gleaming pile. He demands that Wotan cover them with the Tarnhelm, and, reflecting, like Alberich, that as long as he has the ring he is secure, Wotan complies.

Now Fasolt intervenes. He can still see one of Freia's lovely eyes through a crack in the wall of gold. This crack must be stopped up with—Wotan's ring!

Wotan refuses. Despite the entreaties of all the other gods, he is intransigent: He will not surrender the ring.

Suddenly the sky grows dark and an eerie bluish light glows from a mountain cleft. A beautiful woman in a robe of leaves emerges with a warning: "Yield, Wotan, yield! Escape from the ring's curse. To dark destruction its possession dooms you!"

Even the ruler of the gods is shaken by this apparition. He asks her identity. "I know whatever was, whatever is, whatever shall be: The eternal world's first ancestress, Erda, warns you. My womb bore three daughters, conceived before the start of time; what I see, the Norns nightly tell you. But direst danger today brings me to you. Hear me! All that is shall come to an end. I charge you, shun the ring!"

Wotan cannot take such words lightly and after a long moment, he calls to Freia to join the gods and tosses the ring upon the golden hoard.

While the siblings rejoice in their reunion, the businesslike Fafner begins to load the treasure into a huge sack. His brother ceases his mournful contemplation of Freia in time to notice Fafner's efficient packing, and at once, the two giants begin to argue over the division of the spoils. Their squabble quickly escalates and, with hardly a word of warning, Fafner kills his brother. Tearing the ring from Fasolt's finger, Fafner continues his packing.

Shaken by the scene he has witnessed, Wotan declares that he must return to the world to find Erda and learn more from her about the fatal ring. Fricka urges him to come home, but he responds gloomily, "With unclean wages I have paid for that building!"

Untroubled by Wotan's dread, the other gods collect clouds into a storm with a curving rainbow. All gather to traverse this bridge to their new fortress, but as the immortals enter their new home, from far below them come the laments of the Rhinemaidens, mourning their lost gold. ⁓ᴽ᷎

# DIE WALKÜRE

~⁂~

Decades have passed since the gods entered Valhalla. Wotan, as promised, has sought out Erda for more information about the power of the ring, but their conversation clearly took other turns, for he has produced nine equestrian daughters by her. These are the Valkyries, for whom the opera is named, goddesses who fly through the clouds on their horses to earthly battlegrounds, where they rescue fallen heroes and import them to Valhalla for guard duty. The youngest Valkyrie is Brünnhilde, Wotan's favorite.

Fricka's grievances begin to seem justifiable when we learn that Wotan has also fathered a race of mortals, the Wälsungs. His offspring from this episode are twins, Siegmund and Sieglinde, who know their father as a mortal named both Wälse and Wolfe. These human children have been less fortunate than their divine half-sisters; indeed, they have been separated forcibly from one another. Left at home alone one day, Sieglinde was abducted by and forced to marry the brutish Hunding. Soon afterward, Siegmund lost sight of his father in the midst of a battle and now wanders through the forest, attacked by enemies.

## ACT ONE

As a storm rages, Siegmund enters a hut that has been fashioned around and within the trunk of a giant ash tree. Exhausted, he collapses before the fire, where his dazed repose is soon interrupted by a beautiful young woman. This is Sieglinde, and while her brother does not recognize her, he feels an instant attraction. Their increasing interest in each other is abruptly arrested by Hunding, who glowers at his unexpected guest, though ancient laws of hospitality oblige him to provide the stranger with a meal. Sieglinde hastily sets food upon the table and as the two men sit down to eat, Hunding notices the resemblance between his wife and his guest. He demands to know the stranger's name and story.

Siegmund replies that he is the son of Wolfe and tells of the day he and his father returned from the hunt to find their home burnt to ashes, his mother murdered, and his sister gone. Shortly afterward, his father disappeared as they fought a gang of villains, and in wandering the forest in search of him, Siegmund has collected nothing but enemies. Even this day, he defended a girl from a forcible marriage, only to have her betray him to her kinsmen. Alone, Siegmund had fought until his sword and shield were cut from him and he retreated, wandering until he arrived at Hunding's hut.

Hunding realizes that his guest is the very man he had been pursuing that day. Avowing his hatred for the Wälsungs, Hunding warns Siegmund that though he may sleep on his hearth tonight, Hunding will avenge his slain kinsmen in the morning. For Siegmund, with neither sword nor shield, this is tantamount to certain death. Silently, Sieglinde attempts to direct the stranger's eyes to a spot above the hearth, but Hunding notices her glance and roughly orders his wife to retire. With a final threat to his guest, Hunding follows her.

Alone before the fire, Siegmund extols Sieglinde's beauty and bemoans his swordless state. As if in answer to his lament, the dying fire flares suddenly, illuminating the hilt of a sword driven into the ash tree, and Sieglinde tiptoes in. She has given Hunding a sleeping potion, and she begs the stranger to save himself. Pointing to the sword's handle, she tells him of her dark wedding day. As the bandits who had stolen her caroused with her new husband, a travel-worn elder had entered the hut. His hat covered one eye, but the bitterness of the other made the roomful of men fall silent with fear. The stranger had approached the hearth and plunged his sword into the tree trunk, saying that the weapon would belong to the man who could pull it out. The guests had vied with one another, but none succeeded in budging the sword. Sieglinde has long sighed for a champion who would retrieve the sword and rescue her from dishonor.

Confessing their growing attraction, the pair embraces, and the door of the hut flies open to reveal the moon-bathed spring night. Ecstatically, the two trace their resemblance to each other and realize that they are the children of the sword bearer, Wolfe the Wälsung. This discovery does nothing to check their mounting passion and Siegmund, transformed, strides to the hearth to draw out the sword. "*Notung,* Needful, I name you, sword! Show your sharpness, precious blade," he declares. "You see Siegmund the Wälsung, wife! As wedding gift he brings this sword, so he weds the fairest of women. Now follow me far from here."

Together the lovers make their escape into the silver night.

# ACT TWO

Against the background of a storm-whipped sky, Wotan stands upon a mountain peak with his spear in hand. Hunding is in hot pursuit of Siegmund and Sieglinde, and Wotan directs his favorite, Brünnhilde, to ensure Siegmund's victory in the coming combat. With a wild battle cry, Brünnhilde leaps from crag to crag to greet the warriors, but her eyes falls upon Fricka, Wotan's wife. Brünnhilde wisely departs as Fricka descends on her husband in a rage. As the guardian of wedlock (and, incidentally, the opponent of her husband's illicit progeny), she is infuriated by Wotan's protection of the adulterous Siegmund and Sieglinde, and she has promised Hunding revenge. Fricka righteously points out that he is making a laughingstock of sacred marriage bonds; does he wish to flout his own rules to protect his vulgar human children? "Go on, do it; trample on the wife you have cheated."

Beleaguered Wotan tries to argue that Siegmund must win the fight because only a hero free from divine protection can retrieve the ring from Fafner's grasp (Wotan himself cannot challenge Fafner, remember, because he has entered into a contract with the giant). Fricka instantly points out that Siegmund's success is guaranteed only by the intervention of Brünnhilde and the magical sword Notung. Thus, she concludes, Siegmund's triumph would be nothing more than Wotan's creation.

Wotan is vanquished. Bitterly, he agrees to sacrifice Siegmund. As Fricka departs in triumph, Brünnhilde comes whooping back to her father, eager to join in battle. Wotan tells her that he has been caught in his own trap and recounts the history of the ring, concluding with Erda's warning to him that if Alberich or his Nibelungs once again attained the ring, the doom of the gods would be imminent. Desperate to recapture the ring from Fafner, Wotan had fathered the mortal Wälsungs to seize the golden treasure. "Only one person can do what I may not: a hero whom I have never stooped to help. Only a stranger to the gods, free from immortals' favors, unwitting and unprompted, with his own weapons, can do the deed that I must avoid, and that I

can never suggest—even though it is my only wish." Wotan then directs Brünnhilde to kill Siegmund and procure victory for Hunding.

Frantically, Brünnhilde protests. She knows her father loves Siegmund, and so does she—she cannot kill him. Exhorting her not to provoke his anger, Wotan leaves her with a fearful decision.

All too soon, Siegmund and Sieglinde appear on the mountain crag. Exhausted, Sieglinde begs her husband to leave her to her fate. She blames her shameful marriage for their misfortunes, but Siegmund reassures her that he will avenge her. Though filled with dread, Sieglinde allows her lover to soothe her and soon falls into a fitful sleep.

Now Brünnhilde appears before Siegmund. He will die, she says, and be transported to Valhalla, which she describes in all its glory. Siegmund does not shrink from death, but asks if Sieglinde might accompany him. No, Brünnhilde replies; Sieglinde must remain on earth to bear his child. But Siegmund defiantly declares that he would rather go to the underworld with his love than to the home of the gods without her and raises his sword to kill Sieglinde that they might be joined in death. Astonished by the power of mortal love, Brünnhilde is moved to a dangerous act of rebellion. "Stop, Wälsung! Sieglinde shall live and Siegmund live with her. It is decided: I'll change the outcome of the fight." Flying away, she bids him prepare for battle.

Siegmund kisses the sleeping Sieglinde and leaves to join Hunding in fight. As the sky explodes with thunder and lightning, the two warriors meet atop the mountain crag. Brünnhilde hovers near Seigmund, urging him on, but suddenly a red light glows: Wotan has arrived. As Siegmund leaps forward to strike a mortal blow, Wotan thrusts his spear between the two men and Notung is shattered on it. Hunding takes the opportunity to plunge his sword into his foe and Siegmund drops lifelessly to the ground. Realizing that she is about to face the consequences of her defiance, Brünnhilde takes flight, stopping only to rescue Sieglinde. As the storm rages, Wotan turns contemptuously to Hunding and kills him before racing off in pursuit of his disobedient daughter.

# ACT THREE

As Brünnhilde races through the sky seeking shelter for Sieglinde, her Valkyrie sisters are assembling, each bearing a dead hero for Valhalla's guard. First four, then eight dash across the mountaintops, calling to one another with their powerful cry (The Ride of the Valkyries). At last, Brünnhilde joins them, bearing not a warrior but Sieglinde, and begs her sisters to help her conceal the woman from Wotan's wrath. Aghast that she has defied their Battlefather, the Valkyries decline to assist her, but they hastily tell Sieglinde to go east. She will find Fafner, now a dragon, dwelling there, guarding the ring, and Wotan will not dare venture near his cave. Brünnhilde gives Sieglinde the pieces of Siegmund's sword along with the prophecy that her son will someday reassemble them. Revived by this new mission, Sieglinde hurries away.

Now a furious Wotan arrives on the scene. At first, the Valkyrie sisters attempt to hide Brünnhilde, but Wotan's rage quickly puts a stop to any idea of reconciliation. Bravely, Brünnhilde steps from her hiding place to bow before her father. Wrathful Wotan banishes her from the gods; she will no longer be a Valkyrie but a mere mortal woman. She will be left in enchanted sleep on the mountaintop, to be carried off by the first man who finds her, whom she will be condemned to serve for the remainder of her pitifully short life.

The eight other Valkyries beg their father to reconsider, but he is adamant—Brünnhilde must be cast out. The sisters, weeping, are ordered away, leaving Brünnhilde and Wotan alone. Sadly, he tells her that they must be parted forever, and sadly, she accepts her fate.

But knowing that Sieglinde will beget a heroic son, Brünnhilde begs one final favor from her father. She asks him to set a ring of fire around her resting place so that only a fearless, unrestrained hero might be the one to find her. Agreeing, Wotan embraces her and calls upon Loge to encircle his most beloved child. As fire springs up around Brünnhilde's form, Wotan utters one final incantation: "Whosoever fears the tip of my spear shall never pass through this fire!"

# SIEGFRIED

~⦿~

Some years have elapsed since the events of *Die Walküre*. Sieglinde, directed to the land of the Nibelungs by the Valkyries, found her way to the cave of Mime (Alberich's oppressed brother dwarf from *Das Rheingold*), where she died giving birth to Siegfried. With her last breath, she consigned the baby to Mime's care, along with the fragments of Siegmund's sword, Notung. As *Siegfried* begins, the baby has grown into a healthy, heedless young man who likes nothing more than sporting around the forest with the birds and animals and nothing less than his foster father, Mime.

## ACT ONE

In keeping with the traditional occupation of the Nibelungs, Mime is at his anvil, forging—and complaining bitterly that his labors are fruitless. All the swords he makes for Siegfried are instantly destroyed by the headstrong boy. As Mime whines on, he reveals his true motive in raising the child, which is to lure him into killing Fafner, who harbors the magical ring. Once a giant, Fafner has used the Tarnhelm to transform himself into a dragon in order to protect his loot. But rather than enjoy his riches, the dragon has spent the last decades fast asleep on his hoard. Mime senses that Siegfried, armed with Notung, is the one person who might kill the beast. However, the sword has resisted all the dwarf's efforts to repair it.

In the midst of Mime's sour reflections, Siegfried enters. Carelessly, the young man makes fun of his foster father, while Mime bemoans Siegfried's lack of gratitude for all the delicious dinners, the soft bed, the careful instruction—

"What you've most sought to teach me I never succeeded in learning," Siegfried interrupts: "how to tolerate you." Ignoring Mime's wounded sniveling, Siegfried says that what he would really like to know is who his mother is. Mime tries to dissemble, but when Siegfried threatens him, he reveals how he found a woman in the throes of childbirth and helped her as best he could. Dying, she named her son Siegfried and gave him to the dwarf. Siegfried demands to know his mother's name and the reluctant dwarf finally reveals it, saying he never knew who Siegfried's father was. Full of suspicion, Siegfried accuses Mime of making the story up, so as proof Mime shows him the pieces of the sword that Sieglinde left with him.

Joyously, Siegfried takes up the fragments and commands Mime to make out of them a sword. Armed with this weapon, he knows that he will be liberated from the crabbed Nibelung. Invigorated, Siegfried dashes out, leaving the dwarf looking after him in consternation. How, reflects Mime, will I ever get him to Fafner's cave now?

As if in answer to his question, an old gentleman in a long blue coat enters. Though it should be easy to recognize Wotan behind the disguise, Mime fails to do so and tells him to take himself off. The Wanderer suggests instead that Mime ask him three questions; if he fails to answer them correctly, his host may have his head. Irritably, Mime poses three questions to his guest, all of which, of course, the Wanderer answers correctly. Then the stranger suggests that the dwarf answer three queries himself.

"Which is the race that Wotan oppressed and yet whose life is dearest to him?" the Wanderer asks.

Mime answers correctly that Wotan loved the Wälsungs, Sieglinde and Siegmund, though he punished them. It appears that he knows a great deal more about Siegfried's family history than he had claimed to the boy.

"What sword must Siegfried now brandish to kill Fafner?" asks the Wanderer.

"Notung," answers Mime promptly.

The third question is more difficult. "Who will weld the splinters of Notung back into a sword?" Affrighted, Mime admits defeat, but the Wanderer kindly answers the question for him. "Only one who has never felt fear shall forge Notung anew."

*The gap between his creative vision and its realization on the stage at the first Bayreuth Festival left Wagner in a profound depression. In addition to contemplating emigration to America, he made long lists of the elements that had failed to meet his expectations, among them, the Valkyrean mountaintop in* Die Walküre. *"I'll change that someday," he told his wife, Cosima, gloomily, "when I produce* Walküre *in heaven, at the right hand of God, and the old gent and I are watching it together." He found solace only in working on his long-planned opera,* Parsifal, *but even the joy of creation was tarnished by the specter of production. "Oh, I shudder at the thought, especially of the costumes—and the grease paint! And when I think how these characters like Kundry are to be fitted out, my mind immediately goes back to those ghastly artists' balls; after creating the invisible orchestra, I would now like to invent the invisible theater," he said, adding, "and perhaps the inaudible orchestra."*

Left alone, Mime is overcome with terror. Soon he has so thoroughly frightened himself that he is hiding behind the anvil when Siegfried comes bounding back to the cave to demand his new sword.

Mime confesses that he has been unable to manufacture the sword, as "only one without fear" might do so. This mention of fear intrigues Siegfried, and he asks to be acquainted with this concept. Chastising himself for failing to teach the boy fear, Mime attempts to instruct him in the art of being scared. But even his description of the forest's nighttime gloom, a wild approaching roar, and flashing flames fail to evoke any terror in Siegfried. It all sounds perfectly delightful to him. "This shivering and shuddering, burning and swooning, hammering and beating, I'd like to feel this alarm!" he exclaims.

Seizing an opportunity, Mime offers to guide him into the presence of Fafner so that he might learn fear. Siegfried eagerly acquiesces, "Quickly, then," he orders the dwarf. "Make the sword." Mime repeats that he cannot and Siegfried contemptuously declares that he will do it himself. Mime is full of professional advice, all of which Siegfried ignores. With great zest, he hammers at the metal, calling out the weapon's name, "Notung! Notung! Trusty sword!" As the sparks fly, Notung regains its form.

Mime, watching from the sidelines, spins out a new scheme: After Siegfried slays Fafner, he will offer the young warrior a refreshing drink. This, a sleeping potion in disguise, will overcome the boy, permitting Mime to kill him with the sword and steal the ring and treasure for himself. Siegfried, oblivious of Mime's growing excitement, exults over his completed weapon.

# ACT TWO

Alberich, as bad-tempered and repugnant as ever, is crouched near Fafner's cave, waiting for his opportunity to steal back the ring. His solitude is soon shattered by the arrival of Wotan. Neither is particularly pleased

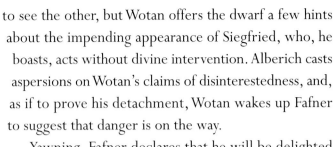

to see the other, but Wotan offers the dwarf a few hints about the impending appearance of Siegfried, who, he boasts, acts without divine intervention. Alberich casts aspersions on Wotan's claims of disinterestedness, and, as if to prove his detachment, Wotan wakes up Fafner to suggest that danger is on the way.

Yawning, Fafner declares that he will be delighted to kill Siegfried when the time comes—then rolls over and goes back to sleep. Unfazed, Wotan departs.

Soon enough, Siegfried and Mime come traipsing through the forest, Mime solicitously describing the perils of the dragon's tail, the dragon's mouth, the dragon's spittle—but Siegfried merely wants to know the location of his heart, so that he may pierce it with Notung. With unaffectionate adieus, Siegfried sends his foster father off and sits down to await Fafner's daily excursion to the watering hole. While he waits he tries vainly to converse with the birds singing around him but sadly concludes that he can't understand them. However, his attempts wake the dragon, who lumbers out of his cave with bloodcurdling groans. Unalarmed, Siegfried demands to be taught fear and threatens to cut Fafner into shreds should he fail to do so.

Thus challenged, the dragon roars, "I wanted a drink; now I've also found food!"

Still fearless, Siegfried makes a great leap and thrusts his sword into Fafner's heart, killing the massive beast. With his last breath, the dragon eulogizes his race and warns Siegfried about the curse of the ring.

Once the beast is dead, Siegfried tastes a bit of the dragon's blood. Suddenly, the song of the birds becomes comprehensible. "Hey! The Nibelung's treasure now belongs to Siegfried," a bird announces. "If he wants to take the Tarnhelm, it will help him perform wondrous deeds, but if he could get the ring, it would make him ruler of the world!"

Thanking the bird for her useful counsel, Siegfried marches jauntily into Fafner's lair. No sooner has he gone than Mime and Alberich emerge from their respective hiding places, ready to get their hands on the loot. Each is outraged at the temerity of the other and, certain that Siegfried will be satisfied with baubles, they argue vociferously about who deserves the Tarnhelm and who the ring. Imagine their fury when Siegfried appears at the mouth of the cave with the Tarnhelm at his belt and the ring on his finger.

The forest bird speaks again to Siegfried, warning of Mime's plot against him and performing a magical trick that allows the young hero to hear Mime's true thoughts. The dwarf opens his mouth to fawn and wheedle, but what emerges is a magnificent jumble of compliments and murderous truth. "You are tired from your great efforts; your body must be burning. I have brewed for you this restoring broth; drink it now, and I will win your sword, the helmet, and the treasure."

"I'd gladly take a good drink," says Siegfried, leading him on. "How has this been made?"

"Hey! Just drink it. In murk and mist your senses soon will sink unwaking. And with the sword that you made so sharp, I'll hack off the boy's head: then I'll have peace and the ring too! Now, my Wälsung! Drink and choke yourself to death."

With one final look of loathing, Siegfried lifts Notung and delivers a violent blow to the dwarf, who falls dead. Alberich's squealing laugh resounds through the forest.

After the flush of triumph has ebbed, Siegfried turns again to the forest bird. But now he asks the bird to help him find a companion. The bird tells him of a wonderful woman who lies asleep on a rocky height, surrounded by a wall of fire. "He who can break through the blaze and wake the bride—Brünnhilde will be his!" exults the bird.

Siegfried is captivated by the idea, and when he learns that Brünnhilde is accessible only to one who has never felt fear, he is fired by a desire to find her.

## ACT THREE

Amid a great, swirling storm, Wotan looms at the base of a forbidding mountain. Raising his voice above the tempest, he calls upon Erda, the earth goddess, to wake from her brooding sleep.

In a cloud of bluish light, Erda appears, protesting this rude awakening. Wotan seeks her knowledge, but she refuses. Erda advises him to seek enlightenment from his daughter, the Valkyrie Brünnhilde, and Wotan is forced to reveal that she has been stripped of her immortality. Disgusted with such capricious rulership, Erda returns to her eternal meditation, while Wotan, alone aware of Siegfried's destiny, resigns himself to the triumph of the human race and the twilight of the gods.

*Karl Marx, who was traveling through Germany on a holiday during the 1876 premiere of the* Ring, *was quite put out to find every hotel bed in Bavaria occupied by ardent Wagnerians. After passing a cold night on a railway bench, Marx became a bitter opponent of the master, particularly as he found himself pestered everywhere he went with the question, "What do you think of Wagner?" He took to responding sourly that the extended Wagner family was every bit as queer as the Nibelungs and merited its own opera.*

The clouds lift and the sky grows lighter as Siegfried, led by the bird, appears on the scene. The bird flutters away, leaving the youth with an old man whom he does not recognize as his grandfather. With sorrow and affection, Wotan begins to question the young man, but Siegfried is too impatient to tolerate much conversation and eagerly demands to be shown the way to the sleeping Brünnhilde. Wotan suggests that he show more respect for his elders, an idea that Siegfried dismisses instantly: "All my life an old man has stood in my way. If you persist in obstructing me, watch out!" Still, Wotan insists on talking to the boy about obscure events and concludes by holding out his spear to bar him from the path to Brünnhilde.

This is the last straw for the impetuous Siegfried. He lifts Notung and shatters Wotan's spear to splinters. In that instant, the rule of the gods is destroyed, but Siegfried knows nothing of this and dashes forward to seek his companion.

With the dawn breaking forth in rosy clouds, Siegfried attains the mountaintop and stands dazzled by what he sees. There, encircled by the fire begun by Wotan, sleeps Brünnhilde, clothed in her glistening armor. Crossing through the flames, Siegfried approaches the slumbering figure. Carefully, he lifts her helmet, and masses of golden hair tumble out, but, never having seen a woman, Siegfried believes her to be a man. Anxious for his comfort, Siegfried removes the figure's constraining breastplate, and leaps back, stunned by the new emotions that course through him. Imagining that he is finally experiencing fear, he calls upon his mother to guide him in this new world of love, but he soon gathers enough courage to kiss the sleeping maiden ardently.

Waking from her long night, Brünnhilde rapturously greets the sun, the glorious day, the gods, the world, and the hero who rescued her from eternal slumber. When she learns that her savior is none other than Siegfried, she rejoices: "O Siegfried, blessed hero! Waker of life! If you but knew how I have always loved you!" Suddenly, sublimely, supremely in love, Siegfried and Brünnhilde delight in one another until a dark realization shadows Brünnhilde's joy: Love is an emotion belonging to mortals, and she mourns her lost divinity. She recognizes that she is now a human woman, vulnerable to male desire and her own. But Siegfried's fervor inspires her and, giving herself up to passion, she accepts her fate: "Laughing, I must love you, laughing, I will bear my blindness! Farewell, Valhalla's glittering world! May your end be blissful, immortal race! You Norns, snap your rope of symbols! Dusk of the gods, let your darkness descend! Siegfried's star now shines upon me: He is mine forever, my inheritance, my one and all; radiant love, laughing death!" ∿

# GÖTTERDÄMMERUNG
## — The Twilight of the Gods —

## PROLOGUE

Far below Brünnhilde's summit, the three Norns, Erda's daughters, crouch in a dark cavern weaving the golden rope of fate. As they twist the strands, they recount the mournful tale of Wotan's rise and fall: how he broke a branch from the world ash tree to fashion his spear, how the tree then faded and died. Now, says the second Norn, Wotan's spear has been pulverized by the brash young hero, bringing his power to an end. Wotan has sent the Valkyries' heroes down to gather the withered boughs of the world ash, and these he has heaped up around Valhalla. There the gods sit, continues the third Norn, awaiting their annihilation at the hands of Loge, the fire god.

As the three sisters tell the tale of Alberich's theft of the Rheingold and its ensuing curse, their golden rope suddenly snaps. Terrified, the Norns rush to the underworld to rejoin their mother. As they flee, day breaks upon the great mountain and welling music lifts the scene to Brünnhilde's cave, whence the onetime Valkyrie is emerging with her hero, Siegfried. Of course, a hero must perform heroic deeds, so Siegfried is preparing to depart, but before he leaves, he gives the ring to Brünnhilde as a pledge of his love and she, in turn, gives him her horse, Grane. With many rapturous protestations of love, they part, and Siegfried rides toward the Rhine and the mortal world.

## ACT ONE

At about the time that Sieglinde gave birth to Siegfried, the loathsome Alberich sired a son by mortal woman, in order to better contend with the Wälsungs for the ring. Named Hagen, this child has grown into a scheming, evil-hearted villain. By some stratagem, Hagen's mother succeeded in raising him alongside of her legitimate children, Gunther and Gutrune. Now Gunther has succeeded his father as the chieftain of his tribe, the

Gibichungs, and the three siblings live together. Though Gutrune is pretty and Gunther is a solid, even-tempered fellow, it's obvious that Hagen is far their superior in cunning and intelligence, if not in noble blood.

Now the three Gibichungs are sitting in the great hall. Gunther is eager to extend his renown, but is not quite sure how. Hagen announces that both Gunther and Gutrune must marry. This, Gunther concedes, is a splendid idea, but whom shall he marry? Craftily, Hagen describes the world's finest woman, who dwells in the rocky heights, surrounded by a fire that can only be penetrated by a hero.

Gunther wonders if he is the man for the job, and Hagen assures him that he is not. No, only Siegfried, the slayer of Fafner, can undertake such a feat. Hagen gives a digest of Siegfried's heroic deeds, including his capture of the omnipotent ring. Though Gutrune is intrigued, Gunther is discouraged. "Why," he demands of Hagen, "do you arouse my desire for what I cannot obtain?"

Hagen unveils his plot. Siegfried will bring Brünnhilde to Gunther in order to win Gunther's permission for Gutrune's hand!

Now it is Gutrune's turn to be discouraged. Why would Siegfried, the world's mightiest hero, desire to marry her?

The wily Hagen reminds her of the magic love potion left them by their mother. When Siegfried drinks it, he will forget every woman but her. Thus, the plan is laid, and the rulers of the Gibichungs will extend their domain. As Gutrune and Gunther rejoice in their half-brother's cleverness, a horn is heard from the Rhine, announcing the arrival of Siegfried himself.

Siegfried, bounding into the great hall, is greeted warmly. After Gutrune retires in pretty confusion, Hagen steers the conversation to the subject of the dragon's treasure. Siegfried naively admits that he took from the cave only a helmet—the Tarnhelm—and a golden ring that now adorns the finger of a "wondrous woman."

Gutrune returns with a drinking horn and ceremoniously offers it to her guest, who proceeds to gulp down a sizeable quantity of magic love potion. At once, Brünnhilde is erased from his memory and, seized with passion for Gutrune, he offers himself to her. Gutrune retires again in pretty confusion and the men get down to brass tacks. Gunther graciously bestows his sister on Siegfried, on the condition that Siegfried help him obtain the woman he has set his heart on, who dwells high upon a rock in a circle of fire. Proving the potion's efficacy, this rings no bells with Siegfried, and he vows to win Brünnhilde for Gunther if he may marry Gutrune. He decides to assume Gunther's form through the powers of the Tarnhelm, though he will retain his own magnificent fearlessness, and with much satisfaction the two men swear a blood oath of good faith and brotherhood.

With characteristic impetuosity, Siegfried is ready to embark on his quest the moment the oath is sworn. Picking up his shield and sword, he directs Gunther to his boat, and the two men sail off in pursuit of Brünnhilde, leaving Hagen to break to Gutrune the news of her impending marriage.

Far above the meandering course of the Rhine, Brünnhilde gazes
at the ring on her finger and contemplates her love for Siegfried.
Her thoughts are interrupted by distant thunder, and she hears
for the first time in twenty years the sound of a sister Valkyrie. As
Waltraute swoops out of the sky, Brünnhilde greets her joyously.
But Waltraute's anguish ends her enthusiasm. She describes a
waning Valhalla, where Wotan sits silently on his throne awaiting
his doom. She has come, she reveals, because only Brünnhilde can
reverse the gods' inexorable extinction by returning the ring to the
Rhinemaidens.

But to Brünnhilde, the fortunes of the gods no longer matter. "Go back to
the holy council. Tell them I will never renounce love, and they shall never wrest
love from me, though Valhalla's splendor collapses in ruins!" Waltraute departs in despair,
and all too soon Brünnhilde hears the call of a hunting horn. A dreadful figure breaks through the wall of flame
that surrounds her. It is Siegfried, but changed into Gunther's form. As Brünnhilde shrinks back, terrified to
find her sanctuary invaded by a stranger, Siegfried proclaims in Gunther's voice that he has won her for a wife.

Desperately, Brünnhilde protests that she is inviolate as long as she wears the ring, but Siegfried's response
is to tear it from her finger and seize her. Terrified, she struggles with him but is soon overcome. Brutally, he
drives her into the cave, but before he enters himself, Siegfried unsheathes Notung and vows that the sword
will separate him from Gunther's bride throughout the night.

# ACT TWO

Outside the hall of the Gibichungs, Hagen sits, fast asleep. Moonlight reveals Alberich's figure, squatting
before his son. Hagen's glittering eyes spring open and he greets his father joylessly. Alberich is concerned
only with the ring. Carefully, he retells the story of its theft by Wotan and its acquisition by Siegfried. He urges
Hagen to procure it from the young hero, who, he says, is so naive that he has no idea of the ring's power.
Exhorting his son to be bold and loyal, Alberich disappears as the sun rises.

Siegfried marches in, once again his own self and ready to claim Gutrune. Hagen summons the girl, and
the pair listens as Siegfried tells of his exploits—with special emphasis on his gentlemanly behavior in the
cave. When Hagen sights a sail down the river, Siegfried announces that the boat carries Gunther and his new
bride. Hagen calls on the vassals to prepare a feast to celebrate their leader's marriage, and the Gibichung
men march down to meet their chieftain at the shore.

Gunther proudly escorts his bride through the throng and leads her into the hall. Pale and downcast,
Brünnhilde follows him obediently until the fateful moment when Siegfried steps forward to greet her.

Astonished, she lifts her eyes to those of her true husband and sees no recognition. When her despairing gaze falls upon the ring that he wears, this final sign of betrayal fairly maddens Brünnhilde, and she bursts forth in a torrent of accusations. Her avowal that Siegfried was her husband before Gunther is misinterpreted by the Gibichungs to mean that Siegfried was not as chivalrous as he had earlier sworn and they, too, accuse him of betrayal. Hagen accuses him of stealing the ring, the bride, and his friend's honor. Gunther, thoroughly confused, turns to Siegfried: Is it true? Is Brünnhilde Siegfried's wife? Siegfried, eager to placate his friend, takes an oath that he has never been married to Brünnhilde. Moved to new heights of fury, Brünnhilde takes an oath of her own. Grabbing Gunther's spear, she dedicates its power to Siegfried's downfall: "I bless your blade that it may pierce him!" she cries in ringing tones.

With the blithe assurance of a man without a memory, Siegfried manages to convince Gutrune and the vassals of his innocence, and leads them off to begin the wedding party. The unhappy triumvirate of Gunther, Brünnhilde, and Hagen remains behind. At least, Gunther and Brünnhilde are unhappy; Hagen's mask of gloom covers his elation that the ring is so close to his grasp. With reptilian cunning, he approaches Brünnhilde, whispering "Trust me, wronged wife! I will take revenge on your betrayer!"

Beguiled by this, Brünnhilde heedlessly reveals that Siegfried is vulnerable on his back. The rest of him she shielded with her magical powers, knowing that her hero would never turn his back on an enemy. Hagen seizes on this information, and, calling Gunther into their confabulation, they agree that Hagen will kill Siegfried the next day, with a spear to the back, while the men are out on a hunt. After some vacillation, Gunther agrees, especially after Hagen promises him the ring from Siegfried's finger. Together, the vengeful Brünnhilde and the hapless Gunther swear, "So be it! Siegfried shall die!"

Mark Twain, a Wagner aficionado, attended Bayreuth in 1891 and came away with a characteristically contrarian assessment of the affair. "The entire overture, long as it was, was played to a dark house with the curtain down. It was exquisite; it was delicious. But straightway thereafter, of course, came the singing, and it does seem to me that nothing can make a Wagner opera absolutely perfect and satisfactory to the untutored but to leave out the vocal parts. I wish I could see a Wagner opera done in pantomime once. Then one would have the lovely orchestration unvexed to listen to and bathe his spirit in, and the bewildering beautiful scenery to intoxicate his eyes with, and the dumb acting would not mar these pleasures, because there is not often anything in the Wagner opera that one would call by such a violent name as acting; as a rule all you would see would be a couple of silent people, one of them standing still, the other catching flies. Of course I do not really mean that he would be catching flies; I only mean that the usual operatic gestures which consist in reaching first one hand out into the air and then the other might suggest the sport I speak of if the operator attended to business and uttered no sound."

# ACT THREE

In a wooded valley of the Rhine, the three Rhinemaidens cavort happily in the water, singing of the lost ring and the hero who may bring it back to them. Right on cue, Siegfried, the ring on his hand, comes wandering through the woods. This is the day of the fateful hunt, but, in his pursuit of a bear, Siegfried has become separated from Gunther, Hagen, and their vassals. The Rhinemaidens, ever flirtatious, coax him to return the ring to them, but when their teasing is met with good-humored rejection, they become serious and warn Siegfried of the curse that attends the golden band, prophesying that he will die that very day. Siegfried dismisses their cautions, and the three sisters swim away.

Soon Hagen and Gunther join Siegfried with their men. Perceiving Gunther's melancholy, Siegfried offers to entertain him with stories of his boyhood, and soon he is telling the tale of the surly dwarf who raised him from a baby; of his sword, forged from the splinters of his father's blade; and of the journey to Fafner's cave, where he slew the dragon and captured his treasure. Caught up in his story, Siegfried hardly notices when Hagen gives him a draught that restores his memory, but continues recounting how upon the taste of dragon's blood, he could suddenly understand the birds, who bid him to find his bride, Brünnhilde, on the rocky summit. Slowly, thoughtfully, he tells how he passed through a wall of fire, "and I found a wondrous woman asleep, clad in shining armor." With a rush of memory and increasing joy, Siegfried cries out, "I loosened the glorious maid's helmet; my bold kiss awakened her: oh, how ardently was I enfolded in Brünnhilde's arms!"

Astonished by this evidence that Brünnhilde's avowals are true, Gunther springs to his feet, but Hagen is too quick for him. Pointing to two black ravens circling above, he asks whether Siegfried can understand their cry. Leaping up to look after them, Siegfried turns away from Hagen, who yells, "To me they cry revenge!" and plunges his spear into Siegfried's back. Siegfried turns to engage Hagen, but his strength fails and he drops back on his shield. As Gunther and the vassals look on helplessly, Siegfried returns in a vision to the radiant Brünnhilde. Then, as his eyes grow dim and fail, he dies.

Within the hall of the Gibichungs, Gutrune waits uneasily for Siegfried. Instead of her husband, Hagen arrives, eager to bring bad tidings. Hardly bothering to disguise his glee, he tells Gutrune that Siegfried has been killed by a wild boar. Gunther arrives, accompanied by the corpse of Siegfried, and divulges that Hagen himself was the wild boar. The two begin to quarrel about who shall inherit the ring. Gunther is strongest, but Hagen is the most vicious, and, amid the screams of the Gibichungs, Hagen strikes his brother dead. Snarling, he reaches to tear the ring from Siegfried's finger, but falls back in terror as the dead hero's hand rises against him with a menacing gesture.

Into the crowd of terrified vassals strides Brünnhilde. Commanding silence, she reveals to the sorrowing Gutrune that she was the hero's true wife. As the anguished girl curses Hagen and his potion, Brünnhilde directs the vassals to build a massive pyre on the banks of the Rhine. As they do so, she calls upon the gods to witness the outcome of their evil deeds, and, taking the ring from her husband's finger, she resolves to return it to the Rhinemaidens.

Brandishing a lighted torch, Brünnhilde directs the ever-present ravens to return to Valhalla: "Fly home, you ravens! Pass by Brünnhilde's rock: Direct Loge, who still blazes there, to Valhalla, for the end of the gods is nigh. Thus do I throw this torch to Valhalla's vaulting towers!" Flinging the firebrand onto the pyre, Brünnhilde watches as the flames rise into a great conflagration, and then, with a cry of joy, she leaps on her horse and rides to her death.

The flames lick upward until they fill the scene, as the Rhine, seemingly in response to the fire, overflows its banks. Summoned by Brünnhilde's vow to return the ring, the three Rhinemaidens reappear in the flooding waters. Hagen, watching from the shore, grows frantic with anxiety and greed, and he plunges into the river to seize back the ring. But Woglinde and Wellgunde twine their arms around his neck and drag him to a watery death, as their sister triumphantly displays the ring for all to see.

The flames of Siegfried's funeral pyre have reached into the sky to ignite Valhalla. The gods and goddesses look on impassively while bright flames engulf their fortress. The rule of the gods has come to an end, and a new world, created in the image of Brünnhilde's great love, has begun. ∽◈

# RIGOLETTO

❦

By 1842, Italian opera was in a shambles. Rossini had retired from music, the exquisite Bellini had long since expired, and though Donizetti was busily at work on *Don Pasquale,* it was to be his last composition. For a country that staged fifty new operas each year, the dearth of composers was catastrophic. Every self-respecting Italian city boasted a good, sometimes excellent, opera company. Needless to say, the competition for audiences was fierce, and any composer with drawing power was besieged by desperate impresarios. One such impresario was Bartolomeo Merelli of the Teatro alla Scala in Milan, who found himself, in 1841, with a very nice libretto on the subject of Nebuchadnezzar and no one to set it to music. Finally, he thought of Giuseppe Verdi, a young composer whose first opera had been a mild success and his second an unmitigated failure. Verdi's wife had died suddenly during composition of this second work and in the intervening months, Verdi had given himself over to depression. He was on the verge of renouncing composition altogether when Merelli ran into him one day and began telling him about the libretto. At Merelli's insistence, Verdi took the book home, where, according to his own account, it fell open, and "I gazed at the page that lay before me, and read the line *'Va, pensiero, sull'ali dorate'* (fly, thought, on wings of gold)." Unable to resist the poetry, Verdi read through the manuscript in one sitting. But when he returned to Merelli the next day, he refused to consider composing the opera. Infuriated, Merelli thrust the libretto into Verdi's pocket, pushed him out, and locked the door in his face. "What," Verdi recalled in a memoir, "was I to do? I returned home with *Nabucco* in my pocket. . . . Little by little the opera was composed."

*Nabucco* was a smash hit from its first performance, in 1842. The great chorus of the Jewish captives (the very same *Va, pensiero*) became the anthem of the Italian nationalist movement, the tune on everyone's lips, and Verdi, overnight, was transformed from an obscure prodigy to the patron saint of Italian opera, the darling of the working class and the cultured alike. What followed were fourteen operas in ten years, some of them enduring, some not so enduring, but all part of Verdi's great upward trajectory.

That arc culminated with *Rigoletto* (1851), which was the apotheosis of all that had gone before it in Italian opera; a perfectly proportioned dramatic and lyrical structure housing a multitude of inspired musical developments. Revolutionary in certain respects, it eschewed such venerable traditions as ensemble finales and conventional recitative. The combination of tradition and innovation, as well as the unflagging precision and effectiveness of the composition, has made *Rigoletto* the musician's favorite among Verdi's oeuvre. Even Verdi, when asked which of his operas he liked the best, said, "Speaking as a professional, *Rigoletto;* as an amateur, *La Traviata.*"

# ACT ONE

The Duke of Mantua is an inveterate womanizer and an all-around snake in the grass, and everyone knows it. However, everyone also knows that the insatiable Duke has not the slightest scruple about imprisoning his enemies, and his courtiers have therefore grown adept at pretending not to notice when their wives are appropriated by him. Even now, as he strolls into the great hall of his magnificent palace, where a splendid party is in full swing, the Duke is confiding to his friend Borsa his plans for the capture of a pretty young girl he has noticed at church. Before long, the festive tunes distract him, and as he looks about the room thoughtfully, his eye falls on the wife of one of his closest advisors, Count Ceprano. Borsa warns him that his dalliance might be discovered by one of his other mistresses, but the Duke scoffs, *"Questa o quella . . .* This one or that one, it's all the same to me. Each is exactly like the rest, and I never give up my heart to any one. Fidelity I shun like a bad disease."

Count Ceprano is keeping a close eye on his wife, but his vigilance does him no good, for the Duke soon approaches the Countess with fulsome compliments. Before the Count can do more than swear softly, she has been whisked away.

Off in a corner, a small, hunchbacked figure has also been watching this little drama. It is Rigoletto, the court jester, and now, with a twisted smile, he approaches the helpless Count. "What's that you have on your head," he asks tauntingly, making a pair of horns with his fingers. As the Count stalks stiffly away, the courtiers burst into malicious laughter. Rigoletto, satisfied, departs.

Marullo, the court poet, enters the hall in a state of excitement. He has discovered an incredible secret about Rigoletto—the deformed old monster harbors a lovely young mistress. As the courtiers titter and wonder, the Duke returns, trailing Rigoletto and Ceprano. "No one is such a bore as Ceprano," the Duke sighs to Rigoletto, "and his dear wife is such an angel."

Rigoletto coolly recommends abducting the wife and imprisoning the bore. Or perhaps chopping the bore's head off altogether. This light talk is too much for the long-suffering Ceprano, and in a rage, he draws his sword on the jester. But Rigoletto has the Duke's protection, and he laughs at Ceprano's humiliation. Stepping into a cluster of friends, Ceprano vows to get revenge on the jester. His vendetta has no lack of

Rigoletto *was based on a play by Victor Hugo entitled* Le roi s'amuse, *"The King Enjoys Himself," which told the story of King Francis I and his jester Triboulet and ran for exactly one night before it was closed down by the French government on the grounds that it defamed the sacred institution of the monarchy. Verdi seemed to think that the Italian censors would be more liberal than the French, but his optimism proved ill founded. Even as he was in the midst of the composition, the Military Governor of Venice issued a rousing condemnation of the whole project. However, the manager of Il Teatro La Fenice, one Marzari, concocted a new plot, relieved of all offensive royal shenanigans and pretty much everything else, too. Verdi's opinion of this expurgated version may be deduced from his response to Marzari:*

> *"In its present form . . . the dramatic moments leave one completely cold. . . . The Duke has no character. The Duke must definitely be a libertine: Without this there is no justification for Triboletto's fear that his daughter might leave her hiding place, and the drama is made impossible. What would the Duke be doing in the last act, alone in a remote inn, without an invitation, without a rendezvous. I don't understand why the sack has gone. Why should a sack matter to the police? . . . But let me say this: Why do they think they know better than I do about this? . . . With that sack removed, it is improbable that Triboletto would talk for half an hour to a corpse, before a flash of lightning reveals it to be his daughter. Finally, I see that they have avoided making Triboletto an ugly hunchback!! A hunchback who sings? Why not? . . . Will it be effective? I don't know. But, I repeat, if I don't know, then they who propose this change don't know either. I thought it would be beautiful to portray this extremely deformed and ridiculous character who is inwardly passionate and full of love. I chose this subject precisely because of these qualities and these original traits, and if they are cut I shall no longer be able to set it to music."*

*In the end, Verdi had his way. True, Francis I was changed into a defunct Duke. The title, too, was changed. But in all other essential ways, the plot returned to its original form, and Verdi's adherence to his principles was rewarded by the smashing success that* Rigoletto *has enjoyed since its first performance.*

supporters, for they have all felt the sting of Rigoletto's acid tongue, and the group agrees to meet the next night. Before long, intimations of jealousy and revenge are forgotten in the gaiety of the party. Dancers turn and glide, and the ducal palace seems the very kingdom of pleasure.

Suddenly, the dark figure of Count Monterone punctures the festive scene. He has come to confront the Duke, to demand vengeance for his daughter's seduction. But the Duke finds the accusation and the accuser merely tiresome, and it is Rigoletto who comes forward to greet the Count with mockery. Insolently, he advises the Count to cease his complaints: "What madness takes you, that you chatter on about your daughter's honor?"

"One more insult!" exclaims old Monterone, firmly declaring his intention never to give up his campaign.

"Enough!" cries the Duke in exasperation. "Arrest him!"

"He's mad," agrees Rigoletto with a snicker.

"May both of you be damned!" bursts out Monterone. "To unleash your hounds on a dying lion is cowardly, O Duke!" And, turning to Rigoletto, he adds, "And you, serpent, you who laugh at a father's grief, my curse upon you!"

At these words, the blood drains from the jester's face. "Oh, horror!" he whispers to himself fearfully, as Monterone is led away by two soldiers.

A small, comfortable house stands on a quiet street of Mantua; from within its walled courtyard the grand palace of Ceprano can be seen.

The twilit quiet is broken by Rigoletto, who hurries along the street, glancing fearfully behind him, for he is being followed by a gaunt, heavily cloaked man. As it turns out, his shadower is Sparafucile, a hired assassin, who offers to kill Rigoletto's enemies for a fee. The jester shows an eager interest: How much? How much more for a nobleman? Half in advance, half on delivery? Well, and how shall he be found, should the need arise?

Laconically, Sparafucile answers Rigoletto's questions, even revealing his method of ensnaring his victims—his pretty sister dances in the street, luring the quarry home with her. With a final promise that he will appear each night, in case the jester wants to make an order, Sparafucile takes his leave.

Rigoletto watches the cloaked figure walk unhurriedly down the street. *"Pari siamo . . .* We are alike," he reflects. "I with my tongue, he with his dagger. O nature, in me, you did create a vile scoundrel. To be a buffoon! No other duty, but to laugh! I lack the heritage of every man—tears. But here," he turns toward the quiet house, "here, I become another person!" Opening the gate with his key, he enters the courtyard.

Immediately, a lovely young woman runs out of the house and flies into his arms. This is his secret, his daughter Gilda. Fiercely protective, he tells her nothing of the court, of his past, of her mother, whose death marked the end of his greatest happiness. Gilda peppers her father with questions, but the jester only repeats that she is his whole world and tells her for the millionth time that she must never leave the house, except, of course, to go to church. Tormented by the fear that his Gilda will be seized by his enemies, Rigoletto questions Giovanna, the servant, whose job is to keep the girl locked in the house day and night. Except, of course, for church. Patiently, Giovanna answers: No one has come in. The gate is always locked. No one has followed them to church.

During this interrogation, the Duke, disguised as a simple bourgeois, passes quietly through the street, sneaks into the courtyard, and conceals himself behind some shrubbery. Clearly, he has some purpose in mind, for he tosses a purse of golden coins at Giovanna's feet to buy her silence. But the Duke is astonished to discover his jester Rigoletto in the very garden he has taken such trouble to find.

"Now, if anyone knocks on the door, you must not open it," Rigoletto is warning Giovanna.

"Not even for the Duke?" asks the servant laughingly.

The jester's face darkens. "Especially not for him. My daughter, good night."

"His daughter?" whispers the Duke wonderingly.

Father and daughter embrace, and the jester departs.

After a troubled silence, Gilda confesses to Giovanna that she is ashamed not to have mentioned the youth who followed them to church.

Fingering her purse, Giovanna ventures that he seems a fine young man, a real gentleman. But Gilda swears she would love a poor man more. "Asleep and awake, I am always calling him," she muses, "and my soul cries out, 'I lo—'"

"—I love you!" cries the Duke, rushing from his hiding place. Gesturing at Giovanna to make herself scarce, the nobleman kneels before the girl and repeats, "I love you! Speak these words again, and a heaven of joy will open before me!"

Terrified, Gilda calls for Giovanna and laments to find herself alone with this importunate suitor. But soon, the Duke's honeyed words begin to melt her heart, and after he tells her, with assumed humility, that he is Walter Malde, a poor student, she is persuaded to reveal that she loves him.

At this moment, a more sinister assembly is gathering in the street outside. Ceprano, Borsa, Marullo, and a band of courtiers have come to wreak their revenge on Rigoletto by abducting the beauty whom they take to be his mistress. The Duke and Gilda, alarmed by the noises on the street, quickly swear eternal devotion before he pads off into the night. "Walter Malde," says Gilda dreamily. "Walter Malde. *Caro nome* . . . Beloved name, the first that ever brought the pulse of love to my heart." Taking up a lantern, Gilda ascends the stairs to her room, utterly unaware of the eyes observing her from atop the garden wall.

"Look at her," says Ceprano.

"Like a fairy or an angel," says Marullo pensively. Transfixed, the men make no move to carry out their plan.

Suddenly, the spell is broken by the abrupt return of Rigoletto. In the thick blackness of the night, the jester jostles against the interlopers and jumps back, crying, "Who's there?"

Recognizing the voice of Rigoletto, the men are recalled to their malevolence. Marullo suggests that it would make an excellent joke to dupe Rigoletto into helping them abduct his own mistress! Shielded by the night, he approaches the jester to reassure him—it's just he and some courtiers, come to play a prank on Ceprano by carrying off his wife from the nearby palace. Assuming his professional character, Rigoletto volunteers gleefully to join in the fun.

But he must be masked, Marullo insists, for the rest of them are. And atop the mask, he ties a thick cloth over Rigoletto's eyes and ears. "You shall hold the ladder," he commands, and the befuddled Rigoletto, believing himself to be at the walls of Ceprano's palace, obligingly holds the ladder firm as the courtiers ascend his wall. Barely able to suppress their triumphant laughter, they climb onto the terrace outside Gilda's bedroom.

With callous efficiency, they break down the door and pull Gilda out, gagging her with a handkerchief

and spiriting her down the staircase and into the garden. Outside, her father grips the ladder firmly, unable to hear her muffled cries through the wadded cloth around his head. Then he realizes that his mask is really a blindfold. Overcome with terror, he pulls it from his face, only to hear Gilda's calls for help fading into the distance. Looking desperately around him, he sees Gilda's scarf lying in the street. In one horrible moment, he realizes that his worst fear has come true, and he stands holding his heart as though he has been stabbed. "Gilda! Gilda!" he screams. Shaking his fists, he cries out despairingly, "The curse!" before falling insensible to the ground.

# ACT TWO

In an elegant salon within the ducal palace, full-length portraits of the Duke and Duchess look serenely out over the room, with its velvet hangings and massive dining table. Much less serene is the actual Duke, who is fuming about the sudden disappearance of his latest conquest. "She has been stolen from me! Her gate opened! Her house deserted! Where can that beloved angel be, she who has inspired such a faithful love in me! *Parmi veder* . . . I seem to see before me her lovely face in tears, and she, calling for her Walter in vain."

Much pleased by the pathos of this vision, the Duke is smiling when Ceprano, Marullo, Borsa, and the other courtiers arrive with the news that Rigoletto's mistress has been carried off.

"Splendid!" he cries jovially. "From where?"

"From his house," they reply, and as they cheerfully discuss the abduction, the Duke puts two and two together. The mistress in question is none other than his own lost conquest. And when he learns that this trophy has been hidden in his own palace, he is exultant. As the Duke strides out of the room in search of Gilda, Rigoletto enters it. While the courtiers smirk knowingly, the jester prowls about the grand chamber with painfully assumed indifference, looking for some evidence of Gilda. Ceprano and Marullo rejoice in such signs of Rigoletto's inner torment, but their glee is interrupted by a page who comes with an urgent message from the Duchess: She needs to speak to the Duke immediately. Various excuses fail to placate the page, and finally the courtiers are reduced to broad hints about the Duke's current occupation.

The lurking Rigoletto seizes on this clue. "Ah, she is here then! She is with the Duke," he bursts forth.

"Who?" say the courtiers mockingly.

Thwarted by their bland denials, Rigoletto can no longer hide his breaking heart. He begs for his daughter's return, but is met only with scorn. Now, tormented by the certainty that Gilda is being ravished, perhaps in the very next room, Rigoletto dashes toward the door leading to the Duke's chambers, but a phalanx of courtiers blocks his way. Goaded beyond endurance, Rigoletto's fragile composure is shattered. *"Cortigiani, vil razza damnata . . ."* he rages, "Vile, damnable race of courtiers, how much were you paid for my only treasure?" Again, his assault on the door is repulsed by the smiling aristocrats. "Assassins!" he screams, "open that door!" But his rage is met with cool disregard, and, defeated, Rigoletto weeps.

As he kneels before his enemies, a small door opens and Gilda rushes into her father's arms. The sight of her dismay finally brings a sense of shame to the snide courtiers, and they depart. Left alone with her father, Gilda tells the sad story of her undoing: how the handsome youth she had seen at church came to see her the previous night to confess his love, and how her heart had opened to hope. Then, abduction and shame.

As they weep together, the old Count Monterone is led into the salon by two guards. He is bound for the dungeons, but first, he halts before the Duke's portrait, lamenting that his curse has proved useless and the Duke lives on untouched. As he watches the old man being pushed from the room, Rigoletto makes a passionate vow of revenge.

# ACT THREE

On a dark and deserted street stands a house so dilapidated that any passerby may see its interior simply by looking through the wall's gaping cracks. It is a tavern, and at a long splintering table sits Sparafucile, the hired killer. Outside are Rigoletto and Gilda, who watch Sparafucile unobserved. Rigoletto seeks to make good his plan for vengeance, but he is restrained by Gilda, who loves her seducer more than ever.

"Even if you were sure that he is unfaithful, would you still love him?" asks her father with a voice full of pity.

"I can't know, but I am certain that he adores me," she replies.

Hoping to cure her of her passion, Rigoletto leads her closer to the tavern, where the Duke, disguised as an officer, now bounds through the door, in high spirits and singing a charming little song about the inconstancy of women, *"La donna è mobile . . .* Woman is fickle as a feather in the wind, simple in speech and simpler in mind."

Sparafucile brings his raffish customer a bottle of wine, then calls his sister downstairs. Maddalena, a ripe young woman in gypsy costume, appears with a beguiling smile, and the Duke immediately tries to avail himself of her charms. While she flirts within, Sparafucile goes outside to consult with Rigoletto. "Is that your man? Shall he live or die?"

Rigoletto, torn by his knowledge of Gilda's love for the Duke, postpones the decision. He and his daughter watch as the seduction proceeds inside the tavern—the Duke avows, in familiar tones, his eternal love, and Maddalena, no fool, laughingly disparages his fine falsehoods. Outside, Gilda's heart is breaking, and Rigoletto swears once more that he will be revenged. Sending his betrayed daughter home with a command to don man's attire and travel to Verona where they will meet again, the jester goes in search of Sparafucile. After a quick exchange, the two men agree that Rigoletto will return at midnight to receive the body of the Duke.

As the Duke and the decoy continue their flirtation, the sky grows thick with storm clouds, and a strange moaning wind fills the night. Sparafucile suggests that the officer might like a bed for the night, rather than braving the storm. Eyeing Maddalena, the Duke agrees enthusiastically and follows his host up to an open loft. Stretching out on a thin pallet, the Duke soon lulls himself to sleep singing his little tune about fickle women.

Below, Maddalena is awaiting her brother's return. She doesn't want such a handsome fellow to be killed, she protests. But Sparafucile is insistent, so Maddalena soon creeps up the stairs to relieve the Duke of his sword.

Meanwhile, Gilda, costumed as a man, walks slowly toward the tavern. Pausing outside the walls, she listens as the assassin commands his sister to mend an old sack for him. Maddalena continues her campaign as she sews—the lad is so handsome, he loves her, he is sleeping, he must not be killed. Exasperated, Sparafucile informs her that the sack she is sewing will contain her suitor's body after his throat has been cut.

Gilda's cry of horror is drowned out by Maddalena's pragmatic suggestion that he kill the hunchback instead. That way, her brother will have the money, and she'll have the handsome fellow. But no, Sparafucile has his professional ethics and refuses to do any such thing. However, to placate his sister, he develops an alternate plan: If another guest shows up before midnight, Sparafucile will kill him and leave the handsome officer alone.

Against the background of the roiling storm, Gilda gathers her resolve and knocks on the door of the tavern. Begging for a little shelter, she is eagerly greeted by Maddalena. Calmly, Sparafucile unsheathes his dagger and approaches his new victim with silent efficiency. While the storm wails wildly, Gilda receives her death blow.

Soon afterward, Rigoletto returns, hurrying along the riverbank toward the tavern. Grimly, Sparafucile emerges from his darkened home and hands the jester a bulky sack.

Rigoletto is exultant. "He is in there! Dead!" cries the jester. "Now look upon me, O world! Here is a buffoon, and here is a mighty prince!" Nearly dancing with delight, Rigoletto turns to drag the sack toward the river, when he is arrested by the faint sound, now clearer, then clearer still, of singing.

"La donna è mobile . . . " It is the Duke, and Rigoletto screams in terror. Fumbling to open the sack, he pulls out the body within, only to discover that it is Gilda, near to death. Desperately, he begs her to speak, to tell him what happened.

In a weak and halting voice, Gilda confesses that she died to save her lover and asks for her father's forgiveness.

"Do not die," begs her father. "You must not leave me! Do not die—or let me die with you." But his words are futile; Gilda utters a final good-bye and dies, and Rigoletto, alone and lost, screams to the heavens, "Ah! The curse!"

# IL TROVATORE

~·O·O·~

**A**s so many critics—from Lord Chesterfield to Bugs Bunny—have pointed out, opera is preposterous, irrational, and absurd. And nowhere is its inherent absurdity more apparent than in Giuseppe Verdi's *Il Trovatore*. The opera is a catalog of implausible plot twists, flat characters, and unlikely singing opportunities—and it includes the redoubtable "Anvil Chorus," during which eighteen anvils are rhythmically walloped by gypsy blacksmiths in honor of gypsy maidens who have absolutely nothing to do with the story at hand. The story at hand is fairly strange, for the most exciting bits seem to have occurred about twenty-five years prior to the first act. Stage time is given over primarily to reflection about the past events. Such duels, elopements, and executions as do take place generally occur offstage.

And yet, *Il Trovatore* is equally a catalog of all that is luscious and loveable about opera: noble passions and passionate nobles, lurid pasts and dire futures, revenge, jealousy, desperate love, and, above all, thrilling, melodious music, not least of which is that same irrepressible "Anvil Chorus." Implausible, illogical, immoderate, yes—but also vigorous, extravagant, and deeply enjoyable, *Il Trovatore,* first performed in 1853, is the last great efflorescence of the Italian Romantic tradition that began with Rossini and was about to be washed away by the sea change of *La Traviata*.

## ACT ONE: THE DUEL

The Prince of Aragon may be the master of Aliaferia Palace, but our story concerns a young nobleman in his service, the Count di Luna, who cherishes an unrequited passion for Leonora, a lady-in-waiting to the Princess. The Count di Luna has spent many nights beneath Leonora's balcony, lying in wait for his shadowy rival, the Troubadour, *il trovatore*. And tonight is no different; the Count's soldiers and servants are sitting in the anteroom to the Count's apartments, where they must await his return. Yawning, they beg Ferrando, a grizzled old officer, to help them stay awake by recounting the dreadful history of the Count's brother.

Ferrando begins. The old Count di Luna was happy, proud of his two fine sons, but his contentment was short-lived. One morning, the nurse who cared for the younger child woke to find a foul gypsy peering into the cradle. The nurse's screams summoned the household, and though the old gypsy proclaimed her innocence, it was clear she had bewitched the boy, for he soon grew languid and weak. In despair, the old Count ordered that the gypsy be found and burned at the stake. But he had reckoned without the gypsy's daughter, who avenged her mother's murder by abducting the sickly baby. Searching for the child, the Count's men found a smoldering fire on the very spot where the old gypsy had been burned—and in the fire, a child's bones, half-burnt!

The soldiers and servants cry out in horror, but Ferrando continues. The old Count lived but a few days after this tragic discovery, but as he lay dying, he had faith that his baby was not dead, and he begged his older son to continue the search. However, all efforts to find the child or the gypsy daughter proved vain. Thoroughly terrified by the story, Ferrando's men scatter as the midnight bell chimes ominously.

Meanwhile, out in the dark gardens, Leonora waits and wishes for her Troubadour. She describes to her friend Inez her first meeting with the mysterious knight. At a tournament a stranger wearing black armor swept all before him. As Leonora placed the victory wreath upon his head, she lost her heart. But soon afterward, the civil wars erupted, the knight disappeared, years passed, and then—

"What happened?" asks Inez, as a confidante should.

"*Tacea la notte placida* . . . the peaceful night lay silent, when suddenly the quiet was broken by the sweet sound of a lute, and the voice of a troubadour sang out." There, beneath Leonora's balcony, stood the very same knight. "Then there came joy such as only angels feel." Despite Inez's warnings, Leonora declares as they enter the palace that her heart will belong to the Troubadour forever.

No sooner has she departed, than the Count arrives, drawn by the flickering light in Leonora's apartments. He vows that he must see the woman he loves, but his steps are arrested by the sound of a lute. It is his rival, the Troubadour, and the Count trembles with fury at each sweet note. Suddenly Leonora reappears and, mistaking the Count's dark figure for that of her Troubadour, and flings herself upon him with words of love.

"Faithless one!" hisses the Troubadour's voice from the bushes.

Realizing her error, Leonora throws herself at her beloved's feet, declaring her remorse and devotion. The Troubadour raises her tenderly up, and they are united in an embrace that is soon checked by the Count, who demands to know the name of his opponent. The Troubadour proudly declares that he is Manrico. This incenses the Count still further, for he knows Manrico to be a warrior in the army of Urgel, Prince Aragon's enemy. Immediately, he threatens his opponent with death, and the rivals are soon set upon a duel.

Exchanging insults, di Luna and Manrico dash away, swords drawn, leaving Leonora aswoon on the terrace.

# ACT TWO: THE GYSPY

In the windswept mountains of Biscay, the clustered gypsies greet the dawn with enthusiasm, banging cheerfully on their anvils to a rollicking tune about the delights of gypsy life and gypsy girls. Somewhat apart from this raucous crowd, the gypsy woman Azucena rests near the fire with Manrico, her son. As she stares at the writhing flames, Azucena is transported, and she begins to chant a strange song. *"Stride la vampa! . . . The flames roar, the crowd runs toward the fire, the murderers lead their victim in."* As though hypnotized, she paints a scene of horror: a woman burned to death as a mob cheers.

Manrico begs his mother to tell him the sad story behind her song. Azucena acquiesces. "This is a bitter tale of how my mother died," she begins, recounting the same story that Ferrando told. "They drove her into the flames, the murderers! As she died, she cried out, 'Avenge me!'"

"And did you avenge her?" asks Manrico.

"I managed to steal the Count's son, and brought him to my mother's pyre." Ignoring Manrico's shocked cry, Azucena tells how, half-crazed with grief and horror, she wildly threw the small bundle into the flames. Some while later, as her delirium ebbed, she turned away from the conflagration—only to see the Count's small son lying safe in the grass. "My son, my own baby—I had cast him into the flames!" moans Azucena.

Manrico gasps—but soon another thought occurs to him. "Am I not your son? Then who am I?" he asks in confusion.

Azucena realizes she has revealed too much. "You are my son," she says hastily, assuring him that the other story was just imagined. "Haven't I always been a loving mother?" she insists. Certainly Manrico cannot deny it, for recently she rescued him from the battlefield of Pelilla, where he had been wounded and left for dead, the sole survivor of an attack by the Count di Luna's forces.

"And that's the thanks the scoundrel gave you for sparing his life in the duel. What strange pity blinded you that night?"

Even Manrico cannot explain it. As di Luna lay helpless on the ground and Manrico lifted his sword for the deathblow, a strange chill ran through him. "Do not strike," intoned a voice from heaven. Manrico swears, though, that he will have his revenge at their next encounter. Their conversation is interrupted by Manrico's henchman, Ruiz, who says that rebel forces have taken the fortress of Castellor, and that Urgel commands Manrico to defend it. Furthermore, Ruiz's message reveals that Leonora, assuming her Troubadour to be dead at Pelilla, plans to take the veil that

very night in a nearby cloister. Manrico lets out an anguished cry at the thought of losing his beloved, and he rushes away to save his Leonora.

Manrico is not the only one who wishes to save Leonora from the nunnery. The Count di Luna and his men enter the convent courtyard under the cover of night. As the Count explains to Ferrando, he had thought that Manrico's death would remove all obstacles to his courtship. Determined now to have Leonora, di Luna has come to capture his prize. Moving cautiously, the Count and his followers conceal themselves in the shadows to await the postulant.

Soon a procession of nuns approaches, leading Leonora to the chapel. All her hopes have been destroyed, she tells Inez, and she will now devote herself to God. The Count, overhearing, bursts out of his hiding place with a resounding, "Never!"

Just as the Count leaps forward among the shocked nuns to seize his quarry, Manrico hurls himself into the scene from atop the convent wall. A moment of general astonishment gives way on Leonora's part to tremulous joy and on the Count's to dire fury. Leonora, uncertain whether she is in heaven or on earth, flees into Manrico's arms. But the Count will not be dissuaded by the resurrection of his enemy; brandishing his sword, he attempts to rip Leonora from Manrico's embrace. Just at this moment, Manrico is joined by his faithful lieutenant Ruiz and his followers, who have come to announce that Urgel has achieved victory. Thus surrounded, the Count resigns himself to defeat.

Blissfully, Leonora leaves on Manrico's arm, guarded by Ruiz and his retinue as the Count looks on helplessly, issuing bitter threats of revenge.

# ACT THREE: THE GYPSY'S SON

Outside Castellor, di Luna's forces are preparing for a counterattack on Urgel's troops, which occupy the city. Eager for the call to arms, the soldiers while away the hours. Now Ferrando emerges from the Count's tent with good news: The battle will take place tomorrow! The soldiers exult at the prospect: "*Squilli, echeggi la tromba guerriera* . . .Let the warlike trumpet sound the call to battle! May our banner tomorrow be firmly planted on those distant towers!" Filled with a new sense of purpose, the troops disperse.

Alone, the Count emerges from his command post and glowers at the fortress of Castellor, which harbors Leonora and Manrico.

Di Luna's dire ruminations are interrupted by Ferrando, who appears with the news that his men have found a suspicious-looking gypsy lurking nearby. Azucena is brought in, her hands bound. Convinced that she has been spying, the Count interrogates her, though she pleads innocent to his accusations. However, once she reveals that she comes from the lands near Biscay, Ferrando scrutinizes her face. Pretending idle interest, the Count asks her if she knows about the son of a count, stolen as a baby by a gypsy.

A cabaletta *is a short, high-powered aria that delivers a quick shot of virile intensity at the end of a slower passage. Manrico's passionate "Di quella pira," as he resolves to rescue his mother from her death sentence, is considered the apotheosis of the genre. By definition, a* cabaletta *requires a repeated refrain, but most tenors find it difficult to produce more than one round of* "Di quella pira," *due to the astonishing high Cs that make the aria a virtuoso showpiece. Remarkably, the gravity-defying Cs were not scored by Verdi; they were an interpolation by a tenor named Tamberlick, who politely asked the composer's permission to include the note because, he explained, it was in great demand with the public. Verdi replied pragmatically, "Far be it from me to deny the public what it wants. Put in the high C, if you like, provided it is a good one."*

Azucena stutters, "Who are you?" Noticing her ill-concealed terror, Ferrando voices his belief that she is the gypsy in question. Seizing on this opportunity to avenge the ancient crime, the Count gleefully sentences her to death.

Trembling with terror, Azucena invokes her son: "Are you not coming, Manrico? Won't you save your poor mother?"

"Manrico's mother!" cries di Luna. "And in my power! I shall use your agony to pierce his heart!" And, as Azucena is dragged away, the Count sets his trap for Manrico.

Meanwhile, next to the chapel in Castellor, Manrico and Leonora prepare for their marriage. Leonora's heart fails her at the prospect of the imminent battle, but Manrico assures her that her love has strengthened him. "But if it is my fate to die on the enemy's sword, my last thoughts will be of you."

Their moment of happiness is shattered by Ruiz, who arrives to tell his master of Azucena's arrest and death sentence. Cursing this new infamy, Manrico resolves to liberate his mother, no matter what the peril, *"Di quella pira . . .* The terrible flames of that pyre consume my own being!" As Leonora weeps for her beloved's safety, Manrico and his soldiers fly to Azucena's defense.

# ACT FOUR: THE ORDEAL

Atop the highest tower of Aliaferia Palace is a tiny barred cell that holds Manrico and Azucena, now imprisoned together. Manrico's sortie to save his mother has failed, Urgel's forces have been routed by di Luna, and all appears to be lost. But in the dark, Leonora creeps across the ramparts, guided by Ruiz and fired by the belief that she can save her lover. "Have no fear for me," she assures the trusty Ruiz, "my defense is quick and sure." As if to strengthen her resolve, she gazes at a large jeweled ring she wears.

As the funeral bells toll and the monks in the chapel chant the prayer for the dying, Leonora realizes with horror that Manrico will soon be executed. As if he could read her thoughts, Manrico, from within his tower, bids farewell to his lost Leonora, and against the somber background of the monastic dirge, the two avow their love for all eternity.

The Count strides across the ramparts, directing his lackeys to behead Manrico at dawn and to burn his mother at the stake immediately afterward. As the servants depart, di Luna permits himself a moment's reflection: "I abuse, perhaps, the power entrusted to me by the Prince. Ah, to what ends have you drawn me, Leonora!" As he broods on her disappearance after the recapture of Castellor, Leonora steps out of the shadows. "Why have you come here?" he asks grimly.

"He is about to die, and you ask why I have come?"

Furiously, di Luna rejects her pleas; he will never take pity on his rival, and the more she begs, the more outraged he grows. In desperation, Leonora offers her own life in exchange for the Troubadour's.

"If only I might find some crueler death for him," di Luna cries. "The more you love him, the more my fury blazes!"

In anguish, Leonora plays her final card—she offers herself to the Count in exchange for Manrico's freedom.

Though he scarcely believes her, the Count agrees feverishly. Leonora requests that she be allowed to speak to Manrico one last time before he escapes and the Count claims her. This the Count concedes, but while he is giving orders to the prison guard, Leonora quickly lifts her ring to her mouth and swallows the poison it contains. "You shall have me, but cold in death," she whispers.

Inside the dark cell, Azucena lies on a thin pallet, while Manrico sits nearby. The old woman, growing more distraught as her death draws near, describes once again the scene of her mother's burning. Manrico comforts her, hoping to lull her into sleep, and bit by bit, she drifts off.

The cell door opens, and Leonora flies to Manrico's side. The Troubadour's rapture is short-lived, however, for when Leonora urges him to make his escape posthaste, he demands to know why she isn't coming with him. Though she tries to evade his questions, Manrico soon guesses the bargain she has made with di Luna and turns on her with contempt. "This wretch has sold the heart she swore was mine!" he fulminates. "Go—I despise you, I curse you!"

Leonora's protestations are mixed with the sleeping Azucena's dreams of the mountains of home, but Manrico is not recalled to tenderness. Finally, falling at Manrico's feet, she cries, "No more! This is not the moment to revile me, but to pray for me!"

A sudden realization stops Manrico's heart, and he turns to see Leonora collapsing. He drops to her side, begging her forgiveness, and it is this scene that greets di Luna as he strides into Manrico's cell. Together the enemies look on in helpless despair as Leonora bids them farewell and dies.

The Count immediately turns to his guards. "Take him to the block," says he, pointing to his rival.

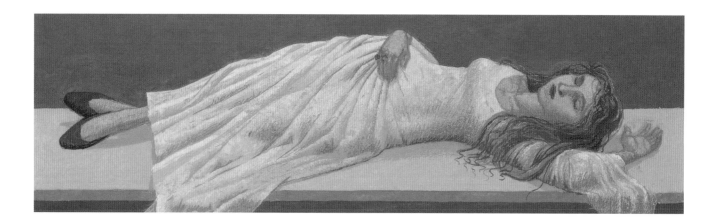

As he is dragged away, Manrico calls out to Azucena.

Waking with a start, she cries, "Manrico! Where is my son?"

"Going to his death!" shouts the Count, and, pulling the gypsy up to the window, he cruelly forces her to watch as the ax falls on Manrico.

Azucena turns and gives the Count a long look filled with hatred. "He was your brother," she says with such force that di Luna knows her words are true.

"Oh, horror!" he whispers.

Azucena emits a wild, howling laugh. "You are avenged, O mother!" she cries, and then falls lifeless to her pallet.

For a long moment, the Count simply stares at the old woman's corpse. Finally, he turns to leave. "Yet," he says quietly, "I must live."

# LA TRAVIATA

*~⊙⟩⟨⊙~*

It's hard, now, to imagine the powerful effect of *La Traviata* when it burst forth on the world in 1853. The fallen woman with the heart of gold is now an archetype, but then she was a shocking development. Violetta's death from consumption, tragic and touching to us, was at that time an uncomfortable slice of realism, rather like the spectacle of someone dying of lung cancer would be for us today. Furthermore, the contemporary setting was an innovation so nerve-wracking that, for the opera's premiere, the action was thrust back to the year 1700.

Startling as these elements were, they represent only one part of the transfiguration of opera wrought by *La Traviata*. The other, more truly far-reaching development is less tangible: the introduction of intimacy into a genre previously dominated by the monumental, the monstrous, or the farcical. Here we have no grand pageants, rebellious armies, vicious tyrants, noble nobles, foul murders, wily servants, or caprices. Instead, we have three characters who love and torment one another, who are torn between what they desire and what they know, whose flesh is both demanding and decaying—three characters, in short, who live in the same world we do. Violetta Valéry, though tragic, is not improbable, which is what makes her story heartrending and completely satisfying. It is also what makes the role both a great opportunity and a treacherous snare for a soprano. Violetta depends on dramatic ability; a mediocre singer with superior acting skills can triumph in the role, while a soprano with a lovely voice and a wooden delivery will fail. Those who combine voice and dramatic talent—Maria Callas, for instance—are the immortal Violettas.

In the tried-and-true tradition of all artistic innovations, *La Traviata* was a flop at its premiere. Nobody has ever pinpointed the reasons: Some say that the Germont was in bad voice, some say that Violetta's profession outraged the critics and that the Violetta was, at 285 pounds, too fat to authentically portray a consumptive. With admirable concision, Verdi announced the failure to his friends: "*La Traviata* last night a fiasco. Was the fault mine or the singers? Time will decide." Time did. A year later Verdi and his Violetta swept into the halls of triumph with a new batch of singers, and there they have remained ever since.

# ACT ONE

In her gilded apartments, Violetta Valéry is holding one of her famous soirees. Brilliantly dressed women and laughing noblemen stroll the rooms, drinking champagne. Violetta, dazzling in a black and silver gown, rustles forward to greet the latest arrivals: her friend Flora Bervoix, who is accompanied by her lover, the Marchese, and Violetta's own protector, the extremely rich and dour Baron Douphol. As the company settles into an evening of pleasure, two new guests arrive: Gaston, an old and platonic friend of Violetta's, has brought Alfredo Germont, who has been longing to meet her. Introductions soon give way to a lavish supper, and, seating herself next to Gaston, Violetta learns that Alfredo, though a stranger to her, had called every day upon Gaston during her last illness to ask about her progress.

Wonderingly, Violetta turns her luminous eyes upon the young man. "But why? I don't understand." Blushing, Alfredo confirms the report. Violetta says with gratitude, "I thank you." To her lover, she adds teasingly, "You, Baron, were less attentive."

"I have only known you a year," replies the Baron.

"And he for just a few minutes," says Violetta lightly. Displeased, the Baron shoots Alfredo an acid look and mutters darkly, but the guests banter on cheerfully around him. The wine flows, and a toast is certainly imperative, but the Baron declines the honor. Urged on by Gaston and Violetta, Alfredo rises to the occasion: *"Libiamo, ne' lieti calici . . .* Drink from the joyful glass resplendent with beauty! Drink to the spirit of pleasure that enchants a fleeting moment!" The crowd joins him. "Drink, for wine will warm the kisses of love!"

Laughingly, Violetta stands to offer a toast of her own. "Everything in life is folly—except for pleasure!" she exclaims. "Let us be joyful, for love is fleeting and short-lived!" She invites her guests to continue the revelry with a waltz.

"With pleasure!" they cry, dashing madly from the salon.

As she begins to follow, Violetta suddenly turns pale and reaches for a chair to steady herself. Alfredo, observing her closely, hangs behind the others and watches as Violetta, thinking herself alone, turns to a mirror. "How pale I am," she whispers, touching her reflection. A slight movement catches her eye and she turns to see Alfredo, his eyes filled with concern. He begs her to take care of herself, to abandon her hectic life, but Violetta dismisses his advice blithely.

"If you were mine, I would watch over you," says he.

"What do you mean? No one cares what happens to me," she assures him with a laugh.

"That's because no one in the world loves you—except me!" declares Alfredo passionately.

Though she tries to deny it, Violetta's heart is touched. "Have you been in love with me for long?" she cannot help asking.

"For a year," he replies. *"Un dì felice, eterea . . .* One day you passed by me, happy and light as air, and ever since, even without knowing it, I loved you with the love that is the very breath of the universe, mysterious

and noble, at once the torment and ecstasy of the heart."

For a moment, Violetta stares at him. "If this is true," she begins haltingly, "then you must leave me, for I can offer you only friendship." But Alfredo presses on, and Violetta finds herself wavering, perhaps even falling—but no! "No more love, then!" she says with false brightness. "Do you accept the pact?"

Alfredo sadly acquiesces. "I shall leave."

But Violetta cannot bear for him to do so. She pulls a white camellia from her hair, saying, "Come back when this has withered."

Joyously, Alfredo takes the flower. "Tomorrow!" Hastily gathering his things, as if he could hurry the next day into existence, Alfredo leaves in a haze of love. The other guests, too, return to make their good-byes, for the dawn is breaking.

Left alone, Violetta muses on the possibility of love, *"È strano! È strano! . . .* How strange! His words are burned upon my heart! No man has ever made me feel this love!" Rapidly, she paces back and forth. *"Ah fors'è lui . . .* Perhaps he is the one . . . he came while I lay sick, awakening a new fever—of love. Love that is the very breath of the universe, mysterious and noble, at once the torment and ecstasy of the heart." Starting suddenly, as though she had touched a flame, Violetta presses her hands over her eyes. "Folly! Folly! This is madness! Delirium! A poor woman alone in this desert people call Paris! What can I hope for? What should I do? Enjoy myself! *Sempre libera . . .* Forever free, I will rush from pleasure to pleasure unceasingly!"

But breaking into her declaration comes Alfredo's voice beneath her window. *"Amore, amor è palpito . . .* Love is the very breath of the universe, both mysterious and noble, the torment and ecstasy of the heart."

Stubbornly resisting, Violetta reaffirms her dedication to freedom at all costs, resolving to pursue only pleasure. But as his tantalizing words wind their way into her heart, her resolve begins to crumble.

# ACT TWO

Nearly a month later, Alfredo and Violetta are settled in a comfortable country house an hour or two away from Paris geographically and a million miles away in spirit. Removed from the social whirlwind, the two live only for each other. But living on love alone is notoriously nonremunerative, and Violetta is secretly making plans to raise money by selling off her possessions. As the sun floods in the windows, Alfredo, unaware of her scheme, wanders about the drawing room reflecting smugly on his new life. He is like a man reborn, he declares, the violence of his spirits tempered by the tenderness of her love. His reverie is interrupted by Annina, Violetta's maid, whose traveling attire catches his eye. Violetta's plans come to light and Alfredo, ashamed of his obliviousness, resolves to raise the necessary money himself. Swearing Annina to silence, he leaves at once for Paris.

Soon after his departure, Violetta enters. On learning that Alfredo has gone to Paris, she turns her attention to the papers she carries. One is an invitation from Flora to an elegant supper party of the very sort that

Violetta used to frequent and she tosses it aside, relieved to be free of such frivolities.

When her servant announces a gentleman, Violetta presumes that her visitor has come on business, but the man who enters—stern in dress and expression—introduces himself as Alfredo's father. "I am father of this reckless lad, who is rushing to his ruin because of you!" Giorgio Germont says bitterly.

Flushing, Violetta rises from her chair. "Sir, I am a woman and in my own home. Now please excuse me," she says.

Germont, who cannot help admiring her spirit, reaches out to stop her departure. He tells her that his son is on the verge of making over all his property to her.

Violetta dismisses this rumor with such authority that Germont cannot doubt her. And yet he knows that the luxury he sees around him must come from somewhere. Violetta, eager to win his approval, shows him the documents that reveal her plan to sell all she owns.

Germont is astonished at her selflessness. This is not what he expected. Understanding now that he is dealing with a woman of noble sentiments if not noble birth, Germont broaches the purpose of his visit: "I have come to ask a sacrifice—"

A shadow of dread crosses Violetta's face. "Oh no, do not say it! I knew it—I expected you—I was too happy," she stammers.

Gently, Germont tells her that he is the father of a daughter as well as Alfredo, *"pura siccome un angelo . . . as pure as an angel,"* whose engagement and future are compromised by Alfredo's liaison with Violetta.

Violetta is silent for a moment. "I understand," she says finally. "I must leave Alfredo for a time. It will be painful for me, yet—"

"That is not what I ask," interrupts Germont.

Violetta recoils. Her lips can hardly form the words. "You want me to give him up forever?" she whispers.

"You must!" insists Germont.

"No!" cries Violetta in despair. "Never! No!" She pleads with him: Can't he see how much she loves Alfredo, she who has no one and nothing else? Doesn't he know that she is dying, that she has only a short time to live? How can he be so cruel?

Sympathetic though he is, Germont discounts her illness as imaginary and patiently repeats his request, assuring her that such a young and beautiful woman will find another love. Violetta vows that she could never love anyone else.

Inexorably, Germont begins to assault her newfound trust in love. Men are often fickle, he points out. Once the first flush of love is over, and their relationship begins to grow tedious, she will have no marriage vow to depend on.

"It's true!" Violetta groans.

So, Germont urges, she must cease living this delusion, and become the angel of his family by abandoning her claims on his impressionable son.

*Maria Callas's phenomenal acting ability was at least as important as her voice in securing her place as the foremost soprano of her time, and nowhere was this ability put to better use than in her interpretation of Violetta. For the Callas aficionado, each performance of* La Traviata *was an epic in itself, to be savored, analyzed, and compared to previous appearances. Each exegete had his favored performance, the lustrous details of which were recounted time and again. One such aficionado was Harold Rosenthal, who in his memoirs recalled Callas's five Violettas in the Covent Garden season of 1958 with lapidary precision: "The way Callas found the right 'tone color' for certain phrases marked her as someone unique in our day. Single words and phrases would take on a new meaning—the emphasis she put on the word* due *in the phrase 'Di due figli?' when Alfredo's father, Giorgio Germont, tells her that Alfredo is not his only child; or 'È vero, è vero,' uttered in a resigned tone when Germont pointed out that one day she would grow old and that Alfredo would tire of her, will, I know, never be equalled. Nor the way she started 'Dite alla giovine' when the phrase sounded as if it was suspended in mid-air.*

*"Callas's last act was superb. One suffered with the dying Violetta as she dragged herself from bed to dressing-table, from dressing-table to chair; 'O come son mutata,' she gasped, as she looked at her wan reflection in the mirror. When her faithful maid, Annina, told her that Alfredo had arrived, she hurriedly tried to tidy her hair and look her best; then came the reunion of the two lovers, with Violetta's hands (and how Callas made use of her beautiful long fingers throughout her performance) clasping at the longed-for happiness and hardly believing that Alfredo was really a flesh-and-blood figure. 'Ah! Gran Dio! Morir sì giovane' (Oh God, I am too young to die) was sung with terrific intensity—and at the final performance, Callas took the whole phrase in one breath. As the drama moved to its close and Violetta gently gave Alfred her locket, it was impossible to keep back my tears. The death scene was almost horrific, the last 'È strano!' was uttered in an unearthly voice, and as Violetta rose from her chair to greet what she thought was a new life, a glaze came over her eyes and she literally became a standing corpse."*

Wretchedly, Violetta acquiesces. But, she begs, *"Dite alla giovane sì bella e pura . . . Tell your daughter, so lovely and pure, that a miserable woman, who has but one precious thing in life, will sacrifice it for her—and then die!"*

Benevolent in his victory, Germont reaches out to comfort her, assuring her that he understands the enormity of his request. Knowing he does not, Violetta makes one last entreaty: "Let him know the sacrifice that I made for love, for my life's last breath will be for him alone."

Knowing that a delay will only destroy her resolve, Violetta hastily scribbles a note to Flora and instructs Germont to wait in the garden for his son's return. Germont takes his leave and Violetta begins the torturous task of writing Alfredo a letter that will turn his love to hate. Weeping as she writes, she completes her letter, just as Alfredo returns. Dismayed to find his beloved in tears, he begs her to tell him her trouble, but

Violetta hides her letter and dries her eyes. "See? I am smiling—see?" She babbles frantically, "I shall always be here, near you, among the flowers. Love me, Alfredo, love me as much as I love you!" Overcome, she hurries away to begin the journey that will break her heart.

Alfredo, oblivious, reflects happily on her devotion and wonders when his father will arrive for his much-dreaded visit. His paradise is short-lived, however, for a messenger arrives with a letter from Violetta, who is reported to be on her way to Paris. Alfredo assures himself that business matters provide a reasonable explanation for this sudden flight, but nonetheless, the sight of the envelope fills him with dread. Trembling, he rips it open and reads Violetta's farewell. With a cry, he turns, sees his father, and throws himself into his arms.

Seeking to relieve his son's suffering, Germont gently reminds him of his home. *"Di Provenza il mar, il suol* . . . The sea and hills of Provence, have they been erased from your heart? Remember what joy warmed you there."

But Alfredo is in no mood to be consoled by cozy visions. Catching sight of Flora's invitation on the table, he instantly deduces that Violetta has been seduced by the promise of dissipation and pleasure; boiling with rage, he resolves to exact his revenge. He rushes from the room, and his father anxiously follows.

Violetta *was* headed to Flora's party. Against the background of a magnificently decorated salon, Flora, the Marchese, and Dr. Grenville, their old friend, are gossiping about the prodigal's return. Their tête-à-tête is interrupted by an exuberant band of gypsies—really demimondaines in disguise—who dance for the assembled crowd and tell a few pointed fortunes. Then come a swarm of matadors—the gentlemen this time, with Gaston in the lead—who sing lustily of Spain. As their song comes to a riotous end, the company prepares for the next entertainment: gambling. Into these revels, Alfredo enters, looking haggard, though he tries to affect a casual air.

His assumed nonchalance is tested when Violetta appears on the arm of the saturnine Baron Douphol. Equally shaken is Violetta. As she seeks to calm herself, Alfredo, pointedly ignoring her, begins to gamble—and win. Soon a cluster of onlookers has gathered to watch his progress. "Those who are unlucky in love are lucky in cards," explains Alfredo bitterly.

A tense exchange of words with the Baron brings Alfredo a new opponent. His winning streak continues, much to the Baron's displeasure, and the increasingly charged contest is brought to a halt only by the announcement of supper. The guests swarm into the dining chamber, leaving Violetta lingering behind, for she has secretly asked Alfredo for a word.

In an instant, he is at the door, glowering at her. "Please leave," she falters, "you are in danger."

"So you think I am a coward?" he returns.

She protests that it is the Baron she is afraid of, but Alfredo rebuffs her warning. Suddenly seizing her hands, he begs her to run away with him.

"No, never," replies Violetta, trembling.

Alfredo, beside himself with jealousy, cannot see her despair. He asks her roughly if she loves the Baron, and, forcing the words, Violetta replies, "I love him, yes."

In a fury, Alfredo rushes to the door and calls the guests back into the salon.

"Do you know this woman?" says Alfredo, pointing coldly at the weeping Violetta.

"Who? Violetta?" reply the bewildered guests, crowding into the chamber.

"This woman was about to lose all she owns for love of me, and I, blind and vile, accepted it. But now it's time to clear my name, and I have called you here as witnesses that I have paid her everything I owe!" In a brutal gesture of contempt, he throws his winnings at Violetta, but she has fainted in Flora's arms.

The guests draw back in revulsion at Alfredo's cruelty, revealing Germont, who has heard the end of his son's speech and now denounces him, even as he begins to regret the part he has played in the whole affair. The sight of Violetta's limp body returns Alfredo to his senses, and a wave of remorse washes over him, just as the Baron challenges him to a duel. Reviving, Violetta tells Alfredo that he will never know how much she has suffered for him, and, supported by Flora and Dr. Grenville, she leaves the room.

# ACT THREE

Only a few months have passed since Flora's party, but they have wrought a ghastly change in Violetta. Her world has contracted to the sparsely furnished bedroom where she is living out her final illness. There, in the dim light that gleams through the shutters, she lies asleep in a small bed, her thin hands resting atop a worn

blanket. Annina dozes in a chair, and a fire burns low in the grate.

The quiet is broken by the arrival of Dr. Grenville. With much effort, Violetta walks slowly to a sofa to greet him and responds cheerfully to his searching questions. She has slept well; she has seen a priest. Assuring her that she will be better in no time, Dr. Grenville gathers his hat and gloves. Stopping at the door, he speaks in a low voice to Annina: "She has only a few hours to live."

Unaware of her death sentence, Violetta listens dreamily to the sounds of jollity in the street. It is carnival, and all of Paris is going mad. Violetta sends Annina to distribute the last of her money to the poor; left alone, she pulls a well-worn letter from her dressing gown. It is from Giorgio Germont and it tells her the events that followed Flora's party: The duel between Alfredo and the Baron left the Baron wounded, though not mortally, and forced Alfredo to flee the country to avoid arrest. Regretting his part in Violetta's misfortune, Germont revealed her sacrifice to his son, and, he concludes, both of them will return as soon as possible to beg her pardon. "It is late," says Violetta with a sigh.

"I wait, and they never come." She looks at herself in a mirror, and sighs again. "How I have changed! *Addio, del passato bei sogni ridenti . . .* Farewell to the happy dreams of the past."

In the street, the merrymakers break into riotous Bacchanalian chant, and Violetta smiles. Suddenly, Annina returns, in obvious haste. Begging her mistress not to become overexcited, she hints at a joyful surprise.

"A surprise?" repeats Violetta, lifting her head eagerly from her pillow. "Alfredo!"

*Adelina Patti, who generally did not choose to act her parts at all, was not known for her* Traviata, *nor, indeed, for any particular role. She was instead seen as a great natural phenomenon, the possessor of so magnificent a voice that she blessed whatever song she sang. However, it was in the role of Violetta that Madame Patti's pragmatic nature was most famously displayed. She was touring in the United States with the British impresario and producer Colonel James Mapleson, who found himself running short of funds on the afternoon of Patti's scheduled appearance in* La Traviata. *Patti required the payment of her fee of 1,000 pounds sterling before she would condescend to go on stage, and Mapleson knew it. Scraping together £800, he begged her agent, Signor Franchi, to convince the soprano to extend his credit until after the evening's performance. According to Mapleson's memoirs, Signor Franchi reappeared two hours later in high spirits:*

" 'I cannot understand,' he said, 'how it is you get on so well with prima donnas, and especially with Mme Patti. You are a marvelous man and a fortunate one, too, I may add. Mme Patti does not wish to break her engagement with you, as she certainly would have done with anyone else under the circumstances. Give me the £800 and she will make every preparation for going on the stage. She . . . will be at the theatre in good time for the beginning of the opera, and she will be ready dressed in the costume of Violetta, with the exception only of the shoes. You can let her have the balance when the doors open and the money comes in from the outside public; and directly she receives it she will put her shoes on and at the proper moment make her appearance on the stage.'*

"After the opening of the doors I had another visit from Signor Franchi. By this time an extra sum of £160 had come in. I handed it to my benevolent friend and begged him to carry it without delay to the obliging prima donna, who, having received £960, might, I thought, be induced to complete her toilette pending the arrival of the £40 balance.

"Nor was I altogether wrong in my hopeful anticipations. With a beaming face, Signor Franchi came back and communicated to me the joyful intelligence that Mme Patti had got one shoe on. 'Send her the £40,' he added, 'and she will put on the other.'

"Ultimately the other shoe was got on; but not, of course, until the last £40 had been paid. Then Mme Patti, her face radiant with benignant smiles, went on to the stage; and the opera already begun was continued brilliantly until the end.

"Mme Adelina Patti is beyond doubt the most successful singer who ever lived. Vocalists as gifted, as accomplished as she might be named, but no one ever approached her in the art of obtaining from a manager the greatest possible sum he could by any possibility contrive to pay."

And there is Alfredo, at the door. He runs to her arms and they embrace rapturously, begging each other's forgiveness and swearing eternal love.

"We will leave Paris, dearest, and live our lives together," exclaims Alfredo. "We will make up for all our sorrow, and your health will return. You will be the light of my life, and the future will smile upon us!"

Violetta echoes his words dreamily. But she is not languid for long; suddenly she is taken with the idea that they must go to church and thank God for their reunion. Struggling to rise, she sways and falls into a chair, nearly fainting. Shocked, Alfredo lifts her up, realizing for the first time the extent of her illness. Violetta insists, calling Annina to bring her a dress. But try though she will, she is too weak to put it on, and she drops back, crying, "Dear God! I cannot!"

Appalled, Alfredo orders Annina to call the doctor immediately. "Yes," says Violetta from her sofa, "tell him that Alfredo has come back to his love. Tell him that I want to live again. But," she says confidingly to her beloved, "if in returning you have not saved my life, then nothing on earth can save me." All too soon, her joy is broken by a spasm of pain, and, with a gesture of despair, she gives up the pretense, crying, "Ah, dear God! To die so young, when I have suffered so long! It was but a dream."

Frantically, Alfredo seeks to restore her hope, but at last he breaks off, admitting defeat with a groan.

"What a cruel end for our love," mourns Violetta.

Now Giorgio Germont appears in the doorway. Like his son, he enters full of plans, prepared to welcome Violetta into his family as his son's wife.

"Alas, you have come too late," Violetta says simply, and Germont, looking now at the pale wreck that is Violetta, finally believes that she is dying. Overcome with remorse, the old man begs her forgiveness.

With her last vestiges of energy, Violetta wrenches open a secret drawer of her dressing table and removes a locket bearing a portrait of her in better times. She begs Alfredo to keep it; and, she continues, if he should fall in love with some young girl, he should give the portrait to her, telling her it is a gift from one who prays for her and her beloved Alfredo. Holding the locket in hands that seem too weak to support it, she gives her last gift to her beloved, and drops back, her eyes retreating to their own visions.

Terrified, Alfredo entreats her not to die, and Germont despairs at the thought of his part in her decline. Lost in the labyrinthine passages that precede death, Violetta seems to hear nothing, but suddenly, startlingly, there is a change. A new light fills her eyes and Violetta lifts her head, looking about the room in wonder. "How strange! The pain has ceased! A new strength is bringing me back to life! Oh!" she exclaims, "I shall live! Oh, the joy——" But this rebirth is only the beginning of her death, and a moment later she falls back, dead. ⁓⧉

# AIDA

~⧼⧽~

$A$ida was Verdi's most spectacular foray into Grand Opera, and also his last. This Egyptian epic features the Pharoah's palace at Memphis, an imposing Temple of Vulcan, a triumphal arch in Thebes, the Nile, and a subterranean tomb, not to mention dancing slaves, chanting priests and priestesses, cheering Egyptian soldiers, downcast Ethiopian captives, and assorted royal functionaries. Sometimes, depending on a theater's resources, elephants thunder across the stage. The musical requirements are likewise monumental: For the Italian premiere, Verdi requested a chorus of one hundred, a twenty-six-piece stage band, and a string section composed of twenty-eight violins, twelve violas, twelve cellos, and twelve double basses, among other elements. With *Aida,* Verdi became nearly Wagnerian in his attentiveness to every facet of the production. From the ornamentation on Amneris's mourning dress to the coaching of the singers, Verdi did not rest in his pursuit of a perfect opera.

There is a long-standing tradition that *Aida* was commissioned by the Khedive, Egypt's Viceroy, for the opening festivities of the Suez Canal, but this is mere myth. *Aida* was born, instead, in the researches of Auguste Mariette, a serendipitously successful nineteenth-century archeologist who happened upon the Temple of Serapis and consequently became the foremost Egyptologist of his day. The Khedive promptly hired Mariette to oversee all of the country's excavations, but, much to Mariette's dismay, the position turned out to be significantly less ornamental and more arduous than he had anticipated. The story of *Aida,* which Mariette said he had based upon a real incident that took place "in the time of the Pharoahs," was to be his ticket home to Paris. He submitted a sketch of the plot to his friend, Camille du Locle, who was the director of the Opéra-Comique, and, incidentally, a close friend of Verdi's. "Now, if . . . you agree to do the libretto," Mariette wrote to du Locle, ". . . you must write to me that the subject chosen is so . . . Egyptological that you can't write [it] without a full-time policeman at your side; and besides, that my presence in Paris is absolutely necessary . . . If I could get to Paris this summer, my goal will have been attained." Mariette got his

wish with a vengeance: Verdi agreed to write *Aida,* and the Khedive agreed to bankroll the whole production for the opening of his new opera house in Cairo. Accordingly, Mariette was sent off to France in the summer of 1870 to review the costumes and sets, but instead of the respite he had hoped for, the unfortunate fellow ran smack into the Franco-Prussian War and, during the long, cold, rat-eating winter of the siege of Paris, he, the costumes, and the sets remained trapped in the capital, a turn of events that delayed the Cairo premiere for nearly a year. Despite this setback, the momentous first performance in 1871 was greeted with wild enthusiasm, as were the successive stagings in Italy.

# ACT ONE

The Pharoah's palace at Memphis glows with color: Lapis lazuli and gleaming gold burnish the massive colonnade, the walls are festooned with intricate murals, and exotic flowers curl through the open-air hall. In the distance, silent and strange, the golden pyramids can be glimpsed.

Amid this splendor, the young general Radames is deep in conversation with the venerable High Priest Ramfis. Egypt has been invaded by its age-old enemy, Ethiopia, and the city of Thebes is in imminent danger. Ramfis confides that Isis is even now being consulted about the best choice for a commander to lead the army against the invading forces. He hints that Radames himself will be the choice. After the High Priest departs, Radames is lost in thought. To be the leader of the army is his secret wish, for he knows that military victories are the only path to the prize he truly longs for, the hand of Aida. *"Celeste Aida . . .* Heavenly Aida, mystic garland of light and flowers, you are the queen of my thoughts."

Radames will need the aid of the gods, for his beloved is a slave, and an Ethiopian slave at that. Aida was captured by Egyptian soldiers, and her beauty and grace won her a position as handmaiden to Amneris, the only daughter of the Pharoah. And though she returns Radames's love, Aida has not revealed even to him the secret of her identity: She is the daughter of Ethiopia's king, Amonasro. Neither Radames nor Aida yet suspects that the greatest danger to their future lies in the beautiful, imperious Princess Amneris, who cherishes a great secret herself: She is madly, wretchedly in love with Radames. Now, moving swiftly along the colonnade, Amneris comes upon the solitary young general. Her darting eyes note his abstraction; why, she wonders, is he so impervious to her charms? A sudden thought sends the hot blood of anger to her face: Could it be, she thinks incredulously, that he loves another woman?

Disguising her fears, Amneris extracts from Radames the cause of his preoccupation. He was dreaming of leading the Egyptian legions, he confesses; but this is not enough for Amneris. Perhaps, she suggests, he was dreaming of something, or someone, sweeter, here in Memphis? Radames, aghast, strives to conceal his feelings, but his efforts are vain, for just then, Aida enters the hall, and delight can be read in his face as he greets her. Amneris's suspicion crystallizes into bitter hatred as she turns to see the answering rapture on her servant's face. But Aida's cheeks are wet with tears, and, counterfeiting affection, Amneris draws her near and begs to know the reason for her sorrow. Aida answers that she is weeping at the news of warfare between her native country and Egypt, but Amneris is not deceived. "Tremble, slave," she mutters to herself, "for the truth is clear to me when I see your tears and blushes."

Reading the poison in the Princess's eyes, Radames grows fearful for his beloved and his future, but these worries are interrupted by the entrance of the Pharaoh and his retinue, as well as the stately Ramfis in his sacred vestments. Their procession ends with the Pharaoh seated in his throne, preparing to receive a messenger from Thebes. The report is gloomy: The Ethiopians, led by the warrior king Amonasro, are marching now upon the city. Aida's gasps are drowned in general cries for revenge, but the Pharaoh holds up a silencing hand. Holy Isis has chosen Radames to lead the Egyptian forces. The crowd cheers their new general, and Radames, exhilarated, offers thanks to the gods, while Aida turns aside, stricken with fear.

With stately dignity, the Pharaoh directs Radames to the Temple of Vulcan, where he will be anointed for his great task. Then, turning to his soldiers, he calls on them to save their country. *"Su! del Nilo al sacro lido* . . . Onward! Go forth, Egyptian heroes, to the sacred banks of the Nile. From every heart let the cry sound out—War and death, death to the invader!"

Taking up the cry, ministers, captains, guards, and soldiers vow to rout the enemy. The frenzied cries soon dissolve into a single word: "War!"

Radames, fired with passion, leads his soldiers off to prepare for battle, and as he goes, Amneris steps forward, calling, *"Ritorna vincitor!* Return victorious!"

"Return victorious!" roars the crowd.

Soon, the throngs have departed, and Aida stands alone against the massive colonnade. "Return victorious," she repeats, shuddering. "My lips have spoken the traitorous words! Victorious over my father, victorious over my brothers. All so that I may see Radames, stained with the beloved blood, welcomed in triumph back to Egypt! O gods," she cries in agony, lifting her arms to the skies, "destroy the legions of the oppressors! Oh, but my love! Can I forget this love that burns inside, that I welcomed like a ray of sun?" Falling to her knees, Aida whispers a hopeless prayer, "O gods, have pity on my suffering!"

That night, in the cavernous Temple of Vulcan, Radames is consecrated to his task. Bathed in a mystical blue light, a multitude of priests and priestesses perform their ancient rituals before the colossal altar of Vulcan. Half-obscured by the curling smoke of incense, Ramfis stands upon a dais, invoking the great god Phtha, and Radames is led into the temple, his face solemn, while the priestesses perform the sacred dance honoring the god of war. As the priests place a veil of silver over Radames's head and a sword in his hand, the mournful chanting of the priests and priestesses fills the looming shadows.

# ACT TWO

Word has come to Memphis that Radames and the Egyptian forces have triumphed. In her luxurious apartments, Amneris is being dressed and beautified for the great victory celebration. As her handmaidens cluster about her with perfumes and unguents, her exuberant Moorish slaves break into a beguiling dance.

Neither the ministrations nor the entertainment can relieve Amneris's dark jealousies, and when Aida appears, she summarily dismisses the other slaves, ostensibly to soothe her favorite handmaiden, who must be distraught about the defeat of her people. Her true motive is to learn the state of Aida's heart. To Amneris's solicitous inquiries, Aida protests that she is tormented by anxiety about her family, but Amneris is not so easily dissuaded. "Among those brave men who conquered your homeland, was there perhaps one you loved?" she asks slyly. Aida's stammering response inspires Amneris to new cruelty. With a sugary smile she says, "After all, not all our soldiers died on the battlefield as our fearless leader did."

Aida's howl of anguish is all the evidence Amneris needs. Grasping the sobbing girl by the shoulders, Amneris gives her a violent shake and tells her the truth: Radames is alive.

"Alive? Praised be the gods!" gasps Aida.

"Yes, you love him!" hisses Amneris. "But I love him too. I am your rival, I, the daughter of the Pharaohs!"

Drawing herself up, Aida is on the verge of answering with the hauteur befitting an Ethiopian princess. Just in time, she remembers that revealing her identity will mean her death. Hastily she abases herself, begging her mistress to remember that while she, Amneris, is all-powerful, her handmaiden has nothing to sustain her but her love.

"Fear me, you slave!" spits Amneris. "Let your heart break; this love may mean your death. My heart rages with hate and vengeance!" She stalks away from the terrified Aida as the returning soldiers begin to march through the city gates, their voices raised in triumph.

Just within the monumental gate of Thebes, the Temple of Ammon stands, glowing golden in the brilliant sun. In the distance, the avenue of the sphinxes can be glimpsed. A great throne has been set down before the temple, and there the Pharaoh sits, surrounded by his retinue, awaiting the arrival of his troops. Next to him sits Amneris, arrayed in a headpiece of gold and turquoise. Flags flutter from every tower and rampart, and, as the crowd of onlookers swells, the air crackles with excitement. Priestly prayers are nearly drowned in a fusillade of trumpet calls. Then come chariots, foot soldiers with their lances, and troops bearing sacred vessels and statues. A graceful band of dancers displays treasures captured from Ethiopia. At the end of this great parade, Radames arrives, borne on a litter carried by twelve captains; the sight of their conquering hero drives the crowd wild with delight, and even the Pharaoh rises to greet his general.

After inviting Radames to accept a triumphal wreath from Amneris, the Pharaoh promises to grant him whatever he desires. Radames hesitates. "Before I reply, let the prisoners be brought before you."

A band of weary-looking captives, bound with chains, is led before the Pharaoh. One man's majestic bearing catches Aida's eye. It is none other than Amonasro, though he is dressed as an officer rather than a king. "My father!" she cries, running toward him.

"Her father!" echo the courtiers incredulously.

Embracing his daughter, Amonasro whispers, "Do not betray me," for his captors do not know that he is the King of the Ethiopians.

The Pharoah, interested in this coincidence, calls Amonasro to him. "Who are you?" he asks.

With great dignity, Amonasro claims Aida as his daughter and recounts the story of his defeat and bondage. Turning to the Pharoah, he adds, "You, O King, look with mercy on these captives. Today we are laid low, but tomorrow, this could be your fate."

Aida joins her father in pleading for the prisoners' lives, though Ramfis and the other priests urge the Pharaoh to put them all to death. Radames, observing Aida's impassioned pleas, becomes even more besotted, and Amneris, her glinting eyes fixed on his face, is quick to see his passion and curses Aida under her breath. But Radames is speaking. "O King," he says evenly. "You swore to grant me my wish. I ask you, then, to free these prisoners, for if Amonasro, their king, is dead, they can no longer hope to fight us."

Satisfied with this logic, the Pharaoh agrees to grant Radames's request, with one stipulation: Aida and her father must remain in Egypt as a pledge that their countrymen will not rise again. "Now," says the Pharaoh, "I give you an even greater pledge of peace. Radames, the fatherland owes everything to you. The hand of Amneris shall be your reward. One day, with her, you shall rule over Egypt."

Stricken, Radames attempts to look grateful, though inwardly he cries that the throne of Egypt is not worth Aida's heart. Amneris casts a triumphant glance at Aida, who struggles to maintain her composure. Meanwhile, the Pharaoh, the priests, and the populace rejoice in the happy union of hero and princess, while the newly freed prisoners exult in their liberty.

Aida prays only for oblivion, but her quiet anguish is interrupted by her father's hand on her arm. "Be brave," he says softly. "Wait patiently for happier days for our land. For us the day of revenge is already dawning."

# ACT THREE

It is the eve of Amneris's wedding to Radames. Near the lush palms and rocks of the Nile's banks stands the Temple of Isis, glowing white in the light of a full moon; there Amneris arrives to pray for the goddess's blessing on her marriage. Surrounded by women and guards, she is greeted by Ramfis, who will join her in prayer until the dawn breaks.

As Amneris disappears into the temple, Aida steals into a clearing near the river's edge. She is awaiting Radames, who has asked her for a last farewell. And then, she vows, she will cast herself into the Nile, for

One of the more celebrated performances of Aida took place when a company from Italy arrived in Rio de Janeiro in 1886. Neither the singers nor the orchestra were particularly notable; it was the conductor who made history. The company had been touring Brazil under the baton of a Rio native named Leopoldo Miguez. Relations between conductor and orchestra had been strained from the beginning: He considered them uncooperative and they considered him incompetent. Performing throughout the country to lukewarm reviews and gleeful gossip, the troupe struggled along until they came to Rio. Here, on the afternoon before the first performance, the conductor resigned. The impresario decided to soldier on, replacing the errant Miguez with the Italian second conductor.

However, the audience, furious that their native son had been so ill used, made such a racket that not a single note could be heard. The substitute retired from the podium to a chorus of jeers, spitting, and stamping. The impresario was on the verge of canceling the performance and the tour, when a few of the company made a suggestion. Why not send out the new cellist? He knew the whole score and had been coaching the singers. The desperate director grasped at this straw, and the nineteen-year-old cellist was commanded to march out before the roaring crowd and conduct Aida. So Arturo Toscanini strode to the podium, slammed the score shut, sat down upon it, and lifted his baton. The house fell silent, and the gentle opening notes of Aida, magnificently conducted, began to swell.

now that her love is thwarted and her dreams of returning to her homeland blighted, she hopes for nothing but death. As Aida muses on the beauties of Ethiopia, now lost to her forever, Amonasro appears. He comes to the point: He has seen that his daughter is wasting away with love for Radames, and he for her. But she has a powerful rival, the Princess of a hated race.

"And I am in her power," cries Aida indignantly. "I, the daughter of Amonasro!"

"In her power? No! If you wish, you can defeat your rival—and fatherland, throne, and love will all be yours." Amonasro paints a seductive picture of the blessings Aida might enjoy if Ethiopia could overthrow the Egyptian tyrants. Dilating on the depravity of their oppressors, Amonasro deliberately arouses Aida's indignation and patriotism. The Ethiopian troops, he confides, have armed themselves. All they lack, he says meaningly, is the knowledge of the enemy's whereabouts.

"Who could get such information?" asks Aida innocently.

"You could!" explodes her father. Radames loves her and would tell her anything.

Horrified, Aida swears she could never do such a thing.

Amonasro looks at her coldly. "Arise then, soldiers of Egypt! Sack and burn our cities! Spread terror, rape, and death!"

In vain, Aida begs him for forgiveness. He spurns her frantic entreaties contemptuously. "Because of you, our country dies," he intones remorselessly, pushing her away. "You are not my daughter. You are the slave of the Pharoahs!"

His hatred is more than Aida can bear, and filled with anguish, she accedes to his commands. He hides himself as Radames approaches, and the two despairing lovers rush to embrace and comfort each other on the impending marriage that will bring their secret romance to an end. Radames, ever hopeful, believes that he may be called to battle before the wedding can take place. Then, he says confidently, the Pharaoh will give him anything.

Aida is, reasonably enough, doubtful that this plan will succeed, and she tremulously suggests they flee. Radames is dumbfounded. Eagerly, Aida describes the sweet-smelling forests of her native land, where they will forget the world together. "You're asking me to abandon Egypt?" he repeats, aghast.

Remembering her duty, Aida feigns indignation. She accuses him of not loving her, astonishing the young man still further. He protests his undying love, and Aida goads him to prove himself by escaping with her to Ethiopia. Confused and infatuated, Radames surrenders to her will. They will flee to the perfumed land of love and flowers. "But now," says Aida cozily, "how can we avoid the Egyptian legions?"

This is certainly not a problem, Radames assures her. The troops will not be moving through the Napata Pass until tomorrow.

Amonasro leaps from the concealing palms with a cry of triumph. "My men will be there!"

Radames jumps to his feet. "Who has overheard us?"

"Aida's father, the King of the Ethiopians!" calls Amonasro proudly.

Aida clings to Radames. "Be calm!" she begs. "Trust in my love!"

Radames is not to be consoled. "I am dishonored! Dishonored!" he raves. "For you, I have betrayed my country!"

Amonasro himself is touched by the young man's wild grief. "You are not guilty. It was the will of fate. But come," he coaxes. "Come beyond the Nile, where my men are waiting."

The little group in the clearing is unconscious of the clouds of doom that have gathered around them. Amneris, Ramfis, and a band of guards have emerged from the temple; there they stand still, watching and listening.

The silence is sundered by Amneris's scream. "Traitor!" she cries, pointing at Radames.

Instantly, chaos reigns: Amonasro throws himself on Amneris with his dagger drawn, but Radames impetuously inserts himself between the weapon and its target, crying, "Stop, madman!" Seizing the older man by the arm, he pushes him toward Aida. "Run! Quickly!" he commands.

Amonasro takes his daughter by the arm and begins to flee, with the guards in hot pursuit. Radames looks after them longingly but makes no move to follow. Turning to Ramfis, he says with quiet resignation, "Priest, I am in your hands."

# ACT FOUR

In the farthest reaches of the Pharoah's palace lies the chamber of judgment. Dark and somber, the room is overshadowed by a vast portico. The walls, dimly seen in the gloom, are rich with images of the sphinx and the deities of justice. Before them paces Amneris, like a lion in a cage. She is torn, for Radames's fate is being decided within, and she alone might save him by testifying that he is innocent. Admitting that she loves him still, she commands the guards to bring him to her.

Radames enters, stiff and silent. "Defend yourself," she begs, "and I will ask the Pharoah to pardon you."

But Radames refuses bitterly: "The source of all my joy is gone. I wish only to die."

At the thought of his death, Amneris sheds the remnants of her pride, declaring that she loves him, that she would give up everything, anything, for him.

He answers coldly. "You took Aida from me. Perhaps, because of you, she is dead—and you offer me my life?"

"No, she is alive!" cries Amneris frantically. "Only her father died!" Radames looks up, interested for the first time. She feels the familiar stab of jealousy. "But if I save you, swear to me that you will never see her again!" she commands.

Radames's face once again grows cold. "I cannot." With increasing desperation, Amneris begs him to let her save him, but he refuses again and again. Finally, he departs, heavily guarded, for his cell, and Amneris collapses into a chair, reviling herself for her jealousy.

Ramfis and his priests call for Radames, who is led into the vault where his fate will be decided. His voice grave, Ramfis reads the three accusations against Radames, each time calling upon the prisoner to defend himself. But Radames remains silent. As Amneris, listening from without, weeps in despair, the priests pronounce him guilty of treason and subject to a traitor's death: entombment alive beneath the altar of Vulcan.

Radames is unmoved by his ghastly sentence, but, as the priests march solemnly from the chamber, they are assailed by the enraged princess. "You have committed a crime," she spits. "Infamous, bloodthirsty beasts—you outrage the gods and man!"

"He is a traitor. He shall die," they repeat impassively.

Now the moment of the interment has come. Above, the Temple of Vulcan is bathed in golden light, but below, the vault's colossal arches recede into the gloom and the air is dank and still. Radames sits on the steps that he has just descended, looking up at the last vanishing sliver of light as the priests carefully seal the crypt with a massive stone.

His impending death matters very little to him. His thoughts are with his lost love. "Aida—where are you? May you at least live happily, never knowing my fate." A whisper of air draws his attention to a dark corner. He looks again, and cries out. It is Aida, weak and faint, but living. Radames rushes to her side, begs her for a sign that she lives.

"In my heart," she begins, "I knew your fate. Secretly, I stole into this tomb, opened as it was to receive you. And here we shall die together."

"To die," says Radames wonderingly. "So pure, so lovely! To die, for love of me! Heaven created you for love, yet I, in loving you, have killed you!"

His remorse falls on deaf ears, for Aida is now in the delirium that precedes death, and, as the priests and priestesses above pray to Phtha, Aida sees the gates of heaven open to receive her. Distraught, Radames races up the stairs and attempts to remove the stone that imprisons them.

"It is useless," Aida says. "On earth, all is finished for us."

"It is true," he replies sorrowfully.

"*O terra, addio* . . . Farewell, O earth, farewell, vale of tears, dream of joy that vanished into sorrow, farewell." Wrapped in each other's arms, the lovers bid good-bye to life with peaceful resignation.

Above, Amneris, dressed in mourning, enters the temple to pray, and with the priestly voices soaring behind her, she prostrates herself upon the stone that seals the tomb, crying out in agony. ᴥ

# OTELLO

~⊙⊙~

The prevailing wisdom among the cognoscenti is that Verdi saved his best for last. In fact, the only Verdians who don't consider *Falstaff* the composer's masterpiece are those who give the laurels to *Otello.* Certainly, the composition of *Otello* was a labor of love. In the fourteen-year silence that followed *Aida,* the Maestro resisted time and again the efforts of his friends, publisher, and public to entice him to further operatic composition. He was tired, he told them, and depressed. There were no good libretti. He didn't want to leave home. But there was one temptation that overcame these real and pretended objections: Shakespeare. Verdi had always revered the "great poet of the human heart," as he called him. Early in his career, his attempt to adapt *King Lear* to the operatic form had foundered, and although his *Macbeth* of 1847 had improved with the revisions he made eighteen years later, evidence suggests that Verdi was never satisfied with it.

It was at a carefully planned dinner party in 1879 that Guilio Ricordi, Verdi's publisher, began to lure the composer toward *Otello.* Ricordi later told his young protégé, Puccini, "I chanced to turn the conversation on Shakespeare and Boito. At the mention of *Othello* I saw Verdi look sharply at me, with suspicion but with interest. He had certainly understood. He had certainly reacted." Arrigo Boito was a composer, poet, and all-around cultural maverick; he was also, by far, the best librettist Verdi ever worked with. When the Maestro saw Boito's scenario for *Otello,* his resistance crumbled, and he began to make music once again. He clearly felt no need to hurry as he had earlier in his career. The composition took two years, partly the result of his fanatic attention to detail. But he also lingered because it was work he loved. When the opera was performed to wild acclaim, Verdi said to a visitor, "How painful to have finished it! I shall now suffer such loneliness. Till now I used to wake each morning and return to the love, anger, jealousy, deceit of my characters. And I would say to myself: I have this scene to compose. . . . And then, when the opera was finished, there were the rehearsals . . . and I was not conscious of fatigue and I did not feel my age. But since *Otello* now belongs to the public, it has ceased to be mine . . . I now feel an enormous void, which I think I shall never be able to fill."

# ACT ONE

*—— Note: Because singing takes more time than speaking, Boito was obliged to compress Shakespeare's* Othello *for its operatic incarnation. His most notable elision was the removal of the entire first act of the play, and with it, Venice and Brabantio. The opera, therefore, opens as Othello regains Cyprus from the Turks. ——*

Upon the ramparts that surround the governor's castle, hundreds of anxious eyes are fixed on Othello's ship as it tosses in the roiling sea amid a great battle. A raging thunderstorm attacks the warring ships, and the citizens of Cypress watch in the split-second revelations that come with each flash of lightning. There are moans as Othello's vessel is engulfed in waves, cheers as she is spotted again, rising from the deep. A mighty, gusting roar breaks the mainsail and sends the ship careening to the rocks. While the Cypriots around him lament, a small man, narrow and pale, says in a cool undertone to his friend Roderigo, "May the belly of the sea be her tomb." This is Iago, watching with a slight smile.

But he does not get his wish, for Othello's ship somehow manages to attain the shore, and a short time later, he bursts onto the ramparts with a retinue of soldiers and sailors. *"Esultate!* Rejoice! The Muslims' pride is buried in the sea," proclaims Othello proudly, "ours and heaven's is the glory!"

The Cypriots exult in their liberation from the Turkish oppressors. Jubilantly, they celebrate Othello's victory, even as the storm begins to fade.

Iago does not join in the general gaiety. Instead he chides Roderigo for his infatuation with Othello's new

bride, the lovely Desdemona. All he need do is wait, Iago sneers, for Desdemona will soon grow tired of Othello's kisses. Iago offers to devote himself to sundering the knot that binds them, for he has his own reasons to hate Othello: Cassio, a young captain, has been promoted by Othello while he, Iago, languishes as an ensign. But, reflects Iago dispassionately, "'Tis true that, were I the Moor, I would not wish to see an Iago about me."

Amid the clusters of joyful Cypriots and soldiers, Iago and Roderigo weave their way toward the table where Cassio is sitting with his friends. "Roderigo," exclaims Iago, "let's drink! A cup here, Captain." He offers a brimming glass to Cassio.

"I drink no more," replies Cassio. But it does not suit Iago's purposes for Cassio to refuse. Repeatedly, he presses wine on the captain, but it is only when he proposes a toast to the brand-new marriage of Othello and Desdemona that Cassio agrees to join in, for his admiration of Desdemona knows no bounds. Drinking, Cassio sings her praises, arousing the jealousy of the thick-headed Roderigo.

Iago whispers to Roderigo that he has a rival in his seduction of Desdemona. Better get him drunk, advises Iago, filling glasses all around. His face cracks into a convivial grin. "Drink hard, drink deep!" he commands. "Beva, beva, beva . . . Drink, drink, drink with me!"

Cassio, already tipsy, quaffs wine with abandon and joins Iago in his song, though he gets the words a bit confused, and the onlookers begin to chuckle.

Meanwhile, Iago is doing his best to spur Roderigo on. "Force a quarrel upon him," he whispers. "A brawl will ensue. Think—you will be able thus to trouble the happy Othello's first night of love."

The festival of drinking is interrupted by Montano, erstwhile governor of Cyprus, who has come to call Cassio to oversee the changing of the guard. The young captain agreeably begins to stagger off to the ramparts, a spectacle that sends Roderigo and his friends into gales of laughter. Now Cassio is drunk enough to be mortally offended by such laughter, and he hurls himself upon Roderigo. Montano dutifully comes between the two combatants, but all he receives for his pains are insults from Cassio. The exasperated Montano dismisses the invective as a drunkard's babbling, which enrages Cassio further. Drawing his sword, he leaps on Montano and a vigorous fight commences.

Iago has been watching with sparkling eyes. Now he turns to Roderigo, ordering him to alert the castle, to spread alarm throughout the city. As bystanders run shrieking, Iago pleads with the combatants to stop fighting, making sure to stay well out of their way. Now Cassio has succeeded in wounding his foe, but still he rampages on. Screams of terror and calls to arms resound against the castle walls. All is chaos and frenzy.

"Put down your swords!" roars Othello, striding swiftly to the center of the terrace. A sudden silence descends. Cassio stands frozen. Demanding an explanation from his soldiers, Othello suddenly notices the wounded Montano and explodes in anger. The appearance of Desdemona, wakened by the melee, provides a further indictment of Cassio. "How now? My sweet Desdemona, too, roused from her slumbers? Cassio, you are captain no longer."

Stunned, Cassio lets his sword drop to the ground. Iago darts forward and picks it up, hiding his triumphant smile. Calmer now, the General directs Iago to restore the town to peace. One by one, soldiers and Cypriots depart, until Othello and Desdemona are left alone in the cool night. Smiling, they turn to each other, certain in their love. Wrapping herself in her husband's arms, Desdemona reminisces about their courtship, how she was wooed by Othello's stories of his exile, his griefs, his adventures, his triumphs.

"Your lovely face ennobled the story," replies Othello fondly, "and on my darkness glory descended."

"And from your dusky temples I saw the eternal beauty of your spirit shine," returns Desdemona, gazing up at her beloved.

"And you loved me for the dangers I had passed and I loved you that you did pity them," says Othello.

"And I loved you for the dangers you had passed and you loved me that I did pity them," she says softly.

"I am filled with such intense joy," Othello sighs, "consumed with such breathless longing. A kiss . . . a kiss . . . and yet another kiss. . . ."

Slowly, they walk back toward the castle, clasped in each other's arms.

# ACT TWO

On a terrace overlooking the castle gardens, Iago and Cassio are in conversation. Though Cassio despairs of regaining his post, Iago assures him that his rift with Othello will soon be healed if he enlists the aid of Desdemona, for she is "the leader of the Leader." Cassio, cheered by this plan, leaves at once to find his intercessor in the shade of a little grove, where she rests at noon with her lady-in-waiting, Emilia, who is Iago's wife.

Snickering, Iago looks after the departing Cassio. "Go, then. I see your end already." Pacing about the shady terrace, Iago dismisses Cassio, for his downfall is only incidental to Iago's plans. *"Credo in un Dio crudel* . . . I believe in a cruel God, who has created me in his image. I am evil because I feel within me the primeval slime. This is my creed, and I believe it with a firm heart. I believe man to be the sport of an unjust fate from the germ of the cradle to the worm of the grave. After all this mockery comes Death."

Iago takes up his post and watches as Cassio humbly approaches Desdemona in the garden. Sympathetically, she listens and soon they are deep in conversation, all under Iago's sharp gaze.

Moments later, an even greater piece of good fortune befalls Iago: Othello walks out onto the terrace. Seeing his ensign, he approaches him just in time to hear Iago murmur, "I like not that."

"What do you say?" asks Othello.

Iago starts. "Nothing, nothing. An idle word." But his anxious face belies his words.

Othello looks to the garden. "Was not that Cassio parting from my wife?"

"Cassio? No," says Iago with a great show of confusion. "That man shook like one guilty when he saw you coming."

And so, with a single sting, the poison enters Othello's blood. Smoothly, simply, in a guise of regret and compassion, Iago constructs Desdemona's hidden liaison with Cassio. In the course of a few moments, Othello's peace is destroyed, his vision clouded, his heart shattered.

With a secret smile Iago leans forward for one last bit of advice. "Beware, my lord, of jealousy. 'Tis a dark hydra, malignant and blind."

No, Othello agrees dully. Vain suspicion is useless. Proof is necessary before—

Of course, Iago agrees, and therefore his master must be on his guard, must watch Desdemona's every move, observe her every word.

His instructions are interrupted by the sounds of a song. The people of Cyprus have come to serenade Desdemona in her garden, and she greets them sweetly and tenderly. Looking down at her lovely face, Othello is almost convinced of her innocence. However, when the serenade is over, Desdemona comes into the castle to plead for Cassio's restoration. Her timing could not be worse, for her words seem to prove Othello's darkest fear. Angrily he rejects her petition; surprised at his unwonted harshness, she innocently inquires if he is in pain.

"My forehead is burning," replies Othello shortly.

Desdemona takes her handkerchief from her pocket. "The tiresome ache will pass if I bind your brow with this soft kerchief," she says sympathetically.

Furiously, Othello tears the cloth from her hands and throws it to the floor. "I have no need of that!" he cries.

Emilia stoops to retrieve her mistress's handkerchief while Desdemona gazes unhappily at Othello. "If, unwittingly, I have sinned against you, husband, grant me the sweet and happy word of pardon."

But Othello is lost in miserable speculation: How could he have been so foolish, so betrayed? "Perchance because I have declined into the vale of years, perchance because I have upon my face this dark hue, perchance because I do not understand the subtle deceits of love, she is lost and I am mocked and my heart is broken."

The premiere of Otello in 1887 was an international event on the scale of a world exposition. Critics and audiences gathered in Milan from all over Europe and the Americas for the occasion, and as the opening approached, ticket prices reached fantastic heights. On the great day, the streets around La Scala were impassable, and elegantly clad ladies and gentlemen had to abandon their carriages and wade through the crowds. Every seat was taken a full hour before the performance was scheduled to begin—an unheard-of break with Italian tradition.

Apparently, Otello met and surpassed every expectation. The audience went mad with delight; in the course of the first act, they twice tried to call Verdi to the stage to receive their ovations. When, at the first-act curtain, the composer was finally compelled to appear, one reporter recalled, "one immense simultaneous shout makes the theater rock. Verdi slightly bends his head and smiles, the frantic enthusiasm of the assembly bringing tears to his eyes." At the end of the last act, the fervor continued unabated; Verdi was called out on stage twenty times, and when he finally was allowed to leave the theater, his admirers unharnessed the horses from his carriage and pulled the Maestro themselves, accompanied by thunderous cheers. One British journalist reported: "At five in the morning I had not closed my eyes in sleep for the crowds still singing and shrieking 'Viva Verdi, viva Verdi!'"

All in all, the premiere was deeply gratifying for everyone, with the possible exception of Verdi himself, who returned to his farm at Sant' Agata with a sigh of relief after attending the requisite three performances.

Iago, meanwhile, is engaged in an oblique tussle with his wife over the handkerchief. He wants it; she, certain he is up to no good, refuses to relinquish it. But his threats frighten her and in a few moments, Iago is the triumphant possessor of Desdemona's handkerchief, which he plans to hide in Cassio's quarters.

After Othello brusquely orders his wife away and Iago has enjoined Emilia to silence concerning the handkerchief, the two men are alone. Iago watches with sly pleasure as Othello paces back and forth, groaning. The cancer is growing, and Othello cannot rid himself of the horrible vision Iago has painted for him. First he mourns his lost love, then he lashes out at Iago for his insinuations, then he believes Desdemona a whore, then he thinks she's true. Finally, he wants proof, and he wants it quickly.

Iago is all too eager to provide something very like it: He says that he has heard Cassio talk in his sleep of a secret, ecstatic love, invoking Desdemona's name. But that's not all, he assures Othello. Casually he asks if Desdemona has a silken handkerchief, very finely wrought?

"'Tis the handkerchief I gave her, my first pledge of love," Othello breathlessly replies.

"That handkerchief, I saw yesterday in Cassio's hand," Iago avows.

At this seemingly incontrovertible evidence, the Moor's torment turns to overpowering rage. "Ha!" he roars, "God grant him a thousand lives! One is a poor prey to my fury! Iago, I have a heart of ice. The hydra entwines me in its snaky coils. Oh, blood, blood, blood!"

Kneeling, he swears vengeance. Iago, thrilled by what he has wrought, promises to dedicate himself to the prosecution of Othello's bloody desires.

# ACT THREE

In the great hall of the castle, Iago explains the plan to Othello. He will bring Cassio nearby and provoke him to gossip. Othello will be able to overhear any revelations he lets slip. While Iago is off hunting down his quarry, Desdemona enters the hall in search of her husband.

Othello greets her gravely, and, in her uneasiness, she renews her petition for Cassio's restoration to favor. Othello ignores her words. Instead he complains of headache and asks her to bind his forehead.

Eagerly, Desdemona steps forward, but Othello stops her hands. "I want the handkerchief I gave you," he says.

Innocently, she says she does not have it with her, and the Moor flies into a rage. Frightened, she assures him that it's not lost, that she'll get it presently; and, hoping to distract him, she brings up Cassio yet again. Nothing could rouse Othello's ire more. "The handkerchief!" he bellows, seizing her roughly by the chin. "Look me in the face! Tell me what you are!"

"Othello's faithful wife," Desdemona replies, her mouth quivering.

"Swear it! Swear it and damn yourself! I believe you false!" cries Othello.

"God help me!" she cries, terrified. Again and again, she protests her innocence, swears that she is his alone, but her husband's fury only builds and he rages at her like a madman, accusing her of being a "vile courtesan."

Poor Desdemona cannot even bring herself to repeat the word. "I am not the thing that horrid word expresses," she says, looking earnestly into Othello's eyes.

Othello's wrath gives way to a frightening calm. Taking Desdemona by the hand, he leads her to the door with elaborate politeness. "Give me again your ivory hand. I would make amends. I had thought you that cunning whore who is Othello's wife." Abruptly, he pushes her out and returns alone to resume his pacing. "My God, you might have tried me with afflictions of poverty, of shame, made of my brave triumphal medals a heap of rubble and a lie, and I would have been resigned to the will of heaven. But, O grief, O anguish! Torn from me is the mirage wherein I quieted my soul. Quenched is that sun, that smile, those rays by which I live, that give me joy!"

Iago slips into the hallway and at the sight of him, Othello's thoughts turn to revenge. "She shall confess her sin and then die!" he declares.

Iago has brought Cassio as promised and Othello hastily hides himself. Taking care that Cassio is not too near Othello, Iago begins to banter with the young man about his paramour, Bianca. Vain Cassio is quite ready to ridicule the girl for her flirtatious ways, but Othello believes that it's his wife who's being mocked. Smoothly, Iago leads Cassio to confide that he seeks a purer love, that he has reason to believe that some fine lady admires him, for only yesterday he found a strange sign: a handkerchief, left in his lodgings by an unknown hand.

Almost too eagerly, Iago asks to see the cloth. Of course, it is Desdemona's exquisite handkerchief, and, distracting Cassio with questions about the state of his heart, Iago waves it behind his back for Othello to see.

"All is over," Othello tells himself desolately. "Love and pain. Nothing can touch my soul anymore."

As Cassio exclaims over the beauty of the needlework and Iago cautions him against falling into a trap, a cannon is heard, signaling the arrival of the ambassador from Venice, come to congratulate Othello for his victory over the Turks.

Cassio departs and Othello leaps from his hiding place. "How shall I murder her?" he begins, ignoring the calls to receive the ambassador.

A chorus of Cypriots is shouting for their liberator. "Long live the Lion of St. Mark!"

Iago pretends to consider. "'Twere best to strangle her in her bed, there, where she has sinned."

Othello nods, satisfied. "From this time, Iago, you are my captain."

"I thank you," says Iago. "Here are the ambassadors. Welcome them. But to avoid suspicion, Desdemona must show herself to these gentlemen." He is sent to retrieve her.

Soon, a vast retinue of dignitaries, soldiers, courtiers, and Cypriots has gathered in the great hall to witness the exchange of pleasantries between Lodovico, the Venetian ambassador, and Othello, the "Lion of St.

Mark." Amidst the pomp and pageantry, Desdemona struggles to conceal her sorrow and Othello his murderous anger. As the Moor reads a communication from the Doge, he is distracted, then provoked to fury by his wife's conversation with Lodovico about Cassio's troubles. Finally, his simmering fury explodes. "Devil, hold your tongue," he roars, thrusting her roughly away.

The assembly is shocked at this brutish treatment of the gentle Desdemona, but Othello continues his business unmoved. He announces that the Doge has recalled him to Venice and Cassio is to be his successor as governor of Cyprus.

Lodovico, horrified at Desdemona's plight, begs Othello to have pity on his wife. "We shall sail tomorrow," responds the Moor coldly. Then, pushing his wife to the floor, he sneers, "Down on your knees and weep!"

Desdemona can do nothing else. Bewildered, heartbroken, and tormented by her husband's unjust accusations, she weeps for her lost love, as her friends look on in consternation.

Iago, meanwhile, roused to new heights of malice by Cassio's promotion, promises Othello that he will take care of Desdemona's lover himself. Turning to Roderigo, who is mourning the imminent departure of his beloved, Iago whispers to the impressionable young man that if Cassio should be injured or killed, why then, Othello and the lovely Desdemona would be forced to stay in Cyprus. Without a moment's hesitation, Roderigo seizes on this scheme as the solution to his troubles and vows to kill Cassio that very night.

Displeased by the pleading and scheming that seethes around him, Othello harshly orders the people to disperse. Alarmed, they stammer and flutter about, irritating him until he can no longer contain his wrath and begins to fly at the crowd. As they scatter, Desdemona makes a last attempt to approach her husband and is met with a vicious curse. All beat a hasty retreat, except Iago.

He stands by quietly, watching his general lose his mind. Othello reels from subject to subject, word to word, drowning in a sea of passion. Wildly pacing, he spits and rages until his battered frame finally collapses and he falls to the floor, insensible. Far below, the sounds of the Cypriots' cheers can be heard: "Long live the Lion of St. Mark!"

Iago smiles, looking down at Othello's unconscious figure. "Who can prevent me from pressing this head beneath my heel?" he murmurs, placing a foot on Othello's neck. "Behold the Lion!"

"Long live Othello!" come the cries from the shore.

# ACT FOUR

In Desdemona's room, Emilia readies her mistress for bed, for Othello has bade her to await him there.

Desdemona sits before a mirror, unseeing. Idly, she recounts the sad tale of Barbara, the poor maid whose lover abandoned her. As Emilia brushes her hair, Desdemona sings the mournful "Willow Song," as the lonely Barbara did. A sudden noise distracts her, but it is only the wind knocking.

Her toilette completed, Desdemona embraces her faithful friend. "Emilia, farewell. Good night. Farewell," she calls after the departing figure. Then, kneeling before the image of the Madonna, she recites her prayers, her head resting on her hands. " . . . Pray for us always and in the hour of our death, pray for us, pray for us, pray," she repeats.

Desdemona rises and goes to bed. A long silence is broken by Othello's entrance. He comes in stealthily and blows out the light, leaving the room illuminated by a single candle. Drawing near the bed, he looks at the sleeping Desdemona, and something makes him lean down for a kiss. On the third kiss, she wakens.

Heavily, he asks her if she has prayed, and she realizes that her husband means to kill her.

"Think of your sins," Othello commands her.

"My sin is love," Desdemona replies.

"For that you die."

"Because I love you, you kill me?"

"You love Cassio," he says coldly.

Repeatedly, wretchedly, she denies the accusation, but Othello cannot hear her words. He is intent, fiercely intent, on her death and will not be turned from his purpose.

"Let me live—let me live a little longer—let me live," she begs.

But her pleas only fuel his ire. "Down, down with you, strumpet!" he orders.

"An hour," she asks.

"No!"

"A moment?"

"It is too late!" he roars, wrapping his massive hands around her neck. A moment later, she is limp and still.

Silence. "Quiet as the grave," mutters Othello to himself, but the peace is shattered by Emilia. Bursting into the room, she tells Othello that Cassio has killed Roderigo, but she is interrupted by a faint moan from Desdemona. Rushing to the bed, Emilia ascertains that her mistress is dying.

"Dear God!" exclaims Emilia. "Who has done this? Who?"

"No one," gasps Desdemona, protecting her beloved Othello with her last breath. "I myself . . . "

"Liar! I killed her!" says Othello, and, as if to justify the murder, "She was the mistress of Cassio. Ask Iago."

"Iago?" says Emilia incredulously. "You believed him?"

Othello lunges forward to strike the woman and she calls for help. Her cries are answered by Lodovico, Cassio, and Iago, who fall back in horror at the sight of Desdemona's corpse. And so it all comes out. Emilia bitterly reveals that Iago stole the fateful handkerchief. Cassio explains that he found it in his house. Montano, entering the chamber, discloses that the dying Roderigo has confessed that Iago was the mastermind behind a plot to murder Cassio.

With growing fear, Othello hears each revelation. In panic, he turns to Iago. "Refute these charges," he commands, pleadingly.

Just for a second, Iago smiles. "No!" he cries, dashing out of the room with guards in hot pursuit.

Betrayed, brokenhearted, tortured with remorse, Othello walks slowly to the bed that holds his beloved Desdemona, lost to him forever. Pulling a dagger from his doublet, he stabs himself mortally before the onlookers can stop him, and pulls himself next to Desdemona. "I kissed thee ere I killed thee. No way but this, killing myself, to die upon a kiss . . . another kiss . . . and yet another kiss." ❧

# FALSTAFF

❧⟨◊⟩❧

Two years after the triumph of *Otello,* seventy-five-year-old Giuseppe Verdi was again lured out of retirement by Arrigo Boito and Shakespeare. Typically, Verdi resisted the temptation for as long as he could: "When drafting *Falstaff,*" he wrote to Boito, "did you ever think of the enormous number of my years?" Boito replied with a mix of affection and intelligence: "Writing a comic opera, I believe, would not tire you. Tragedy makes the one who writes really suffer. . . . But the fun and laughter of comedy exhilarate body and soul. . . . There is only one way to end better than with *Otello,* and that is to end victoriously with *Falstaff.* Having made all the . . . lamentations of the human heart resound, to end with an immense outburst of cheer! That will astonish!"

And it does, of course. It is astonishing that the bubbling jollity of *Falstaff* comes from the same hand as the tragedies of *Traviata* and *Otello,* but equally astonishing to find that the opera is tighter and more developed than the work that preceded it. Musically, *Falstaff,* which premiered in 1893, is a galloping plunge forward. The second-act finale, for instance, in which the opera's nine voices join in an ensemble, is a giddy explosion of themes combined, sundered, transformed, and reborn with increasing complexity and dynamism as the scene reaches its climax. It is one testament among *Falstaff*'s many that Verdi's age brought a distillation rather than a diminution of his powers.

Boito's *Falstaff* retells the story of *The Merry Wives of Windsor,* with a few elisions as well as a few choice additions from both parts of *Henry IV.* His Sir John is an entirely ridiculous character, fully deserving of every ounce of punishment he receives, rather than the pathetic old Falstaff of *Henry V.* We may, therefore, laugh without guilt, and Sir John laughs with us, for, as he says, "Every mortal being laughs at every other, but the best laugh of all comes at the end."

# ACT ONE

Inside the Garter Inn, the redoubtable, corpulent, monstrous Sir John Falstaff is sealing two identical letters. He leans back in his chair with the satisfied sigh of one who deserves a long, presumably catered, rest, but his peace is shattered by the arrival of Dr. Caius, shrieking in fury. It seems that his servants have been beaten, his horse worn out, his house turned upside down—and it's all Falstaff's doing!

Falstaff regards Caius calmly. "Here's my answer: I did do all those things you said."

"And so?" says Caius triumphantly.

"I did them on purpose," replies Falstaff, sending Caius into a rage again. Enter Sir John's faithful henchmen, Pistol and Bardolph, who are even less scrupulous than their master. Caius accuses the pair of getting him drunk and picking his pocket, and they blandly agree that they did. Poor Caius is now just as infuriated by their equanimity as by the crime itself, and he showers them in wrath. Falstaff, however, has grown bored with his insults and sends him packing. He has more important matters on his mind; to wit, his empty purse. He is being ruined, he moans, by the appetites of his friends. "You are eating up my substance," he glowers at Pistol and Bardolph. "If Falstaff ever got thin, he wouldn't be himself, and nobody would love him. In this great abdomen are the thousand tongues that proclaim my name!" He pats his belly. "This is my kingdom, and I will make it greater."

He has been concocting a plan: The merchant Ford is possessed of a large fortune and a lovely wife who is in charge of the money box. The fair Alice—eyes like stars! neck like a swan! and lips! lips like a laughing flower!—is burning up with love for—guess who!—Falstaff.

Bardolph and Pistol are suitably impressed, but imagine their astonishment when Falstaff modestly reveals that the comely Meg Page, who also keeps the key to her husband's bulging money box, has displayed an unmistakable interest in his immense attractions. These two lovelies will restore his fallen fortune, crows Falstaff, and he has written them each a letter. Bardolph is to deliver one and Pistol the other.

Here, unexpectedly, Falstaff encounters a hitch. First Pistol and then Bardolph decline to participate, the former on the grounds that he is not a panderer and the latter on the grounds that his honor forbids it.

The mention of honor sends Falstaff into a fit. *"L'onore! Ladri!* . . . Honor! You thieves! Your honor! What honor! What humbug! What nonsense! Can honor fill your empty paunch? No. What is it, then? A word. What is there in this word? Poof. There's some air that floats away. What a fine invention! Flattery inflates it, pride corrupts it, and calumny sickens it. And I'll have none of it!" He snatches up a broom and begins to wallop his cringing companions. "Get out of here, you thieves! Get out!" Bardolph and Pistol scramble out the door and Falstaff follows, still bellowing.

A small convocation of women has gathered in Ford's garden: Meg Page and Mistress Quickly, Dr. Caius's servant and friend to all, have come bustling over with news for Alice Ford and her daughter, Nanetta.

But, says Alice, she was just coming out to share a laugh with *them*.

Tell us, tell us! they clamor. And, in a few short moments, Falstaff's ignominy is laid bare, for Meg and Alice compare their missives and find that Sir John has had the impudence not only to woo both of them but also to woo both of them in the same words. The insolence! The outrage! In no time, Meg and Alice decide that Falstaff must pay for this indignity.

"We must cheat him," says Alice decidedly.

"And make a show of him," adds Nanetta.

"And make a fool of him," Alice declares.

"What revenge!" nods Meg, and the four women move inside to refine their plans.

Meantime, Ford enters his garden, surrounded by a hubbub. Bardolph and Pistol have joined forces with the still-outraged Caius and are eagerly revealing Falstaff's plan to bed Ford's wife and steal his fortune. Young Fenton, interested in ingratiating himself with Nanetta's father, offers to skewer the fat knight. Protesting, expostulating, and decrying Falstaff's indecency, they urge Ford to take immediate action. Just then the four women return to the garden. Both parties lapse into guilty silence and hurry away, with the exception of Nanetta and Fenton, who delightedly seize the opportunity for a little flirting, an embrace, two—no, three—no, four—kisses. Their romance, with its obligatory blight of parental disapproval (Ford wants his daughter to marry Dr. Caius), is progressing by leaps and bounds when they are interrupted by the return of the Merry Wives and Quickly, who are putting the finishing touches on their vendetta. Mistress Quickly is to visit Sir John to offer him a rendezvous with Alice.

Giggling, Meg, Alice, and Quickly depart, but Nanetta lingers. Fenton emerges from his hiding place in the shrubbery, but before he achieves more than one kiss, the return of all the others necessitates a retreat. The men cluster around Ford, offering advice as he resolves to foil Sir John's invidious plans. The women cluster around Alice, offering advice as she plots to defeat the amorous knight. "We'll see that terrible belly puffed up with pride," Alice warns.

"Puffed up and then popped!" shriek Meg, Nanetta, and Quickly, doubled over in laughter.

# ACT TWO

Sir John Falstaff is sprawled in his chair at the Garter Inn, alternately guzzling sherry and dozing. His labors are disrupted, however, by Bardolph and Pistol, satisfyingly penitent. Falstaff welcomes them back with lordly generosity, and they announce the arrival of Mistress Quickly, who ever-so-coyly charges Sir John with being a great seducer.

"I know it," he replies grandly. "Continue."

Alice, she informs him, is in a terrible state of love for him. And her husband is always gone from two to three o'clock.

Falstaff accepts this assignation with maximum nonchalance. But, says Mistress Quickly, she has another message for him: Poor Meg brokenheartedly must inform him that her husband goes from home very seldom. "You bewitch them all," adds Quickly.

"There's no witchcraft in it; only a certain personal fascination that I have," Falstaff assures her. "But tell me, does the one know about the other?"

"Oh, no no no," Quickly replies, and, with much bowing and scraping, she departs.

Alone, Falstaff struts about the room. *"Va, vecchio John, va . . .* Go on, old John, go on your way. This old flesh of yours can still squeeze out a little sweetness for you!"

His panegyric is interrupted by Bardolph, come to announce an unexpected visitor, a Master Fontana who longs to make Falstaff's acquaintance. Fontana, who happens to be Master Ford in disguise, comes forward carrying a large bag of money, which, he intimates, he would be more than happy to give to Falstaff, in exchange for his assistance with a certain problem. Falstaff, eyeing the bag greedily, begs to know his desire.

It's a woman, a lady of Windsor, named Alice, the wife of a certain Ford, begins Fontana. This Alice, confesses Fontana, has spurned him. He loves her, but she doesn't love him. He searches for her and she eludes him. He has showered her with treasure, but in vain.

Falstaff sympathizes, but what, he asks, has this to do with him?

Fontana shoves the bag of money across the table. "I ask you to conquer Alice!" He explains that once Falstaff has triumphed over the fair Alice's virtue, she will succumb more easily to his, Fontana's, advances.

Preening, Falstaff assures Fontana that his longings soon will be satisfied. "I'm already pretty far advanced," he confides. "In a half an hour, she will be in my arms!"

The Ford underneath the Fontana nearly explodes with rage and dismay at this precipitous courting. After Falstaff sweeps away with the money bag, a disconsolate Ford bemoans his fate. *"È sogno? O realtà? . . .* Is it a dream or is it real? Two enormous horns are growing from my head . . ."

When Falstaff returns, decked out in his most alluring attire, the two pretenders take elaborate leave of each other, and Sir John makes his way to Ford's house for his assignation.

Inside this very house, Mistress Quickly is regaling her confederates with the tale of her meeting with Sir John. All are convulsed—except Nanetta, who bursts into incongruous sobs. Tearfully, she confesses that her father wants her to marry Dr. Caius, and she would rather be stoned to death.

A chorus of sympathy from Meg, Alice, and Quickly comforts the girl, and they return to their plans for Sir John: placing an ingenuous lute, setting up a strategic screen, and carefully arranging a giant basket of dirty laundry. Alice is to play the scheme's central role, of course, but the others will be on guard outside the door.

When Falstaff's monumental tread is heard, the four women fly to their posts. As he opens the door, he is greeted by the sight of doe-eyed Alice plucking a lute, the very picture of amorous possibility.

Sir John begins whispering winning words into the lady's pearly ear. Encouraged by her coy smiles, the knight soon attempts to pull her into the cushiony recesses of his embrace, but she resists. No matter, Falstaff has moved on to a subject that interests him more: himself. *"Quand'ero paggio . . .* When I was the Duke of Norfolk's page, I was slender, I was a vision, pretty, light, gentle, charming."

Firmly, Alice returns to the subject of love. As Falstaff reassures her that she needn't be jealous, the rendezvous is interrupted by Quickly and Meg, who announce, loudly, that Alice's husband approaches, threatening to cut his rival's throat.

Taking a moment to ascertain that this report is actually true, Alice quickly urges Falstaff to hide himself behind the strategically placed screen. No sooner has he wrapped the screen around himself than Ford, Caius, Fenton, Bardolph, and Pistol storm into the room, determined to discover Alice's seducer.

With admirable dispatch, Ford tears apart the great laundry basket, but finds no lover within. "Shirts! Skirts!" he curses. "Oh, I'll skin you, you scoundrel! Sheets! Nightcaps! He isn't there!" Shouting, he and his cohorts run wildly from the room in search of Falstaff.

Shaking with terror, Falstaff emerges from the screen and pleads with the assembled women to save his life.

"We could put him in the basket," suggests Meg.

"No, he can't get into it," replies Alice. "He's too fat."

"Yes I can! I can get in it," cries Falstaff, and with difficulty and much assistance, he lowers himself in, hiding among the dirty linen.

As pandemonium reigns, Fenton and Nanetta arrange themselves behind the screen for a bit of billing and cooing. Soon the room is again invaded by Ford and his confreres, who have concluded that the lover must certainly be there. They attack the cupboard vigorously—but find no Falstaff. Then their attention is caught by the screen—why, they think they hear a kiss!—and they move stealthily toward it. Meanwhile, Meg and Alice stand guard over the monstrous basket, from which the Falstaff's head emerges every few minutes to cry, "I'm roasting! I'm stifling!" Ignoring his moans, the merry wives push him back down.

Nanetta and Fenton are comparing the airy spirit of their ardor with the thunderous mayhem that surrounds them. As they exchange promises of lifelong love, their screen collapses in front of the furious Ford. The lovers scatter, the manhunt continues, and Alice and Meg decide that enough is enough. Calling the servants, Alice directs them to dump the laundry out the window. The basket, however, is terribly heavy.

"Keep it up!" cries Meg.

"Listen to the bottom crack!" exclaims Nanetta.

*Falstaff was Verdi's last opera, but not his last composition. As he wrote to a friend, "With my tongue hanging out like a mad dog, I'm fated to work until my last gasp." His chief work in the seven years that intervened between the premiere of* Falstaff *and his death in 1901 was the celebrated* Te Deum *that is the last of the* Quattro Pezzi Sacri, *a work that he called "a thanksgiving not on my part but on the part of the public who is now set free after so many years from having to hear new operas of mine."*

*When, at the age of eighty-seven, Verdi succumbed to a cerebral hemorrhage, Italy was plunged into mourning. Verdi had specified in his will that his funeral was to consist of "one priest, one candle, one cross," and his wishes were respected. But a month later, when the remains of the composer and his wife were transferred to their final resting place at the Casa di Riposi in Milan, the opportunity to celebrate Verdi's life was too tempting to resist. Arturo Toscanini conducted an orchestra and an eight-hundred-voice choir in selections from the Maestro's operas, but Verdi's place in the Italian heart was more tellingly revealed when the crowd of some three hundred thousand spontaneously broke into the famed chorus from Nabucco, "Va, pensiero, sull'ali dorate . . . fly, thought, on wings of gold," the anthem of Italian independence and, in some ways, of Verdi's astonishing career.*

"Up! Up! Up!" they call in unison as the basket is lifted aloft.

"Victory!" sings Alice, as the basket, the laundry, and the immense Sir John Falstaff go tumbling out the window into the river below.

# ACT THREE

On a bench outside the Garter Inn sits Falstaff, somewhat damp and wholly disenchanted. "Innkeeper! A glass of hot wine!" he calls. "I, after so many years as a knight both brave and gay, am to be carried off in a basket and thrown to the water as if I'd been a cat! If this superb belly had not buoyed me up, certainly I would have drowned." On and on he mutters, until a ray of sunlight in the form of a big glass of wine appears on the bench beside him. "Hm, let's pour a little wine into the Thames water," he mumbles, sipping. "Ah! Good wine dispels the stupid gloom of discouragement"—his weakened voice grows stronger—"lights up the eyes and the wits; from the lips it goes up to the brain and there awakens the little maker of thrills; the gay wind flickers with the thrill and the mad globe quivers with a thrilling madness!" And Falstaff stands, renewed, revitalized, reborn—

Mistress Quickly is approaching. She has come, she says, with a message from the lovely Alice.

"You and your lovely Alice can go to the devil!" shouts Falstaff.

"Oh sir, you've made a mistake!" quavers Quickly, as, one by one, the heads of Alice, Meg, Nanetta, Ford, Caius, and Fenton pop out from behind the house opposite. "The fault was with those damnable servants. Alice

is weeping, moaning, praying to her saints. She loves you." She hands him a letter from her co-conspirator.

Joyfully, the onlookers see that Falstaff has swallowed the bait. Snatching the paper, he reads assiduously: Alice has arranged for another tryst; this one will be at the Royal Park, and Falstaff is directed to appear in the guise of the Black Knight, underneath Herne's Oak, at the stroke of midnight. Helpfully, Mistress Quickly explains that the Black Knight hanged himself there, and some people say that when the chimes of midnight sound, why, troops of ghosts fall back in horror to watch the grisly remains of the Black Hunter make his way, slowly, slowly . . .

Quickly and Sir John move inside the Garter to plan the details of the rendezvous, while Alice, Nanetta, and Meg lay their trap. As Falstaff approaches the oak, they will disguise themselves as fairies and wreak havoc on him. Ford, who has humbly begged his wife's pardon, joins in planning the masquerade. Nanetta is to be the Queen of the fairies, the other women will be nymphs, and the men shall play imps and elves. Together, they will bedevil the fat knight until he confesses his wickedness and pleads for forgiveness. Laughing merrily, Meg, Alice, Nanetta, and Fenton depart, leaving Caius and Ford to do a little plotting of their own. The two agree that Ford will marry his daughter to Caius during the night's festivities. All Caius needs to do is grasp the Queen of the fairies firmly by the arm and bring her toward Ford. Little do they know that their machinations have been overheard by Mistress Quickly. With eponymous haste, she runs after Nanetta to concoct a counterplot.

It is a silvery, moonlit night in Windsor Park, and from afar, the sounds of guardsmen's horns can be heard. From behind the great, snarled trunk of Herne's Oak steps Fenton, who looks about him in wonder. Always the dreamer, he is inspired by this enchanted scene: *"Dal labbro il canto estasiato vola . . . A* song of ecstasy leaves my lips in this silent night and flies to meet other lips." Nanetta tiptoes in on the final line and the lovers embrace, but Alice breaks up the romantic moment. This is no time for shilly-shallying, she reminds them, handing Fenton a monk's robe and cowl. Fenton, bewildered but agreeable, dons the costume and promises to follow instructions. Meg, running in, reports that the imps are well hidden.

"Silence!" hisses Alice. "The big fish is coming!"

And, indeed, Falstaff is lumbering toward the oak, sporting a pair of stag horns on his head as directed. The midnight bells toll and Falstaff concludes that the moment of love is at hand. Sure enough, Alice emerges from a shrub. The sight of her inflames Falstaff and, declaring his passion, he attempts to seize her. Avoiding his embrace, Alice responds with a coy, "Sir John!"

This, to Falstaff, is tantamount to capitulation. "I am your slave! I'm your frisky stag! Now let it rain truffles, radishes, and fennel. They will be my fodder! And love will overflow! We're alone!" he exults.

Alice demurs. Actually, she reports, Meg will soon arrive.

This is even better than Falstaff expected. "The adventure's doubled!" he cries. "Quarter me like a buck at the table! Tear me to pieces! I love you, I love you!"

Suddenly, an earsplitting shriek rises from the surrounding woods. It's Meg. Alice pretends to shrink in horror, and Meg screams again, "The witches are coming!"

Falstaff looks around fearfully. "Where are they?" he squeaks, and sits down with a thump.

Alice flees in a fine imitation of terror, while Nanetta, in an unearthly voice, begins to summon the nymphs, dryads, elves, fairies, and sirens. An enchanted chorus of whispers, echoes, calls, and songs resounds through the forest, and Falstaff throws himself facedown on the ground, convinced that anyone who looks upon fairies will die. This is just what the merry wives were counting on. Quickly they array themselves: Nanetta as the Fairy Queen, Bardolph in a monk's habit, Pistol as a satyr, Alice as a fairy, Meg as the Green Nymph, Caius in a gray habit, Fenton, likewise in a habit, Mistress Quickly in a witch costume, an undisguised Ford, and a troop of little girls and boys dressed as fairies and imps.

This magical assembly advances on the great quivering mass lying at the foot of the tree. Pistol and Bardolph begin the sport by poking their former protector with sticks, and the imps, spirits, and fairies follow suit, egged on by Alice, Meg, and Nanetta.

"Ay! Ay! Ay!" moans Falstaff, as they roll him over and over.

"Filthy wretch!" shout Caius and Ford. "Glutton!"

"Big belly!" cry Bardolph and Pistol. "Scoundrel! Crusher of beds!"

"Splitter of waistcoats!" calls Quickly.

"Barrel-emptier!" yells Pistol.

"Chair-breaker!" taunts Meg.

"Destroyer of mares!" spits Caius.

"Triple-chinned!" adds Ford.

"Say you repent!" they all chime.

"Ay! Ay!" groans Falstaff. "I repent!"

But the maddened crowd of magicals continues to torment him until, in the heat of the moment, Bardolph's cowl falls back.

"Hell fire! Sulpher and blazes!" roars Falstaff, getting up. "I recognize Bardolph! Spit of hell! Dried herring! Vampire! Basilisk! Hired assassin!"

Throughout this hue and cry, Dr. Caius has been searching for a particular fairy queen. Now, as Ford reveals himself to Falstaff as the erstwhile Fontana, Quickly draws Bardolph aside and covers him with a shimmering white veil. Falstaff, meanwhile, is learning his lesson. Looking around at the familiar faces, he says, slowly, "I begin to perceive that I have been an ass." To a chorus of agreement, he smiles. "Every sort of common clown makes fun of me. But I'm the one who makes them so clever. My wit creates the wit of others!"

"Bravo!" the others shout.

Ford breaks in with studied casualness. "And now, let us crown our masquerade with the betrothal of the Fairy Queen. Here comes the engaged couple! Attention!" Indeed, a figure veiled in shimmering white approaches, firmly held by a gray monk.

"Another pair of lovers wants to be admitted to the happy betrothal!" calls Alice, pulling forward a figure in a thick blue veil and a monk clad in black.

"Let them come," says Ford with dignity. "May heaven unite you in marriage."

As the crowd breathes a sentimental sigh, the concealing veils are removed. Pandemonium! Caius has married Bardolph, and Fenton has married Nanetta!

A beaming Falstaff calls out, "Good Master Ford, tell me, who is the dupe now?"

Thus, the fateful night ends in a swelling laugh, as the merry wives, their friends, lovers, and the immense Sir John himself celebrate the resounding success of all their schemes. Opening his arms wide, Falstaff declares: "*Tutto nel mondo è burla* . . . All the world's a joke, and man is a born joker, pushed this way and that by faith or by reason. Every mortal being laughs at every other, but the best laugh of all comes at the end." ∼⬥

# FAUST

Charles Gounod had the misfortune to write the most successful opera of the nineteenth century: *Faust.* Between 1860 and about 1920, it was performed with stupefying regularity at all the great opera houses of Europe and the Americas, receiving little more than critical contumely for the duration. A good portion of the sneers centered on Gounod's evisceration of Goethe's revered play; indeed, the Germans were so sensitive to this desecration that they refused to call the opera *Faust,* and it's retitled *Marguérite* when performed in Germany. Gounod's easy tunefulness provided another target: How could anyone respect the composer who packed so many hits into one work? Then there was the pious sentimentality, the sudden eruption of duets, trios, and quartets where none should, dramatically, exist, and the egregious excess of Méphistophélès's Walpurgis Night fest—in short, the sheer enjoyability of the whole affair made it suspect. For, as generations of opera-goers have known, *Faust* is the most enjoyable of operas. Featuring the Devil incarnate, a pure heroine, a conflicted hero, various stirring choruses, charming country traditions, rousing drinking songs, tender love scenes, a fatal duel, seduction, madness, jail, infanticide, a witch's sabbat, and, finally, a rousing damnation, *Faust* contains something for everyone, all set against a background of music that wells when you expect it to well and lulls when you expect it to lull. It was enough to make a critic mad.

Let the critics pickle themselves in vitriol; the audiences loved it. *Faust* was a welcome relief from the excesses of Grand Opera. Its intimacy and poetry enchanted the war-weary refugees of *Les Huguenots;* its sentimental psychology appealed to the conventional morality of the average Victorian (including Queen Victoria herself); and its melodic and easily understood music presented a pleasing contrast to the explosions of contemporaneous French and German works. As a result, its success was undeniable and unwavering. Throughout the late nineteenth and early twentieth centuries, *Faust* was the great operatic certainty. If the season's offerings weren't drawing crowds, impresarios simply replaced the lineup with *Faust.* After the Metropolitan

Opera House, which was inaugurated with *Faust* in 1883, performed the opera twelve times in a single season, it became known as the *Faustspielhaus.* It was the most frequently presented opera in London in the final third of the nineteenth century. In Italy, only *Aida* surpassed it in stagings. As for France, it soon acquired the status of a national monument; by 1934, Parisians had enjoyed over two thousand performances of this quintessentially French masterwork. It's no wonder that George Bernard Shaw complained in 1893 that a professional music critic "has to spend about ten years out of every twelve of his life listening to *Faust* . . . I am far from sure that my eyesight has not been permanently damaged by protracted contemplation of the scarlet cloak and red limelight of Méphistophélès."

# ACT ONE

"Nothing!" cries the lonely old man in his study. "I know nothing!" Crabbed with age and broken by the futility of philosophy, Faust watches the sky lighten to dawn as he resolves to end his life. He lifts the beaker of poison to his lips, but his hand is stayed by the songs of the harvesters in the field below his window. Listening to their praise of God and nature, Faust sets down the poison in despair. "A curse on happiness, a curse on science, prayer, and faith! Satan, come to me!"

The invitation was all he needed. "Here I am!" calls out Méphistophélès gleefully, looking quite the fashionable young seventeenth-century gentleman, except for the curious scarlet cape he wears.

The old doctor tries to dismiss his guest, but the devil will have his day: Méphistophélès offers him riches, glory, and power, and Faust is lured into his tragic bargain. Greedily, he cries, "I want youth! Then pleasures will be mine, and so will young mistresses! Mine their caresses! Mine the powerful instincts and the orgy of heart and senses!" Méphistophélès assures Faust that all his wishes can be gratified, for a slight consideration. He brings forth a parchment.

Faust quails. But Méphisto conjures up a vision of a girl as beautiful as the day. It is Marguérite, her blue eyes and golden hair dazzling against the dull background of the room where she sits spinning. "Youth is calling you," whispers the devil.

Transfixed by Marguérite's loveliness, Faust signs the pact without hesitation. Now Méphistophélès invites his convert to sample the beaker's contents. No longer poison, the potion transforms Faust into a young and elegant nobleman, eager to meet the flesh-and-blood counterpart to his vision. Faust and his diabolical companion dash away to find their victim.

# ACT TWO

At the town gates, the Kermesse, or Easter Fair, is in full swing. The tavern is particularly popular with the students, who lustily proclaim their devotion to excess. One particularly rambunctious youth named Wagner encourages his fellows to drink anything but water. Inspired, the soldiers join in, and then the respectable burghers. As the celebration reaches its apex, a young man enters the square. This is Valentin, Marguérite's brother. About to depart for war, he confides his concern for his sister to her ardent admirer, a young boy named Siebel. Valentin feels a rush of dread at the prospect of leaving her alone and defenseless. *"Avant de quitter ces lieux . . .* Before I leave this place, my forefathers' native land, to you, King of Heaven, do I entrust my sister. I beg you to defend her from every peril." Valentin's presentiments are interrupted by the irrepressible Wagner, who rouses him from his gloom with a foolish song about a rat.

Before Wagner can get his tune fully underway, his performance is halted by the appearance of a smiling stranger in a red cloak. Although his grin is cheerful, there is something discomfiting about him, and Wagner quickly cedes his stool. Méphistophélès, for of course it is he, throws himself into a different song with gusto: *"Le veau d'or est toujours debout . . .* The golden calf is still standing." On he goes, singing his little ditty about the triumph of idolatry.

Wagner politely invites the stranger to join them, but his courtesy is ill rewarded when he passes the glass to Méphistophélès, who grabs Wagner's hand and pronounces him doomed to be murdered. The lad Siebel is likewise informed that flowers will wither in his hands. "No more nosegays for Marguérite," chortles Méphisto.

The mention of his sister's name offends Valentin to the core, but his outrage is met with the prophecy that he will be killed by an acquaintance of the stranger. With a laugh, Méphistophélès disparages the wine and magically replenishes the barrel with a better vintage. But when Méphistophélès has the effrontery to toast Marguérite, Valentin can stand it no longer; leaping up, he draws his sword and challenges the stranger. Unconcerned, Méphistophélès draws a circle around himself with his own sword. As Valentin lunges across the line, his weapon falls to pieces. The crowd gasps, certain now that they are in the presence of the devil. They back away in horror, while Valentin, retrieving the pieces of his sword, forms a cross of the shards to protect himself. Even Méphistophélès is no proof against the power of the cross, and he shrinks fearfully into a corner as the students and soldiers, bearing their inverted swords as crosses, leave him alone in the empty tavern.

Here is where Faust finds him. Eager to begin his amorous escapades, the newly young man begs Méphistophélès to produce the lovely Marguérite. Quickly regaining his good humor, the devil leads his pupil outside, where a crowd swirls in a festive waltz.

Sure enough, Faust soon spies Marguérite making her way among the dancers and chivalrously offers to escort her. She demurely refuses his arm, leaving him more captivated than ever. Spurred by Méphisto, Faust pursues her, while the dancers whirl on, oblivious of their brush with the devil.

# ACT THREE

Into Marguérite's cottage garden creeps young Siebel. With devotion, he picks first one flower and then another, begging each to whisper his love to Marguérite, but Méphistophélès's curse clings to his hands and the blooms wither. After a moment's consternation, the resourceful youth dips his fingers into a font of holy water on the cottage wall, which miraculously cures him. Leaving a bouquet at Marguérite's door, he departs, resolving to warn her against Mephisto the next day.

Alas, the next day will be too late, for who is lurking in the bushes? Méphistophélès and Faust. Casting a cynical eye at Siebel's posies, the devil offers to supply Faust with a more toothsome enticement. Faust, though, is enchanted and enmeshed in love—a state that brooks no interference, not even from the devil. Impatiently, Faust tells his mentor to make himself scarce. Alone in Marguérite's twilit garden, Faust is overcome with reverence for her simple home. *"Salut! demeure chaste et pure . . .* Hail, chaste and pure abode, lighted by the presence of an innocent and holy soul."

Faust's tender reflections are shattered by Méphistophélès, now bearing a casket of jewels so rich that the devil vows they will corrupt even Marguérite. His victim appears in the garden, singing a little ballad, though she keeps interrupting herself to rhapsodize about the handsome gentleman who offered her his arm. Her eyes fall on Siebel's bouquet, but she is immediately distracted by the sight of a golden chest. *"O Dieu! que de bijoux! . . .* O gracious! What jewels!" she exclaims. With growing excitement, Marguérite decks herself in the dazzling gems.

*One of the great sopranos of the belle epoque, Nellie Melba was a walking definition of the term* prima donna. *Her contracts stipulated that none of her fellow singers should receive as high a fee as she; accordingly, the great Caruso had to be satisfied with £399 to her £400. She traveled in regal splendor, her train compartment appointed with scented bed linens and silken pillows. And she never, ever permitted herself to be upstaged or outsung, even going so far, during a performance of* La Bohème, *as to join in a secondary soprano's aria when she felt that the girl was receiving too much applause. Stage managers and conductors quailed before her imperious confidence in her voice and musicianship, and only a fool would have tried to criticize her to her face.*

*Once, a certain fool did. He was Kaiser Wilhelm II, who fancied himself quite the musical authority, and one evening, after a performance of* Faust *featuring Melba as Marguérite, he was pleased to offer the diva his opinion of her singing. "Don't you think, Madame Melba, that you took the 'Jewel Song' at much too fast a tempo?" he asked.*

*Melba was not one to coddle kaisers. "No, your imperial majesty," she replied firmly, "I do not. I sang the part of Marguérite according to the instructions of the composer himself, M. Charles Gounod, who was pleased to express his entire satisfaction with my interpretation and to compliment me on it."*

*And that was that. The Kaiser stormed out of the room in a huff, leaving Melba, as usual, victorious.*

Her fun is interrupted by her neighbor, Martha, a good-natured, gossipy old soul, who assures Marguérite that the treasure must come from a lovelorn nobleman. Méphistophélès and Faust choose this moment to emerge. Faust and Marguérite stare foolishly at each other, their hearts pounding, and the devil toys shamelessly with Martha, who is soon flirting like a teenager. As the young couple strolls through the garden, Marguérite tells the story of her lonely life—her mother long dead, her brother gone to be a soldier, and her beloved baby sister just taken by death—while Faust listens with rapt admiration. Though she knows she should resist him, Marguérite can't stop herself from listening to his declarations of love; even as she begs him to leave, she can feel her resolution crumbling.

Méphistophélès, escaping from the clutches of his aged sweetheart, calls on his diabolical powers to overcome Marguérite's scruples. "Love, make their ears deaf to untimely remorse! And you, scented flowers, bloom under this accursed hand of mine and put the last touch to Marguérite's undoing!"

Marguérite, falling prey to the enchantment of the garden, languorously plucks the petals from a daisy to determine her fate: "Loves me! Loves me not! Loves me!"

Faust passionately confirms the flower's message, but Marguérite summons her last vestige of resolution to beg him to leave and return tomorrow. Truly in love by now, Faust agrees; but as he departs, he runs afoul of the diabolical debaucher. Subtly guiding Faust near Marguérite's window, Méphistophélès urges him to take one last look. In the pale moonlight, Marguérite confesses her rapture to the stars. Faust calls her name, and all is lost. As Satan roars with laughter, Marguérite is undone.

# ACT FOUR

Months have passed since Marguérite's seduction. Now, deserted by her lover, she sits alone in her room, cast out by her one-time friends. Only Siebel has remained loyal, but when he offers to avenge her, she gently dismisses him, admitting that she still loves Faust.

Convinced that she has committed a mortal sin, Marguérite departs for church to pray for forgiveness. Even there, she is tormented by Méphistophélès, who warns of the eternal suffering she will endure in hell. As the church choir intones the *Dies Irae,* Satan's demons call out, and Méphistophélès cries, "Marguérite! Be accursed! Hell awaits you!"

With a heartrending scream, Marguérite falls to the floor in a faint.

The soldiers are coming home, singing a rousing tune about the glories of war. Valentin, unaware of what has occurred, greets Siebel affectionately and invites the boy to accompany him home. Siebel's discomfort is palpable and Valentin demands an explanation. Stammering and stuttering, Siebel begs his old friend to be merciful and runs away. Filled with suspicion, Valentin enters his house.

Now Faust and Méphistophélès appear. Faust has some compunction about his behavior, and approaches

Marguérite's home with a mixture of shame and tenderness. Rolling his eyes, Méphistophélès bursts into a mocking serenade. "Don't open the door, my pretty one, till the ring is on your finger," he bellows.

The newly enlightened and enraged Valentin bursts out of the front door to ask them what they mean by this insult, and he challenges his sister's seducer to a duel. The devil goads the two men into fury, laughing all the while. Valentin unsheathes his sword and the two men begin to fight. But Méphisto soon grows impatient and, shoving Valentin's sword aside, he allows Faust to plunge his sword into his enemy's heart.

As Faust and Méphistophélès scurry away, old Martha and a group of townspeople rush to Valentin's aid, but he is near death. Marguérite comes running, only to be cruelly rebuffed by her brother, who adds to her shame by announcing that he has been wounded by his sister's lover. Pulling himself to his knees, he spits out his final words to Marguérite: "Go! Shame now crushes you! But the hour will strike at last! Die! And if God forgives you, may you be cursed in this world!" The bystanders gasp, and, steeped in bitterness, Valentin dies.

# ACT FIVE

Deep in the Harz mountains, witches and demons are gathering for their Walpurgis Night celebration, and here Méphistophélès guides his protégé. Though Faust is conscience stricken and protests that he is in no mood for festivities, the devil has a particular distraction in mind. At a sign from Méphisto, the mountain opens to reveal a glittering golden palace hall. Seated at a richly laid table is an alluring collection of history's great wanton women. Beauties such as Cleopatra and Lais ply Faust with drink while dancing girls disport for his amusement. Faust soon forgets Marguérite's tribulations in a sea of drink and lust, and the whirling dance grows giddier.

Suddenly, the brilliant light grows harsh and Faust sees Marguérite in a prison cell, pale and wan, the scarlet ribbon around her neck eerily resembling a gash. The courtesans vanish and Faust is once more in the dark mountains with his diabolical companion, who does his best to dismiss the specter as mere witchcraft. But Faust remains disturbed and demands that Méphisto take him to Marguérite.

Obediently, Méphisto transports him to Marguérite's cell, where she lies in restless sleep, condemned to death for murdering her baby. Méphistophélès urges Faust to help his lover escape, but Faust is immobilized by terror and regret, realizing for the first time the magnitude of the tragedy he has caused. As he whispers her name, Marguérite awakes, joyfully recognizing her beloved's voice. Elated, Faust reaffirms his love, and Marguérite tenderly recalls their first meeting. Faust urges her to escape with him immediately.

Marguérite talks on as though she has not heard him: the delightful garden, the roses, the evening . . .

Faust begs her to hurry, but again, she babbles on, and Faust realizes she has gone mad. Méphistophélès reappears, exhorting the couple to hurry. But Marguérite now recognizes her lover's friend for what he is, and she calls upon God to protect her. As Faust tries to drag her to freedom, she prays for forgiveness, and her lover's damnation is revealed to her. "Why are those hands red with blood? Go away!" she screams. "You fill me with horror!" Pushing Faust away from her, she falls dead.

"Judged!" cries Méphistophélès triumphantly, but he has not reckoned on God's grace, and to the swelling refrains of an angelic choir, Marguérite ascends to Heaven. ⁓⬥

# THE TALES OF HOFFMANN

## — *Les contes d'Hoffmann* —

The history of *The Tales of Hoffmann* offers composers a valuable moral: Never die before your opera is finished. Jacques Offenbach, creator of more than one hundred feather-light and melodious operettas, was quite possibly the most beloved composer in France in the late nineteenth century. Dubbed "the Mozart of the Champs-Elysées" by the eternally epigrammatic Rossini, Offenbach pleased aristocratic audiences, who savored his satire, as well as the more plebian theatergoers, who hummed his tunes. His hits, such as *La Belle Hélène, The Grand Duchess of Gerolstein,* and *La Périchole,* were more or less in perpetual performance from the moment of their premieres onward.

But it wasn't enough. Offenbach longed to compose in a more serious vein. In 1877, already gravely ill with the heart disease that would kill him, he began to write *The Tales of Hoffmann,* his last work and only true opera. It is a dark, fantastic vessel for all that he had been forced to jettison in his lighter works; its richly discursive music is matched with a series of three mad fables about love and betrayal. Featuring murder, insanity, seduction, a maniacal musician, a gorgeous golem, and a diabolical doppelgänger, not to mention a few quotations from *Don Giovanni,* this final effort was a world apart from Offenbach's earlier compositions.

By 1880, *Tales of Hoffmann* was in rehearsals at the Opéra-Comique, and Offenbach was laboriously adapting his music to the specific talents of the cast and the requirements of Léon Carvalho, the impresario. "Make haste and produce my opera," he wrote to Carvalho. "I have not much time left and my only wish is to see the first performance." However, he died on October 5, 1880, with his wish unfulfilled and the orchestration incomplete.

Delighted to have an opportunity to hew the opera of their dreams out of Offenbach's lapidary construction, the impresario, the composer's son, and the musician hired to complete the work got out their hatchets. Roles were chopped in two, then in three. Dialogue was added and subtracted. The chorus of the first act was cut. A piece of the second-act *romance* was hacked off and reattached elsewhere in the act. Stella, the love interest of the fifth act, became a nonsinging role. Most egregiously, the entire fourth act was removed, its major tunes—including the famous barcarole—dispersed through the rest of the opera wherever there seemed to be enough room. By the time of its wildly successful premiere, in early February 1881, *Tales of Hoffmann* was a compact little show, with a running time of just over two and a half hours. Offenbach wouldn't have recognized it.

After a long period of further meddling and inappropriate musical-theater staging, a restoration movement began, but after so many years and so many manuscripts, it was difficult to discern what the composer's original intentions had been. However, the musical scholars persevered, and in current productions, the missing fourth act is usually reinstated (although sometimes it becomes the third act). Some adventurous companies even seek to fulfill Offenbach's initial dream of casting one soprano for all four of Hoffmann's loves and a single baritone for all four villains, though this is rare (it takes quite a toll on the soprano). It is difficult to know if the repairs are complete, but it is certain that *The Tales of Hoffmann* now approaches in some measure the vision of its author.

*—— There was once a man named Hoffmann. He was an artist, a musician, and a weaver of tales so strange that those who heard his stories could never forget them. In fact, they had nightmares about them for years. Nonetheless, in a certain tavern in Berlin, crowds gathered, waiting for Hoffmann to arrive. Jealously they watched as he drank, first one glass and then another and another and another. Only then, as his imagination soared, would he begin to spin his weird legends. ——*

# ACT ONE

It is night and the moon gleams silver through the windows of Luther's Tavern, shining its pale light on rows of bottles, small barrels, casks, and an assortment of small tables and benches scattered in haphazard fashion around the room. Out of the shadows, thin voices begin to rise, and a mouse scurries for cover. But the lilting song is coming from the barrels and bottles themselves: It is the spirits of wine and beer, extolling their charms—how they banish care, remove worries, alleviate boredom.

In a shower of blue light, the Muse arrives. She is an exasperated muse, for her charge, Hoffmann, is once again about to lose his heart and neglect his art. Vowing to rescue him from the distractions of love, the Muse dons the appearance of Nicklausse, a young companion of Hoffmann's. With firm orders to the bottles to ply her charge with drink, the Muse-Nicklausse departs to the opera house next door, where Stella, Hoffmann's temptress, is singing in *Don Giovanni*. The spirits of wine, feeling expansive, continue to sing their own praises.

They stop abruptly, though, when the door bangs behind Councillor Lindorf and Andrès, who just happens to be Stella's servant. From him, Lindorf, who is also smitten with Stella's charms, learns that Hoffmann is his rival and, moreover, that he seems to be gaining the upper hand, for Stella has sent him a key to her dressing room. Pocketing the key and the letter that accompanies it, Lindorf sends Andrès on his way. With a few remarks about the foolishness of preferring a drunken poet to a clever fellow like himself, Lindorf creaks over to a corner table to await his enemy.

The performance next door has reached its intermission, and now throngs of students barge cheerfully into the tavern demanding drink. As Luther and his waiters bustle about filling orders, the students sing the praises of the divine Stella until the door crashes open and Hoffmann, with his faithful friend Nicklausse at his side, enters.

The students shout out greetings, but their beloved Hoffmann is in a foul mood, his spirits darkened perhaps by the freezing cold or by a drunkard asleep outside the tavern door. "Give me something to drink!" he demands roughly, "and let me sleep in the gutter, like him!" Trying to cajole him out of his gloom, the students ask him to sing "The Legend of Kleinzack," and Hoffmann, relenting suddenly, agrees. As he finishes the last verse, he throws his glass against the wall and resolves to get drunk. His friends vow to join him, but their hilarity is cut short by the crabbed Councillor Lindorf, who taunts Hoffmann for his low pleasures. It is clear that the two are old enemies, and Hoffmann responds insolently. They exchange elaborately polite insults, culminating in a toast to their respective demises. But Hoffmann, growing serious, tells the students that Lindorf has always been a harbinger of bad fortune to him, especially in love.

The students commiserate, but Hoffmann dismisses their measly affairs, utterly dissimilar to his grand amour, the incomparable Stella, who is three women in one, an artist, a young girl, and a courtesan. Why, says he, she is the embodiment of all the women he has ever loved, a trio of enchantresses who shared his life between them. Smiling, he leans back and asks, "Would you like to hear the story of these mad loves?"

"Yes! Yes! Yes!" chorus the students.

In vain, Luther warns them that the opera is about to resume. The students would rather miss it all and listen to the tales of Hoffmann.

"The name of the first was Olympia . . . " he begins.

# ACT TWO

A thin, nervous old man carefully lowers a tapestry curtain that leads from his study to a long gallery. "There! Sleep in peace!" he mutters, adjusting the fabric by a fraction. Rubbing his hands, the inventor Spalanzani paces about the book-lined room, muttering anxiously about his marvelous creation, the exquisite Olympia, who walks, sings, dances, just like a real daughter. Her talents will display his genius and, he hopes, restore the fortune he has lost from the bankruptcy of the moneylender Elias. The only cloud on the horizon is the wicked old doctor, Coppélius, who has not yet been paid for the beautiful blue eyes he provided Olympia. Spalanzani frets that this outstanding bill might allow Coppélius to claim rights to the wondrous doll, but his worrying is interrupted by the appearance of Hoffmann.

The life of the actual E. T. A. Hoffmann was only slightly less strange than its operatic version. Born Ernst Theodore William Hoffmann in Germany in 1776, as a young man he exchanged William for Amadeus in homage to Mozart. A talented musician and artist as well as a writer, Hoffmann was forced into an extremely uncongenial career as a bureaucrat for the Prussian government in Poland, which gave him a fractured double life as a functionary by day and hard-drinking artist by night. In addition to causing him much despair, Hoffmann's administrative job landed him squarely on the wrong side during Napoleon's invasion of Warsaw. Deported with the rest of the Prussian bureaucracy, Hoffmann was separated from his Polish wife and nearly starved to death in the upheaval of war. For several years he managed a number of theaters and wrote music criticism, as well as painting scenery, conducting, and composing.

In 1814, Hoffmann was appointed a councillor of the Prussian Supreme Court; his real work, however, was writing. During this period, he composed many of the macabre, Romantic tales for which he is justly famous, including those upon which the three episodes of The Tales of Hoffmann were based: "The Sand-Man," "Automata," "Councillor Crespel," "Der Magnetiseur," and "The New Year's Eve Adventure: The Story of the Lost Reflection." Just like his operatic alter ego, Hoffmann often recounted his tales to enthralled listeners at his favorite tavern. As the years went on, both the stories and the teller became increasingly bizarre, and Hoffmann's fame as a spectacle almost surpassed his fame as an author. He died in 1822, of alcoholism, shortly after dictating his final tale, "The Recovery."

Our friend Hoffmann, a somewhat younger version of his tavern-frequenting self, is deeply, desperately in love—with Olympia. Having caught sight of the beautiful figure reclining with regal poise in the professor's sitting room, Hoffmann has abandoned poetry and art to devote himself to Spalanzani's favorite subject, physics, in order to come into closer proximity to the girl. For his part, Spalanzani is delighted to have such a susceptible subject upon which to test his automaton's wiles, and the two men exchange numerous congratulations on their new partnership. But Spalanzani is distracted, for he has invited a glittering array of guests to a reception where he will present the marvelous Olympia and, he hopes, reap some rewards for his inventive genius.

As Spalanzani departs to prepare Olympia for her debut, Hoffmann stands, dazed with love, in the middle of the room. His rapture is interrupted by Nicklausse, whose good advice he spurns, and by a strange old man, who offers to sell him some eyes. This is Coppélius, stooped under a bulging sack. Slyly, the wizened creature slips a pair of magic glasses on Hoffmann's eyes, glasses that make Olympia seem all the more real. Stealing a magically enhanced glance at his inamorata, Hoffmann is enchanted anew and willingly surrenders the three ducats requested. Pocketing the coins, Coppélius gets down to his real business, which is extorting money from Spalanzani. Accosting the professor as he returns to the study, the mad doctor demands his share of the money, for after all, Olympia has his eyes. Spalanzani, desperate to be done with Coppélius, writes him a note for five hundred ducats, payable from Elias, and the gratified Coppélius shuffles off. And none too soon, for a throng of richly appareled guests starts to arrive. Filled with admiration for the professor's home and for his lavish hospitality, they chatter among themselves about the promised performance by Spalanzani's daughter. "They say she is ravishing!" "Lovely! Without vices!" they whisper with excitement.

Finally, the paragon is brought forward; just as expected, she is perfectly lovely, though her wide blue eyes seem to lack expression. Her proud father suggests that she display her singing talents, and she complies with a charming air. "*Les-oiseaux-dans-la-charmille* . . . The-birds-in-the-bower-the-sun-in-the-heavens . . . " Hoffmann stares at her with adoration, never noticing the tiny whirring sound of a spring that seems to come from her back as Spalanzani winds her up.

After this demonstration of Olympia's talents, the wily old professor announces supper. As the guests cluck approvingly and depart for the table, Spalanzani touches Hoffmann on the shoulder. Would he mind, asks the old man, keeping Olympia company as she is rather too tired to eat?

But of course. Nothing could be more delightful. Once they are alone, Hoffmann kneels before his angel in an ecstasy of excitement. "Oh, my Olympia!" he exclaims. "Let me admire you and bask in your charming gaze!"

"Yes! Yes!" she replies.

"Is this not a feverish dream? I thought I saw you sigh!"

"Yes! Yes!"

"Sweet pledge of love! You are mine! Our hearts are united!" cries the infatuated young man. Drawing Olympia into his arms, he vows a lifetime of love; but as his hands clasp hers, she jumps away, careening around the room in various directions before making an abrupt departure by walking directly into a curtained doorway. Poor Hoffmann, certain that he has offended his Olympia somehow, calls after her. Though the faithful Nicklausse tries to warn him that the girl is rumored to be a mechanical doll, he swears to defy all nay-sayers in the pursuit of his love. From the next room, dance music wells, and Hoffmann dashes away, eager to waltz with the peerless Olympia.

Before the assembled guests, Hoffmann waltzes ecstatically around the room with Olympia in his arms, circling to and fro as the crowd admires her dancing skill. Every step is perfect, but the mechanism grows overheated, and the doll and her partner begin to whirl faster and faster—

The old professor leaps forward and touches his daughter's shoulder, bringing her to a precipitous halt and hurling Hoffmann onto a nearby sofa. Recollecting his charade, the professor hastily pats his Olympia on the shoulder. "There now! That is quite enough, my daughter."

Olympia responds with a series of increasingly explosive "Ahs!" and her father sends her off for a rest.

Hoffmann, reviving, finds that only his glasses have been broken in the melee; but the general relief is short-lived, for a servant enters the room at a run to tell his master that Coppélius has returned.

The blood draining from his face, Spalanzani rushes toward the gallery where Olympia is stored, but he is too late: The harsh sounds of springs snapping and wood cracking meet his ears. "She is broken!" screams Spalanzani.

With a wild cackle, Coppélius enters to confirm the suspicion, "Yes!" he cries exultantly, "smashed to bits!"

Hoffmann, starting up in terror, dashes into Olympia's room as the two old men lunge at each other. He returns, white as a ghost, his illusion destroyed. "A mechanical doll!" he says incredulously, " a robot!"

At this, the assembled guests burst into laughter. "The bomb goes off! He loved a mechanical doll!" they jeer. Spalanzani and Coppélius, meanwhile, are exchanging blows and threats. "He loved a doll, a mechanical doll," repeats the crowd with rising hilarity, as Hoffmann, brokenhearted, stares blankly at the wreckage of his dreams.

# ACT THREE

Councillor Crespel's music room seems to have been furnished by someone who loathes music, for a collection of violins are mounted inaccessibly on the walls, and the furniture is placed precisely to discourage listening. A long portrait of a beautiful woman hangs between two doors, and her cool glance seems to overshadow the whole room. Only the harpsichord is open, and there sits Crespel's daughter, Antonia, singing herself a lonely song.

Scarcely have the last exquisite notes died away when her father enters the room abruptly. "My dear child!" he exclaims. "Did you not promise me that you would sing no more?" The Councillor is tormented by the memory of his wife, who, though wasted with consumption, refused to abandon her career as a singer, leaving her husband to watch in agony as the effort of each song pushed her a little closer to collapse. His anxious eye has detected traces of the same disease flushing his daughter's cheek; without revealing his fears, he has exacted from her a vow never to sing again.

Sadly, Antonia renews her pledge and leaves the room disconsolately.

Grinding his teeth, Crespel curses Hoffmann, whose memory has provoked his child's rapturous singing. "Because of him I have had to flee here to Munich," grumbles the Councillor, as he calls in his servant Frantz to give him stern orders not to admit a soul while he, the Councillor, is gone from home.

Frantz nods vigorously, but alas, Frantz is hard of hearing and has no idea what his master has requested. Accordingly, soon after Crespel's departure, Hoffmann makes his entrance, accompanied, as ever, by Nicklausse. Hoffmann, fervently in love with Antonia, has been seeking her for the better part of a year and is exultant that he has finally found her. Sending Frantz to announce his arrival, Hoffmann swears that he must know the reason why she and her father left him behind. Nicklausse attempts to dampen his friend's ardor with a mention of the Olympian fiasco, but Hoffmann is undaunted. Seating himself at the harpsichord, he begins to play the music he finds there, *"C'est un chanson d'amour . . .* This is a love song that soars, sometimes sad, sometimes mad with passion."

At the sound of his voice, Antonia bursts into the room and the long-separated pair embrace. Hoffmann begs to know why he was abandoned, but Antonia confesses that her father will not tell her. Unable to penetrate this mystery, the lovers content themselves with a joyous reunion, and Hoffmann promises to marry her the next day. Forgetting her promise to her father, Antonia eagerly offers to sing for Hoffmann, and together they embark on the *chanson d'amour.* As their voices rise and mingle, Antonia cheeks grow flushed and she puts her hand on her heart. Hoffmann, noticing her trembling, breaks off. "What is wrong?" he inquires anxiously.

Nothing, she protests; then the sounds of her father returning send her running from the room. Hoffmann, much disturbed by his beloved's agitation, hides himself behind a curtain in order to get to the bottom of the matter.

Crespel enters, but his solitude is soon broken by Frantz, who announces the arrival of Dr. Miracle. "That scoundrel," cries Crespel. "Shut the door quickly! That grave digger, that assassin, who would kill my daughter as he killed my wife!" Shuddering, the Councillor runs to bar the doors, but he is too late.

A grim laugh precedes Dr. Miracle into the room. He is a thin man and pale as death. Clothed from head to foot in ancient black, he doffs his hat with exaggerated courtesy at Crespel. "Well now, here I am! In person! To ward off danger, you must recognize it."

Something about his tone freezes Hoffmann's heart with fear, and Crespel, too, seems paralyzed with terror. Imperturbably, Dr. Miracle continues. Pointing toward Antonia's room, he begins an examination of the girl as though she were really present, seeming to coax her, soothe her, take her hand, and seat her in an armchair. "How old are you, please?" he begins. "Twenty? Ah. The springtime of life! Let me see your hand." Taking out his watch, Miracle counts her pulse. "Can you sing?"

"No!" breaks in the agonized Crespel. "Do not make her sing!"

"Sing!" commands Miracle.

And from Antonia's room comes a brilliant flourish.

Miracle smiles a diabolical smile. "Look how flushed she is and how her eyes sparkle. She clutches her hand to her pounding heart!" Unctuously, he offers her father his special medicine, which comes in certain milky flasks, flasks he begins to click like castanets between his fingers.

Finally, shouting curses, Crespel succeeds in driving Miracle out of the room inch by inch, leaving a shaken Hoffmann behind, certain that he has been in the presence of Satan himself.

Hoffmann resolves to save Antonia by persuading her to renounce singing, and when Antonia enters, Hoffmann sorrowfully asks her to relinquish her singing and her glorious future. After a long silence, Antonia acquiesces. Kissing her hands, Hoffmann takes his leave.

Poor Antonia, deprived of her lover and her singing, wanders about the room in tears. As she looks longingly at the music resting on the harpsichord, a gaunt black figure rises from the floor behind her. Leaning close to her ear, Dr. Miracle whispers a song of seduction. "Will you never sing again? Do you know what a sacrifice is being imposed on your youth, and do you understand the extent of it? Your grace, your beauty, your God-given talent! All the blessings heaven entrusted to you, must they be buried in the shadow of family life?" On and on he goes, cataloging the fame that would have been hers.

Antonia struggles to ignore the strange messages that fill her head, but the doubts unfurl inexorably in her mind—"What sort of love is this? Hoffmann sacrifices you to his own brutal desires"—and she is powerless to resist them.

Frantically, Antonia calls on her mother's spirit for support, but for Miracle, nothing is sacred, and, with a single flick of his finger, he summons up a specter to speak in the dead woman's voice. This false spirit, too, urges her daughter to renounce her vow: "Dearest child, whom I call as I used to do. Heed your mother's voice!"

"Sing along with her!" hisses Miracle, seizing a violin from the wall and playing a frenzied accompaniment to the voice from the grave.

Antonia is powerless to resist the combined forces of her mother's commands and Miracle's temptations. Surrendering, she sings as she has never sung before, ecstatically greeting her mother's spirit, their two voices mingling with the dark tones of Dr. Miracle. Vainly, the girl attempts to quit the song, but she is instead driven

Jacques Offenbach and Richard Wagner represented opposing poles of music in the late nineteenth century. Needless to say, each despised the other's work. Offenbach was uncharacteristically harsh in his assessment of Wagner: After hearing Tannhäuser, he wrote, "To be erudite and boring is not the equivalent of art." Wagner was equally sour: Offenbach's operettas, he said, were "a dung-heap upon which all the swine of Europe wallowed."

It was left to the erstwhile champion of Wagnerism, Friedrich Nietzsche, to provide a surprise: "If by artistic genius we understand the most consummate freedom within the law, divine ease and facility in overcoming the greatest difficulties, then Offenbach has even more right to the title of genius than Wagner has. Wagner is heavy and clumsy; nothing is more foreign to him than the moments of wanton perfection which this clown Offenbach achieves as many as five times, six times, in nearly every one of his buffooneries."

to sing higher and higher, and finally she collapses to the floor, unconscious and near death.

As the strains of her last notes reach him, Crespel rushes into the music room to find his beloved daughter breathing her last. Frantically, the old man dashes around, calling for blood, and when Hoffmann, too, appears, Crespel sets upon him with a knife. Only Nicklausse's intervention saves his friend, for Hoffmann is distracted by the sight of Antonia's prone figure. "A doctor! Call for help quickly," he exclaims.

"Here I am," intones a soothing voice. It is Miracle, who bends over the girl and feels for her pulse. "Dead," he announces with cruel satisfaction.

"Antonia!" Hoffmann calls out in despair.

# ACT FOUR

The scene has changed to Venice, luxurious, dissolute Venice. Here, in a gilded palazzo overlooking the Grand Canal, the courtesan Giulietta is holding court, surrounded by a swarm of frivolous young men and women that includes Hoffmann, Nicklausse, and Pitichinaccio, one of Giulietta's most durable admirers. The guests are drinking and gambling and carousing, while Giulietta and Nicklausse, reclining on a silken sofa, amuse themselves by singing an enchanting, undulating barcarole: *"Belle nuit, ô nuit d'amour . . .* Lovely night, O night of love, smile upon our pleasures. Night, more beautiful than day, O beautiful night of love . . . "

The guests are pulled into the dreamy spell of the music, all except Hoffmann, who dismisses love as a moral error and extols the virtues of wine instead. Laughingly, the crowd professes agreement with his cynical view, but the fun is interrupted by the appearance of Schlemil, a saturnine, unattractive man who is Giulietta's official lover. As the assembly moves off toward the card tables, Nicklausse once again attempts to warn his friend away from love.

Hoffmann protests. May the devil damn his soul if he is ever such a fool as to fall in love with a courtesan, he avows. And, there, off in a corner of the golden room, a thin, elegantly dressed man appears. His name is Dapertutto, and he eyes Hoffmann with amusement.

All unaware, Nicklausse and Hoffmann follow the guests. Dapertutto, left alone in the salon, pulls a brilliant, gleaming diamond ring from his pocket. Laughing to himself, he twirls the jewel on his finger. As though hypnotized, Giulietta enters the room. Never removing her eyes from the glittering gem, she crosses over to Dapertutto and asks him what he requires. Placing the ring on her finger, Dapertutto congratulates her on her success in stealing Schlemil's shadow. But now, he continues, he would like her to obtain Hoffmann's reflection.

With glowing eyes, Giulietta agrees to the bargain, just as Hoffmann reenters, followed by a jubilant Schlemil. The latter has found the card tables immensely cheering, for he has just won every cent that Hoffmann possesses. Schlemil crows about his triumph, but Dapertutto silences him with an alarming magic trick at his expense.

The other guests, left alone, are calling for Giulietta's return, so the gambling begins anew. Once again, Hoffmann and Schlemil take up their cards, and Giulietta, casting ardent glances at Hoffmann, begins to sing a sinuous love song. The ever-impressionable Hoffmann cannot resist Giulietta's manufactured passion, and he clasps her in his arms, confessing that he loves her. As they kiss, they are discovered by the rest of the company, and Schlemil explodes in rage, vowing that it would be better to see Giulietta dead than in the arms of another man.

Ignoring the gawking crowd, Giulietta whispers softly to Hoffmann that it is his job to retrieve the key to her room from Schlemil. Then, transforming once again into the smiling hostess, she begins bidding her guests farewell, for gondoliers singing the languorous barcarole can be heard approaching in the distance. Hoffmann and Schlemil wait in icy silence until the others are gone, and then the poet turns to his rival. "Would you be kind enough to give me a certain key I desire?"

"You shall have this key only with my life," cries Schlemil in a fury.

Hoffmann shrugs, "If that's what you want, I will have both."

Dapertutto, who has been lingering in the shadows, efficiently provides Hoffmann with a sword, and the two men repair to a small garden, brilliantly illumined by moonlight. To the soothing strains of the gondoliers' song, the rivals remove their jackets and prepare to fight; but Hoffmann, glancing about, is shaken to see that Schlemil casts no shadow on the garden wall. He hesitates, but Schlemil thrusts his sword forward impatiently. Their brief parry ends as Hoffmann's rapier bestows a mortal wound to the older man; leaning over the dying figure, Hoffmann coolly divests him of the key and makes away to Giulietta's room.

Dapertutto emerges from his dark corner. Placing his hand over Schlemil's dead heart, he begins to laugh uproariously.

In her satin-draped boudoir, Giulietta pleads with Hoffmann to save himself, for he will undoubtedly be arrested if he stays. Delirious with passion, her lover refuses. *"O Dieu! de quelle ivresse embrasses-tu mon âme . . . My God, with what intoxication have you inflamed my soul?"*

Entwining her arms in his, Giulietta murmurs, "Strengthen my resolve by giving me something that belongs to you." Leading him to her mirror, she appeals for the gift of his reflection. Startled at first, Hoffmann is soon lost in a tide of rapture and willingly relinquishes his image to her mad desire.

The moment he succumbs, Dapertutto rises as if by magic in the shimmering boudoir. With a flick of his fingers, the reflection of Hoffmann, bent over Giulietta's pliant body, disappears from the mirror. Half-unconscious, Hoffmann falls onto a sofa. Giulietta looks coldly down at him. "I leave it to you," she snaps to Dapertutto, and turns to greet Pitichinaccio, who is slipping in by a small side door.

Hoffmann, reviving, is aghast to find himself surrounded by people, and even more alarmed when Pitichinaccio solicitously hands him a mirror, that he may regard his reflectionless self. As Hoffmann looks uncomprehendingly from one to another, Nicklausse rushes in, determined to extract Hoffmann from

Giulietta's house before the police arrive. And now the guests, too, come scurrying back, eager to see one more drama before the night ends.

Slowly, the truth of his situation begins to dawn on Hoffmann. He has been betrayed again, by yet another diabolical plot. Enraged, he turns to Giulietta. "Wretched woman! Did you feign the language of sacred love to rob me of my soul, my life, and my blood? You viper, I will destroy you!" Pulling a dagger from his pocket, he rushes toward her.

"Powers of hell, blur his vision," Dapertutto intones, and Hoffmann, blinded, searches helplessly for Giulietta while the guests burst into laughter. As Nicklausse attempts to lead his friend away, the harsh voices of the police are heard below, but Hoffmann continues to brandish his dagger as he runs about the room blindly.

"There she is!" he exclaims, catching hold of the giggling Pitichinaccio and stabbing him repeatedly.

"My 'Naccio!" screams Giulietta. "My heart!"

The guests begin to roar with laughter.

## ACT FIVE

Back at Luther's Tavern, everyone is seated precisely as they were when Hoffmann began to speak, hours before.

Hoffmann pushes back his chair with a rough gesture. "There you have the story of my loves," he says, standing. "Their memory will live in my heart forever."

At this, Nicklausse is struck with an idea. "I know," he exclaims. "Three dramas in one: Olympia, Antonia, Giulietta are one and the same woman—Stella!"

Hoffmann turns furiously on his comrade. "One more word and I swear on my soul that I will smash you to bits—like this!" He seizes a glass and hurls it to the floor, where it shatters into a thousand pieces. Cloaking his rage with hilarity, Hoffmann turns to the gathered students. "I am insane! Let ours be the divine delirium of alcohol, beer, and wine! Let drunkenness and folly reign, and then the nothingness that allows us to forget!"

Not only the students, but the spirits of wine and beer join in this plan with gusto, and a great deal more drink is consumed by everybody, particularly Hoffmann, who collapses onto a table just as the tavern door opens to reveal Stella, swathed in the lace veils of Donna Anna. The students brashly shout her name, but Hoffmann remains oblivious to her presence until her servant Andrès approaches his table to announce, "You are making us wait for you."

This remonstrance precipitates another fury. Hoffmann jumps to his feet, his eyes flashing at the diva. "What do you want? What am I hearing? What is your name? Good public, be courageous!" he hisses bitterly. "Strew flowers at her feet as she passes! Intoxicate her with your bravos! You don't know what these creatures leave along their paths of death and debris. Nor how contemptible they are!"

Drawing herself up, Stella turns away. "You may not use my love for your ridicule," she says with dignity. "Your nights will be haunted by my beauty that you have spurned. Farewell to your heart forever!" When she reaches the tavern door, the diva stops and looks at Hoffmann one last time. Moved by memories, or perhaps pity, she tosses a flower from one of her bouquets at his feet. Hoffmann watches her silently, while the students jeer, and Stella departs.

Some time later, Hoffmann is in his study, fully absorbed in his writing. Nicklausse, transformed back into the Muse, stands triumphantly behind him, while weird images and wraithlike dreams called up by the poet dance about the room. Hoffmann, the prisoner of his imagination, attempts a final, drastic escape in suicide, but the implacable Muse arrests his hand. "You ingrate!" she cries. "What about me? Me, your faithful friend, whose hand has wiped away your tears? Am I nothing to you? May the tempest of passions subside in you! The man is no more: Poet be reborn! I love you, Hoffmann! Be mine! Rekindle your genius from the embers of your heart! Smile serenely at your sorrows! The Muse will soothe your great suffering! One is made great by love and greater by tears!" ⁓◦

# DIE FLEDERMAUS

### — *The Bat* —

Until the middle of the 1860s, Johann Strauss the Younger was content to be the Waltz King of Vienna, the highly paid idol of the frivolous society that danced away the twilight years of the Austro-Hungarian Empire. But after countless triumphs, including a tour of America during which he was so hounded for locks of his hair that he took to passing out clippings from his Newfoundland dog, Strauss found his dance tunes being upstaged by the stage. Operettas were taking Vienna by storm, and, after much urging from his wife—and even from his rival Jacques Offenbach—Strauss set to work on composing for the musical theater. His first effort was immensely popular, as were his numerous other forays into light opera, but few have withstood the ravages of time and music critics. An exception is *Die Fledermaus,* which has enchanted audiences since its first performance in 1874. With a plot as frothy as the champagne it exalts and a cascade of lilting, danceable tunes, *Die Fledermaus* is charming, silly, festive—in short, everything anyone could want in an operetta. Which is not to say that it's simple. Strauss's masterpiece requires consummate vocal artistry, particularly in the roles of Adele and Rosalinda, and his social satire is readily apparent in his casting of the decadent Prince Orlofsky as a mezzo-soprano and, indeed, in all his characters' flamboyant lack of virtue. Finally, the structural importance of the orchestra, which tends in many operettas merely to underpin the vocal numbers, ensures the place of *Die Fledermaus* in the repertory of even the most august companies.

## ACT ONE

Everyone at Eisenstein's house is scheming. Alfred, the music teacher, is down on the street, serenading Rosalinda, who just happens to be Eisenstein's wife. Adele, the chambermaid, has just received a letter from her sister, Ida, inviting her to a magnificent party at Prince Orlofsky's, and she must quickly finagle the night off. But Rosalinda has no patience for Adele's hastily manufactured story, for her husband begins his five-day jail sentence this very night and she requires Adele's attendance in her despair. Unfortunately, Rosalinda finds herself distracted from her sorrow when Alfred bounds in, begging for a rendezvous while her husband's in jail. As he scampers away, promising to return, Rosalinda implores the heavens for a reprieve for her husband. Otherwise, she knows, her virtue is lost.

But what's this? Eisenstein is returning from the courts, his outraged shouts revealing that, instead of winning the expected reprieve—his crime, after all, was only offending an official—his sentence has been lengthened, owing to the incompetence of his lawyer, Dr. Blind. Eisenstein excoriates the addled advocate, and Rosalinda adds her two cents before flouncing from the room. After Dr. Blind totters away protesting, Eisenstein receives a new guest, his old friend Dr. Falke, who has a magnificent plan to cheer up his pal. It seems that Eisenstein is not actually due in jail until six the next morning, plenty of time for him to accompany Falke to the Grand Ball at Prince Orlofsky's. "There will be girls there," says Falke slyly. "Ballet girls, every one of them!"

Eisenstein needs no more persuasion. Taking out his watch, he calculates how long it will take him to get ready—

Falke eyes the pretty little watch enviously. He knows it well, having seen it used to capture the attention of countless girls. The two plan how Eisenstein will tenderly take leave of Rosalinda and sneak off to the ball. Falke obligingly agrees to introduce Eisenstein as the Marquis Renard and takes himself off, promising to meet his friend later.

Immensely heartened, Eisenstein repairs to his dressing room to don his evening clothes. Rosalinda, coming upon him, is taken aback at the vast wardrobe he is packing. "You are dressing for prison?" she inquires.

"Noblesse oblige," he replies, bustling out of the room with his valise.

Rosalinda looks after him in astonishment. "He seems almost glad to be going to jail," she says. But soon she is hatching a plot of her own. When Adele comes in to announce supper, Rosalinda benevolently if belatedly gives her the evening off. As Adele expresses her thanks, Eisenstein, resplendent in white tie and tails, comes in to take his leave. What a touching scene ensues! The husband and wife can hardly bear to be parted! They groan together, while Adele wrings her hands at the tragedy of the separation. Rosalinda waxes poetic about how she will be so brokenhearted at the sight of his empty cup at breakfast that she'll drink her own coffee without sugar. From such devotion, Eisenstein somehow manages to tear himself away, with Adele beating a hasty retreat right behind him.

The bereft wife has only a few moments to despair before Alfred pops in, so full of bravado that he dons Eisenstein's dressing gown and nightcap and settles down for a cozy evening. Rosalinda summons up some halfhearted outrage, which Alfred recommends that she douse with drink. Demonstrating the remedy, Alfred tosses down a few glasses while Rosalinda alternately protests and plays along.

Once Alfred is truly drunk, their tête-à-tête is interrupted by Herr Frank, the governor of the prison to which Eisenstein is condemned. He has come to collect his prisoner himself and reasonably mistakes the drunk fellow in the dressing gown for Eisenstein. At first, Alfred protests—he's not Eisenstein, no sirree!—but Rosalinda rapidly conveys to him the importance of being Eisenstein, for, after all, her reputation is at stake.

Frank is quite confused by Alfred's denials. Could he possibly have the wrong man?

"My dear sir," begins Rosalinda smoothly, "by voicing doubts of that kind you truly cast aspersions on my honor." Besides, she points out, who but a spouse would be yawning and gaping while she sat across from him? Who but a husband would look so bored?

Frank decides that she has dispelled all his qualms. Let the couple make their farewells, then, for he must be on his way to a grand party.

Here Alfred begins to see a silver lining: the good-bye kiss.

Rosalinda gulps: the good-bye kiss.

And, as Frank describes the lovely accommodations in his jail, the counterfeit husband and wife resign themselves to giving a very good impression of a passionate kiss.

*Just what is it that separates operetta from opera? There is no simple, scientific answer; the distinction depends on such nebulous terms as* charming, frivolous, *and* light. *Operetta as we know it originated more or less in reaction to the French opéra comique of the mid-nineteenth century, which, after years of rubbing up against the massive style of Grand Opera, was virtually indistinguishable from it. In 1855, the young composer Jacques Offenbach noted that "the Opéra-Comique was no longer the home of true comic opera; that really gay, bright, spirited music . . . was being forgotten. Composers for the Opéra-Comique were simply writing small 'grand' operas." His antidote was* Orphée aux Enfers, *featuring the scandalous can-can dance, an even more scandalous parody of Gluck's* Orphée et Euridice, *satirical commentary on the French government, and a succession of appealing tunes. It was an immediate sensation, and Offenbach's work became the definition of the form: witty, tuneful, fast-paced, and pleasing. One hallmark of operetta is its improbable story, featuring highly unlikely characters whose convoluted fortunes are resolved by a series of ridiculous coincidences. Another is the use of spoken dialogue to further the plot. Still another trait is the primacy of the songs; orchestration is generally kept to a supporting role, so that the hits can be easily heard. But though one may offer these definitions, the true character of operetta rests in its ineffable grace and charm.*

# ACT TWO

Finally we arrive at Prince Orlofsky's party! In a glittering golden salon, beautiful girls flutter about. Weaving in and out of the crowd are servants bearing silver platters of ices, chocolates, canapés, and the ever-present, effervescent champagne. Only Prince Orlofsky fails to be amused, for, as he is telling Falke, he is permanently bored.

But Falke has promised to make the Prince laugh tonight, by arranging a little farce for his entertainment. It all began three years before, Falke relates, when he and Eisenstein attended a masked ball. Dressed as a bat, Falke had enjoyed himself mightily, getting ever drunker as his friend Eisenstein refilled his glass time and again. After the party ended, the thoroughly soused Falke hadn't noticed that Eisenstein was driving him to the woods instead of to his house; no, he had simply snuggled under a tree and fallen asleep. But when he awoke the next morning and found himself miles from home, he was forced to walk through the city wearing only his bat costume, subjected to the ridicule of every passer-by.

But tonight, he crows to the Prince, he will have his revenge! A complicated plot has been set into motion, beginning with Adele, who is just finding out that it wasn't Ida who summoned her to the party. Quickly adapting, Adele makes a deep curtsey to her host and introduces herself as Olga, an actress.

And here is Eisenstein, or Marquis Renard, as Falke presents him to Orlofsky. Smiling, the Prince welcomes the newcomer with a few house rules: No one is allowed to be bored or stop drinking; otherwise the Prince will have to throw him out personally.

Olga, née Adele, resplendent in one of her mistress's ballgowns, is just whirling by. "Why," exclaims Eisenstein, "that's Adele!"

"My gracious mas—" begins the girl, but she is smoothly interrupted by Falke, who offers to introduce Mademoiselle Olga to Marquis Renard. Catching herself in the nick of time, Olga haughtily asks why Eisenstein stares at her.

Stuttering, he replies, "I only thought I saw a resemblance to a . . . a . . . chambermaid—"

"I, a chambermaid? Ha!" shrieks the outraged Mademoiselle Olga. Together, the Prince and his guests laugh heartily at Marquis Renard's ridiculous, not to mention ungallant, blunder.

Now, a new actor in Falke's farce appears, the Chevalier Chagrin, otherwise known as Frank, the prison warden. He is followed by a masked Hungarian Countess, whose renowned beauty, Falke confides to Eisenstein, must be disguised because of her husband's extreme jealousy. Of course, this countess is none other than Rosalinda, who has been summoned by a note from Falke.

With one outraged glance, Rosalinda takes it all in: There is Eisenstein, with a lady on his arm. And it's Adele! In one of Rosalinda's own dresses! Quickly, the good Rosalinda resolves to teach her husband a lesson. Donning her mask, she assumes an air of mystery, and Eisenstein is immediately smitten. Leaving Adele, he saunters toward the masked lady and launches his campaign by consulting his watch in an obvious manner.

Rosalinda looks covetously at the little watch—what an excellent piece of evidence!—and embarks upon a scheme to acquire it. Flirting for all she's worth, she has soon lured the so-called Marquis into her trap. She stops, breathes heavily, and passes her hand before her eyes. "Oh!" she cries, "everything is getting blurred and I'm having palpitations!"

Eisenstein congratulates himself for having such an effect on the lady.

"It's an old complaint," the Countess confides, "but it's always quick to go. All's well if my heartbeats match the ticking of a watch."

With maximum solicitude, Eisenstein produces his watch and begins to count. But the Countess finds the numbers terribly confusing and begs to look at the hands of the watch herself. Eisenstein is only too glad to oblige, and—at last!—the Countess pockets the treasure. "Ha ha! Dear Marquis, I thank you for this charming watch!"

Eisenstein gasps and burbles, but in the next moment, a swarm of guests buzzes into the room, and the Countess proposes to entertain them with a little Hungarian song. This interlude is followed by a renewed burst of festivity, wherein all the guests, led by Prince Orlofsky, toast King Champagne the First and dance in his honor. Amid the melee, Eisenstein/Renard and Frank/Chagrin become sworn and eternal friends, without discovering their true identities.

"What a touching reunion there's going to be in jail," Rosalinda whispers to Falke and Orlofsky, watching her husband stagger about with his warden.

Tolling bells announce the hour: six in the morning. Restored to reality with a lurch, Eisenstein and Frank dash frantically about.

"I'm due in jail!" shouts Eisenstein.

"I should have gone home hours ago!" hollers Frank.

Arm in arm, the new friends depart, leaving the rest of the guests to waltz toward the day.

# ACT THREE

At the jail, Frank's assistant, Frosch, has been in charge throughout the night. Fortified by slivovitz, he is in fine spirits, except for the annoyance of Alfred's incessant singing.

But now Frosch's prestige is coming to an end, for Frank is stamping through the door, a bit woozily to be sure and blabbering foolishly about the charming Olga, but the warden nonetheless. Oops, he falls asleep in his chair. Frosch, entering, wakes him with the information that four ladies are waiting for him, or perhaps only two, since the slivovitz makes Frosch see double.

Yes, it's only two, Olga and Ida to be exact. They've come with a confession. Olga, they admit, is really not an actress, but a chambermaid. Frank recoils, but not much. They've come, they say prettily, because Olga is simply dying to go on the stage, and if only he would, well, help . . .

"Hm. Has she any talent?" inquires Frank.

"Have I talent? I'll show you!" announces Adele, and proceeds to demonstrate her range: queen, ingenue, aristocrat—she can do anything!

Frank is duly impressed, but Frosch interrupts to announce a Marquis Renard. Disposing of the young ladies, Frank welcomes his friend with the news that he is Frank the prison warden, not the Chevalier Chagrin. Eisenstein receives this disclosure hilariously. "Enough of this marquis business!" he laughs. "My name is Eisenstein, and I'm here to serve my sentence."

"I can prove you're not Eisenstein," Frank retorts with a guffaw. "I personally arrested Eisenstein last night and brought him here!" Laughing, he details Eisenstein's tender parting from his wife, while Eisenstein grows increasingly irate.

Enter Dr. Blind, the lawyer, who has been called to defend the faux Eisenstein, Alfred. The real Eisenstein resolves to change clothes with the lawyer and cross-examine the imposter together with the latest newcomer, Rosalinda. Under his questioning, Alfred and Rosalinda reveal the whole story, though they are increasingly disgruntled by the outbursts of their lawyer. Finally Eisenstein, overcome by rage, pulls off his disguise to accuse his wife of unfaithfulness.

"You have the audacity to reproach me?" she exclaims, producing the little watch.

As the imbroglio reaches its climax, Falke arrives, eager to enjoy the spectacle he has conjured. Joined by the Prince and a pack of his guests, Falke explains his hoax to Eisenstein, and, after Rosalinda swears that her dalliance was mere playacting, the butt of the joke joins in the general mirth. To wrap up the festivities, Prince Orlofsky declares that he will support Adele's theatrical career, and the bubbly story ends with a great chorus in praise of champagne. ⌇

# CARMEN

❧

*C*armen may well be the perfect opera, as Friedrich Nietzsche famously claimed. It possesses everything an opera connoisseur could desire: a rich mezzo-soprano lead; orchestration that emphasized wind instruments for the first time; a magnificent, pulse-pounding overture; and brilliant Spanish rhythms integrated into its musical themes. Likewise, *Carmen* also possesses everything an opera neophyte could desire: a sexy heroine; a story rife with lust, betrayal, madness, and murder; and some of the most memorable tunes in the operatic repertoire: Carmen's devil-may-care *habanera,* the seductive *seguidilla,* and, of course, the "Toreador Song," which may be the most irresistible whistling tune ever written. As with all great art, every moment and every note of *Carmen* seems ordained by fate, and the audience watching Don José's descent into the nether realms of obsession is pulled into an equally inexorable musical current that rushes forward to its thrilling climax.

Why, then, was *Carmen* damned as a failure after its premiere at the Opéra-Comique in 1875? For so it was, and its composer, the talented and underappreciated Georges Bizet, died four months later without any idea that he had written what would become one of the most popular operas of all time. The problem lay with Carmen herself. Picture the immaculately dressed bourgeois, with his beruffled wife and demure daughter, settled into the velvet loges of the Opéra-Comique. Picture their consternation at the appearance of a gypsy girl who saunters about, brushing up against various and sundry men while declaiming her inviolable right to sexual gratification. And that was just the first scene. The critics fulminated: "A plague on these females vomited from hell! . . . she should be gagged, a stop put to the unbridled twisting of her hips; she should be fastened into a straitjacket after being cooled off by a jug of water poured over her head." Audiences were shocked, journalists outraged, even the choruswomen revolted by the brutality of the scenes they had to play. Fiasco! Indignity! Horrors!

Except that the opera was a masterpiece. And, in a development that has encouraged visionaries ever since, *Carmen* could not be sunk. After its first run in Paris, it was performed in Vienna, where it was an immediate sensation, then in London, Dublin, New York, St. Petersburg, Marseilles, Hanover, Mainz, and Berlin. Everywhere, it triumphed; even, some eight years after Bizet's death, in Paris itself.

# ACT ONE

Seville in 1820 is a dusty, sleepy town of small plazas and magnificent palaces crumbling under a brilliant Mediterranean sun. In one particularly shabby square, a small contingent of soldiers lounges outside the guardhouse. There is no one to guard and they are spending the morning smoking, gossiping, and tossing stones at the neighborhood cats. Nothing ever happens in their square.

Except—there's a pretty girl approaching the guardhouse. Furiously stroking his moustache, Corporal Morales offers assistance. She is looking, she replies timidly, for Don José. Though he draws out the conversation, Morales is finally obliged to admit that Don José will be coming shortly, when the guard changes. The girl refuses the soldiers' pressing invitation to be their guest and departs, leaving them to their boredom.

Sure enough, a military air is soon heard, and the relief guard marches in. Lieutenant Zuniga, Corporal Don José, and a contingent of dragoons step smartly into the square. After salutes and formalities, Morales tells Don José about his visitor.

A smile warms Don José's face. "That must be Micaela."

As the tramping footsteps of the departing soldiers fade, a harsh bell rings, marking the lunch hour for the girls who work in the cigarette factory across the square. At once, the place is filled with young men, laughing, jostling one another, and waiting for the girls.

Here they come, an eddy of them, smoking, giggling, and glancing flirtatiously. The soldiers emerge from the guardhouse to watch. Only Don José is indifferent to the scene; he sits composedly in a chair outside the guardhouse, cleaning his gun.

A buzz of disappointment rises from the crowd: "But where is Carmen? We don't see Carmencita."

"Here she is!" someone cries.

A lithe, dark-haired girl paces languorously into the light, then stretches a little, arching her back. Her dress is cut a shade lower than those of the other girls, and in her bodice, she wears a blood-red flower. Instantly, she is surrounded by clamoring boys. Smiling and laughing, she flirts with them until she notices Don José, who is still calmly cleaning his gun. Even when she walks near him, he remains absorbed, simply unaware of her.

Carmen begins to sing a sultry *habanera*. "*L'amour est un oiseau rebelle* . . . Love, love is a capricious bird that no one can ever tame. . . . Love me not, then I love you; if I love you, you'd best beware." The local boys are thrown into a frenzy, but she breaks through the crowd and stands before Don José, who looks up inquiringly to find himself the center of attention. Never removing her eyes from his, Carmen plucks the scarlet flower from her bosom and tosses it at his feet. Don José leaps up, his chair toppling behind him, and reaches out to catch his temptress—but the bell clangs, and with a toss of her head and a final glance, Carmen retreats with the other girls into the factory.

Breathing unevenly, José looks after her, then picks up the flower. Its perfume is heady, dizzying, and the corporal tucks the blossom in his jacket. His reflections are interrupted by the arrival of Micaela, his sweetheart from home, who brings a letter from his mother. Micaela's simple charm restores José to his senses, and after a few moments of conversation, Carmen's brashness seems repellent.

Leaving him to read his letter, Micaela departs. Fortified by this recollection to homespun charms, José pulls Carmen's flower from his jacket. "So much for your flowers, you filthy witch," he cries, preparing to grind the bloom under his heel. But his movements are arrested by a sudden scream from the factory. Alarmed, Lieutenant Zuniga and his troops run out of the guardhouse to be greeted by a swarm of factory girls pouring into the square, screaming for help and arguing vociferously.

Confusion reigns until Zuniga, exasperated, sends José into the factory to find out what's happened. A few moments later, the corporal returns, leading Carmen behind him.

"Sir, it was a quarrel," he reports. "Words first, then blows. One woman hurt."

"By whom?" inquires Zuniga.

"Why, by her," replies Don José, jerking his head toward Carmen.

Zuniga turns toward the perpetrator threateningly and begins to interrogate her, but try as he might, he cannot make her answer his questions—or even inspire any fear in her. "Since you take this tone, you can sing to the prison walls," he says briskly. "Tie up her pretty arms," he commands José, and he retires to the guardhouse to write up her arrest.

Unabashed, Carmen gives José a long look. Prison sounds less than appealing to her, but José is resolute. He can do nothing for her, he says stiffly. This she dismisses. Of course he will help her, since he is in love with her. José denies it vehemently. Carmen only smiles and moves a little nearer to her captor. *"Près des remparts de Seville chez mon ami Lillas Pastia . . .* Near the walls of Seville, at Lillas Pastia's tavern, I'll go dance the *seguidilla* and drink Manzanilla," she sings, "but all alone, I'd be bored, so to have some company, I'll take my lover with me. Who wants to love me? I'll love him. You've come at a good moment."

Outraged, José commands her to be quiet.

"I'm not talking to you," she retorts. "I'm singing to myself! And I'm thinking of a certain officer who loves me and whom I might very well, yes, might very well love in return."

"Carmen!" cries José.

"My officer is not a captain," she says, laughing, "not even a lieutenant, he is only a corporal; but that's enough for a gypsy."

José looks down at her, dazed. Then, feverishly, he begins untying the cords around her wrists. "Carmen, I am like a drunk man! If I agree, if I give myself to you, will you keep your promise? If I love you, Carmen, my Carmen, you will love me!"

"Yes," replies Carmen briefly, and renews her song. "We will dance the *seguidilla* and drink Manzanilla . . ."

When Zuniga returns with the papers for her imprisonment, Carmen leans toward José. Speaking in a rapid whisper, she says that she will push him as hard as she can, and he is to fall, allowing her to escape. José, utterly under her spell, agrees, and Carmen is soon running like a deer as a crowd roars with laughter at the spectacle of Don José toppled by a woman.

# ACT TWO

At Lillas Pastia's infamous tavern, Carmen watches a pair of gypsy girls dancing to guitar music. Her friends Mercédès and Frasquita lounge nearby, flirting with soldiers and officers, and Carmen herself is the object of Lieutenant Zuniga's persistent attentions. But her energies are focused on the music, and soon her clicking castanets lead the revelers into a swirling gypsy dance.

Finally, the tavern has to close, and Zuniga tries once more to persuade Carmen to accompany him home. She refuses, but is delighted when he reveals that Don José has finished serving his sixty-day jail sentence for allowing her to escape.

Their conversation is interrupted by the sounds of a parade in the street: Escamillo the toreador, winner of the bullfights in Granada, is returning home in triumph. Glowing with success, Escamillo enters the tavern and proudly recounts his victory. Vividly, he reenacts the scene of his triumph, and Carmen, enthralled, pours the hero a drink. He eyes her appreciatively, but Carmen is loyal to Don José, at least for the moment, and turns away from the torero.

Both repudiated by the bewitching Carmen, Lieutenant Zuniga and Escamillo hie themselves away, leaving Carmen and her friends alone with the ancient Lillas Pastia. With the stealth of thieves, which they are, El Dancairo and El Remendado enter.

They have in mind a smuggling venture, which they feel certain they can pull off if they have the assistance of Carmen, Mercédès, and Frasquita. Preening, the girls assure the thieves that nothing could possibly be well stolen without them. Carmen, however, objects to traveling just now. When pressed for a reason, she admits that she's in love. This news is met with general disbelief, but she assures them it is so. They urge her to combine love with duty, but Carmen says she intends to wait for Don José.

And who should be heard in the distance but José himself, singing a military air as he hastens toward the tavern. With a brief exhortation to Carmen to bring her sweetheart into their merry band, Remendado, Dancairo, and the two gypsy girls hurry away.

Carmen greets her lover with a reprise of her brilliant gypsy dance. As she sways and circles, her castanets keep up a fiery, staccato pace and José watches, hypnotized. Suddenly, a distant bugle call breaks through her song, and Don José recognizes the summons to return to quarters. Awkwardly, he tells Carmen he must leave.

"To quarters!" she cries bitterly. "After I went to such trouble to entertain the gentleman? I sang! I danced! I even think that I did a little more—I loved him! Taratara! There's your bugle calling!" she says mockingly, throwing his helmet at him.

José stands, irresolute. "It's cruel of you, Carmen, to make fun of me," he begins, but Carmen tosses her head.

In vain, José begs her to listen. He loves her, he wants her, she knows he does. But Carmen will not be placated. "Listen to me," he pleads, taking a withered red flower from his jacket. *"La fleur que tu m'avais jetée* . . . the flower that you tossed to me stayed with me in my prison cell," he begins, telling her how he was tormented by her vision, how he was consumed by the desire to see her again.

His passionate words move Carmen not at all. She insists that if he loved her he would abandon the army and come away with her, to the mountains, to freedom!

Don José begs her to have mercy. He will not desert his army, he avows. "Farewell," he says, "farewell forever!" Just as Don José turns to leave, however, the tavern door bursts open to reveal Lieutenant Zuniga, who has come to try again for Carmen's favor. His lip curled, Zuniga takes in the scene and orders Don José back to barracks. But José refuses to obey this preemptory command. In a moment, the two men have drawn their swords. Carmen flings herself between them, calling for help. Dancairo and Remendado appear in a flash and efficiently hold a gun to Zuniga's head, suggesting that he might like to take a stroll with them. Left alone with Carmen, Don José gloomily reflects that now he has no choice but to join the band of thieves. Carmen urges him to rejoice in his new career: "You will see how marvelous it is, a life of wandering, all the universe your country, your own will the only law, and above all, freedom, freedom!"

# ACT THREE

Night has fallen in the mountains, and the band of smugglers led by Dancairo and Remendado is taking an hour's rest before the final leg of their journey past the border guard.

Carmen casts a keen glance at Don José, who stands on a rocky promontory, lost in thought. "What are you looking at?" she asks.

"I am thinking of my mother in her village far below," replies José morosely.

Exasperated by his woeful manner, Carmen brusquely suggests that he go back to her. Don José is shocked by her casual suggestion that they separate, but their brewing quarrel is forestalled as Carmen flounces over to Frasquita and Mercédès, who are reading their fortunes with cards.

Carmen deals out the cards for herself, only to find, again and again, death. Accepting her fate with her customary fortitude, she says, "If you must die, you can cut and shuffle twenty times, and the pitiless card will continue to repeat the truth—death!"

Now it is time for the smugglers to make the final assay. Carmen and her friends assure Dancairo and Remendado that they will easily take care of the customs guard, for after all, he's a man. The smugglers move off down the mountain and for a few moments, all is quiet. But soon Micaela appears; she has crept up to the hideaway in search of Don José. Just as she has summoned up her courage to call to him, a shot rings through the crag and Escamillo hurries into the pass. "A shade lower and I was done for!" he shouts cheerfully.

Don José, surprised by his target's good humor, puts down his knife, and the two men greet each other. Escamillo reveals that he has come in search of a gypsy girl he's crazy about named Carmen. He continues obtusely, "She had a lover, a soldier who deserted for her, but it's finished, I think. Carmen's love doesn't last more than six months."

Don José's face grows dangerously quiet. "But you love her?"

"Madly!"

"Then you'll pay for her!" says José, drawing a knife. Escamillo is not one to refuse a challenge, and two knives are soon flashing in the moonlight. Fired by rage, Don José out-maneuvers his opponent, and the

*Impresario James Henry Mapleson recounts in his memoirs a particularly tense production of* Carmen. *Soprano Minnie Hauk was renowned in the lead role, and in 1886, she toured with one Luigi Ravelli as Don José. One night, writes Mapleson,* "in the middle of the third act, when Ravelli was about to introduce an effective high note that generally brought down the house, . . . Carmen rushed forward and embraced him—why, I could never understand. Being interrupted at the moment of his effect, he was greatly enraged, and by his movements showed that he had resolved to throw Madame Hauk into the orchestra. But she held firmly onto his red waistcoat, he shouting all the time, 'Laissez-moi! laissez-moi!' until all the buttons came off one by one, when she retired hastily to another part of the stage. Ravelli rushed forward and exclaimed, 'Regarde, elle a déchiré mon gilet!' (Look! She's ripped my waistcoat!) and with such rage that he brought down thunders of applause, the people believing this genuine expression of anger to be part of the play . . .

"The details of the affair soon got known and were at once reproduced in all the papers. . . . What could the public think of an opera company in which the tenor was always threatening to murder the prima donna, while the prima donna's husband found himself forced to take up a position at one of the wings bearing a revolver with which he proposed to shoot the tenor the moment he showed the slightest intention of approaching the personage for whom he is supposed to entertain an ungovernable passion?"

torero falls to the ground; but as José lifts his arm to deliver the deathblow, Carmen and the smugglers jump between the men.

"How enchanting," remarks Escamillo from the ground, "that you should be the one to save my life, Carmen." Getting to his feet, he invites one and all to his next bullfight and, with compliments all around, takes his leave.

At this juncture, Micaela is discovered among the rocks. She has come, she says, from José's mother, who begs him to return.

"Go!" says Carmen scornfully, but Don José, certain that she is planning a tryst with Escamillo, declares that he will never leave her.

Micaela, seeing that José is unmoved by her pleas, reveals that his mother is dying. Shocked into compliance, Jose prepares to depart immediately, but before he goes, he makes one last threat to Carmen: "Go ahead, be happy that I'm gone, but remember, we shall meet again!"

From far down the mountain, Escamillo can be heard singing the refrain of his toreador song. Carmen lifts her head and begins to run after him, but quick as lightning, Don José blocks her way, his knife bared.

## ACT FOUR

Outside the walls of the arena, the square is bright with color and clamorous with noise. Oranges, fans, water, wine, cigarettes—all are being hawked with cries and shouts. Excited children are rushing about, and the crowd swarms through, gossiping, making bets, and displaying their holiday finery. Today is the magnificent day of the bullfights.

Escamillo enters the square with Carmen on his arm, glorying in the crowd's adoration. With repeated avowals of love, Escamillo departs to prepare for the bullfight, and Carmen is left alone on the steps of the arena.

Frasquita and Mercédès approach, filled with alarm. Don José is here, they warn her. Calmly, Carmen surveys the crowd. Yes, there he is, pale and haggard, his mouth set. "I am not a woman to tremble before him. I'll wait and talk to him," she says proudly.

Soon the two are face-to-face. Around them, people stream into the arena, but Carmen stands coolly before her former lover. José, gray faced and shaking, begins with a plea. "I make no threats—I implore, I beg. What's happened between us, I forget. Let us begin another life, under other skies!"

Irritation tightens Carmen's lips. "You ask for the impossible," she bursts out. "I have never lied; between us, everything is finished!"

José's pale cheeks flush, but he contains his anger. Reaching out a hand to detain her, he cries, "There's still time. Let me save you. I adore you!" But Carmen dismisses him contemptuously.

Hoarsely, Don José promises that he will do anything, anything to win her back.

"Carmen will never give in!" she cries, "Free she was born, and free she will die!"

A roar erupts from the crowd inside the arena, "Viva! Viva! Victory!"

At the sound, Carmen throws back her head in delight and turns to run into the stadium, but Don José seizes her arm, his face rigid with fury. "You'll not go in there, Carmen!" he hisses. "It's me you'll come with!"

Outraged, Carmen tears her arm from him. "Never, never!" she cries.

"For the last time, demon, will you come with me?"

"No!" she spits, tearing a ring from her finger. "This ring—you gave it to me: Here!" She hurls to the ground at his feet.

Maddened by this insult, José rushes toward Carmen, and, as the crowd inside the arena explodes into cheers, he lunges and sinks his dagger into her back. With a great scream, Carmen falls dead at the foot of the steps.

Pouring from the arena, the crowd is halted by the terrible sight of Carmen's blood-drenched figure. Don José stands swaying before them. "You can arrest me. I killed her," he says to the stunned audience. Then, throwing himself on Carmen's body, he screams, "Carmen! My beloved Carmen!" ⌇

# BORIS GODOUNOV

~◈~

**M**odest Moussorgsky's only complete opera, *Boris Godounov,* is often classified by music historians as an exemplar of naturalism, the late-nineteenth-century cultural trend that is also found responsible for *Carmen* in France and for *verismo* shockers such as *I Pagliacci* in Italy. Moussorgsky's Russian naturalism, unlike the Western European brand, did not focus on the randy inclinations of the lower classes, but instead took historical events for its subject and the Russian people as one of its protagonists. Musically, too, Moussorgsky was defiantly un-Western, eschewing arias, identifiable tunes, and heartwarming conclusions for a single-minded devotion to the text of Pushkin, the truth of history, and the suffering strength of the Russian populace. As a result, *Boris Godounov* is an austere, if powerful, night at the opera: The orchestration is bald by Italian standards, and the instrumental counterpoint is nearly nonexistent. Most of the color, mood, and atmosphere are, therefore, conveyed by voice alone. Led by Boris's tormented bass and the haunting choruses of the people, *Boris Godounov* is worlds away from the polish and lyricism of its Western European contemporaries.

And therein lay the rub. The moment Moussorgsky finished composing *Boris Godounov,* people began trying to change it. The first round of revisions, at least, came from Moussorgsky himself. Advised by the Imperial Theater that his opera could not be performed without a female lead and something recognizable as a love story, the composer went back to the historical sources and came up with the "Polish Act," which features the romance of Marina Mniszek and the False Dmitri. With the addition of a harrowing final scene in the fourth act, this second version of *Boris* was deemed palatable enough for staging in 1874, when it was received with outrage by the musical establishment and some appreciation by the public. Accordingly, it remained in the Imperial Theater's repertory until 1882, the year after Moussorgsky's death at the age of forty-two. At that point, the composer's friend Nikolai Rimsky-Korsakov undertook to correct what he and others regarded as the opera's flaws. As a result, the dissonances, the sparse orchestration, and the uningratiating vocal writing gave way to a slicker, more harmonious *Boris*. In this guise, the opera became known throughout the world (though a redaction by Dmitri Shostakovitch held sway in the USSR) until about 1976, when Moussorgsky's second version was rehabilitated and restored to the international repertory.

*—— When Tsar Ivan the Terrible died in 1584, he left behind him two sons, the feeble-minded Feodor, who succeeded him, and a child named Dmitri, who died in 1591 at the age of nine under mysterious circumstances. After Feodor succumbed to general debilitation in 1598, the throne was, for the first time in the history of the Muscovite Empire, without a natural heir. All eyes turned to Boris Godounov, Feodor's regent and brother-in-law. It is at this perilous moment that our story begins. ——*

# PROLOGUE

In the courtyard of the Novodevichy Monastery near Moscow, small groups of peasants cluster outside the walls, gossiping about the boyars, or noblemen, who hurry by. Their whispering ceases with the appearance of an irritated policeman. Quickly, they gather into a tight, watchful group, but not quickly enough to please the policeman, who brandishes his truncheon fiercely. "What's the matter with you?" he hollers. "Get down this instant!"

With defiant slowness, the peasants kneel on the stones and begin a droning, mournful prayer to Boris Godounov to accept the throne. "We beseech you with burning tears in our eyes," they wail toward the monastery where Boris has immured himself. But once the police officer has walked away, the moans become less heartrending.

"Hey Mitiuka, what are we yelling for?" calls out one peasant.

"How do I know?" Mitiuka returns. Various distractions interrupt the wailing, and, just as they decide to take advantage of the policeman's absence by retreating, he returns and commands them to continue pleading—or else! They take up their keening anew.

"Silence! Stand up!" growls the officer suddenly, for Tchelkalov, the secretary of the Duma, or parliament, has appeared at the monastery gate. Boris, he announces, is obdurate in his refusal to become tsar, intending instead to devote himself to a life of prayer. After a short, fervent application to God to change Boris's mind, Tchelkalov withdraws.

Out in the square, the people are bewildered: Are they supposed to moan some more? From a short distance away comes the sound of pilgrims singing. The peasants listen reverently to the approaching monks. These monks just happen to be singing a hymn about the perils of anarchy and the importance of a strong tsar. After passing out amulets and icons, they, too, disappear into the monastery, presumably to plead with the intransigent Boris.

Mitiuka and the rest of the peasants prepare to go home, but the police officer pops out of the convent for a final directive: They are to be at the Kremlin tomorrow—or else!

The peasants shrug at one another indifferently. "If they order us to wail, we'll wail in the Kremlin, too."

Apparently Boris did not long remain obdurate, for the next thing we see is his coronation procession in the Kremlin Square. There, hundreds of commoners kneel in obeisance to their new tsar, singing his praises against a background of pealing bells. A solemn parade of bodyguards, soldiers, and boyars winds among them. Prince Shuisky carries the imperial crown. Slowly, they file into the Cathedral of the Assumption.

"Long live Tsar Boris Feodorovich!" roars Shuisky to the crowd.

"Long live our gracious tsar!" the people call back.

When the new ruler of Holy Russia finally appears before the crowd, he looks speechlessly for a full moment at the great sea of humanity below him. "My soul grieves," he begins. "Involuntary fear has gripped my heart." Striving for hope, he calls upon God to bless his throne, his land, and his people. Then, following ancient tradition, he invites the populace to partake of a great feast and turns to lead the way.

Distinctly energized by the prospect of a free meal, the crowd surges forward, and, within moments, police officers are laying about them with their cudgels. Impassively, Boris and his retinue march on.

# ACT ONE

Four years later, in the Monastery of Chudovo, the aged monk Pimen is writing deep into the night. His cell mate, young Grigory, wakes with a start from a dreadful nightmare and is comforted by Pimen. Their talk turns to Pimen's youth, and thence to the piety of Tsar Feodor, who was succeeded by the monster Boris. "We have angered God," Pimen concludes passionately. "We have nominated a regicide as our tsar!"

Grigory, listening intently, begs the old monk to tell him the story of the Tsarevich Dmitri's death.

"Oh, I remember," begins Pimen, who had been called to Uglich on that bloody day, "during mass, I heard bells sounding the alarm. There were shouts and cries. The tsarevnas came running into the courtyard; I saw the murdered tsarevich lying in a pool of blood. His mother, the tsaritsa, was lying in a faint over him. And suddenly, the frenzied people seized the villains. . . . 'Confess!' thundered the people. And in terror, under an ax, the villains confessed and named Boris the murderer."

"How old was the murdered tsarevich?" asks Grigory ruminatively. Upon learning that the murdered Dmitri had been exactly his age, an idea begins to take root in the young monk's mind. Slowly, his vision grows in glory and daring: He himself will avenge Dmitri's murder and punish the usurper by assuming the guise of the dead tsarevich. He will spin a tale of surviving the terrible attack, of being hidden away for eleven years, and of a heroic resolve to claim his heritage. And perhaps he was, after all, the tsarevich—who could tell? Picturing the fanatical devotion of his followers, Grigory grows more and more certain of his destiny.

Some time later, in a small inn on the Lithuanian border, an old innkeeper is startled by the appearance of three strange men. She is quite relieved to learn that they are monks. At least that is what the two older ones say; the young one remains silent.

Gladly, the old woman invites them in for a rest, and gladly do Missail and Varlaam accept the invitation. Grigory, their companion, enters hesitantly, looking about with caution. An escapee from the monastery, he has disguised himself as a peasant to elude the police, who are searching for a shadowy figure who calls himself the Tsarevich Dmitri and is stirring up rebellion in the populace. With a rapidly increasing band of believers, Grigory is planning to cross the border into Lithuania to gather forces for a campaign against Boris.

With extravagant expressions of regard for their hostess, the two old monks are drinking up as much free wine as they can swallow. Only Grigory does not partake of the wine. Instead, he asks how far away the border of Lithuania lies. Very close, the innkeeper tells him. So close that he could get there by evening if it weren't for the roadblocks.

"Roadblocks? What roadblocks?" asks Grigory.

"Oh, someone's escaped from Moscow," she explains, "and the orders are to check everyone at the border." But they will never catch anyone, she is certain, for it is simple to elude the barricades. Innocently, she gives Grigory the very details he has been seeking. Varlaam and Missail, who have been drinking themselves into a stupor, are now roused by a knock on the door. Two red-faced policemen stand at the threshold, looking at the three men with unfriendly expressions. The two drunks hasten to reassume their monkish identities, but Grigory, in a casual manner, announces that he is just a poor peasant on his way home. The head policeman accepts this story without a moment's doubt, but he continues to stare meaningfully at the two monks. He announces that he's in search of a heretic named Grishka Otrepiev, whom the Tsar has ordered to be caught and hanged. The more the head policeman stares at Varlaam and Missail, the more certain he is that one of them is the miscreant himself. However, the head policeman cannot read, so he is not sure which one of them matches the description in the warrant.

Grigory kindly offers to read the document for him. "The unworthy monk, Grigory Otrepiev," reads Grigory, "under the devil's instructions, has resolved to disturb the holy brotherhood of the Monastery of Chudovo with all manner of temptations and acts of lawlessness. And he, Grigory, has escaped to the Lithuanian border and the Tsar has ordered him to be caught—"

"—and hanged!" interjects the head policeman gleefully.

"It doesn't say hanged here," notes Grigory drily, and continues his reading. "He, Grisha, is about—" he looks ruminatively at Varlaam— "fifty years old. He has a gray beard, a fat belly, and red nose . . . "

"Seize him!" shriek the policemen, falling upon Varlaam.

"What are you doing, you rogues!" yells Varlaam, tearing the warrant out of Grigory's hands. "Brother, you are too young to play tricks on me! I may not be able to read, but I can at least sound out the syllables. I'll decipher it! Here . . ." He squints mightily at the paper. "He's . . . a-bout . . . twen . . . twenty. Twenty!

Where does it say fifty? He . . . has . . . li-light . . . brown . . . hair. On his nose . . . he has . . . a, a wart! And one of his . . . arms is shorter than the other . . . But wait. Isn't that . . . isn't that . . . ?" Varlaam looks suddenly toward Grigory.

But the resourceful Grigory has pulled out his dagger, and with a mighty leap, he jumps out the window and is gone.

# ACT TWO

The walls of the Imperial Apartments are hung with tapestries and the rooms appointed with velvet sofas and carved furniture, but a lowering cloud of gloom hangs over the Tsar's palace. In the schoolroom, Boris's daughter Xenia is weeping over a portrait of her dead fiancé. Her brother, Feodor, and her old nurse try to comfort her, but Xenia remains disconsolate. The nurse and Feodor join together in a riotous folk song, but in the middle of it, the Tsar slips in the door, and the nurse is too flustered to continue. Embracing his daughter, Boris, too, offers words of sympathy for the girl's loss.

After Xenia leaves with the nurse, Boris turns to his son, who is studying his geography lesson. Maps of Russia's vast territory are spread across the table, and Boris praises him on his understanding of the realm that he will someday command. Turning to his own thoughts, Boris ruminates on his reign: He has reached supreme power, his lands are at peace, the astrologers predict a long, untroubled rule—but he is tormented by dark thoughts. Having begged God for peace, he has instead received God's curses: sedition among the boyars and intrigues in Lithuania; famine, plague, earthquakes, and poverty ravaging his country; his name reviled by the people. "And even sleep evades me," mutters the Tsar, "for in the night, a blood-smeared child rises up and, pressing his hands together, his eyes ablaze, he begs for mercy! The terrible wound gapes open! I hear his last cry—Oh Lord! My God!—"

A squeal from the hallway interrupts Boris's agonies. The sounds of a scuffle can be heard, and Boris stiffens in fear. But instead of assassins, a courtier enters the room and announces the arrival of Prince Shuisky, along with a whispered caution that the Prince is rumored to be plotting the Tsar's downfall. Boris is stunned at this new evidence of treason within his ranks, but he is momentarily diverted by Feodor, who runs in to tell his father the cause of the commotion: a parrot with a vengeful character.

Boris embraces the boy, sighing, "If only I could see you as the Tsar, with what delight would I exchange the imperial scepter for that bliss." But, he warns Feodor, beware of advisers such as Shuisky, wise, perhaps, but also wily and malicious.

"Great sovereign, my homage," says Shuisky, bowing deeply. He has heard every word, but without apparent rancor, he informs his Tsar of a new and formidable threat. A pretender has appeared in Poland, where he has won the support of the King, the noblemen, and even the Pope.

Wearily Boris asks who the villain has proclaimed himself to be. When, after many circumlocutions,

Shuisky admits that the imposter has resurrected the name of Dmitri, the name is like a stab to his heart. "Tsarevich, leave!" he commands Feodor in a hoarse voice.

Once the boy has departed, the Tsar leans toward Shuisky, his eyes burning. "Take measures this instant! See that Rus is fenced off from Lithuania. Not a soul is to cross this frontier . . . Go! . . . No! Wait!" The Prince turns, his face impassive. "Have you ever heard of dead children rising from their coffins to accuse lawful tsars?" A strange howl comes from Boris's mouth. "Well? Isn't it funny? Why aren't you laughing?" Shuisky bows, his face grave. Boris continues in a whisper. "Listen, Prince! When the great crime was committed, that child . . . who perished . . . was . . . Dmitri?"

"It was," replies Shuisky firmly. "I visited the child's corpse in the Cathedral of Uglich some five days later. Around him lay thirteen bodies; they had begun to decay, but the Tsarevich's face was radiant, clear, and pure. The terrible deep wound was gaping, but there was a lovely smile on his lips. It was as though he was sleeping—"

"Enough!" breaks in Boris, signaling with a wild gesture for Shuisky to leave him. Alone, the Tsar gasps raggedly. "Oh, I can hardly breathe! O cruel conscience, how terrible your punishments are! . . . If there is even a single accidental spot, your soul is consumed with fire." Boris clutches his hands to his head, writhing in agony. "It becomes so hard, with reproaches and damnation hammering away in your ears, and something stifles you, stifles you. . . . Again and again you see a child," he moans, "a child covered in blood! Over there . . . there in the corner, it's swaying, growing, drawing close! Keep away!" he screams in terror, glancing frantically around the room. "It was the people, not I! The will of the people! Keep away! Lord! You do not want a sinner to die! Have mercy on the soul of the criminal tsar, Boris!"

Shuddering and weeping, Boris Godounov falls to the floor.

# ACT THREE

Meanwhile, in Poland, the False Dmitri has been raising an army with the not entirely disinterested support of the governor of Sandomierz and assorted other noblemen. The governor also has supplied him with a candidate for Tsaritsa in his beautiful daughter, Marina Mniszek, whose combination of steely ambition and breathtaking allure Dmitri finds irresistible.

As befits an aristocrat, Marina is being serenaded by her handmaidens as she completes her toilet. They sing paeans to her beauty and deck her with a diamond crown, but Marina is nonetheless profoundly bored. "Enough!" she calls out. Their flattering words have displeased her, she announces. Dismissing them, Marina sighs gloomily. The days have dragged by since Dmitri has gone. "My Dmitri, awesome, merciless avenger," she rhapsodizes. "God's judgement and God's punishment for the Tsar." Soon, her thoughts turn toward her future, when she shall be tsaritsa of Russia: "I shall shine like the sun in my gold-embroidered purple robe! And the dull-witted Muscovites will glorify me!" Bursting into triumphant laughter, Marina walks to the mirror

and turns this way and that, the better to admire every facet of her beauty. Suddenly, she gasps—a dark figure has slipped silently into the reflection. "Oh, it is you, Father!"

A thin, sallow man in the garb of a Jesuit priest has entered her apartments. It is Father Rangoni, Marina's confessor and confidante. Like Marina herself, Rangoni is ruthless in his pursuit of his goal, which is the conversion of the Russian state from Orthodox Christianity to Catholicism. Eyes burning with fanaticism, he calls up the image of God's Church, abandoned and defiled by the heresy of Russian Orthodoxy. He conjures up a vision of the Church restored to its glory by Marina's influence, expanding on his theme until the young noblewoman is transported with religious fervor. "Proclaim the righteous faith to the heretic Muscovites," intones Rangoni, flushed with ardor. "Show them the way of salvation, and the angels of the Lord will glorify the saintly Marina!"

Abashed, Marina protests that she is unworthy to lead such a Crusade, but Rangoni presses on, straight to the heart of her greatest weakness. "Captivate the Pretender with your beauty," he hisses, "subjugate his reason with your fiery gaze and enchanting smile! Do away with false maidenly shame! Seduce him, and when he lies exhausted at your feet, speechlessly awaiting your commands, demand a vow of propagation of the faith!"

"What?" asks Marina incredulously.

Father Rangoni will not have his ambitions thwarted: "You dare to oppose the Church?" he snarls. "You must sacrifice your honor!"

Marina is outraged at this base command. She curses Rangoni and orders him away. But the priest knows his target well. Coolly, he remarks that he sees a change in her looks, that the spirits of darkness are possessing her, and that Satan is hovering over her soul.

Even Marina Mniszek is no proof against the threat of eternal damnation. Sobbing, she falls to the floor at Rangoni's feet. He stands above her, exultant. "Entrust to me all your thoughts, desires, and dreams: Be my slave!"

"At midnight . . . in the garden . . . by the fountain . . ." murmurs Dmitri to himself as he steps into the moonlit garden of Sandomierz Castle. Rapturously he awaits his rendezvous with his beloved. But, though he calls cautiously through the screen of leaves, Marina's window remains dark. Instead, the insidious figure of Father Rangoni glides through the shadows and rises at Dmitri's side.

"You again!" cries Dmitri, startled. "You follow me like a shadow!"

Rangoni merely nods, and reports that though Marina's trysts with Dmitri have made her the target of malicious gossip, she loves him still, loves him passionately. Filled with rage at the thought of her suffering, Dmitri vows eternal love for Marina and promises to exact revenge on her adversaries by elevating her to the imperial throne, where she shall rule over all Russia at his side.

Rangoni, seeing that he has hit the bull's-eye, expatiates on Marina's torments at the hands of jealous courtiers, and Dmitri, his fury building, makes all sorts of impetuous promises. Expert manipulator that he is, Rangoni seizes the opportunity to exact a vow of protection from Dmitri. By now the Pretender is nearly mad with impatience to see his beloved, but Rangoni urges caution and leads Dmitri to a hiding place from which he may glimpse Marina, who is engaged in some obligatory flirting with a toothless old general.

The flirting, obligatory or not, infuriates the False Dmitri, and when Marina finally breaks away from her guests to keep her assignation with her lover, he greets her with a remonstrance. The haughty Marina taunts him for his callowness. Only one thing interests her: When will he be Tsar in Moscow?

Although her cold lust for power repels Dmitri, her charms ensnare him; as she winds her arms through his, he begs her not to reject his love.

Exasperated, she breaks out of his embrace. "I feel sorry for you," she says bitterly. "Love for your Marina has exhausted you. Night and day you dream about her, and you have forgotten about the struggle against Tsar Boris. Be off, vagrant! Serf!"

Dmitri responds bitterly, warning her that when he takes the throne of Russia, he will laugh at her misery. "O, how gladly shall I watch you, crawling toward the foot of my throne—then I shall command one and all to laugh at the Polish fool!"

Sensing danger, Marina quickly tries to repair the damage she has done, assuring her betrothed that she meant only to spur him on. Kneeling before him, she feigns weakness. "My Tsar!" she intones humbly, and Dmitri succumbs anew, vowing to make her his tsaritsa.

As the lovers kiss, Father Rangoni emerges from the nearby shadows to watch. A thin smile of delight curls his lips; Russia will be his.

# ACT FOUR

Far beneath the swirling, parti-colored domes of Saint Basil's Cathedral in Moscow, a miserable band of beggars clusters against the walls. They call out their greetings to some friends emerging from the cathedral's great doors, "Is the mass over?"

"Yes, and Grishka Otrepiev has been cursed."

A heated argument ensues: What good does it do to damn Grishka Otrepiev when the insurrection is being led by Tsarevich Dmitri? But they've just sung a mass for the repose of the Tsarevich's soul! But he's alive! Alive and about to give Boris what's coming to him!

The argument sinks to whispers: They say he's nearly at Kromy. He'll be marching on Moscow any day!

For all its scenes of blood-curdling madness, pretenders, and sedition, the most astonishing aspect of Boris Godounov is how much of it is based on verifiable historical fact. No one could possibly make up a plot that would exceed in brutality and strangeness the true story of Russia in the early seventeenth century.

The death of the Tsarevich Dmitri is one of the great mysteries of Russian history. Though Boris Godounov was certainly implicated, modern scholars tend to believe that he did not murder the boy; they point to Dmitri's relatively small chance of inheriting the throne. It seems unlikely that Boris would have opened himself up to the accusation of murder to get rid of such a weak rival. Most historians now believe that Dmitri was not murdered at all, but succumbed to a self-inflicted knife wound sustained during an epileptic fit.

Moussorgsky's False Dmitri is patterned closely on the original. Scholars agree that the Pretender was in fact a delusional monk named Grigory Otrepiev who left his monastery and began to foment rebellion against Boris Godounov in 1602. While raising an army in Poland in 1603, he did indeed fall in love with a beautiful Polish aristocrat named Marina Mniszek. Late in 1604, an army led by Dmitri invaded Russia and had the unbelievable luck to approach Moscow just as Boris Godounov expired. Godounov's commander immediately defected to the Pretender, and, together with boyars, he led the rebellion against Godounov's young son, who was murdered shortly after his father's death. On June 20, 1605, the False Dmitri entered the capital in triumph, and the ever-pragmatic Prince Shuisky recanted his previous testimony and vowed that he had never seen the corpse of Dmitri at Uglich, thus bolstering the Pretender's claims. The Tsarevich's mother was extracted from her nunnery long enough to have a touching reunion with her long-lost child.

Unfortunately, the honeymoon was brief. Though he refused to honor his promise to convert his domain to Catholicism, Dmitri surrounded himself with Polish and Catholic advisors. His marriage, in 1606, to the redoubtable Marina further exacerbated anti-Polish sentiment among the boyars, and soon afterward, Prince Shuisky led a coup against the new Tsar. The False Dmitri attempted escape, but he was captured and returned to his enemies, who once more brought forth Dmitri of Uglich's mother, who now swore that the Pretender was an imposter. After the wily Prince Shuisky ascended to the throne, the False Dmitri was murdered, then burned, and his ashes were fired from a cannon in the direction of Poland. This valiant effort to eradicate future Dmitris proved futile, however, for before 1607 was over, another False Dmitri had appeared, claiming once more to be the rightful heir to the throne. Primarily because of the disarray that existed in Russia at the time, this Dmitri, too, enjoyed a certain success. Marina Mniszek, always a realist when power was at stake, recognized him as her husband, and the mother of the original Dmitri joyfully identified him as her offspring. Though the second False Dmitri established a stronghold near Moscow, he was never formally crowned Tsar. Basil Shuisky fought hard for his throne but finally lost it in 1610, when a council of clergy, boyars, gentry, and commoners deposed him and forced him to become a monk.

Now comes a diversion. The neighborhood simpleton totters into the square, his shackles clanking, hoping to escape the pack of boys who routinely torment him.

"I've got a kopeck, you know!" announces the Fool proudly.

"Impossible!" cry the boys, gathering round the poor simpleton, who produces the coin. The boys snatch it from his hand and dash away, screaming with laughter, while the onlookers shake their heads.

"Oh! Oh!" moans the Fool, oblivious to the imperial procession coming down the cathedral steps. "They've offended God's Fool! They've taken my kopeck!"

As Boris, followed by Shuisky and some boyars, marches past, the beggars plead for alms, but the Tsar's attention is caught by the Fool's lament. "What is he crying about?" asks Boris curiously.

"The boys have taken my kopeck," wails the Fool. "Have them killed as you did the little Tsarevich."

"Silence!" hisses Shuisky. "Seize the Fool!"

"Don't touch him!" Boris says quickly, and, turning back to the simpleton, he says gently, "Pray for me, blessed one," before he hurries away.

"No, Boris, I can't," the Fool protests, as the courtiers brush hastily by him. "I can't pray for a Tsar Herod. The Mother of God will not allow it."

Deep within the Kremlin, an extraordinary session of the Boyar's Council is in progress, yet the boyars are, as usual, mired in vacillation and petty disagreement. The secretary of the Duma, Tchelkalov, reads an edict denouncing the Pretender, and the boyars argue vigorously about how the traitor should be put to death, ignoring the fact that the Pretender hasn't been caught. They develop an exquisite menu of torture, but it needs, they reflect mournfully, the approval of Prince Shuisky.

In strides Shuisky, apologizing for his lateness. With oily smoothness, he turns the discussion to the Tsar. A few days before, he happened to look through a chink in the palace wall, and what did he see? Boris, shivering and muttering. "All of a sudden, his face darkened and he began staring at a corner, groaning terribly and stepping back in horror! 'Keep away! Keep away!' he cried—"

Shuisky stops, for Boris has entered the boyars' chamber. His eyes are glazed and staring; he has no notion that he is surrounded by people. "Keep away! Keep away!" he shouts hoarsely.

"Keep away, child!" repeats Shuisky, attempting to lead him to confession.

"Keep away!" Boris looks about wildly. "There is no murderer. He's alive, the little child is alive!" Suddenly, the Tsar realizes where he is. Shaking his head violently, he returns to his senses. "And Shuisky is to be quartered for perjury!" he adds bitterly.

Somewhat taken aback, Shuisky changes the subject: There's an old man who is waiting to present himself to the Tsar, for he has a great secret to reveal.

Hoping for some good news, Boris commands him to be summoned. The guest is none other than the monk Pimen, who tells the Tsar of a miraculous event. An old shepherd, blind since childhood, was commanded in a dream to journey to the town of Uglich and pray upon the grave of Dmitri. As soon as he did so, his sight was restored.

A sudden dagger thrust of guilt and despair causes Boris to fall back in his chair. "Oh," he cries. "I cannot breathe. I can't breathe. Take me into the light!" Collapsing into the arms of his attendants, he gasps for air. "The Tsarevich, quickly!" he begs, and the room erupts into confusion. Some boyars leap to do his bidding; others whisper among themselves; still others stand gaping.

Feodor comes running in with Shuisky at his side and embraces his father. "Farewell, my son," Boris begins weakly. "You will begin to reign now. Do not ask me how I came to the throne. There is no need for you to know." Desperately, the Tsar gives advice and instruction to the boy and prays to God to protect his child. As a nearby choir calls him to heaven, Boris makes one last attempt to rally. "Oh, spiteful death, wait a little. I am still the Tsar!" But, clutching his heart, he falls back into a chair. "Forgive me!"

The boyars stand frozen, watching the death agonies of their ruler. Feodor bows his head and weeps. The vast chamber is silent as Tsar Boris Godounov takes his final breath.

Snow lies thick on the ground in the forest near Kromy, and in the still air, shouts and cries can be heard. A ragged pack of peasants moves into the clearing, pushing a boyar before them with sticks and cudgels. They have beaten him half to death, but they aren't finished with him yet; propping him up against a tree, they gag him and taunt him cruelly, for upon him they propose to avenge all the wrongs they have suffered at the hands of the landowners.

Bands of vagrants drift out of the trees to join in the retribution. The simpleton, still pursued by his tormentors, shuffles into the clearing. Missail and Varlaam, too, wander into the scene, offering dire warnings about the consequences of Boris's sinful rule. "The sun and the moon have grown dim," they intone. "The stars have vanished. Boris's grave sin has caused the universe to tremble. Beasts never heard of before are being born and devouring human bodies."

The assembly calls for an uprising and hails the rebel forces as saviors. Working up a fever, the crowd turns on two Jesuit priests who happen onto the scene, but, just as they are about to be hanged, trumpets herald the arrival of Tsarevich Dmitri. A moment later, the clearing is filled with soldiers bearing torches, and the Pretender arrives on horseback. The populace cheers him, and he returns their salute: "We, Dmitri Ivanovich, by God's will Tsarevich of All Rus, Prince from the family of our ancestors, invite you who have been persecuted by Godounov to join us, and in return promise you charity and protection!"

Inspired, zealous, the people throng to Dmitri's side; even the beaten boyar declares his devotion, and, as bells clang in the distance, these new converts follow their leader towards Moscow. The clearing empties, the sounds of trumpets, horses, and voices dies away, and only the Fool is left, sitting on a stone. He begins to chant, "Flow, bitter tears. Weep, weep, Orthodox soul! Soon the enemy will come and darkness blacker than night will descend. Woe is Rus! Weep, Russian people! Weep, famished people!"

# I PAGLIACCI

## — *The Clowns* —

*I*Pagliacci is considered the arch-example of *verismo,* or realism, a movement that took Italian opera by storm at the end of the nineteenth century. Following the precepts of Zola, veristic composers abandoned aristocratic anguish and offered, instead, "a slice of life." That was the theory, anyway. It's true that *Pagliacci* features no aristocrats, taking its plot from the doings of a poor troupe of strolling actors. Otherwise, this blood-drenched, passion-driven opera, featuring adultery, vengeance, deformity, and murder, presents little in the way of everyday life. This failure to adhere to theory hardly mattered to *Pagliacci*'s audience, who lapped up the sensational story with gusto and made the opera one of the most phenomenally popular of all time, despite critical sneers and jeers.

The composer of *Pagliacci,* Ruggiero Leoncavallo, who began his musical career as an ardent Wagnerian, suffered the fate of being labeled a one-hit wonder: Though he wrote and wrote, his later work never achieved even a fraction of the acclaim his suffering clowns have been awarded since they first took the stage in 1892.

## PROLOGUE

The theater is not yet dark. People are still coming in, settling themselves in their chairs, shifting, rustling, smoothing their coats. They greet one another, hand sweetmeats back and forth. Now the lights dim, and the audience looks expectantly, appreciatively, toward the stage.

A face peers out between the curtains, then disappears. A short, hunched figure limps out toward the footlights. It is Tonio, waving his hands to silence the audience. "If I may? Ladies and gentlemen, I am the Prologue. As you can see, the author wishes to remind you of old traditions, but also to bring you some new ones. Ours is not a drama in the old style; we will not show you feigned tears and false suffering. No, the author has sought instead to show you a bleeding slice of life, for he has only one conviction, and it is this: He must write for people like you and me." Here, Tonio smiles enigmatically, then continues. "Therefore, you will see how humans really love each other, see the sad fruits of hatred, spasms of sorrow and agony, shouts of anger, and cynical laughter. Instead of our poor costumes and poses, consider our souls, because we are men of flesh and bones, and just like you, we breathe the air of this inhospitable world. So, now, I've given you the idea. Just watch how it unfolds."

# ACT ONE

In a small, dusty village in the Italian countryside, a long holiday afternoon is drifting slowly by. Suddenly the quiet is ruptured by the rattling of cart wheels, followed by cheers and cries, faint at first and then growing louder, as a little band of players marches into town. The townspeople call to one another and the village boys scramble after the small wagon that serves the company as stage, dressing room, and transportation. Beppe, who drives the donkey, and Canio, the lead actor and manager, swat cheerfully at the rambunctious boys, which deters them not at all. "Three cheers for the clowns!" bellow the boys.

"Bravo!" holler the villagers. "What's the play?"

Canio steps forward with an elegant mock bow and wallops a huge drum to silence the crowd. The great performance begins at seven, he tells them, and they are all cordially invited. Jubilant at the prospect, the crowd begins to disperse, excepting the cluster of boys, who linger, attracted to the glamour of the theater. They watch as the hunchbacked actor Tonio moves to help the leading lady, Nedda, down from her seat and is quickly slapped for his trouble by Canio, her husband. "Get out of here!" Canio orders Tonio, and the boys giggle.

Tonio's bitter glance follows Canio's retreating back. "You'll pay for that, villain," he mutters darkly.

An old villager invites Canio and his company to come for a drink. Canio and Beppe accept with alacrity, but Tonio begs off. At this uncharacteristic abstemiousness, the boys call out teasingly to Canio, "Be careful, clown! The only reason Tonio is staying behind is to flirt with Nedda."

Canio's easy smile fades and his cheerful face becomes grim. *Un tal gioco . . .* If that's a joke, believe me, it's better not to joke with me," he warns them. "The theater is not the same as life. On stage, the clown may find his wife with a lover in her room, he gives a funny speech, and you all applaud. But if Nedda gave me such a surprise, the story would end differently!"

Nedda, looking innocent, murmurs, "I don't understand," and Canio departs with his pals.

But now a little procession of pipers is marching toward the church for vespers, and, beckoned by the resounding call of the bells, the villagers flock after them.

Left alone, Nedda reflects anxiously on Canio's jealous nature, but such dark thoughts are anathema to her light heart; warmed by the afternoon sun, she cheers herself by watching the birds flying freely through the air. She envies them their freedom, their adventures, their abandon—

Nedda gasps, for the dark figure of Tonio appears suddenly at her side. "Is that you?" she says harshly. "I thought you had gone."

The hunchback moves closer. "Your singing," he says hoarsely. "You fascinate me, enchant me!"

Nedda laughs cruelly, and she carelessly orders him to leave. "You can tell me that you love me tonight, on stage!" she sneers.

"Don't laugh, Nedda," Tonio warns, but she continues to mock him, his deformity and his love, until he can bear it no longer and his soul turns dark with rage. "Wretch! By God, you'll pay for this!"

"You're threatening me?" asks Nedda, with an incredulous smile. "You want me to call Canio?"

"Not until I kiss you!" replies Tonio, lunging for her.

But Nedda is too quick for him; grabbing a whip from the wagon, she lashes Tonio fiercely. Screaming in pain, he falls back and stands glowering at her. "Nedda, I swear it. You'll pay!" he growls, stumbling away.

Nedda looks after him, slowly recovering from her shock.

"Nedda!" calls a voice softly.

Turning, she sees her lover, Silvio, sidling close to the wagon. "Silvio! Now? You know it's not safe," she remonstrates. But she cannot resist him, and they begin to talk, quietly, urgently. She tells him of Tonio's attack and her reprisal, and Silvio begs her to leave the company and find refuge with him.

"Don't tempt me," she cries. "Do you want to get me killed? It's crazy!" But as Silvio repeats his pleas, Nedda's resolve crumbles. Giving herself up to his arms, she kisses Silvio passionately. Neither of them sees Tonio, who looks on with a bitter smile from the shadows of the trees. Silently he departs.

"If you're leaving tomorrow, why do you kiss me like this?" demands Silvio. "You must have forgotten our secret hours, but I have not! Your kisses have kindled a fever in my heart!"

"I've forgotten nothing!" protests Nedda. "I want to live only with you, a life of love and peace. I give up!" She capitulates. "You alone will rule me!"

"So you'll come to me?"

"Yes. Kiss me," she replies.

Canio and Tonio are coming toward the wagon. "Walk softly and you'll surprise them," the hunchback whispers.

"'Til tonight," Nedda is calling softly after the departing Silvio, "and then I'm yours forever!"

With a roar of fury, Canio races toward the disappearing figure, determined to catch his rival.

Nedda, terrified, realizes that her secret has been discovered, and the figure of Tonio, standing nearby with a small smile on his face, reveals how. Ironically, she congratulates him on his success.

"You don't know how happy I am," he assures her.

Canio stumbles back, flushed and panting. His pursuit has come to nothing, but he is determined to force a confession from Nedda. "The name, don't delay, woman!" he cries, drawing out his dagger.

"No! I'll never say it!" she hisses, unafraid.

Swearing, Canio lunges at his wife and is only kept from stabbing her by the intervention of Beppe, who rushes in and pulls the knife from Canio's shaking hand. "Sir, my God, what are you doing?" cries Beppe. "People are gathering for the play. Calm down!"

Still, Canio demands the name of Nedda's lover, but she steadfastly refuses to utter it. Finally, Beppe takes matters into his own hands and commands her to dress for her part. Tonio, smiling, assures Canio that he'll keep an eye out for her lover during the performance.

"Come on, boss, get dressed," says Beppe gently. "And, you, Tonio, beat the drum."

Canio stands immobile, unseeing, as the two men leave. Mechanically, he starts toward the wagon, then stops. "Perform! Now? But you must force yourself! Are you a man? You're a clown! *Vesti la giubba* . . . Put on the garb and whiten your face. People pay to laugh at you," he cries, tears streaming down his face. "Turn into a jest your agony and tears, your sob into a funny face. Laugh, clown, over your shattered love. Laugh at the poison in your heart." Slowly, painfully, Canio approaches the curtain that covers the dressing room. Reaching to pull it aside, he breaks down into tears once again, then straightens and enters the theater.

# ACT TWO

The villagers rush forward exuberantly, full of anticipation for the entertainment. Beppe, hurriedly arranging chairs, and Tonio, banging his drum, mingle with the audience, urging them to take their seats. Silvio enters with studied casualness, greeting old friends and surreptitiously eyeing the stage. The crowd buzzes with excitement. Suddenly a bell rings, and the stage curtain rises to reveal Nedda, as pretty, flirtatious Columbina, seated at a table. After casting any number of impatient glances out the window, she finally rises and begins to pace nervously about. Pagliaccio, her husband, she informs the audience, will return late that night, and the time is ripe for a tryst. But her dumb servant, Taddeo, is missing, which is throwing her plans off.

At this moment, the strumming of guitar is heard, and Arlecchino, Columbina's lover, begins to serenade his sweetheart from beneath her window. Columbina's transports of love are interrupted by the return of Taddeo, played by Tonio, who sighs mournfully over his unrequited love for the lady of the house.

Just as in real life, Columbina shows nothing but scorn for the lowly Taddeo and orders him to hand over the groceries he was sent to buy. While Columbina talks chickens, Taddeo attempts to talk love, aggravating the lady no end. Finally, Arlecchino, who has been waiting impatiently for Taddeo to hie himself off, climbs in the window and grabs the ridiculous fellow by the ear. To the delight of the audience, Arlecchino gets rid of the lovelorn Taddeo with a swift kick and is rewarded by a rapturous greeting from Columbina. The lovers happily pull themselves up to the table to sup on Taddeo's chicken, feeding one another morsels as they concoct a plan to poison Pagliaccio, Columbina's husband. The lady is just agreeing to this murderous scheme when Taddeo rushes in, shaking like a leaf. Pagliaccio is coming—he knows everything—he's armed! And Taddeo sprints away in cowardly panic.

Arlecchino, feeling no particular desire to face an enraged husband, also opts for a discreet retreat. "Put the poison in his cup," he calls to his beloved as he lowers himself out the window.

"Until tonight," calls Columbina. "Then I'm yours forever!"

Canio, entering the room, seems to stumble, for those were the very words he heard from Nedda's lips that afternoon. After a long moment, he begins to speak his lines, woodenly, carelessly, his eyes locked on Nedda's averted face.

Awkwardly, the play lurches on: Columbina dismisses Pagliaccio's accusations with a laugh and calls on the fumbling Taddeo to affirm her innocence. The audience laughs happily when the aggrieved Pagliaccio demands to know the name of his rival.

Doggedly, Nedda keeps to her script, cooing "Pagliaccio, Pagliaccio!"

*"No! Pagliaccio non son!"* cries Canio, "I'm not Pagliaccio. If my face is pale, it's with rage for vengeance. Man demands his rights, and a bleeding heart wants blood to cleanse disgrace, damn you. I'm not Pagliaccio! I'm the fool who rescued you from an orphan's life, nearly starved to death, offered you a name, and loved you to the point of insanity!"

Silvio, out in the audience, is now trembling in fear, while the ladies around him twitter wonderingly about this heartrending play. Nedda, onstage, summons her dignity. "Well, then, if you think me unworthy of you, throw me out right now!"

Canio laughs bitterly. "So you can run right to your dear lover? How clever you are! No, by God, you're staying here, and you're going to tell me the name of your lover!"

Vainly, Nedda attempts to continue the play, but Canio prevents her. "His name or your life!" he roars.

"No! By my mother," Nedda cries, "I may be unworthy, if that's what you want to think, but a coward I'm not!"

The audience is now lost in consternation. Are they acting? Are they serious? What is happening? Beppe, horrified, makes a move to intervene and is held down by an exultant Tonio, who watches the stage as though he could never get enough. The craven Silvio looks on in dismay—until the clown reaches for his dagger, and he sees that his beloved Nedda is in mortal peril. Leaping from his seat, he attempts to charge the stage but is restrained by the uncomprehending villagers. Nedda, realizing Canio's desperate intent, makes a frantic attempt to escape, but her enraged husband seizes her and stabs her, once, again, and again.

"Silvio!" screams the dying woman.

Breaking free of his captors, Silvio dashes to save his lover, but he is too late to do anything other than give himself away. "Ah, so it's you!" calls Canio triumphantly, thrusting his dagger deep into Silvio's heart. "Welcome!"

As the villagers scream in terror, Canio drops his knife and turns toward them in his bloodstained clown robes. Quietly, he looks out at his audience. "The comedy is finished," he announces. ~❦

# LA BOHÈME

~⊙⊙~

In 1890, Giacomo Puccini was just another impecunious composer, one of the many candidates in the Heir to Verdi contest that preoccupied Italy for so many decades. His first opera had been moderately successful, but his second was an out-and-out failure, and their author seemed more likely to fade into obscurity than to become the preeminent operatic composer of his day. Yet that is what happened.

Even before his rise, Puccini was renowned for tormented relations with his librettists. During the composition of *Manon Lescaut,* which was to be his breakthrough opera, he cast aside several writers in succession before landing the poet and dramatist Giuseppe Giacosa, who in turn convinced his young colleague Luigi Illica to take on the major burdens of the writing. This triumvirate—Puccini, Giacosa, Illica—proved propitious. Despite years of complaints, disputes, and ruptures, they produced four of the most popular operas ever composed, among them *La Bohème.*

Puccini had been casting about for a subject for some months before he came upon a dramatization of Henri Murger's *Scènes de la vie de Bohème,* a novel based on the author's irresponsible and artistic youth. Together with Illica and Giacosa, Puccini labored for three years to transform the material into its final dramatic form. This required a substantial revision of some of the characters: The poetic Rodolfo, based on Murger himself, was transplanted without much pruning; but the Mimi of the opera is a considerably more delicate creature than her predecessor in the novel, whose tiny white hands were described by Murger as designed "to mutilate the poet's heart with their pink nails" and whose eyes were "overcast . . . by an expression of cruelty that was almost savage." This discrepancy between the original Mimi and the operatic Mimi was a particular source of stress between Puccini and Giacosa, who was outraged at the quantity of revisions demanded by the composer, whose editorial interference he called the "Puccini torture."

Nevertheless, the product of this arduous process was a smashing success. Despite the usual objections of the critics, the public loved *La Bohème,* with its charismatic melodies and pathetic story, and within a few years of its premiere in 1896, it had become one of the most often performed works in the repertory.

# ACT ONE

Paris, Christmas Eve, some time in the 1830s. Snow swirls against the window of a barren attic room where two young artists are hard at work. As Marcello squints at his much-belabored painting of the Red Sea, Rodolfo finally gives up his attempt to write and contemplates the empty fireplace.

"I have something very profound to say," announces Marcello. "I'm frozen stiff."

"Me, too," agrees Rodolfo. "I no longer believe in sweat."

"My fingers are so cold," says Marcello, "I feel as if I've stuck them in Musetta's icy heart."

Always the poet, Rodolfo is compelled to speak of the fire of love—until Marcello interrupts him to suggest that they burn the chair.

Unfortunately, it's their only chair. But Rodolfo has an inspiration. He seizes an enormous sheaf of paper. "I've got ideas to burn!"

"Should we burn the Red Sea?"

"No, no. Paint makes a terrible stink, but this fiery drama will keep us warm!" He hands Marcello part of the manuscript, and together they light it.

As the paper burns, the philosopher Colline enters the garret with a pile of books. "The Apocalypse approaches!" he cries. "Even on Christmas Eve, the pawnbrokers take nothing!" He dumps the pile on the table. "What's this? A fire?"

"Quiet!" commands Rodolfo. "I'm giving my play."

"To the fire," adds Marcello. "I find it inflaming."

"But it doesn't last," says Colline, watching the blaze die.

"Brevity is priceless," says Rodolfo sternly.

Together, they toss the rest of the play into the blaze, applauding enthusiastically. But soon the paper is expended and the crackling flames grow dim.

"What a hollow, empty drama," Colline says bitterly. "Down with the author!"

Just as they are about to return to their freezing state, two messenger boys arrive, bearing food, bottles, cigars, and even wood. The three friends fall upon them as the musician Schaunard comes through the door.

"The Bank of France is now open!" he announces, showering the floor with coins. While Rodolfo, Marcello, and Colline dive for them, Schaunard tells how he came into this fortune. A rich Englishman ordered him to play in the same room with a parrot until it died. After three days of nonstop music, he finally poisoned the parrot with parsley, and—

But the others, rushing to light a fire and set the table, haven't heard a word.

"The devil take you all!" Schaunard shouts. He looks about him. "What on earth are you doing? This food is our insurance against dark days ahead; tonight is Christmas Eve! My friends! On Christmas Eve, you drink at home, but you dine away!"

Seeing the wisdom of this, the friends gather round the bottle, but a sudden knock on the door freezes them in mid-toast. It's Benoit, their put-upon landlord, come to collect the rent. Seeing that they can't evade him, the friends undertake to get the old man drunk. Waving aside his bill, they drink to his health several times. Overwhelmed by their courtesy, Benoit soon loses his indignant air. When they begin to tease him about an imaginary liaison, he acknowledges that he likes his girls not too fat, not too thin. Skinny women are his abomination, he says; his wife, for example—

Marcello feigns horror. "This man has a wife, yet he harbors evil desires!" he shrieks, recoiling.

"He taints and infects this abode of virtue!" cries Rodolfo.

"But gentlemen . . ." wails Benoit.

"Get out of here!" they bellow, bundling him out the door and slamming it behind him.

"There!" says Marcello with satisfaction. "I've paid the rent."

"Café Momus and the Latin Quarter await," intones Schaunard. "Let's go!"

"I'm going to stay a bit longer," says Rodolfo. "I have to finish up my article."

"Hurry!" commands Marcello, putting on his coat.

"Five minutes," replies Rodolfo.

Marcello, Schaunard, and Colline depart, while Rodolfo begins to write. After a few moments of desultory scribbling, he throws down his pen. "Not in the mood," he mutters.

There is a soft knock at his door.

"Who's there?" calls Rodolfo gruffly.

"Excuse me," answers a timid voice. Surprised, Rodolfo opens the door. A delicate young woman stands on the threshold. "I'm sorry, but my candle went out," she says shyly. "Would you be so kind as to—"

"Please have a seat," Rodolfo says, for he can see that she is pale and tired.

"Oh, no, thank you," she replies, but her words dissolve into a fit of coughing.

"Are you ill?" asks Rodolfo.

"I'm only out of breath from the stairs—" she begins, but suddenly she puts her hand to her eyes and falls in a faint. Rodolfo jumps forward to catch her and places her gently in the chair. Finding some water, he touches it to her cheeks.

"What a beautiful girl," Rodolfo says to himself as she slowly revives.

"I'm much better now," she says. "May I light my candle? Oh, thank you. Good night." But no sooner does she go through the door than she is back. "How silly! The key to my room—where did I leave it?" The window shakes with a gust of wind, and her candle flickers and dies. "Oh, heavens!" she cries in consternation.

"Will you light it again? I'm sorry to be such a bother."

Rodolfo surreptitiously blows out his own candle, too. "Confounded darkness," he exclaims in mock exasperation. "I'll find your key," he adds gallantly.

A few moments of searching yield the missing key, which he quickly hides.

"Are you looking?" the girl calls into the darkness.

"Oh yes," replies Rodolfo, continuing his sham hunt. Guided by her voice, he moves toward where she kneels and reaches out to touch her hand.

"Oh!" she cries, surprised.

*Che gelida manina . . .* Your tiny hand is so cold," he says, holding it in his. "Let me warm it. It's useless to search in the dark. But look! We're in luck. It's a moonlit night, and up here the moon is very close."

She tries to withdraw her hand.

"No, wait, signorina!" Rodolfo catches at it. "Wait! Will you give me just a few moments? Let me tell you who I am, what I do, how I live. Please?"

She nods shyly, and Rodolfo begins his story: He's a poet, but despite his poverty, he tells her, he's a millionaire in dreams and

delusions, or, at least, he was—until a moment ago, when all his treasure was taken by two thieves: a pair of beautiful eyes. "When you came through that door just now," he tells her, "all my dreams were stolen. But that is unimportant, because they have been replaced by a very sweet hope." He leans down to look in her eyes. "And who are you? Won't you tell me?" he asks softly.

*Mi chiamano Mimi . . .* they call me Mimi," she responds, "though my name is really Lucia." She's just a seamstress who embroiders flowers on linens and silks. She's content making her lilies and roses and finding happiness in anything that speaks of spring and love, of dreams and illusions, anything that can be called poetry. "I live alone," she continues, "in a little white room that looks out on bare roofs and gray sky, but when spring comes, the first rays of the sun are mine, the first kiss of April is mine! But," she falters, embarrassed, "that's all. Really, I'm just your neighbor who intrudes on you."

Their silence is broken by taunts rising from the street. Rodolfo's friends have returned to see what's taking him so long.

Rodolfo opens the window. "A couple more lines. I'll be there soon."

"What are you doing up there alone?" shouts Marcello.

"I'm not alone," admits Rodolfo. "There are two of us. Go on to Momus and save us a place."

"Hmm," says Marcello astutely, "the poet's found his poetry."

Turning away from the window, Rodolfo catches a glimpse of Mimi in the moonlight. "O, lovely girl," he exclaims, "I see in you the dream that I would like always to have." Together, they reveal the love that has overtaken them, and Rodolfo steals a kiss. "You're mine!" he exults.

"But your friends are waiting," says Mimi.

"You send me away?"

"I could come with you," she offers demurely.

Arm in arm, they depart for Café Momus.

# ACT TWO

The Latin Quarter is alive with students and artists, musicians and streetwalkers, tradesmen and ragged children. The milling throng is irrepressible, singing and calling out greetings. Colline inspects a ragged cloak he hopes to buy, Schaunard haggles over the price of a horn, and Marcello offers his heart to all the beautiful girls passing by.

In their halo of happiness, Mimi and Rodolfo walk dreamily toward the cafe. Ducking into a milliner's shop, Rodolfo buys Mimi a little bonnet decked with roses. She promptly puts it on. "Do you like it?" she asks coyly.

"It gives you lovely color," he replies, looking at her as if he could never look enough.

While the two lovers wend their way through the crowd, Marcello, Schaunard, and Colline commandeer a table at the café, which is so crammed that tables have been put outside, under awnings festooned with lights. They order a splendid supper.

"Here we are," says Rodolfo, arriving at the table with Mimi. Introducing her, he makes no attempt to disguise his euphoria. Soon, the four bohemians and Mimi are deep in a discussion of love. Naturally, Mimi and Rodolfo are ardent supporters of love.

Marcello, though, has reason to disagree, particularly when, as he lifts his glass to drink, he catches sight of a gorgeously dressed woman with a provocative smile coming toward the café. "And for me—poison!" he exclaims.

"What? What's happened?" his friends cry.

"Herself," says Marcello, in a choked voice.

And there she is, his beloved of days gone by, Musetta, arrayed in brilliant silks and accompanied by Alcindoro, a querulous and infatuated old man with plenty of money. She sashays between the tables, making sure that all eyes are upon her. "Come, Lulu!" she calls shrilly to Alcindoro, seating herself next to the bohemians with much fluffing of boas and swishing of petticoats, "Sit!"

"Here? Outside?" says the old man fretfully, turning up his collar.

"Her name is Musetta," Marcello explains to Mimi. "Her last name is Temptation. She's a bird of prey and her daily food is hearts. She eats them, and that is why I have none."

No matter how charmingly she tosses her head, Musetta cannot entice Marcello to glance at her. There he is, chatting away as though she weren't even there. "If only I could fight," she mutters. "If only I could scratch. All I've got is this old pelican here." She squirms with frustration and suddenly grabs a plate from the waiter. "Hey! This dish smells of stale oil!" she screams.

"Quiet, Musetta! Quiet!" begs Alcindoro.

Suddenly, Musetta turns and speaks directly to Marcello. "You won't look at me—"

Rodolfo whispers to Mimi, "I would never forgive such behavior as this."

"I love you and I am yours," she whispers back. "Why all this talk of forgiveness?"

"But I know your heart is hammering," Musetta continues, standing up. "*Quando me'n vo soletta per la via* . . . When I wander through the streets alone, people stare. They drink down my beauty from head to foot—"

"O God, tie me to the chair," cries Marcello.

"And I see the subtle signs of desire flaming in their eyes. You who know, do you think you can avoid me? I know your anguish. You would never reveal it, but I know that inside, you feel dead!"

"This is revolting," quavers Alcindoro.

"The poor girl is crazy about Marcello," whispers Mimi to Rodolfo.

"He's going to capitulate in a minute," observes Schaunard drily.

"Inside, you feel dead," repeats Musetta, her eyes locked on Marcello.

"Quietly, please," pleads Alcindoro.

"This wretched girl, I pity her," says Mimi softly. "Love that's not generous is sad."

"But love without courage is feeble," argues Rodolfo.

"Manners! Grace!" continues Alcindoro.

"Oh, I've got to get rid of this old fool!" mutters Musetta. Suddenly, she utters a piercing shriek, making Alcindoro jump.

"This comedy is splendid," agree Colline and Schaunard.

"My foot! A terrible pain!" She thrusts her foot in her protector's face. "Quick, untie the laces, I beg you! There's a boot shop over there. You must run and buy me another pair. What pain I'm in! Run! Quick!"

The old man fusses off, and Marcello and Musetta face each other. "Oh, my youth, you are not yet dead!" says Marcello. "Nor is my memory of you."

"Marcello!" says Musetta passionately, as they fall into each other's arms.

The waiter approaches with the bill, which is passed round the table like a dish nobody ordered.

"It's high," warns Rodolfo. From the distance come the sounds of a military band. The crowd surges forward to see the parade.

"We're broke," says Marcello.

"Give me the bill," says Musetta. "We'll just add it to the other. The gentleman I was with will pay it," she explains to the waiter.

The bohemians burst into laughter.

"Let's go quickly! Don't let the old boy see us leaving with his prey!" Marcello and Colline say together.

The military patrol enters with a great roll of drums. Musetta, unable to walk in her single shoe, is hoisted aloft by Marcello and Colline and carried through the crowd. "Long live Musetta!" the bohemians cry, marching behind the parade. "The pride and joy of the Latin Quarter!"

A few moments after they depart, Alcindoro returns with the boots, only to be greeted by an empty café and two exorbitant bills.

# ACT THREE

It is now February, and the day dawns cold, the air white with frost and fog. At a tollgate on the road to Paris, several street sweepers and farmers have gathered, waiting for the gate to be opened. Across the small square is a tavern, and above its door swings Marcello's painting of the Red Sea. From within come whoops and laughter mingled with the clinking of glasses. Outside, around a small brazier, the customs guards doze on a bench.

"Hey, we're freezing! Open up!" call the street sweepers.

From inside the tavern, Musetta's voice can be heard, singing a rollicking song.

*Though it was a hit in Italy,* La Bohème *aroused considerable critical ire elsewhere. Only after it received a champion in the form of famed Australian soprano Nellie Melba did the opera become popular throughout the world. Melba was the Mimi par excellence, and when Enrico Caruso joined her as Rodolfo in 1900, their collaboration became one of the most illustrious in operatic history. On May 24, 1902, the pair brought* La Bohème *to Covent Garden in London, where they created a sensation. John McCormack, a notable tenor in his own right, recalled later that when Caruso began to sing, "my jaw dropped as though hung on a hinge. Such smoothness and purity of tone, and such quality; it was like a stream of liquid gold." Soprano Mary Garden was equally astonished by Melba's high C at the end of Act One: "It left Melba's throat, it left Melba's body, it left everything, and came over like a star and passed us in our box, and went out into the infinite. I have never heard anything like it in my life, not from any other singer, ever. . . . My God, how beautiful it was! Since then I always wait for that note when I hear the first act of* Bohème, *and they reach and reach for it, and they scream it, and it's underneath and it's false, and it rolls down the stairs, and never comes out from behind that door, never. That note of Melba's was just like a ball of light. It wasn't attached to anything at all—it was out of everything."*

Finally, the guards open the tollgate, and the peasants and sweepers surge forward toward the city. Mimi, looking cold and tired, enters the square and stands for a moment, glancing about.

"Can you tell me which is the tavern where the painter is working?" she asks a guard.

He points the way, and when a servant emerges from the tavern door, Mimi begs her to fetch Marcello.

As Marcello comes out, Mimi rushes up to him. "I hoped I'd find you here."

"Yes, Musetta and I have been here for a month, at the tavern keeper's expense. She's teaching singing, and I'm painting battle scenes on the walls. It's freezing! Won't you come in?"

"Is Rodolfo there?" Mimi asks hesitantly.

"Yes."

"Then I cannot come in. Oh Marcello, help me!" Between sobs, she explains, "Rodolfo both loves me and wants to run from me. He's consumed with jealousy. Everything makes him suspicious, everything—a step, a word, a kiss, a flower—and we spend our days in quarrels and rages. At night, when I'm pretending to sleep, I feel as though he's trying to pry even into my dreams," Mimi cries disconsolately.

Touched by her despair, Marcello struggles to find words of comfort. "Perhaps a love like yours and Rodolfo's is too intense to continue forever," he suggests.

"You're right," says Mimi sadly. "We must separate. Will you help us? We've tried to help ourselves, but we've failed." Her words end in a wrenching cough.

"My God, what a cough!" exclaims Marcello.

"I've been exhausted since yesterday. He fled from me in the night, saying, 'It's finished!' and when day broke, I came here to find you."

Peering through the tavern window, Marcello sees Rodolfo rising. He warns Mimi, and she hides as Rodolfo emerges.

"Finally, a chance to talk!" Rodolfo begins. "Marcello, I need to separate from Mimi."

"So it's time to have another funeral?" asks Marcello unsympathetically.

"This time, it's forever!" declares Rodolfo, as Mimi creeps closer to listen.

"Only a crazy person would want such a gloomy, dark love! If it doesn't laugh and sparkle, love is weak and brittle. You're a jealous man," accuses Marcello.

"A little," admits Rodolfo.

"You're a bad-tempered maniac, full of prejudices, tiresome and stubborn!" continues Marcello, getting angry.

"Mimi is a tramp," says Rodolfo defensively. "She flirts with everyone. Some damn fop of a viscount gives her the eye, and she shows her ankle."

Marcello looks at him, unimpressed. "Do I even need to say it? You're lying."

The fight dies out of Rodolfo. "You're right. I'm lying." He sits down heavily. "It's no use concealing my real worry. I love Mimi more than anything in the world, but she's so ill. Every day, she gets worse.

The poor girl is dying."

"Mimi?" says Marcello incredulously.

Mimi leans against the wall, trembling.

"That terrible cough is shaking her apart," Rodolfo continues, as if to himself, "and already her cheeks are drained of color."

"Dying?" whispers Mimi, terrified.

"My room is a squalid hovel! I have no fire, and the north wind blows through like it's a mountaintop. Mimi sings and smiles, and I'm sick with remorse, because I'm the cause of her destruction!"

"Poor Mimi," says Marcello softly.

"She's like a hothouse flower. Poverty has robbed it of all its strength, and love is not enough to restore it to life," muses Rodolfo.

Sobbing, Mimi mourns, "Oh, my life! It's finished!" until a spasm of coughing overtakes her and reveals her presence.

"She's heard it all," murmurs Marcello pityingly.

Rodolfo runs to Mimi and holds her. "You heard me? I was just getting panicky about nothing, dear. Nothing."

Musetta's raucous laughter floats out of the tavern. "That's Musetta!" says Marcello irritably. "Who is she laughing with, the flirt?" He marches purposefully to the door.

"*Addio, senza rancor* . . . Good-bye, without regrets," says Mimi quietly. "Though I came to you full of joy, it's time for me to return to my solitary nest, to embroidering my flowers. Gather up my things, and I'll send someone to get them. Under my pillow is the rose-covered bonnet. Keep that, if you wish, as a memento."

"Then it's over?" asks Rodolfo tenderly. "Good-bye, dreams of love."

"Good-bye, quarrels, suspicions, and bitterness. Alone, in the winter, it will be unbearable," sighs Mimi.

"Alone, it's unbearable," echoes Rodolfo.

"When spring comes, we'll have the sun for company," Mimi reminds him.

A tremendous crash of breaking dishes erupts from the tavern, and Musetta and Marcello burst out of the door in a magnificent fight.

Too absorbed in their own nostalgia and sorrow to notice the tempest, Mimi and Rodolfo speak of the spring, the season that she has been longing for. Perhaps they should wait to separate, she thinks, until they can have the comfort of flowers and warmth.

Meanwhile, Musetta is storming, "I'll love whom I please! Musetta goes her own way. I bid you farewell— with pleasure!"

"Your ladyship's servant!" yells Marcello. "I'm off!"

"House painter!"

"Viper!"

"Yes, we'll part in the season of flowers," agree Mimi and Rodolfo. "I wish winter would last forever," adds Mimi.

# ACT FOUR

Some weeks later, in their garret room, Rodolfo and Marcello are again trying to work, but they find it impossible to think of anything but their failed love affairs.

"You saw her in a coupe?" asks Marcello, incredulously.

"With a livery and pair. 'So, Musetta,' I said, 'how's the heart?' 'Can't hear it,' she replies, 'underneath this velvet dress.'"

"Well, that's truly interesting," says Marcello, trying to look amused. "I, myself, met Mimi the other day."

"You saw her?"

"She was in a carriage, dressed like a queen."

"Good. I'm happy for her."

"Liar," says Marcello.

They agree to get to work. But they can't work. They throw down their pen and brush in despair, mourning their lost loves. "Oh, Mimi," whispers Rodolfo longingly, "you are gone. Small hands, fragrant hair, snow-white skin. Mimi, my lost youth!" He draws her little bonnet out of a drawer and touches it lovingly. "What time is it?" he calls to Marcello.

"Time for yesterday's dinner," says Marcello drily.

Right on cue, Schaunard and Colline arrive, bearing four loaves of bread and a single herring. Abandoning sorrow for hilarity, Rodolfo and Marcello pretend that they are enjoying a sumptuous feast, and the other two join in. As the meal concludes, Schaunard suggests that the dancing begin.

"Yes!" cheer Rodolfo, Marcello, and Colline. They shove the table and chairs aside. After squabbling about which dance to start with, Colline and Schaunard begin to squabble about the correct method of performing it. Soon they are in the midst of a duel, Schaunard armed with the poker and Colline with the tongs. Rodolfo and Marcello dance around them as they shout insults and whack away. In the midst of the cacophony, the garret door bursts open—

"Musetta!" cries Marcello.

Breathlessly, she says, "Mimi is here with me, and she is very ill!"

"Where is she?" cries Rodolfo.

"She can't climb the stairs without resting," Musetta replies, and Rodolfo and Marcello rush to help. While they are gone, Schaunard and Colline move the bed to a warmer spot.

Half-carrying Mimi, Rodolfo lays her on the bed. As she begins to revive, she sees him for the first time.

"Rodolfo!" she cries, struggling to sit up.

"Ssh. Rest and be quiet," he responds.

"Oh Rodolfo, do you want me here?" she asks.

"Ah, Mimi, always."

Musetta tells the others what's happened. "A few nights ago, I got word that Mimi had left the Viscount and was terribly ill. I looked for her everywhere, and just a few minutes ago, I saw her on the street, barely able to walk. She said to me, 'I can't last much longer. I want to die with him.'"

"I feel better already," says Mimi contentedly. "How comfortable I am here! Life returns. And you will leave me no more!"

"Blessed lips, you speak to me again," says Rodolfo.

"If only I weren't so cold. A muff would feel wonderful! I think my hands will never be warm again."

Taking her hands, Rodolfo begs her to rest quietly. "Talking tires you, dear."

"I have a slight cough. I'm used to it," she says. Then, seeing her old friends, "Hello, Marcello, Schaunard. Hello, Colline."

"Don't speak. Don't speak," urges Rodolfo.

Away from the bed, Musetta is removing her earrings. "Take these," she says to Marcello. "Bring back a cordial. And a doctor." She looks over at Mimi. "Wait. The poor girl may never ask for anything again. I'll go with you for the muff."

"You are good, my Musetta," says Marcello softly, as they leave.

Taking off his overcoat, Colline looks at it sadly and addresses it: "*Vecchia zimarra . . .* Listen, old cloak, I must remain below, but you will ascend the sacred mountain." Wrapping it in a parcel, he prepares to take it to the pawnbroker. "Schaunard, let's you and I put together two acts of kindness: I, with this; and you, by leaving them to themselves!" Schaunard agrees, and the two depart.

Mimi opens her eyes and smiles gently at Rodolfo. "Are they gone? So many things I must say—or, really, only one, as vast and deep as the sea: you are my love and all my life!"

"Oh, my beautiful Mimi!" cries Rodolfo.

"Am I still beautiful?" she asks.

"As beautiful as the dawn."

She laughs softly. "You must have meant to say 'beautiful as the sunset.'"

Together they reminisce. Rodolfo shows her the bonnet he has treasured, and they speak of their meeting: the candle and the key. But the conversation has worn her out; she begins to cough, and again, she faints.

Musetta and Marcello return, bearing a muff and vial of medicine. Musetta approaches the bed and lays the muff on Mimi's hands. Mimi, now nearly blind, believes that it has come from Rodolfo. "Oh, how beautiful and soft. No more frozen hands now. Are you giving it to me?" she asks Rodolfo.

"Yes," says Musetta quickly.

"You are? Thank you! But it must have cost a lot." She touches his face. "Don't cry. I'm well. Here . . . love . . . always with you," she murmurs drowsily.

Musetta, heating the vial over the lamp, prays for Mimi, while Rodolfo busies himself in creating a makeshift curtain to keep the sunlight away from her face. "I still have hope," he says to Musetta. "Does she seem any worse to you?"

"I don't think so," she says, pityingly.

Returning from his errand, Schaunard approaches the bed and then recoils. "Marcello," he whispers, "she's dead."

Rodolfo, intent on the curtain, doesn't notice Marcello step toward the bed. Colline comes in and places some money on the table. "And how is she?" he asks Rodolfo.

"See? She is calm," he replies, turning toward Mimi. That is when he notices the stricken expressions of Marcello and Schaunard. "Why do you look like that?" he demands.

Marcello approaches him. "Courage!" he says in a broken voice.

But Rodolfo is running toward the bed. "Mimi! Mimi!" he cries. ⁓⊗

# TOSCA

~⦿⦿~

What can one say about *Tosca*? Along with *La Traviata* and possibly *Carmen, Tosca* is the opera most likely to appeal to those who know nothing of opera. This is partly because *Tosca* is a riveting drama, a true spellbinder. The principal characters, too, are appealingly lurid: the demonic, sadistic Scarpia; the passionate, proud Tosca; and the noble Cavaradossi—who can resist becoming absorbed in their fates? Some early critics even complained that *Tosca* suffered from too much dramatic potency, that the story overwhelmed the music.

Such caviling has little currency now, for *Tosca*'s music has proven to be as powerful as the plot. Some of the best known and most beloved jewels in the operatic crown come from the treasure chest of *Tosca*: Tosca's *"Visse d'arte,"* Cavaradossi's *"Recondita armonia,"* and *"E lucevan le stelle."* These are numbers, to be sure, but they are numbers of aching beauty and extraordinary effect, seductive to audiences and singers alike. But the enduring appeal of Tosca—it premiered to immediate acclaim in 1900—does not rest solely on a few big tunes. Puccini's music is carefully constructed, its melodies gracefully exposed—through lietmotivs connected to the principal characters—and leavened with atmospheric byplay. A good performance of Tosca will leave its audience craning forward in their seats, panting with anxiety. Yet the next morning, it will not be the dramatic finale that comes to mind, but those ripe, rich melodies that linger and glow through the years.

## ACT ONE

Inside the Church of Sant'Andrea delle Valle, a painter's scaffold stands empty before a fresco, and the dim light that filters from above gives only a shadowy hint of chapels and lofty columns.

Suddenly, a disheveled man enters with the stiff-legged gait of someone who is forcing himself not to run. He glances around wildly and then sighs with dawning relief. "At last! I was beginning to see a policeman in every face I passed!" He peers closely at the base of a column, and then, with a cry of exultation, pulls a key from a hidden corner. "Just as my sister wrote me. Here is the key," he turns, "and here is the chapel." Hastily, he unlocks the gate to the Attavanti Chapel and disappears within.

Now the Sacristan shuffles in, carrying paintbrushes and mumbling about the chores brought on by painters and dirty brushes. At the sounding of the Angelus, he exchanges one litany for another and is praying fervently when the young artist returns. Handsome, vibrant Mario Cavaradossi regards the Sacristan with fond disdain and mounts his scaffold to continue working on his portrait of Mary Magdalene. The Sacristan is scandalized to discover that the Magdalene of the portrait bears the blond hair and blue eyes of a mysterious girl who has been coming to the church to pray for the last week. Cavaradossi admits it with a shrug and begins painting with intense concentration. But in a sudden shift of mood, he pulls from his pocket a miniature. Looking back and forth between the two images, he muses, *"Recondita armonia . . . The hidden harmony of contrasting beauties! Dark Floria, my love and passion, blended by the mystery of art with this unknown blond. Yet, as I paint her portrait, Tosca, my only thoughts are of you!"*

The Sacristan, further incensed at this sacrilege, takes himself away. Working in silence for a while, Cavaradossi jumps at the sound of the chapel gate creaking and turns to discover the stowaway sneaking past. Startled, both men regard each other for a moment, and then the stranger cries, "You! Cavaradossi! Heaven itself must have sent you!"

"Angelotti?" replies Cavaradossi, astonished. "The consul of the late, lamented Roman Republic?"

As Angelotti reveals that he has just escaped from prison and is being pursued by the police, their hushed conference is interrupted by a sweet, full voice: "Mario!" It is Tosca, the great diva, as passionate in love as in art, and Cavaradossi's delay in answering her—while he rushes Angelotti back into the chapel—has aroused her jealousy. When he finally admits her, she looks around suspiciously, certain that he has a lover concealed somewhere. "Do you deny it?" demands Tosca, drawing herself up.

"I deny it and I love you!" says the artist, attempting to steal a kiss.

But Tosca will have no kissing in the church. First, she must pray. Arising, she arranges a rendezvous with Cavaradossi for that evening, at his villa. But his distracted response doesn't seem enthusiastic enough, and

*Puccini was concerned when no suitable Cavaradossi could be found for the Livorno premiere of* Tosca. *Livorno was, after all, the hometown of rival composer Pietro Mascagni, and Puccini wanted to give the Livornians no excuse to disparage his latest hit. Always helpful in a pinch, Tito Ricordi sent an unknown young tenor named Enrico Caruso to audition for the composer at his home in Torre del Lago. After an unimpressive bit of small talk, Puccini suggested that his guest display his wares, and Caruso obliged with Cavaradossi's "Recondita armonia." At the closing note, Puccini turned to Caruso and said, "Who sent you to me—God?"*

his ill-concealed desire for her departure excites her jealousy once again. A glimpse of his portrait fuels her suspicions; recognizing the Marchesa Attavanti, she is certain she has found her rival.

Cavaradossi soothes her rage with assurances of his love and her beauty. "Where in the whole world are eyes to compare with yours?" he whispers tenderly, embracing her.

Won by his endearments, Tosca nestles against his shoulder. "Oh, how well you know the art of capturing women's hearts! But," she cannot help adding, "let her eyes be black."

Cavaradossi gently mocks her jealousy, and Tosca penitently admits her fault while her lover swears that she is his idol, his eternal beloved. With a final promise of devotion, Cavaradossi sends Tosca away. Listening intently to her receding footsteps, Cavaradossi waits a few moments before opening the chapel gate for Angelotti.

Discussing his predicament with his friend, Angelotti reveals that he may flee or stay in hiding in Rome, for his sister has hidden a disguise under the altar of the church.

At this, Cavaradossi bursts out laughing, for here is the explanation of the mysterious, fervent beauty who has been frequenting the church. He had assumed she harbored a secret love, but he hadn't realized it was the love of a sister.

"Yes," agrees Angelotti fondly, "she has risked all to save me from that scoundrel Scarpia."

"Scarpia?" cries Cavaradossi. "That licentious bigot, who makes both the confessor and the hangman serve his wanton desires? I'll save you if it costs me my life!" He urges Angelotti to use his villa as a hideout and gives him directions. Gratefully his friend accepts the refuge and prepares to depart. "If there's any danger," adds Cavaradossi, "go to the garden well. Halfway down, a little passage leads to a dark room. It's an impenetrable hiding place."

The report of a cannon causes both men to stop in alarm, for this is a sign that Scarpia and his henchmen have discovered Angelotti's escape. In a panic, the prisoner begins to run. "Wait!" calls Cavaradossi, "I will come with you!" The two men hasten away.

Seconds later, priests, novices, and choristers pour into the church from every direction, with the officious Sacristan at their helm, exulting in the latest news: Bonaparte has suffered a defeat. The Catholic Church, to which Bonaparte's *"liberté, égalité, fraternité"* is anathema, will celebrate the royalist victory. The great Floria Tosca will sing that evening at the palace in honor of the triumph, announces the Sacristan, and the choir erupts into joy. "A gala evening! Long live the King!"

"What is this commotion in church?" inquires an acid voice. The laughter and shouts cease abruptly, for Scarpia, the chief of police, stands at the door, eyeing the crowd with cold displeasure. A shiver of fear runs through the assembly; Scarpia's brutality is well known. Without waiting for an explanation, Scarpia turns to his second in command, Spoletta, with quick instructions to search every corner for the escapee. "Where is the Chapel of the Attavanti?" he demands. A moment later, he emerges, thwarted, with a delicate lady's fan in his hand. Furiously, he inspects the object and notices that it bears the crest of the Marchesa Attavanti. His piercing gaze relentlessly examines every inch of the church for clues, until his eyes light upon Cavaradossi's Magdalene, in whose features he recognizes the Marchesa. "Who painted that picture?"

"The Cavalier Cavaradossi," quavers the Sacristan.

"He!" replies Scarpia incredulously. A slow smile, more fearsome than his frown, comes to his lips. "Tosca's lover? A revolutionary?" All of his long-checked lust for the singer wells up in Scarpia's malignant imagination, and he revels in the possibility of having the beautiful Tosca in his power. No sooner has this prospect warmed his lizard's blood than Tosca herself comes rushing in, calling for Cavaradossi. Quickly, Scarpia ducks behind a column to concoct a scheme.

Tosca is easily provoked to a new bout of jealousy by the Sacristan's report that the artist has disappeared. Slyly, Scarpia slips next to Tosca, offering her Holy Water with extreme unction. Distracted by her thoughts, Tosca barely notices his fulsome compliments, until he points to the portrait, purring, "You are not like some strumpets, who have the face of the Magdalene, but come to church to scheme for love."

Tosca turns sharply toward him. "What? Your proof?" she commands imperiously.

Smiling, Scarpia hands her the fan. "Is this a painter's tool?"

Instantly, Tosca identifies the crest as Attavanti's and succumbs to doubt and tears. Under Scarpia's watchful eye, Tosca's passion mounts, and she resolves to catch the lovers in flagrante at Cavaradossi's villa. Jumping up, she leaves the church in great distress. Immediately, Scarpia's mask of sympathy drops and, summoning Spoletta and his men, he instructs them to follow Tosca wherever she goes.

As his henchmen scatter, Scarpia meditates on his plot with sadistic glee. "Go, Tosca! Scarpia digs a nest within your heart. Go, for I have set loose the roaring falcon of your jealousy!" As the Cardinal passes by in stately procession, Scarpia falls to his knees and assumes a prayerful position. But, as the *Te Deum* swells, his thoughts dwell on the pleasures that will come with Tosca's subjugation. "I now take aim at a double target. Oh, to see the flame of those imperious eyes grow faint and languid with passion! For him, the rope, and for her, my arms!" He pauses, imagining the exquisite details. "Tosca, you make me forget God!"

# ACT TWO

In his apartments in the upper reaches of the Farnese Palace, Scarpia paces restlessly, impatient for news of his prey. The strains of an orchestra rise from a lower floor, where the Queen of Naples is giving a party in

Tosca *began its life as* La Tosca, *a vehicle for Sarah Bernhardt by the redoubtable French playwright Victorien Sardou. After Puccini had, by distinctly underhanded means, acquired the rights to make an opera of the play, he went to pay a call on Sardou to reassure him that no undue liberties would be taken with his drama. However, according to a letter Puccini wrote to a friend afterward, Sardou was an enthusiastic advocate of liberties. Puccini politely deprecated his ability to translate Sardou's masterpiece into operatic form by saying, "But my music is tenuous, it is delicate, it is written in a different register."*

*"There are no registers, M. Puccini," Sardou shouted, "there's only talent!"*

*"My previous heroines, Manon and Mimi, are different from Tosca," Puccini persisted.*

*"Manon, Mimi, Tosca, it's all the same thing! . . . Women in love all belong to the same family. I have created Marcella and Fernanda, I have created Fedora, Theodora, and Cleopatra. They are all the same woman," said Sardou emphatically.*

honor of the day's victorious general. The guests are still awaiting the arrival of the evening's star, Tosca. Dispatching one of his flunkies to tell her to wait upon him after her concert, Scarpia seats himself at his desk. "She will come for the love of her Mario! And for the love of Mario, she will yield to my pleasure . . . For me, the violent conquest has a stronger relish than the soft surrender. I take no delight in sighs or vows exchanged at misty lunar dawn. I crave. I pursue the craved thing, sate myself, and cast it by, then seek new stimulants."

Spoletta enters, already cringing, for he is forced to report that though Tosca led them, as expected, to Cavaradossi's villa, Angelotti eluded capture. Cavaradossi himself has been arrested, for he stubbornly refuses to reveal Angelotti's hiding place. As having Cavaradossi in his power is much more useful to Scarpia's licentious plans, this news eases his wrath. Smiling, he orders Tosca's lover to be brought before him.

Cavaradossi arrives, flanked by Spoletta and his hirelings and followed by Roberti, the executioner, and a judge, handily in the pay of Scarpia. Cavaradossi disdainfully refuses Scarpia's unctuously proffered seat. His interrogation has only just begun when it is interrupted by soaring notes sung in the unmistakable voice of Floria Tosca. Cavaradossi is struck silent for a moment.

Scarpia licks his lips and coolly resumes his questioning, but Cavaradossi denies all knowledge of Angelotti. Laughing, he contemptuously dismisses Scarpia as a spy. The chief of police is enraged by this defiance and vows anew that his prisoner shall pay for it. He approaches Cavaradossi again. "Come, Cavalier, you must reflect. This stubbornness is not prudent. A prompt confession saves enormous pain. Take my advice and tell me: Where is Angelotti?"

"I don't know," returns Cavaradossi shortly.

The battle of wills is interrupted by Tosca, out of breath and flushed. She looks wildly about, and, spotting Cavaradossi, runs to his arms. Leaning into her hair, he says softly, "Of what you saw at the villa, say nothing, or you will kill me!" Almost imperceptibly, she nods.

"Mario Cavaradossi," breaks in Scarpia, "the judge awaits your testimony." He nods at Roberti. "First the usual—formalities—and then, as I shall order." A grinning baliff opens the door to the torture chamber and the other officials usher in Cavaradossi. Spoletta stations himself near the door, and Tosca and Scarpia remain alone together. "Come now, don't look so frightened," he begins smoothly.

"I am not afraid," replies Tosca, with her chin held high.

Leaning over the back of her sofa, Scarpia inquires whether she found her rival at Cavaradossi's villa. She stoutly avows that he was quite alone there.

"Alone? Are you sure?"

Again, Tosca swears Cavaradossi was alone. And again.

"You protest too much," Scarpia says coldly.

"It's quite useless," says Tosca, attempting a laugh. "It seems that one must lie to please you."

"No," purrs Scarpia, "but the truth might shorten an extremely painful hour for him."

"A painful hour?" queries Tosca. "What do you mean? What are you doing in that room?"

"It is force that carries out the laws," says Scarpia smoothly.

As the meaning of his words become clear to her, Tosca leaps to her feet, crying, "My God! What's happening?"

Scarpia keeps his eyes fixed on her face in evident enjoyment. "Your lover is bound hand and foot. A ring of hooked iron binds his temples, and at each denial, the blood flows!"

For a moment, Tosca cannot believe him, but a terrible groan from the next room confirms his words. Frantically, she begs Scarpia to have pity, but the villain only replies that Cavaradossi's fate is in her hands.

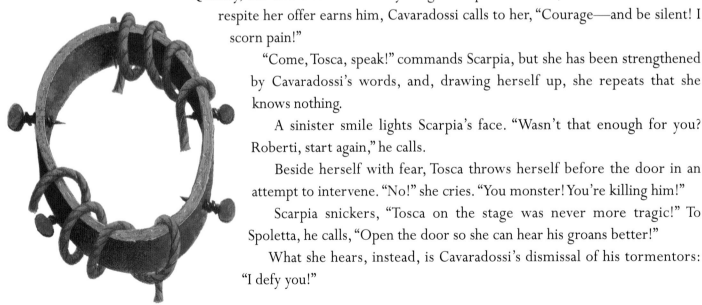

Quickly, she offers to tell him anything to stop the torture, but in the moment of respite her offer earns him, Cavaradossi calls to her, "Courage—and be silent! I scorn pain!"

"Come, Tosca, speak!" commands Scarpia, but she has been strengthened by Cavaradossi's words, and, drawing herself up, she repeats that she knows nothing.

A sinister smile lights Scarpia's face. "Wasn't that enough for you? Roberti, start again," he calls.

Beside herself with fear, Tosca throws herself before the door in an attempt to intervene. "No!" she cries. "You monster! You're killing him!"

Scarpia snickers, "Tosca on the stage was never more tragic!" To Spoletta, he calls, "Open the door so she can hear his groans better!"

What she hears, instead, is Cavaradossi's dismissal of his tormentors: "I defy you!"

"Harder! Harder!" shouts Scarpia.

Tosca is reduced to shivering despair by the decision that confronts her. Sobbing, she begs Scarpia to stop the torture, for she can bear no more. Creeping toward the open door, she catches a glimpse of the ghastly scene within and cries out in anguish. "Mario, let me speak!" she pleads.

"No!" replies Cavaradossi

"I can bear no more!" she weeps.

"Fool! What do you know? What can you say?" he gasps.

Enraged at his victim's defiance, Scarpia shouts, "Shut him up!" and the torture chamber falls ominously silent. Tosca gathers herself up for a final appeal to Scarpia. "What have I done to you in my life? You are torturing my spirit!" she sobs convulsively.

Scarpia steps into the next room and orders a resumption of the torture. As he returns, a piercing scream rings out. Tosca leaps to her feet, gasping, "In the well . . . in the garden!"

Scarpia smiles. "Enough, Roberti!" he calls.

"Murderer! I want to see him!" demands Tosca.

Cavaradossi, unconscious, is borne in by Scarpia's men, and Tosca recoils at seeing her lover's blood-spattered body. Kneeling beside him, she kisses his hand, weeping and ashamed of her confession.

Returning to his senses, Cavaradossi looks tenderly at Tosca. "Did you speak?" he asks hoarsely.

"No, beloved."

"Truly not?"

Scarpia turns to Spoletta, saying loudly, "In the well in the garden. Get him, Spoletta."

Just as he intended, Cavaradossi has heard. He attempts to rise and push Tosca away, but he is too weak and falls back to the sofa, recriminating her.

"Excellency! Bad news!" calls Sciarrone, rushing in to tell his master of a new victory by Bonaparte's forces.

Scarpia, the enforcer for the royalist regime, is discomfited by the report, but Cavaradossi is elated. Rising from his pillow with glowing eyes, he taunts his enemy. "Victory! Liberty returns, the scourge of tyrants!"

Tosca, fearful of Scarpia's revenge, tries to quiet Cavaradossi, but he recklessly continues, and finally Scarpia is goaded out of his reptilian composure. "Go, shout your boasts!" he hisses. "Go, for you die—the hangman's noose awaits you! Take him away!" he shouts to his henchmen. Sciarrone and his flunkies seize Cavaradossi and drag him toward the door. Tosca hurls herself upon her beloved in an attempt to hold him, but she is wrenched away and left, sobbing, alone with Scarpia.

"Save him!" she moans.

"I? You, rather," he replies, returning to the table to attend to his unfinished meal. Nonchalantly, he gazes at Tosca's frozen figure. "Come, sit here. Shall we try to find a way to save him together?"

Tosca's tears cease and she stares at Scarpia. "How much?" she says contemptuously.

He laughs. It is not for money that he lusts, he explains coolly. "I have waited for this hour. Even in the past, I burned with passion for the diva, but tonight, I beheld you in a new role. Your tears were lava to my senses and that fierce hatred in your eyes only fanned the fire in my blood. And when you wrapped yourself around your lover, as supple as a leopard," Scarpia's voice grows thick, "in that instant, I vowed you would be mine!"

Appalled at his brutality, Tosca rushes towards the window, crying, "I'll jump first!"

But she is checked by the knowledge that Scarpia holds Cavaradossi's life in his hands. Thwarted, Tosca drops onto the sofa, her dark eyes burning with fury and contempt. Scarpia, smiling triumphantly, moves toward her. "Don't touch me, you devil!" she cries, enraged. "I hate you!"

"Spasms of wrath or spasms of passion—what does it matter?" he returns. Tosca tears herself away from his hands, but Scarpia reminds her that even as she hesitates, Cavaradossi's gallows are being raised.

Tosca raises tortured eyes to heaven. *"Visse d'arte* . . . I lived for art, I lived for love: Never did I harm a living creature. . . . In pure faith, my prayers rose in the holy chapels . . . Why, then, in this hour of pain, why, Lord, do you repay me thus?" Kneeling before Scarpia, she begs once more, "Look at me! With clasped hands I beseech you!"

He remains unmoved. "You ask me for a life. I ask you for an instant."

Spoletta now bursts into the room with the news that Angelotti killed himself rather than be captured. Scarpia shrugs. "The other prisoner?" he inquires. Spoletta confirms that everything is ready for Cavaradossi's execution.

"God help me!" breathes Tosca.

"Wait," Scarpia says, turning to Tosca. "Well?"

Weeping with shame, Tosca nods her head. "But I demand that he be freed this instant!"

Smilingly, Scarpia demurs, "I cannot openly grant pardon to him. All must believe that the Cavalier is dead. This trusty man will see to it." He indicates Spoletta, who shifts on his feet.

"How can I be sure?" Tosca persists.

"I shall give him the orders in your presence," he purrs. "Spoletta, I have changed my mind. The prisoner shall be shot"—Tosca jerks her head up in terror—"as we did with Count Palmieri." Scarpia gives Spoletta a long, meaningful look.

"An execution . . ." says Spoletta slowly.

"A sham one!" Scarpia says loudly. "As we did with Count Palmieri. You understand?"

"I understand," Spoletta replies.

As Spoletta leaves, Scarpia turns toward Tosca, his face alight with a lascivious glow. "I have kept my promise," he says, advancing on her.

Tosca holds him back with an imperious arm. "Not yet. I want a safe conduct, so that he and I can flee together."

Scarpia cannot object, and goes to his desk to write out the order. As he writes, Tosca approaches the dining table and lifts, with a shaking hand, the glass of wine that Scarpia poured for her. As it touches her lips, her eyes fall on a thin, sharply pointed knife lying on the table. Casting a furtive glance at her enemy, who is still writing, she grasps the knife and quickly hides it behind her back.

The pass complete, Scarpia crosses the room, exclaiming triumphantly, "Tosca, now you are mine at last!"

But his lustful shout ends in a scream, as Tosca plunges the knife into his heart. "This is the kiss of Tosca!" she cries, her voice ringing.

Blood pouring from his chest, Scarpia sways dizzily before her and stretches out his hand. Recoiling in terror, Tosca thrusts her tormentor away, and he crashes to the floor. "Help me!" he chokes, "I am dying!"

Tosca watches with fascinated horror as her enemy thrashes, attempting to lift himself. "Is your blood choking you?" she hisses. "Killed by a woman! Did you torment me enough? Look at me! I am Tosca!" Scarpia falls back one final time, and dies. "Yes! Die!" she cries. "He is dead. And now I can pardon him." She stands, staring at the corpse at her feet. "And before him, all Rome trembled." After a long moment, Tosca goes to the table and washes her fingers with water she finds there. Then she hastens to the desk to search for the safe conduct; not finding it, she turns with a shudder back toward the corpse. There it is, clenched in the dead man's hand. She pulls it free and walks quickly for the door, but a final glance backward gives her pause. She returns to the table and gathers up the candles that flicker there to place next to Scarpia's head. A crucifix from the wall, she lays on his chest. Her duty done, she closes the door behind her.

# ACT THREE

In the prison of the Castel Sant'Angelo, in a small cell with a winding staircase that leads to a platform, the thin, gray light of dawn washes through a casement window, disclosing a jailer drowsing at his desk. Mario Cavaradossi is led into the cell to await his execution. As the jailer enters his name in the register, Cavaradossi begs to be allowed to write a last letter to his beloved. When this wish is granted, he settles himself at the desk and writes hurriedly for a few moments, until his hand is stayed by a flood of memories. *"E lucevan le stelle* . . . The stars shone and the world was drenched in perfume. The gate to the garden creaked and a footstep brushed the path. Fragrant, she fell into my arms . . . oh, soft kisses, oh, sweet abandon, as I discovered her beauty with trembling hands . . . Oh, desperately I die, and never before have I loved life so much!" Dropping his head onto his arms, Cavaradossi weeps.

Quietly, Spoletta appears on the stairs, accompanied by a sergeant and Tosca. Taking the jailer with them, the policemen depart, leaving a single guard behind. Tenderly, Tosca approaches her lover and places her cool hand on his cheek. He lifts his head, then jumps to his feet in astonishment. Tosca wordlessly holds out the safe conduct for him to read. Once and then again, he reads, his eyes resting on the signature. "Scarpia? Scarpia yields? This is his first act of clemency—"

"And his last," says Tosca quietly, and describes the dreadful confrontation that ended in Scarpia's death.

"You!" replies Cavaradossi, amazed. "With your own hand you killed him? You, tender and gentle, did this for me?" Lovingly, he cradles her hands in his.

But Tosca must prepare him for what is to come. She has collected her jewels and gold, a carriage is waiting—but first, he must be shot. In play, she quickly assures him, with unloaded guns. "You must fall down at the shot, then the soldiers leave, and we are safe! Then to Civitavecchia and away to the sea!"

"Free!" cries Cavaradossi joyfully. Together, they make rapturous plans for the future, a life of harmony. Only once is Tosca recalled to the present. She looks around her fearfully. "They still don't come," she says anxiously. "And you must be careful! When you hear the shot, you must fall down at once." Smiling, her lover agrees to make it all look quite natural.

Soon, their reunion is interrupted by the rhythmic tread of approaching soldiers. Tosca whispers final instructions: "Remember, at the first shot, down!"

"Down," repeats Cavaradossi obediently. They look at each other and smile.

Flanked by Spoletta and the sergeant, Cavaradossi is led up the stairs to the platform. Tosca seats herself by the casement window where she can watch. Ever so slowly, the execution commences. Tosca is in a frenzy of impatience and anxiety. "Why are they delaying? I know it is only a comedy, but this anguish seems to last forever!" The sergeant gives final instructions and his soldiers line up before Cavaradossi. "There! They are taking aim!" Tosca says. "How handsome my Mario is!" The sergeant lowers his saber and the soldiers fire. Cavaradossi falls forward to the ground. "There! Die!" says Tosca, satisfied with his performance. "What an actor!"

The sergeant steps forward to examine Cavaradossi, and Spoletta covers him with his cloak. Then all of the soldiers and officials depart, leaving Cavaradossi's fallen figure alone on the platform. Tosca, anxious lest her beloved move or speak before all is safe, cautions him in a low voice, "Mario, do not move. They're going now. Be still!" She advances up the stairs toward the platform, again warning Cavaradossi to remain silent. At the platform, she looks around cautiously and then runs toward Cavaradossi. "Up, Mario! Quickly!" She reaches down to pull him to his feet and suddenly gasps as she sees her hands. "Mario, Mario!" she screams, pulling the cloak aside, her face contorted with terror. "Dead!" Sobbing, she throws herself upon Cavaradossi's body, "Oh, Mario, dead? You? Like this?"

From the courtyard below, shouts and cries suddenly erupt. "Stabbed!" "The woman is Tosca!" "Don't let her escape!" Spoletta rushes in, with Sciarrone close on his heels. "There she is!"

"Tosca! You will pay for his life dearly," shouts Spoletta, charging toward her.

Tosca leaps to her feet and, pushing Spoletta violently aside, screams, "With my own!" She runs to the parapet that borders the platform. Crying, "Scarpia! Before God!" she hurls herself to her death. ∽❦

# MADAMA BUTTERFLY

-ⴰⵏⴰ-

**A**ll opera buffs have their favorite fiasco, and there is a special delectation to the catastrophe if the occasion is also a premiere. There are, therefore, few fiascos to surpass the opening night of *Madama Butterfly*. To be sure, there are rivals: The premieres of *The Barber of Seville, La Traviata,* and *Carmen* were all notable failures. The difference was that these debacles had been, to some degree, anticipated. But there was no sign of trouble on *Madama Butterfly*'s horizon on the morning of February 17, 1904. The premiere was to take place at the most illustrious opera house in Italy, the Teatro alla Scala in Milan, under the baton of the respected Cleofonte Campanini. The cast was stellar, especially the beautiful young Butterfly, Rosina Storchio, a superb singer who, incidentally, was in the midst of a torrid affair with Arturo Toscanini. And as for the opera itself, no one had the slightest doubt that it would take its place in the Empyrean heights next to *La Bohème* and *Tosca,* for everything Puccini touched seemed to turn to gold.

Against this background of assurance and anticipation, the disastrous outcome was particularly painful. The audience took their seats, the curtain rose, and, from the beginning of the opera until the entrance of Butterfly, the entire theater was silent. Absolutely silent. Bear in mind that an Italian opera audience of that era was never silent; they cheered, applauded, booed, threw carrots, tossed bouquets—but they were never silent. Rosina Storchio's first line was received with icy quiet, but as the scene continued, hisses broke out: "That's *Bohème!* Give us something new!" The love duet between Pinkerton and Butterfly passed without a mark of approbation, and when the curtain fell on the first act, the hisses were louder than the scattered applause. The second act was worse. At one point, a draft caused Storchio's kimono to billow out, and a hoarse voice cried, "Butterfly's pregnant!" "Yes!" called another, "with Toscanini's baby!" Hoots and jeers filled the theater. Later still, during the Intermezzo, the sound of twittering birds was supposed to provide atmosphere, but instead caused a storm of barnyard grunts and whinnies in response. The audience found the rest of the act hilarious, and Butterfly's suicide was met with shrieks of laughter. Storchio retired in tears. There was no curtain call.

Clearly, it was a premeditated murder. Puccini's untouchable status deeply irritated his fellow composers and their admirers, and his publisher's tyrannical business tactics caused simmering resentment among the many whom he mistreated. There were plenty of people who wanted them to fail, and plenty who just liked to make a ruckus. Moreover, there were only two acts, and they were far longer than was common. Even the great Verdi had not permitted himself to write an act longer than forty minutes; Puccini's ninety-minute second act was not only a breach of etiquette but also evidence of hubris.

Deeply humiliated, Puccini withdrew the opera the next day, at considerable personal cost. But instead of succumbing to despair, he rewrote the opera, dividing the offending second act into two parts, tightening the makeup scene, and redeeming the loutish Pinkerton with a few moments of remorse, among other changes. The happy result was a second performance three months later in Brescia, to an audience that could not seem to get enough of Butterfly and her sad story. As the curtain rose, the scenery was applauded, and the cheers went on from there. The love duet was greeted with such wild approbation that it had to be repeated. When the curtain went down, Puccini was called to the stage ten times. The audience refused to leave the theater, and backstage, friends, critics, and musicians congratulated the relieved composer.

# ACT ONE

About a hundred years ago, in Nagasaki, an American naval officer named Benjamin Franklin Pinkerton simultaneously acquired a Japanese house and a Japanese wife. Both house and wife were diminutive, charming, and reasonably priced, and Pinkerton was delighted to have obtained such native comforts. His procurer for both was the obsequious Goro, a marriage broker, dapper in his European suits.

As the story begins, Pinkerton is admiring the pliancy of his new house—simply slide the shoji screen over this way and, poof, a bedroom is formed. Proudly, Goro displays the house's other advantages: three dutiful servants. Suzuki, who will wait upon Pinkerton's imminent wife, greets her new employer with a litany of blessings and aphorisms, which soon causes the Lieutenant's face to grow slack with boredom. Alarmed, Goro signals the servants to take themselves away.

Goro peers down the hill, anticipating the arrival of the bridal party. From below comes the roar of an inconvenienced American. "A plague on this ridiculous mountain!" It is Sharpless, the United States consul, come to officiate at the wedding. He arrives in the garden flushed and out of breath.

As Sharpless collects himself, Pinkerton proudly points out to his friend the features of his house. "I bought this house for nine hundred and ninety-nine years, but I have the option to cancel the contract at a month's notice," he chortles. Striding back and forth, he waxes poetic about the intrepid American man: "Life is not worth living if he can't win the best and fairest of each country: the hearts of its women!"

Sharpless looks disapproving. "That easy-going gospel makes life very pleasant, but is fatal in the end—"

Pinkerton ignores this, continuing his disquisition. "Fate cannot crush him, for he tries again undaunted. Which is why," he says, getting down to particulars, "I'm getting married in the Japanese fashion. Tied for nine hundred and ninety-nine years. But free to annul the marriage monthly," he laughs immoderately. "America forever!"

"America forever," repeats Sharpless in a subdued voice. "What madness has seized you? Are you infatuated?"

Pinkerton flushes and makes an impatient movement with his hands. *"Amore o grillo . . .* Love or a whim, I cannot tell you," he says dreamily. "All I know is that she has entranced me . . . like a butterfly, she hovers and settles with so much grace that I am seized by a wild wish to pursue her, though her frail wings might be broken by the capture."

Sharpless, who has seen the girl at the consulate, warns him against breaking her heart, but Pinkerton disparages his gloomy outlook. Pouring the Consul another drink, he jovially toasts his future. "To the day I'll be wed in a real marriage—to a real American wife!"

Their tête-à-tête is interrupted by the sound of the bride's voice, lightly calling encouragement to her friends. Pinkerton and Sharpless retreat to the back of the garden to watch unobserved. Butterfly chatters joyfully about her coming marriage. "I am the happiest girl—in all the world! I have obeyed the summons of love, and all the glory that life or death can offer awaits me."

Butterfly and her friends, clad in flowery kimonos and carrying tinted sunshades, appear at the end of the path. Butterfly instantly spots Pinkerton and drops to her knees. Rising, she meets Sharpless, who finds her enchanting and inquires about her background. Her people, she tells him candidly, were once wealthy. "Say so!" Butterfly commands her friends, and they corroborate her story. But when her family lost its riches, she had to become a geisha to earn her living and support her mother. Pinkerton, utterly unconscious of anything but her beauty, stares longingly at his bride-to-be.

"And where's your father?" Sharpless inquires.

A shadow crosses Butterfly's face. After a moment, she answers tersely, "Dead." Her friends look at the ground, nervously fanning themselves. Perceiving her embarrassment, Sharpless asks her age and is astonished to learn that she is only fifteen.

There is another disturbance at the bottom of the hill, and the officious Goro announces that the High Commissioner, the Official Registrar, and the bride's relations have arrived. With much bowing and greeting, they appear in the garden, casting sidelong glances at the grand American who will be Butterfly's husband. For his part, Pinkerton is vastly amused by this procession. Meanwhile, Butterfly's cousins are making disparaging remarks about Pinkerton to Butterfly, which arouses her indignation. As a storm of criticisms and dire predictions whirls through the garden, Sharpless appeals earnestly to Pinkerton not to trifle with Butterfly's love.

Goro now bustles forth with cakes, wine, tea, and other refreshments. While the relatives munch happily, Pinkerton takes Butterfly's arm. "Come, my beloved. I'll show you our house."

Humbly, Butterfly asks his permission to bring a few treasured possessions into her new home. To Pinkerton's surprise, she is carrying all of them in her sleeves. Shyly, she draws them forth, including a long, narrow case, the significance of which she will not explain, though she declares it her most sacred possession. Goro, however, has no such restraint. "The sword was sent by the Mikado to her father, with a message," he whispers to Pinkerton, miming hara-kiri.

"And her father?" asks Pinkerton softly.

"Was obedient," confirms Goro.

Returning to Pinkerton's side, Butterfly confides she has converted to his God. But her confession is interrupted by the commencement of the wedding ceremony. With all due solemnity, Pinkerton and Butterfly sign the marriage certificate and are united as husband and wife.

Sharpless and the other officials take their leave, and Pinkerton now has only to endure the family's toasts before he can have his bride to himself. Just then, a strange man appears in the garden. "Cio-Cio-San! Cio-Cio-San!" he roars in a voice of thunder. "Abomination!" Whispers of consternation and fear run through the family, for this is the Bonze, who is both a priest and Butterfly's uncle.

The Bonze glares fiercely at Butterfly. "What were you doing at the mission?" he barks. Butterfly hangs her head and remains silent while her people gasp. "Give me an answer, Cio-Cio-San," the Bonze warns, but Butterfly only shakes her head. "She's renounced her true religion!" he shouts into the face of the terrified girl. "May your wicked soul perish in everlasting torment!" Horror-struck, the family recoils.

Pinkerton, understanding only that Butterfly is being abused, seizes the Bonze by the shoulder, growling, "Be silent! Do you hear me?"

At the sound of Pinkerton's raised voice, the Bonze stops short in astonishment. But he soon recovers himself enough to summon the family to leave. "You have renounced us," he announces bitterly, "and we—"

"Renounce you!" cries the family.

Butterfly covers her face and Pinkerton is once again roused to a chivalrous rage. "Leave here this instant! Here, I am master. I will have no disturbance here!" His authoritative aspect terrorizes Butterfly's relations, and they flee, pell-mell, out of the garden and down the path.

In the silence that follows, the only sound is that of Butterfly's tears. As the light fades and stars appear, Pinkerton gently approaches Butterfly and draws her hands from her face. "All your respected tribe and all the Bonzes in Japan are not worth a tear from those dear eyes of yours," he says.

Butterfly, cheered by Pinkerton's affectionate words, stoops to kiss his hand. He pulls her into an embrace. "Alone and renounced," reflects Butterfly. "They've renounced me, and yet I'm happy." Together, they move toward the marriage chamber, which has been arranged to open into the garden.

Pinkerton watches Butterfly with delight, marveling at her delicacy and growing more intoxicated by her charms. "But, dearest, you've not yet told me," he begins, a little hesitantly, "that you love me. Do you think that my goddess knows the words I am yearning to hear?"

Butterfly replies shyly, "She knows, but perhaps will not say them for fear she may die of her love."

"Fear not, dearest, for love does not mean dying, but living!" Pinkerton assures her, and Butterfly confesses that he is the whole world to her now.

"My Butterfly!" exults Pinkerton. "Your name is apt, my gossamer creation!"

But something troubles Butterfly, and she draws her hands from his. "They say that in your country, if a butterfly is caught by man, he'll pierce its heart with a needle and leave it to perish!"

Even her worries beguile Pinkerton. "There is some truth in that. It is so that you may not escape. See?" he says, pulling her close, "I have caught you—I hold you as you flutter—be mine."

"Yes, yours forever," she breathes.

They walk inside, and the maid Suzuki helps Butterfly change into a white kimono that sways with her graceful movements. Pinkerton lolls on a wicker lounge, smoking. Butterfly, completing her toilet, looks toward her new husband and whispers, "Butterfly . . . they've renounced her, but still, she's happy."

# ACT TWO

Three years have passed since Lieutenant Pinkerton left, promising to return with the spring. Butterfly has spent the time waiting, hoping, and weeping, attended only by the loyal Suzuki.

Now, Butterfly is standing in her accustomed position by the window, scanning the harbor below for an American ship. Suddenly she whirls about to face Suzuki. "How soon shall we be starving?" she asks.

Suzuki inspects the contents of a small cabinet, drawing forth a few coins. "Unless he comes, and quickly," she grumbles, "we're in trouble."

"He'll come," says Butterfly decisively.

Suzuki shakes her head in doubt, and Butterfly turns on her indignantly. "I never heard of a foreign husband yet who returned to his nest," observes Suzuki.

"Silence!" cries Butterfly, "or I'll kill you!" Her anger dissipates quickly, however, and she tries once again to persuade Suzuki to believe in Pinkerton with her. He promised, she recalls for the thousandth time, to return with the roses, in the warm season when the robins are busy with their nests. "And," she concludes triumphantly, "he will return. Say it with me," she insists. "He'll return!"

"He'll return!" repeats Suzuki, and bursts into tears.

"You're crying?" says Butterfly, surprised. "Why? You must have faith. Listen. *Un bel dì* . . . One fine day, we'll see a threat of smoke arising on the sea . . . then the trim white vessel glides into the harbor and thunders forth her cannon. Do you see? He is coming! I do not go to meet him. Not I. I stay upon my little hill and wait for a long time. Then, from out of the crowded city comes a man, a little speck in the distance. And when he reaches the top of my little hill, he will call, 'Butterfly.' I will not answer him, a bit to tease him, a bit so as not to die. And then, a little troubled, he will call, 'Dear little baby-wife of mine! Dear little orange blossom!' The names he used to call me." Coming out of her reverie, Butterfly turns to Suzuki. "All this will come to pass, just as I describe." The two women hug, and Suzuki goes to the kitchen to prepare their poor meal. At the same time, Goro and Sharpless approach Butterfly's house.

"Why, here is the Consul," she cries gladly, upon seeing Sharpless. He is surprised that she remembers their meeting. As she scurries about to welcome her honored guest, Sharpless experiences his first misgivings about the purpose of his visit, which is to break to Butterfly the news of Pinkerton's return—accompanied by his American wife.

Gracelessly, Sharpless drops onto a proffered cushion and attempts to come straight to the point, but he is repeatedly thwarted by Butterfly's hospitable small talk. Finally, in desperation, Sharpless says bluntly, "I've got a letter from Pinkerton."

Instantly, Butterfly's attention is undivided. "How is his health?" she asks at once.

"He's quite well," begins Sharpless.

"Then I am the happiest woman in Japan," she sighs. "Would you answer me a question?"

"Gladly," says Sharpless.

"What time of year do robins nest in America?" She explains that Pinkerton's vow to return with the robins had left her wondering how different the habits of American and Japanese robins could be.

Utterly confounded by the prospect of destroying such faith, Sharpless stammers out something noncommittal. Much to his relief, the marriage broker provides a diversion, though Butterfly is by no means pleased to see him. She disdainfully explains to Sharpless that Goro has been pestering her to remarry ever since Pinkerton left.

Goro protests that he is only trying to help. The suitor is the wealthy Prince Yamadori. "She's as poor as can be," he says to Sharpless, "and her relatives have cast her out entirely." The lovesick Yamadori now arrives on the terrace, accompanied by two servants bearing flowers. Seated next to Butterfly, he attempts to reopen negotiations but is met with rebuff after rebuff. She is already married, she says, with the slightly exasperated air of one who has explained this before.

"But the law says," Goro interjects, "that, for the wife, desertion gives the right of divorce."

Butterfly continues, "Yes, of course, to open the door and turn out your wife, *here,* that constitutes divorce. But in America, *my* country, that cannot be done!" She turns to Sharpless. "Say so!"

"Well, yes—but, yes!" splutters Sharpless.

Satisfied, Butterfly leaves the room to make tea. "You hear her?" says Yamadori to Sharpless hopelessly.

"Mr. Pinkerton's ship has already signaled," whispers Goro.

"He doesn't want to see her," Sharpless says quietly to the two men. "I have a letter from him—" Seeing Butterfly return, he breaks off.

After one last rejected plea, Yamadori takes his leave and Goro follows him, leaving Sharpless to try again to relay Pinkerton's message. Filled with joyous anticipation, Butterfly seats herself near Sharpless to hear the letter.

" 'Dear Friend,' " begins Sharpless, " 'I beg you to seek out that child, that pretty flower—' "

"Does he truly say that?" cries Butterfly, her voice rising in excitement.

"Yes, he truly says so, but if you interrupt so—"

"I'll be quiet," she promises. But she cannot contain her joy. In each phrase Sharpless reads, Butterfly finds evidence of Pinkerton's love and a promise of future happiness.

As she grows more and more elated, Sharpless grows increasingly despondent. He cannot bear to deliver the death blow to her illusions. "That fiend of a Pinkerton!" he says to himself bitterly, rising to his feet. But an urge to make her accept reality drives him to say, seriously, "Tell me, Madama Butterfly, what would you do if he were never to return?"

Butterfly freezes, then bows her head and whispers, "There are two things I might do: Go back and entertain with my songs . . . or else—better—to die."

Much moved by her words, Sharpless paces about the room. Finally, he says, "I urge you to accept the hand of Yamadori."

Butterfly looks at him, shocked, then calls Suzuki to show Sharpless to the door. Resignedly, Sharpless prepares to leave, but Butterfly bursts into tears of remorse and begs him to stay. Still, she is shaken by what he's said. "Am I forgotten?" she asks plaintively. Sharpless does not reply, and she runs into the next room. She returns in a moment, bearing a small, sleepy child in her arms. "Look here! Could anyone forget this?" she asks proudly.

"Is it his?" asks Sharpless, touched.

"What Japanese baby was ever born with blue eyes?" she replies. "Such lips, too? And such a head of golden curls?"

"Yes, he's the image of his father," says Sharpless. "Has Pinkerton been told?"

"No. I bore him when he was far off." Butterfly kisses her baby tenderly. "But you will write him that a son is waiting." She settles the boy against a cushion and playfully tells him, "Do you know what that bad man over there had the heart to think? *Che tua madre dovrà* . . . that your mother should put you on her shoulder and wander forth through the town, to try to earn money. That she should dance and sing before the multitude, begging for their pity. No! Never! Not that dishonor! I would rather die than go back to the life of a geisha!" she cries, burying her face in her son's neck.

Sharpless feels tears rising to his eyes. "Poor, faithful soul," he marvels and prepares to take his leave. Kissing the child, he says, "What is your name, sweetheart?"

Butterfly instructs her son. "Say, 'Sir, today my name is Trouble. But write and tell my father that on the day that he returns, Joy shall be my name.' "

"Your father will be told," says Sharpless grimly. "That I promise." He bows and strides away quickly.

But Goro comes back for a final word. In America, he informs her, a child with no father is cast out from society. Enraged by this new insult, Butterfly dashes to the shrine that contains her father's sword and threatens to kill Goro, but Suzuki steps between the two. Seething, Butterfly longs for the day when she will have an avenger.

Her reverie is interrupted by the sound of a cannon shot. Butterfly looks up with a sudden flash of hope. Trembling, she peers through her telescope and sees the very ship she has been awaiting for three years. She begins to dance about the room, babbling feverishly, "He's coming! My love wins the day! He's here! He loves me!" Whirling rapturously out to the terrace, she commands that every flower in the garden be cut and brought into the house, that she may crown her beloved with flowers. "When may we expect him here?" she asks Suzuki, frantic with impatience. "What do you think? An hour?"

"Too soon," replies the servant.

"Yes. Two hours more likely. You go get the flowers. Every flower."

And so the waiting begins. At first Butterfly is busy, carrying and scattering the flowers, entwining blossoms around Pinkerton's chair. Then, of course, she must array herself. She makes her toilette with exquisite care, while Suzuki attends to the child, who must make a fine first impression on his father. While she dons her wedding kimono, she exults in this victory over her enemies. Finally satisfied with her appearance, she decides, "We'll make three little holes in the shoji, so we can look out. We'll watch and wait." She makes one peephole at her eye level and then two lower down for Suzuki and her son.

The minutes move slowly by. After a while, Suzuki and the child fall asleep on their cushions. Only Butterfly remains at her post, motionless.

The night has passed, and as the sky begins to lighten, the clanging of chains and anchors rises from the harbor below. Suzuki, waking with a start, stares confusedly at Butterfly's immobile figure.

"He'll come. I know he'll come," Butterfly mutters, but at her servant's urging, she leaves off her surveillance and retires to her bedroom.

"Poor Madama Butterfly," says Suzuki with a deep sigh. There is a light knock on the door and, to her astonishment, Pinkerton and Sharpless stand before her. Quickly, they enjoin her to keep quiet, not to wake Butterfly. "She was expecting you all through the night, with the baby," Suzuki says tonelessly to Pinkerton.

With a growing sense of guilt and foreboding, Pinkerton looks around the small house, decorated for his welcome. "Did I not tell you?" Sharpless says.

"Oh, torment," Pinkerton murmurs uneasily.

Suzuki catches a glimpse of an American lady waiting in the garden. "Who's that?" she says sharply to Pinkerton.

Sharpless says bluntly, "She's his wife."

Suzuki drops to her knees in distress, but the men beg her to help them prepare Butterfly for the revelations to come. Not only is Pinkerton married, but he also has come to claim his child. At first, Suzuki refuses to take any part in this cruel transaction, but Sharpless presses her, taking her into the garden to meet Kate, Pinkerton's wife.

Pinkerton, haunted by memories, is beginning to understand Butterfly's life of the past three years, and shame floods him. *"Addio, fiorito asil . . .* Farewell, happy home!" he sighs. "I cannot bear to stay! Like a coward, let me fly— farewell!" He rushes from the house, too stricken to do more than look guiltily at Sharpless as he goes.

Kate Pinkerton and Suzuki come in from the garden. "Like my own son, I will tend him," Kate is assuring Suzuki.

"Suzuki, where are you?" calls Butterfly's voice.

In vain, Suzuki tries to prevent her mistress from emerging. But Butterfly, certain that Pinkerton has finally arrived, runs eagerly down the stairs, crying, "He's here. Here is the Consul! And where is—where?" Her eyes dart about the room, seeking her husband— and come to rest on Kate Pinkerton. "Who are you? Why have you come?" She looks wildly to and fro. "Why are you weeping? No! No! Tell me nothing, lest I fall dead at your feet. You, Suzuki, say yes or no, quite softly. He lives?" Weeping, Suzuki nods. "But he'll come no more."

"No more," whispers Suzuki.

Staring at Kate as though hypnotized, Butterfly asks the question to which she already knows the answer. She seems scarcely to hear their gentle, pitying words, but stands immobile, her face expressionless.

"And can he have his son?" Kate whispers to Sharpless.

Butterfly has heard. "His son, I will give to him, if he will come and fetch him. Tell him to climb this hill in half an hour," she says dully.

Suzuki shows Kate and Sharpless to the door and hastens back to Butterfly, who is on the verge of collapse. After a few moments, Butterfly gently removes Suzuki's supporting arm. "Too much smiling spring," she says, looking out the windows. "Close the curtains." Suzuki does so, plunging the room into darkness. "Go and play with the child," Butterfly orders.

Alone, Butterfly wanders over to the image of the Buddha in one corner and bows before it. Pulling a large white veil from a trunk, she drapes it over a screen. Now she carefully lifts her father's sword, pulls the blade from the sheath, and kisses it, murmuring to herself the words inscribed on the steel: "To die with honor when one can no longer live with honor."

The dagger's point rests at her white throat when the door opens and her son runs to her. Butterfly lets the knife fall and seizes her child, smothering him with hugs and kisses. "You beloved idol! Flower of beauty . . . take one last look at your poor mother's face, that the memory may linger, faint and dim. Farewell, beloved. Go." Guiding the boy to a stool that faces the garden, she places in his hands a little American flag and a doll and binds his eyes with a blindfold. Grasping the dagger, she goes behind the screen. A moment later, the knife clatters to the floor. Butterfly emerges, her neck bound with the veil, and stumbles toward her child. She puts her arms around him for one final embrace and falls, dying, to the floor.

"Butterfly! Butterfly!" It is Pinkerton, rushing into the garden. He opens the door with a violent thrust, Sharpless on his heels. But they are too late. Butterfly points weakly at the child and dies. Pinkerton falls to his knees, while Sharpless gathers up the little boy in his arms and kisses him, sobbing. ∼⟲

# TURANDOT

⌘

The years that passed between *Madama Butterfly* and *Turandot* were not kind to Puccini. His chronic indecision about subjects for his compositions became almost pathological, resulting in countless false starts and debilitating anxiety about each new endeavor. Even more discouraging was the reception of the operas he did create. Six years after *Butterfly* came *La Fanciulla del West,* which premiered amid much fanfare at the Metropolitan Opera in New York but never generated the devotion that Puccini's earlier operas did. Then came the long debacle of *La Rondine* in 1917, roundly deplored by critics throughout Europe, followed, the next year, by *Il Trittico,* a triptych of one-act operas that displays Puccini's facility in three different operatic styles. Much to Puccini's dismay, only one of the three, *Gianni Schicchi,* was a real hit. Added to this depressing decline were severe marital troubles and an extremely public scandal involving the suicide of a servant girl. By 1919, Puccini was in dire need of a success, if only to reassure himself of his status as the world's most renowned operatic composer. Thus, once he had selected Carlo Gozzi's eighteenth-century fable *Turandot,* he was in a fever of impatience to begin composition. His letters to his librettists are harrowing: He commands them, he begs them, he appeals to their sense of duty—they must get him a libretto immediately! But even when they finally delivered, Puccini was not satisfied and demanded more and more and *more* revisions. The composition itself was a torment; he agonized over every detail, every note. Still, he battled his way through Acts One and Two. In September, 1924, he was hard at work on Act Three when a persistent pain in his throat was suddenly diagnosed as throat cancer. Immediately, he was sent to Brussels for treatment. His condition was nearly hopeless, but he continued to think about *Turandot*; even from the clinic, he inquired about his librettists' progress. But *Turandot* was to remain incomplete, for Puccini died on November 29, 1924, leaving the final duet, which he considered the culmination of the entire opera, unfinished. A minor composer named Franco Alfano was commissioned to write the duet based on Puccini's notes. Alfano did his best, but the result is far from the soaring climax that Puccini had imagined, and *Turandot* is left strangely arrested in mid-flight, its undeniable magnificence somehow betrayed.

# ACT ONE

Thousands of years ago, the Imperial City of Peking presented a grisly sight to travelers: Arrayed along the massive walls that surrounded the city were the decapitated heads of Princess Turandot's suitors.

"People of Peking!" roars a mandarin from high atop the palace, and the thronging crowd below pauses in its business to hear him announce yet another execution. The Prince of Persia has failed to answer the three riddles set to him by Turandot and so, like his predecessors, must die. The people greet this announcement with enthusiasm and surge toward the palace to watch. Thrust back by the guards, the crowd grows impatient and unruly. Screams can be heard as children are wrenched from their mothers and the weak and elderly are pushed this way and that. One shriek rises above all others: It is a young girl begging for someone to help her old master, who has fallen.

A stalwart young man answers the call, reaches down to assist the old man, and cries out in astonishment, "My father!" For indeed it is Timur, once the King of Tartary, dethroned by invaders and harried from his land. Now blind and helpless, he has been wandering the world in search of his son, Calaf, from whom he was separated in the great battle that ended his reign. His only comfort in the many months of exile and despair, he explains, has been Liù, the girl whose call Calaf answered.

"I fell, exhausted, and she dried my tears and begged alms for me," continues Timur.

"Who are you, Liù?" asks Calaf, regarding her gratefully.

"I am nothing . . . a slave, my lord," replies Liù meekly.

"And why did you choose to share so much suffering?" says Calaf.

"Because . . . once . . . in the palace, you smiled at me," she replies, blushing faintly.

Throughout their reunion, the crowd has been growing more and more frenzied, exhorting the executioner to sharpen his blade further. They invite more would-be suitors to strike the great bronze gong that announces readiness to undertake Turandot's test, for the people want blood. They beg the moon to rise, which will signal the time for the beheading.

Finally, the moon appears in the sky. The hour of death has come. The executioner advances through the crowd. Following behind comes the Prince of Persia, pale, noble, and pathetically young. The people sigh, their blood lust turned to pity at the sight of him. "Oh, a reprieve!" "Mercy on him!" they call.

Calaf is repulsed by Turandot's brutal game. "Let me see you and curse you, cruel princess!" he calls toward the palace.

Suddenly, Turandot appears, far above the crowd. She is as pale and beautiful as the moon that hovers nearby; to Calaf, she seems a shimmering dream that he must somehow bring into the warm light of day. As he looks on, dazzled, the crowd around him drops prostrate to the ground. "Oh, heavenly beauty, oh, wondrous sight! Oh, dream!" he murmurs to himself, as Turandot, unmoved by the appeals of her people, imperiously gestures for the execution to proceed. The Prince, the mandarins, and the executioner move solemnly on, and Turandot, her face impassive, withdraws.

Calaf looks about like one waking from a long sleep. "Did you notice? Her perfume fills the air! It fills my soul!" he sighs rapturously.

Timur gasps in horror. "You are lost! Liù, talk to him," he says, turning trustingly to the girl. In vain, she pleads with Calaf to leave.

"Life is here!" he insists with the vigor of the infatuated.

As if in answer to his words, the strangling death cry of the Prince of Persia is heard in the distance. Clinging to his son to keep him from striking the fateful gong, Timur cries, "Would you die like that?"

"I would conquer, father, for her beauty!" replies Calaf. Tearing himself from his father's arms, he runs once more toward the bronze gong. This time he is apprehended by the Imperial ministers, Ping, Pang, and Pong, who move in graceful unison to block his way.

"Stop! Go away! This is the door of the great slaughterhouse! Fool!" they shout. They enumerate, with gusto, the great variety of ways in which Calaf might be put to death.

"Let me pass!" yells the impetuous Calaf.

"All our graveyards are full!" Pong declares.

"We've enough madmen of our own!" says Pang.

"And we don't want any foreign ones," concludes Ping.

"Let me pass!" roars Calaf.

A coterie of Turandot's ladies rustle in the darkness above. "Silence!" they call reprovingly, "for sleep is descending upon the eyes of Turandot. The darkness is filled with her fragrance." They rustle back indoors.

The thought of Turandot and her fragrance sends Calaf right out of his mind with love, much to the disgust of Ping, Pang, and Pong. Trying another argument, they assure the besotted lover that he will never, ever be able to answer Turandot's riddles correctly. To reiterate the point, the ghosts of the Princess's former suitors appear, drifting along the palace ramparts, moaning over their fatally unrequited love.

To Calaf, these phantoms are only infuriating rivals. "No! No!" he cries. "I alone love her!"

Ping, Pang, and Pong throw up their arms in despair. "You love her! What do you love? You crazy boy! Turandot doesn't exist! Only the void exists in which you will be annihilated!"

Their words fall on deaf ears. "Love is mine!" rejoices Calaf.

Tears trickle down Timur's cheeks as he imagines the weary years he will pass after his son's death. Liù, stricken more by the dire consequences of failure than by Calaf's rejection of her abject love, begs him once more to listen to her. "*Signore, ascolta* . . . Liù can bear no more. Her heart is breaking! Have pity."

Calaf, even in his madness, is moved by Liù's devotion. "*Non piangere, Liù* . . . Do not weep, Liù.

Tomorrow, perhaps, my father will be alone in the world. Do not desert him. Take him away with you!"

Now all of them join forces against him: Timur, Liù, Ping, Pang, and Pong desperately work to convince him, beg him to give up his hopeless plan. Though he hears them and is sorry for their pain, Calaf is resolute. "No power on earth could hold me back," he declares.

The surrounding crowd, catching on to the debate, taunts the enamored Calaf.

Struggling against their restraining hands, Calaf tries to convey his passion. "Every fiber of my being cries with one voice: Turandot!"

"Death!" cry Liù, Timur, Ping, Pang, and Pong.

But now Calaf breaks free and rushes for the massive disk of bronze. He strikes it three times and stands looking toward Turandot's windows. While the crowd predicts death, Ping, Pang, and Pong shrug and depart for home.

# ACT TWO

Ping, Pang, and Pong are settled comfortably in one of the palace's pavilions, discussing the new contender for Princess Turandot's hand. Mournfully, they recall the peaceful China that slept for thousands of years, until the birth of Turandot, with her three riddles and rolling heads. Nowadays, they all agree, they're no more than ministers of the executioner. "Where Turandot reigns, work is never lacking," they complain, and fall to imagining the day when Turandot shall be won. But their visions are interrupted by the sound of hundreds of people gathering in the Imperial courtyard, assembling to watch the newest suitor put to the test. Ping, Pang, and Pong gather up their robes resignedly. "Let's go and enjoy the umpteenth execution," they mutter as they make their way to join the crowd.

A grand marble staircase with three wide landings reaches from the royal apartments down to the teeming courtyard. Eight wise men appear at the top of the stairs, each carrying a scroll upon which is written the answers to Turandot's riddles. As they descend, white and yellow banners flash through clouds of incense, and when the smoke wafts away, the ancient Emperor is seated on his throne.

At the sight of their sovereign, the people prostrate themselves, all except Calaf, who stands at the foot of the staircase, oblivious to everything except the possibility of seeing Turandot. Now the Emperor, adding his voice to the others, begs Calaf not to undertake the murderous test, but Calaf remains obdurate.

Now the mandarin steps forward to read the usual proclamation: "Turandot the Pure will be the bride of the man of royal blood who shall solve the riddles which she shall set. But if he fails in this test, he must submit his proud head to the sword."

Now, as one, the hundreds of people draw in their breath, for Princess Turandot appears, magnificent in a robe of gold, and turns her ravishing face to look upon Calaf. Cold and severe, she tells the story of her peculiar institution. *"In questa Reggia . . .* Within this palace, many thousand years ago, a desperate cry rang out. And down through the generations, that cry has found refuge in my heart. Princess Lo-u-Ling, my serene ancestress, ruled in pure joy."

The people, who know this tale by heart, recite, "It was then that the King of the Tartars unfurled his standards."

Turandot continues, "At that time, war brought horror and the clash of arms. The Empire was conquered, and Lo-u-Ling was dragged away by a man like you," Turandot's eyes flash contemptuously upon Calaf, "who carried her away on that cruel night when her young voice was stifled. O princes, who come from every corner of the earth, I take revenge on you for her purity, her cry, and her death! No man shall ever possess me! Hatred for the villain who killed her lives on in my heart! Stranger, do not tempt fortune! The riddles are three, death one!"

Undaunted, Calaf defies her. "The riddles are three, life one!"

Turandot smiles. Let him accept the consequences.

The test begins. "In the dark night flies a many-hued phantom. It soars and spreads its wings above humanity. The whole world implores it. At dawn, the phantom vanishes to be reborn in every heart. And every night 'tis born anew, and every day it dies."

Calaf knows the answer instantly and jubilantly replies, "Yes! 'Tis born anew! Turandot, it is Hope!"

With quivering hands, the wise men unroll their papers and confirm his answer.

"Yes, hope which leads always to disillusion," says Turandot disparagingly. She descends the staircase to the middle landing, her hands clenched into fists. She begins again. "It kindles like a flame, but it is not fire. At times it is a frenzy. It is fever, force, passion! Inertia makes it flag. If you lose heart or die, it grows cold, but dream of conquest and it flares up."

Calaf pauses, and the crowd shouts encouragement. But the answer comes to him. "Yes, Princess! When you look at me it kindles and grows heavy in my veins: It is blood!"

Excitedly, the Wise Men confirm his answer, and the people cheer. Enraged by this show of support, Turandot runs to the bottom of the stairs. Calaf falls to his knees, overwhelmed by the proximity of his goddess. She stares at him, her face tense, and then offers the final riddle: "Ice which gives you fire and which your fire freezes still more! Lily white and dark, if it allows you your freedom, it makes you a slave; if it accepts you as a slave, it makes you a king!" She smiles at Calaf's confusion. "Hurry, stranger! You turn pale from fear! Ice which gives you fire—what is it?"

There is a long pause, and then Calaf jumps to his feet. "My victory now gives you to me! My fire will thaw you: Turandot!"

The wise men leap from their chairs, screaming "Turandot!" and the crowd bursts into roars of exaltation.

Turandot alone is in despair. Terrified, she turns to the shining Calaf. "Don't look at me that way!" she cries. "I will never be yours! Never! I refuse!"

The death of Puccini left Turandot in disarray. The world premiere was already set to take place at La Scala and Toscanini was already lined up as the conductor, but the roles were not cast and, most seriously, the opera itself was not complete. The Ricordi Company, which had a tender financial interest in its success, suggested another one of their star composers for the job, but the Puccini family found the idea of hiring a competitor repugnant and, on this theory, they advocated the distinctly lesser evil of Franco Alfano. Alfano was well aware that his work would please no one: If he cleaved to the gospel of Puccini's notes, he would be criticized for bald orchestration and thin musical development; if he added material of his own, he would be accused of disrespect. At first, Alfano tried the pure Puccini route, but Toscanini objected. Since there was simply no more Puccini to squeeze out of the brief notes left by the composer, Alfano was forced to add more Alfano. When he submitted this second revision to Toscanini, the conductor grumbled and complained, but ultimately accepted the score, for the premiere date was nearing. The great Puccini's final masterpiece was to be a production to end all productions. Under Toscanini's direction, a stellar cast was assembled, spectacular sets created a truly imperial palace, and magnificent costumes cloaked the singers in silver and gold. Only Alfano's contribution was left ignored and uncelebrated. Finally, after the last dress rehearsal, Alfano approached Toscanini and asked his opinion of the completed work: "What have you to say, Maestro?" And Toscanini replied, "I have to say that I saw Puccini coming out from the back of the stage to smack me." At the premiere, on April 25, 1926, Toscanini's displeasure with Alfano was made even clearer: After Liù's death music came to an end, the conductor laid down his baton and turned to the audience. "Here the Maestro put down his pen," he said and quit the podium, bringing the opera to an end.

But, as the Emperor and the people remind her, an oath is sacred.

Her eyes locked on Calaf's, she says, "Would you have me in your arms by force, shivering with dread?"

The light of triumph goes out of Calaf's eyes. He looks at Turandot's beautiful face with compassion and replies, "No, proud princess. I would have you aflame with love! You set me three riddles and I solved them. I will put but one to you: You do not know my name. Tell me my name before morning, and at dawn I am ready to die!" He stares intently at his Princess. She nods, unable to speak.

"Heaven grant that with the dawn, I may call you son," quavers the old Emperor.

# ACT THREE

Though night has fallen, the streets of Peking are alive with bustling footsteps and hurried whispers, for Princess Turandot has delivered a proclamation to her people: "Tonight no one shall sleep in Peking. Death is the penalty for all unless the name of the Unknown Prince is revealed before dawn." Anxiously, the citizens debate how the secret name is to be learned and grow steadily more frightened by the death sentence that

hangs over them. Only Calaf, far above the crowd on a palace pavilion, is at peace, dreaming of his enchanted future. Even the Princess's dire proclamation seems to him full of promise. *"Nessun dorma! . . .* No one shall sleep! No one shall sleep! You too, O Princess, in your chaste bed, are watching stars that seem to tremble with love and hope. But my secret lies hidden within me, and no one will discover my name! Depart, O night! Hasten your setting, O stars! At dawn, I shall win!"

So absorbed is Calaf that he does not notice the silent figures gathering in the shadows. Ping, Pang, and Pong step out of the crowd, grim faced, and bitterly remind Calaf that his happiness will come at the cost of all their lives. After he categorically rejects their enticements—girls, riches, and glory—their only remaining hope is to appeal to his conscience. Ping, Pang, and Pong describe the horrible tortures, the wretched martyrdom his love will bring down upon the heads of Turandot's miserable subjects. But Calaf remains obdurate.

The crowd is losing patience; they are pressing in on the Prince, daggers drawn, when a group of soldiers rushes in with a new solution: Liù and Timur. The old man and his faithful servant have been recognized as friends of the Unknown Prince. All that remains is to force them to reveal his name, which will be the work of a few moments for the Imperial torturer. Aghast, Calaf swears the pair knows nothing, but of course, nobody believes him.

Like the moon breaking though the clouds, the veiled figure of Turandot glides out on a parapet to watch this new episode in the drama. With disdain, she says to Calaf, "You are pale, stranger!"

"Your own fear misinterprets the light of dawn," he replies. "Those two do not know me!"

Angry at his presumption, she orders Timur to speak, but as her soldiers seize the old man, Liù runs forward. "I alone know the name you are seeking," she shouts at Turandot. The soldiers unhand Timur and start toward her.

"You know nothing, slave!" cries Calaf.

"I know his name," repeats Liù doggedly. "And it is my supreme joy to keep it secret."

Furiously, the crowd demands that she be tortured. Throwing himself in front of Liù, Calaf tries to protect her, but he is forcibly removed and bound as Liù's torment begins. At her first scream, the blind Timur becomes nearly frantic, but Liù reassures him that she is not being hurt. "Go on," she whispers to the soldiers, "but gag me fast, so that he cannot hear."

Burning irons hiss against her flesh, but still, Liù does not break. Turandot, looking down on this cruel scene, is moved to wonder. "What gives your heart such courage?" she calls to the girl.

"It is love," Liù answers simply, but this reply seems to infuriate the Princess, and she orders the soldiers to redouble their efforts. The great executioner Pu-Tin-Pao is called, and Liù, fearful that she will confess, tries to flee. Her attempt fails, and the crowd surrounds her, demanding that she speak.

Turning her bloodstained face to the Princess, Liù speaks. *"Tu che di gel sei cinta . . . You* who are girdled with ice will be vanquished by fire—you will love him, too. Before the break of day, I shall close my tired eyes that he may win again." Then, quick as a deer, she dashes to a soldier, catches hold of his dagger, and plunges the knife into her heart. Dying, she staggers toward Calaf and falls at his feet.

His cry is a moan of agony. "Oh, you are dead, dead, my poor little Liù!"

Timur, dazed by the sudden loss of his best friend, kneels by Liù's body in tears. Even the blood-hungry citizenry is abashed by what they have wrought. Chastened, they lift her figure aloft and carry Liù away with prayers and hymns, leaving Calaf and Turandot alone together.

"Princess of death! Princess of ice! Come down to this earth! See the innocent blood that has been shed for you!" Impelled by love and anger, he rushes forward and tears off her veil.

Turandot recoils. "How dare you, stranger! I am the daughter of heaven, free and pure. You grasp my icy veil, but my soul is above you!"

"Your soul is up there, but your body is close beside me," cries Calaf. "And you shall be mine!"

In vain, Turandot denounces this as sacrilege. Again and again, she asserts that the tragedy of her ancestress will not be repeated, but Calaf is not to be deterred. He seizes her and draws her toward him in a long, passionate kiss.

Turandot rises from his embrace in a daze. "What is happening to me?" she says brokenly. "I am lost! It is dawn! And the setting of Turandot!"

But Calaf is exultant, for as the ice princess melts, the loving woman emerges. "It is dawn," he cries rapturously, "And love is born with the sun!"

Ashamed and frightened of her feelings, Turandot weeps. "My first tears," she says with wonder. Slowly, she confides to Calaf that she feared his power from the first moment she saw him, because she knew that, in his fever of love, he would conquer her.

Now certain of her love, Calaf puts his life in her hands by revealing his name. As the dawn breaks over the Imperial Palace, Turandot and Calaf proceed to the Emperor's pavilion, where her father awaits them in the company of the court and the citizens of Peking.

The vast crowd is silent. Slowly making her way to the throne, Turandot bows before her father. "Noble father," she begins, "I know the stranger's name." There is a gasp. Only Calaf is calm. "His name," she continues, "is Love!" Triumphant and jubilant, Calaf runs swiftly up the stairs to embrace his beloved, while the relieved populace shouts its approval and hurls flowers at their transformed Princess and her Prince. ⚭

# DER ROSENKAVALIER

**B**y 1909, Richard Strauss was renowned—or notorious, depending on your perspective—as the composer of the most shocking operas in the world. At the beginning of his career, Strauss had represented a pleasing amalgamation of the modern and the acceptable. His fervent tone poems, *Aus Italien* (1885) and *Don Juan* (1889), were lauded as revolutionary, but they were also widely performed and well received. Then came the operas. Strauss's first two forays into operatic composition were the usual Wagnerian excursions of a young German, but his third, *Salome* (1905), took the world by storm. Based on Oscar Wilde's somewhat overheated play, Strauss's opera was lurid, raw, and designed to discomfit its audiences (not to mention its cast: Several Salomes refused to carry out the stage directions). Denounced as blasphemous, bestial, and musically "mad," *Salome* was an immense *succès de scandale* and made Strauss a tidy fortune, which he parlayed into immense wealth with a decidedly unpoetic business acumen. His fourth opera, *Elektra* (1909), was exactly that, an electrifying maelstrom of thunderous noise and turbulent emotion. *Elektra* provoked intense admiration and equally intense derision, but even Strauss's most vehement detractors agreed that his genius was incontrovertible.

And then, in late 1909, Strauss suggested to his librettist, Hugo von Hofmannsthal, something truly revolutionary: a comedy. And not only a comedy, but one in the style of Mozart. Hofmannsthal obligingly switched from Sophocles to eighteenth-century Viennese froth, and *Der Rosenkavalier* was born. Though it seems to bear little relation to its elder siblings in the Strauss oeuvre, *Rosenkavalier* displays, beneath its rococo swirls and swaying lyricism, a melancholy fatalism that betrays its twentieth-century parentage, and the Marschallin, with her sensual wisdom, is a creature Mozart could never have conceived. Nonetheless, *Rosenkavalier* was greeted with sighs of relief by Strauss's exhausted audiences when it was performed in 1911. The opera's seeming traditionalism coupled with its charming music permit its listeners to enjoy modernity without undue suffering, and for that, they have rewarded the work by making it the most popular of twentieth-century operas.

# ACT ONE

Awakened by the sunlight streaming through the silken draperies of her bed, the Princess von Werdenberg—known to all as the Marschallin, for she is the wife of Fieldmarshal von Werdenberg—languorously stretches forth one shapely arm and smiles as it is caught and kissed, passionately, by her lover, the seventeen-year-old Count Octavian. He has been kneeling by the side of the bed, watching her jealously as she sleeps, but now that she is awake, his words spill over: He wants to proclaim her perfection from the rooftops, he wants all to know the secret raptures he enjoys! But no! It is better kept a secret, his own secret! For she and he are one! On and on he rants in the delirium of passion, while the Marschallin laughs softly at his fervor.

Equally reluctant to embark on the day that must separate them, the two breakfast in the dilatory fashion of lovers, exchanging tender touches and foolish endearments, until the spell is broken by the Marschallin carelessly remarking that she had dreamt of her husband the previous night.

Octavian can scarcely believe his ears. "Last night you dreamt of him? *Last* night?"

"I do not order my dreams," replies the Marschallin, with a slight edge to her voice. Furrowing her brow in concentration, she begins to recall it. "There was a noise of horses and men in the courtyard, and you were here!" Strangely enough, her words are echoed by a clatter in the courtyard below. The Marschallin looks up anxiously, though Octavian assures her it could never be her husband. He is far, far away, in Raitzenland. But her lover's words do little to allay her fears. "Do you know, Quinquin," she says, her eyes straying to the window nervously, "even if it is far, the Fieldmarshal is very swift, you know. Once—" she hesitates.

Octavian, ever alert to the hint of predecessors, instantly succumbs to a paroxysm of jealousy, but his anguish has little effect on the Marschallin, because she isn't paying any attention. Instead, she stands in the center of her grand room, her face curiously composed, listening to the commotion progress though the halls and chambers of her palace. Just as she had feared, the footsteps are arriving at her dressing room door, not in the antechamber, where merchants and supplicants await her levee. This can only mean one thing: the Fieldmarshal.

The Marschallin flies into action. Grasping her prone lover by the collar, she looks around wildly and points to the curtained bed: "There!"

Torn by the conflicting demands of gallantry and prudence, Octavian hesitates. "I'll stay with you! I'll have it out with him," he declares, brandishing his sword.

"There, in the bed!" repeats the Marschallin firmly.

"If he catches me there, what will happen to you?" asks her lover.

Losing patience, the Marschallin stamps her foot. "Be quiet! I would like to see anyone make a move toward that bed while I stand here!" Octavian subsides into the curtained bed, and bristling with energy, the Marschallin moves towards the door in order to hear better the efforts of her footmen to keep the intruder at bay. They are saying she is asleep; they are saying it stoutly. Another voice objects, objects vehemently. At this, the Marschallin begins to laugh. "That isn't the Fieldmarshal's voice! They're calling him 'Baron'! Quinquin, it's a caller! I know that stupid, loud voice! Who can it be? Oh, good God! But of course! It's Ochs. It is my cousin, Lerchenau, Ochs of Lerchenau! What on earth can he want?" And now, remembering, she begins to laugh in earnest, for Ochs had written to her, yes, some days ago, but she had received this missive while she and Octavian were in her coach and, well, ensuing events had put Och's letter right out of her mind. "For that you are to blame, Quinquin," she calls toward the bed.

"Baron Lerchenau does not hang about in waiting rooms," she hears him bellowing at the servants. He is on the point of bursting through her door when Octavian suddenly materializes from behind the curtains in a demure white dress and cap. With an awkward curtsey, her new servant grins and says, "Teach me my duties, your Grace, for this is my first day of service."

With a kiss for his audacity, the Marschallin whispers a few last-minute pointers: He is to bustle out with the rest of the servants and come back, as himself, as quickly as he can. Octavian hastens to obey, but unfortunately, his urgent desire to depart is equaled by the Baron's urgent desire to arrive, and as he rushes for the dressing-room door, it is finally torn open by the outraged Ochs, who storms in with a phalanx of protesting footmen in hot pursuit, and—crash!

Now, if there's one thing that catches the Baron's attention, it's a pretty young serving girl, and once he gets a glimpse of Octavian's soft white skin and doe eyes, he gallantly offers his hand to assist the little maid to her feet. "Forgive me, my pretty child," he says, chucking her under her chin. Octavian, completely at a loss, tries to turn away, but the Baron is nothing if not persistent, and it is only the regal approach of the Marschallin that recalls Ochs to his purpose.

The Baron bows obsequiously to her, all the while keeping a lusty eye on the pretty little maid, who, having missed his opportunity to depart, is now somewhat desperately fluffing pillows on the bed. The Marschallin, whose enjoyment of Octavian's plight is moderated by its danger to herself, attempts to learn the purpose of her cousin's visit. In between lascivious glances at Octavian, the Baron reveals all: He is to marry (she is already supposed to know that; it was in the letter) a lovely young girl, only fifteen, quite appetizing, fresh from the convent, and, more to the point, the daughter of the immensely wealthy Faninal. The Baron explains the misalliance in his own terms: "The man owns twelve houses in the Wied'n, plus a palace by the Court. And his health is not well spoken of."

"My dear cousin," says the Marschallin smoothly, "I understand what you are getting at." The Baron talks grandly of the concession he is making by joining his blue blood with the common variety before he gets down to business with a thump. He needs the Marschallin's assistance in recruiting a Rosenkavalier, for the tradition of sending a noble emissary to deliver a silver rose along with a proposal cannot be broken, regardless of the pedigree of the Baron's intended.

As Octavian tries once again to leave, the Baron grasps him firmly by the hand, and carries on his conversation with the Marschallin with the maid as his prisoner. He would also appreciate the services of the Marschallin's attorney, he reveals, for the marriage contract. Vainly, she attempts to send her new maid, whom she has named Mariandel, to find said attorney, but the Baron loudly protests: He cannot bear to rob the Marschallin of the services of her maid, no, that would be too uncouth. He grips the white hand even more firmly.

A very tall, very correct Majordomo now enters the Marschallin's chambers to read, with appropriate flourishes, the roster of attendants and petitioners who await the Princess's levee: "Serene Highness has the Attorney, then the Steward, then the Chef; then, sent by His Excellency Silva, a Singer and a Flautist. Otherwise," the Majordomo emits a superior sniff, "the usual rabble."

Of course, the Baron has taken this opportunity to try to arrange a rendezvous with the fair Mariandel. Octavian, warming to his role, pretends alarm at the Baron's rakishness, but the Marschallin, who recognizes the brutality that lies behind the Baron's pursuit of pleasures, bursts out, "No, he goes too far! Leave the child alone."

Unruffled by the Marschallin's indignation, the Baron continues to leer at Octavian. "There's a drop of good blood there, I'll be bound!"

Octavian nearly loses his composure at this, but the Marschallin is more than equal to the moment. "You have a sharp eye," she comments dryly.

The Baron blunders on. "That's as it should be. I find it only right that people of quality should be served by people of noble blood. I myself always travel with one of my love-children with me."

The astounded Octavian croaks, "One of your love-children?"

"My son," replies the Baron pompously. "He has the real Lerchenau features. I keep him as a body-servant, and if your grace would care to see the silvered rose, he will deliver it."

"Mariandel, off you go," commands the Marschallin, "and let them in from the anteroom." Octavian breaks away from the Baron's grip and rushes out the door. The Baron, in hot pursuit, flies after him, only to be buffeted back by the hoard of servants and visitors that pours over the threshold into the Marschallin's apartment. First in line is a decidedly ugly old chambermaid—the Baron shivers—then two footmen bearing a screen behind which the Marschallin retires; then two more footmen carrying her dressing table; then the Attorney, the Head Cook, a kitchen boy carrying a menu book, the milliner, a student with a folio, and an animal trainer with miniature dogs and a small monkey. Two Italians, Valzacchi and Annina, slip in behind the animals, and an aristocratic mother with three daughters, all in deep mourning, set up shop in the center of the floor. The Majordomo, taking offense at such presumption, whisks the tenor and flautist in front of them, and the Marschallin's morning begins.

The orphans begin to sing a dirge, with the object of evoking the Marschallin's pity and purse; the milliner whisks out his newest creation; the animal trainer suggests a parrot; the student struggles to present his tome to her Serene Highness but is shoved aside by Valzacchi, who is hawking the latest scandal sheet. Briefly, the Marschallin emerges from behind her screen, introduces the Baron to her attorney, kisses the children and gives them a purse of money, rejects Valzacchi's tabloid with disgust, and retreats. Now, as the flautist begins his cadenza, a harassed-looking hairdresser rushes in, flanked by a small, merry assistant. As the Marschallin submits to the hairdresser's ministrations, the tenor, stepping forward, begins his aria, all about how his haughty heart was brought low by a fleeting glance, oh, yes indeed, a heart of ice cannot resist the shaft of fire. He repeats this theme several times and finishes with a sob. The hairdresser hands the curling tongs to his assistant and applauds the tenor, who gives a graceful bow.

These elegant proceedings are now interrupted by the appearance of the Baron's servants, who are apparently embroiled in a desperate argument about precedence, for they step on one another's toes and try to push through the door all at the same time. Once assembled in the Marschallin's chamber, their vaunted good blood is nowhere in evidence: The body-servant/love-child is a sallow, lank youth with no chin. The almoner is thick and distractingly squat, and the chasseur is possessed of an interesting twitch. The Baron, looking upon his staff with satisfaction, turns to the attorney and continues his discussion.

The Marschallin picks up her looking glass and regards herself from several angles. "My dear Hippolyte," she says, "you have made an old woman of me today!" Dismayed, the hairdresser works feverishly to rearrange her locks, but the Marschallin's face remains melancholy. "Dismiss them all," she orders the Majordomo.

Forming a human chain, the footmen sweep all the servants and petitioners from the room, though

Valzacchi and Annina take advantage of the hubbub to approach Ochs and offer their services: They will procure for him whatever he desires. For instance, they will watch his new wife with eagle eyes, every coach she takes, every letter she receives, all will be revealed to his lordship. Hm. The Baron doesn't care so much about his new wife, but perhaps they could arrange a meeting with young Mariandel. Eagerly, they agree, though they have never heard of any such person before.

Satisfied that he has made marvelous progress in a variety of departments, Ochs leaves the silvered rose in the Marschallin's keeping, for she will deliver it to her chosen Rosenkavalier, Count Octavian. His errand accomplished, the Baron bids the Marschallin good-day with innumerable creaky bows and departs.

Now, finally, she is alone. She can hear the outer doors slamming behind her cousin, behind his cretinous servants. "There he goes, the bloated worthless fellow, and gets the pretty young thing and a tidy fortune too, as if it had to be. And he flatters himself that it is he who makes the sacrifice. But why do I upset myself? It is just the way of the world. I remember a girl who came fresh from the convent to be forced into holy matrimony." The Marschallin looks into the silver mirror. "And where is she now? How can it really be that I was once the little Resi and that one day, I will become the old woman . . . the old woman, the Fieldmarshal's wife! How can it happen? How does the dear Lord do it? And if He has to do it like this, why does He let me watch it happen with such clear senses. Why doesn't he hide it from me? It is all a mystery, so deep a mystery, and one is here to endure it. And in the 'how' there lies all the difference."

Her reverie is shattered by the entrance of Octavian, restored to his rightful sex, in riding clothes. But not even the appearance of her lover can disperse the mists of melancholy that surround the Marschallin. In the manner of the young, Octavian tries to return to the rapture of the morning with all manner of coaxing, but the Marschallin cannot be enticed. Of course, this only arouses the boy's jealousy, and soon enough, unable to control his feelings, he is weeping in bitter despair. Sighing, the Marschallin strokes his hair and murmurs, "Now I have to console the boy that, sooner or later, will desert me."

"Do you want to drive me away with words," cries Octavian, "because your hands decline to do the deed?"

But the Marschallin only smiles, in love with his love and sure of its end. "The day will come of its own. Today or tomorrow, the day will come." Over his protests, she continues, "I'm not tormenting you, I'm telling you the simple truth. I say it as much for myself as for you. I want to make it easy for you and for me. One must take it lightly, with light heart and light hands hold and take, hold and relinquish. . . . Those who cannot do that will be punished by life and God, and God will have no pity for them."

"You talk like a father confessor today," sulks Octavian. "Does that mean I will never again be allowed to kiss you until you gasp for breath?"

"You must leave now, dearest. In the afternoon, I will send a messenger to you, Quinquin, and perhaps when I am driving on the Prater, you will happen to be there also. Now be good and do as I say."

Brightening a little at the prospect of an afternoon meeting, Octavian says, "As you command," and departs.

Suddenly, the Marschallin jumps to her feet in a panic. "I didn't kiss him!" Ringing wildly for her footmen, she sends them in pursuit of Octavian, but he has already gone. The Marschallin regains her composure and calls for the boy Mohammed. When he arrives, silver bells tingling, she entrusts him with a special commission: He must deliver the case containing the silver rose to Count Octavian. Smiling, the boy runs off, leaving the Marschallin lost in thought.

# ACT TWO

The next day, inside the home of Baron Och's intended, where the draperies are all a little too new and the rugs have most certainly not been in the family for generations, Herr von Faninal is receiving etiquette instructions from his Majordomo. According to custom, Sophie must greet her Rosenkavalier alone, while her father, decked in his most ceremonious garb, is required to retrieve the groom and present him to the bride once she has accepted the silvered rose. While Faninal nervously takes his leave, the family's oldest servant, Marianne, rejoices in the newfound elevation of the Faninals. No one takes greater pleasure in the prospect of this noble marriage than Marianne, and in between peeping out the window to admire her master's new carriage, she extols the virtues of the Lord of Lerchenau (though she has never laid eyes on him) to Sophie, who, in Marianne's opinion, is insufficiently grateful for the honor being done her.

As Marianne gleefully predicts the varying degrees of envy the neighbors will soon suffer, Sophie earnestly repeats her prayers, for she undertakes the state of holy matrimony with the greatest seriousness and devotion. However, when a great commotion in the street announces the arrival of Count Rofrano, the Rosenkavalier, poor Sophie begs the Lord's pardon. "I know that pride is a grave sin, but I can't humble myself now. I simply can't. It is so beautiful, so beautiful," she whispers.

Octavian enters the room, entirely dressed in white and silver, and accompanied by a retinue of regally attired footmen, couriers, and pages. Holding the rose in his right hand, Octavian bows gracefully to the entranced Sophie, though he blushes with embarrassment, and says, "To me has been accorded the honor of presenting, in the name of the Lord of Lerchenau, the rose of his love to his noble and high-born bride."

Taking the proffered rose, Sophie repeats the words she has so carefully learned. "I am much indebted to your Honor. I am eternally indebted to your Honor." Then, in a tone of simple wonder, she adds, "It smells of real roses."

"Yes," replies Octavian, unable to take his eyes from her face, "there is a drop of rose attar in it."

"But like heavenly, not earthly, roses. Like the roses of Paradise. Don't you think so?" She gently holds the rose out to him, and Octavian leans forward to take in its scent, and hers. Watching him, she murmurs artlessly, "It is like a greeting from heaven. Too strong to be endured, drawing me along as if there were reins around my heart. Where was I once before so happy?"

Looking into her wide gray eyes, Octavian repeats, "Where was I once before so happy?" Despite himself, he is falling in love. "If I were not a man, I would faint," he says to himself. "This is a blessed moment."

"This is a blessed moment," Sophie says to herself. Never in her life has she ever dreamed that such a man could exist. Sophie has forgotten all about the unknown man she is supposed to marry; she could easily stand all day in the center of the floor, looking at this beautiful silver-and-white hero who moves her soul so strangely. However, duty calls, and, in accordance with tradition, Sophie and Octavian seat themselves stiffly in facing chairs to converse politely for a prescribed number of minutes. There is an awkward silence, but Sophie, who is by nature rather talkative, breaks it with the confession that she knows all about her Rosenkavalier: his age, his genealogy, his baptismal names, and—she blushes—his nickname, Quinquin. On and on she chatters, while Octavian looks at her in bewilderment, thinking that he has never known anyone so lovely and so innocent.

Their tête-à-tête ends with the entrance of the Baron Ochs, followed by the obsequious Faninal and then the ghastly Lerchenau servants. Approaching Sophie with a thumping gait, Ochs barely waits until Faninal has finished introductions before he begins pawing at the girl. *Delicieuse!* My compliments to you!" he wheezes, kissing her hand and then inspecting it. "Ah! A delicate wrist! That's important to me, and it's a rare distinction in the middle classes."

At the sight of the Baron's lecherous grin, Octavian finds that a fiery rage is mounting within him. Sophie, too, is astounded. "What manners are these?" she whispers to Marianne in consternation. "Is he perhaps a horse dealer? Does he think he has bought me?" Marianne, simpering, advises her that the gentleman is merely affable and spontaneous.

Poor, shocked Sophie looks around wildly for an ally, but her father is in a transport of satisfied snobbery, and Marianne is positively charmed by the Baron's delightful condescension. Only in Octavian's eyes does she see a reflection of her horror, and she takes comfort in that, even as she is slapping away the Baron's groping hand.

"This is a fellow I'd like to meet with my sword handy where no watchman could hear him scream," Octavian is thinking. "Yes! That's all I want! If only I could be far away from here."

"Stop that nonsense!" commands Ochs to his outraged bride-to-be. "Now you belong to me! Just be good!" With an assessing glance, he gloats, "Shoulders like a baby chick! All skin and bones—that doesn't matter—but white, white with a sheen on it. That's what I like. I've simply got the luck of the Lerchenaus!" Sophie stamps her foot at this new familiarity, but her fury only serves to entice the Baron more. Reaching a great paw around Sophie's waist, he pulls her toward him, only to be repulsed by a mighty push.

Pleasure lighting his red face, the Baron congratulates himself, "Really and truly, I have the luck of the Lerchenaus! There is nothing on earth that so excites me, so completely rejuvenates me, as real defiance!" The sight of the attorney, however, reminds him that this marriage is primarily a profit-making venture, and, pinching Sophie's cheek, he relinquishes her to Octavian while he takes care of his business. "I've got nothing against your making eyes at her, good Cousin," he tosses over his shoulder at the young man [the nobility think it a charming custom to call one another cousin, whether there is any relation or not]. "She's a real don't-touch-me, and I think it's all to the good that she's warmed up! Ha! Ha!" The Baron, Faninal, and the attorney leave the room in solemn procession, followed by the servants.

"Are you going to marry that churl, *ma Cousine?*" asks Octavian quietly.

"Not for the world," Sophie replies, looking about to make sure they are alone. "I implore you!"

"What do you implore of me?" he demands eagerly. "Tell me quick."

"Oh, God, that you help me!" she says pleadingly. Their conversation is interrupted by the frantic cries of the Majordomo: It seems that Lerchenau's servants got drunk on the master's wine and are trying to have their way with the maids. Taking advantage of the hubbub to discuss their situation, Sophie and Octavian inch closer and closer to a confession of love. As Octavian promises to help her, Sophie presses his hand to her lips in gratitude, and the impulsive boy, bending down, finds her mouth in reply. Their kiss seals their fate, and, wonderingly, they greet the new world made of one another.

Deep in the far reaches of the chamber, Valzacchi and Annina creep out from behind two armchairs. Silent and unobserved, they move toward the lovers, who are now caught up in a passionate embrace. Then, at a signal from Valzacchi, they leap: Annina seizes Sophie, and Valzacchi grabs Octavian. At once, they begin to screech, "Herr Baron von Lerchenau! Herr Baron von Lerchenau!"

In an instant, the Baron is at the doorway, contemplating the spectacle of his bride-to-be nestled in the arms of his emissary. Contrary to all expectation, a broad smile breaks over his florid face. Nothing could be more insulting to Octavian, who summons up all his dignity and announces, solemnly, "I have to inform your Honor that an important change has occurred in his affairs."

The Baron fails to be impressed. In fact, he bursts into peals of laughter and congratulates Octavian on his flair. Octavian takes a deep breath and begins again. "The young lady does not care for you." The Baron snorts derisively. "The lady has decided that she will let your Grace remain unmarried!" shouts Octavian.

Dismissing this as so much foolishness, the Baron seizes Sophie by the elbow. "Come along," he bellows. "Can't keep the attorney waiting!"

"Hell! You've got a thick skin!" Octavian cries, blocking his path. "You'll not get past me! You are a scoundrel, a dowry hunter, a double-dyed liar, and a dirty boor! And if it comes to it, I'll give you your lesson right here and now!" He draws his sword from its silver sheath.

The sight of the sword gives Ochs the most dreadful turn. Instantly, he sticks his fingers in his mouth and whistles piercingly for his servants. "I should be really sorry if my people here—" he blusters anxiously, racing for the door with Sophie's elbow gripped tightly in his hand. But the door is suddenly crowded with his faithful staff, much the worse for wine. Seeing Octavian and their master at odds, they begin to yell and dance about, taking care to keep well away from the sword.

"You devil! Draw, or I'll run you through!" cries Octavian, rushing toward the Baron. Dismayed, Ochs pulls forth his weapon with a shaking hand and lunges awkwardly toward Octavian's sword, receiving the point in his upper arm. Convinced that the scratch is a mortal blow, Ochs falls to the floor with a shriek, while Octavian keeps the servants at bay with a few quick flourishes of his rapier.

As might be expected, a mighty uproar ensues. In the Baron's supine figure, Faninal sees the wreck of all his most cherished dreams, and only his abject reverence for nobility keeps him from slapping Octavian's face. With excruciating politeness, he suggests that the time has come for the Count to depart. Octavian, loath to leave his love in her present pickle, buys time with an elegant bow. Faninal, distracted by this courtesy from the riot act he is reading Sophie, must bow back.

To preclude further bowing, Marianne shoves Octavian out the door. Soon thereafter, the Baron recovers enough to demand a drink, and Faninal darts from the room to procure the best in his cellar. Ochs spends this interlude uttering threats against Octavian, but once the wine is delivered, a certain mellow cheer overtakes him, and the prospect of Sophie's defiance becomes vastly diverting.

Having directed the Doctor and his servants to oversee the arrangement of his sickroom, Ochs is alone when Annina comes stealing back to his side with a letter in her hand. Much to the Baron's satisfaction, this missive turns out to be a request for an assignation from the Marschallin's delectable maid, Mariandel. The delighted Baron never pauses to consider the probability of such a change of heart; he is too busy congratulating himself on the luck of the Lerchenaus. In fact, he is so busy that he quite forgets—even in the face of substantial hints—to pay Annina for her services, a failure that will bring certain doom to his enterprises, if we are to take warning from the expression on her face as she leaves the room.

Filled with wine and contentment, the rubicund Baron arises from his couch and makes his way to bed.

# ACT THREE

The next day, at a not-very-elegant inn, a private room is being prepared for the great rendezvous of the Lord of Lerchenau and Mariandel. Dimly lit and accoutered with a bed in an alcove, this is a chamber designed for seduction (provided you are not too particular).

But what's this? Annina, dressed in elegant mourning, stands in the middle of the floor, studiously reading a small piece of paper. Valzacchi, hovering beside her, adjusts her veil. Mariandel enters, dressed for romance in a ruffled gown and cap. Valzacchi, recognizing his employer despite his strange costume, makes a

bow and expertly catches the purse Octavian tosses. Annina, disconcerted by the camouflage, forgets to bow and merely stares. Octavian, adjusting his skirts awkwardly, looks at the clock and quickly disappears. Now five extremely suspicious-looking men enter the room, and Valzacchi sets about concealing them behind various trap doors and blind windows. A few minutes later, romantic music begins to ooze into the room from a hidden band.

All is prepared. Valzacchi leaps out into the hall and bows deeply to the Baron Ochs, who enters in a stately march with Mariandel on one arm and a sling on the other. After a great deal of shouting and dismissing and waving of hands, the waiters and the landlord take the hint and depart, leaving the Baron alone with his prey. Octavian, who has been simpering at himself in the mirror, adjusting his cap at ever more enticing angles, suddenly sees a leering face in the glass and shrieks in pretty surprise. It's only the Baron, armed with a large glass of wine.

"Ooooh, nononono, I don't drink wine," trills Octavian. The Baron, ready for business, lunges at the girl, but she flees, stumbling right into the alcove, which precipitates further shrieking. "Jesus and Mary, there's a bed in there, a tremendous big one. Dear me, who sleeps there?"

Soothingly, the Baron leads his Mariandel back to the table, offering her tidbits and tasty morsels, all the while creeping his hand about her waist. Mariandel leans back coquettishly, and the Baron, certain that his moment has come, closes in for a kiss—and is suddenly struck by the girl's likeness to Octavian. Starting back, he grasps his wounded arm and stares at her face in horror. "That face! It pursues me whether I wake or dream!" he gasps.

Octavian giggles coyly, and the Baron reaches anxiously for the wine bottle to aid his recovery. Suddenly, a man's face emerges from the floor, and, just as quickly, disappears. The Baron freezes, him arm outstretched. "I think I'm having a fit," he mutters, taking a large gulp of wine.

Slowly, the Baron collects himself. Pulling off his wig, he prepares for a renewed assault on Mariandel's virtue, but suddenly, he sees another strange face peering at him from the wall. Finally scared out of his wits, the Baron begins to shout. Just at this juncture, the blind window springs open and Annina enters, incognito behind a thick veil.

"That's him!" she cries, pointing at the Baron. "That's my husband!"

"What?" bellows the Baron wildly. But the lady has disappeared.

"This room must be haunted," comments Octavian.

But Annina has returned, with Valzacchi, the landlord, and three waiters in tow, loudly claiming that Ochs is her long-lost husband. The astounded Baron protests that he most certainly is not. But now, somewhat ahead of schedule, four children storm into the room, crying, "Papa! Papa! Papa!" at the Baron. Horrified, he swats at them with his napkin.

Octavian leans toward Valzacchi and whispers, "Has anyone gone to fetch Faninal?"

"He'll be here soon," Valzacchi replies in a reassuring undertone.

With the cool detachment of a casual observer, the landlord suggests that such treatment of his wife and children might land the Baron in trouble. Bigamy is no joke, he adds solemnly.

Hearing these words over the keening pleas of the children, the Baron begins to panic. Tearing open the window, he shouts, "Police! Police!"

Valzacchi turns to Octavian with a look of concern. "Let it happen," whispers Octavian.

And it does. An imperious, self-important Officer and two constables are filling up the chamber in no time. Ochs, who had rather expected some deferential treatment, finds his hopes dashed in the first minute. Instead of recognizing the Baron as a man whose favor must be curried, the Officer treats him like a common criminal. Glaring around the room, the Officer asks if anyone can vouch for this man's identity. All shake their heads soberly.

Octavian, feeling it is time to provide a distraction, begins to run madly about the room, praying God to save her. "Who is that young woman?" asks the Officer coldly.

The Baron, harassed by the specter of bigamy proceedings, even though he knows he's never been married, fabricates hastily. "That is Mademoiselle Faninal, legitimate daughter of the noble Lord von Faninal, who lives in the Court at his own palace," he concludes, proud of his quick wits.

"Yes, yes, I'm here," says a cross voice, and the Baron is terrified to see Herr von Faninal enter the room. "Why did you send for me to meet you at a common pot house?"

It is but the work of a moment for the Police Officer to ascertain that while Herr von Faninal does indeed know the Baron, he has never laid eyes on the wench in the cap. "That mopsy? My daughter?" says Faninal incredulously. "Send my daughter up here! She's sitting downstairs in her sedan!" Turning to the Baron, he storms, "You'll pay for this!" In a rage, he flies at him with his fists clenched. "Oh, you blackguard!" he screams, falling back. "Oh, I'm ill!" Two of his servants run to his side, and Sophie is not far behind. Gently they pick up the old man and carry him to the next room. The Baron, far from being disconcerted by this spectacle, takes exceeding comfort in his wig, which he has just found. Popping it on his pate, he is restored to his customary confidence in the luck of the Lerchenaus. Patting the Police Officer familiarly on the back, he bids him adieu.

"Not so fast," growls the officer.

Octavian steps daintily forward. "Officer, I wish to make a statement, but the Baron must not listen while I make it." The two retreat to the alcove for a conference, leaving Ochs to fuss and fume, until an unexpected diversion occurs.

"Her Most Serene Highness, the Princess von Werdenberg!" announces the Landlord in his deepest voice.

For a moment, everyone stands petrified. And then the Marschallin enters, imparting a sheen of elegance to the dingy surroundings. She stands motionless in the center of the room, looking about her with a faintly bemused expression.

Ochs, uncomfortably aware that the Marschallin's maid is lodged in his bed, wipes sweat from his brow. Octavian, uncomfortably aware that his old love pales beside his new, pops his head out from the bed curtains to ask weakly, "What brings you here, Marie Theres'?"

Only the Police Officer rises adequately to the occasion, saluting smartly at the Marschallin, who recalls with gracious speed that he was once the Fieldmarshal's orderly. The Baron takes advantage of this diversion to signal violently to Octavian to hide, while at the same time edging toward the door that leads to the room where Faninal lies, in order to shut it and his predicament away. As usual, his efforts are unsuccessful, for Sophie is just coming in with a message from her father for the Baron. Unaware of the Marschallin's presence, she gives the Baron his walking papers in decided tones, while Octavian approaches the Marschallin quietly and whispers falteringly, "That is the girl who—for whose sake—"

Without looking toward him, the Marschallin nods. "You seem somewhat impressed, Rofrano. I can well imagine who she is. I find her charming."

The Baron, as obtuse and greedy as ever, announces his willingness to forgive and forget all that has happened.

With quick, precise steps, the Marschallin approaches him. "Make a virtue of necessity," she suggests in a calm, clear voice. "And you will remain—to some degree—a person of rank." The Baron goggles at her, and she turns with charming confidentiality to the Police Officer and says, "You see, Officer, this whole thing was a farce and nothing else."

"Sufficient!" cries the dazzled Officer. "Your obedient servant withdraws!" The law beats an energetic retreat.

"The whole thing was just a farce," repeats Sophie, looking disconsolately at Octavian.

But the Baron is not quite finished. Back and forth between Octavian and the Marschallin his gaze wanders while his fingers rub gently at his chin. "I don't yet know what I ought to think about this quid pro quo," he chuckles.

The Marschallin's eyes rest on his a long moment. "You are, I assume, a gentleman? Then you will think absolutely nothing. That is what I expect of you! Do you not understand when a thing is finished? The whole engagement and affair and everything else concerned with it finishes with this hour!"

"Finishes with this hour," Sophie repeats sadly.

Ochs, utterly disconcerted by this turn of events, looks from the Marschallin to Octavian to Sophie, trying to find a foothold that will allow him to scale the wall of financial gain once more. Just as he is about to make a final assay, Valzacchi and Annina and their retinue troop in, much to the Baron's astonishment. They are followed by the landlord, the musicians, the waiters, a houseboy, and several coachmen, each bearing a long bill. Quickly assessing the situation, the desperate Baron makes a break for it, rushing out the door with the servants, waiters, landlord, and hangers-on at his heels.

And now, finally, Octavian, Sophie, and the Marschallin are left alone to play out an ending and a beginning. At first, Sophie believes she has been deceived, but the Marschallin knows better. Octavian hardly knows how to act his part, for half of him wants to be true to his Marie Theres', and the other half wants to keep on falling in love with Sophie. The Marschallin knows better than that, too. "Go quickly and do what your heart tells you," she commands Octavian. After a few half-hearted protests, obedience and desire propel him toward Sophie, standing wistfully in the middle of the room, and he begins the laborious task of explaining away all that she has seen.

The Marschallin looks on, forgotten by the lovers. "Today or tomorrow or the next day. Haven't I already told myself? This is every woman's destiny. Didn't I already know it? Haven't I made a vow that I would bear it?" Resolutely, she walks toward the reconciling lovers.

Octavian looks up with shining eyes. "Marie Theres', how good you are," he cries. "Marie Theres', I do not know——"

"I know nothing either, nothing!" the Marschallin says impatiently, and signals him to stand near Sophie and take her hand. Watching them, she sighs, "Most things in the world are such that one would not believe them if one were told about them. Only those who experience it believe it and do not know how. There stands my boy, and here I stand, and with that girl there, he will be as happy as men understand happiness."

Meanwhile, Sophie's misgivings are melting like ice under the summer sun of Octavian's ardor. "I feel you and only you, and that we are together," he rhapsodizes with unconscious cruelty. "All else passes like a dream before my senses."

"It is a dream. It cannot be real that we two are together, together for all time and all eternity!" answers Sophie ecstatically.

"In God's name," whispers the Marschallin, disappearing into the next room.

Just as the rapturous lovers are embracing, she reappears, led by a beaming Faninal. All parties bow, with varying degrees of satisfaction, at one another, and Faninal pats his daughter on her cheek. "That's how they are—the young folk!" he smiles.

"Yes, yes," says the Marschallin, gazing at Octavian's joyous face. Gracefully, she and Faninal sweep from the room, leaving the young couple time for a few final moments of blissful adoration. With a quick kiss, Octavian leads Sophie from the room. They depart without a backward glance. ⁓ᷔ

# INDEX